Contrasting Communities

Contrasting Communities

English Villagers in the Sixteenth and Seventeenth Centuries

MARGARET SPUFFORD

*Sometime Calouste Gulbenkian Research Fellow
Lucy Cavendish College, Cambridge, and S.S.R.C. supported
Senior Research Fellow, Keele University*

CAMBRIDGE UNIVERSITY PRESS

CAMBRIDGE

LONDON · NEW YORK · MELBOURNE

Published by the Syndics of the Cambridge University Press
The Pitt Building, Trumpington Street, Cambridge CB2 1RP
Bentley House, 200 Euston Road, London NW1 2DB
32 East 57th Street, New York, NY 10022, USA
296 Beaconsfield Parade, Middle Park, Melbourne 3206, Australia

Library of Congress Catalogue Card Number: 73–83105

First published 1974
First paperback edition 1979

First printed in Great Britain by
Western Printing Services Ltd, Bristol
Reprinted in Great Britain at the
University Press, Cambridge

ISBN 0 521 20323 6 hard covers
ISBN 0 521 29748 6 paperback

Contents

Contents

Maps

Graphs

Tables

Abbreviations

Only abbreviations and the short titles of primary and secondary works more frequently referred to in the footnotes are given below

A Collection: J. Parnell, *A Collection of the Several Writings Given Forth from the Spirit of the Lord, through that Meek, Patient and Suffering Servant of God, James Parnell*, no place 1657

Calamy Revised: A. G. Matthews, *Calamy Revised, being a Revision of E. Calamy's Account of the Ministers and others ejected and silenced, 1660–2*, Oxford 1934

Church Book of Bunyan Meeting: G. B. Harrison, *The Church Book of Bunyan Meeting, 1650–1821, being a reproduction in facsimile of the original folio*, London 1928

Clarke, *A Generall Martyrologie*: S. Clarke, *A Generall Martyrologie, containing a Collection of all the greatest Persecutions which have befallen The Church of Christ . . . whereunto are added the Lives of Sundry Modern Divines*, London 1651

C.R.O.: Cambridgeshire Record Office

C.U.L.: Cambridge University Library

Dedham Minutes: R. G. Usher, *The Presbyterian Movement in the Reign of Queen Elizabeth as illustrated by the Minute Book of the Dedham Classis 1582–1589*, Camden Society, 3rd ser., vol. VIII, London 1905

D.N.B.: *The Dictionary of National Biography*

Early Quaker Letters: G. F. Nuttall, *Early Quaker Letters from the Swarthmore MSS, to 1660*, London 1952

E.D.R.: Ely Diocesan Records

Fenstanton Records: E. B. Underhill, *Records of the Churches of Christ gathered at Fenstanton, Warboys, and Hexham, 1644–1720*, Hanserd Knollys Society, London 1854

Goubert, *Beauvais et le Beauvaisis*: P. Goubert, *Beauvais et le Beauvaisis de 1600 à 1730*, Paris 1960 [translated as 'The French peasantry of the seventeenth century: a regional example', in *Crisis in Europe, 1560–1660. . .*, ed. T. Aston, London 1965]

Glasscock, thesis: R. E. Glasscock, 'The Distribution of Lay Wealth in South-East England in the early Fourteenth Century', unpublished London Ph.D. thesis, 1963

Harrison, 'Grain Price Analysis': C. J. Harrison, 'Grain Price Analysis and Harvest Qualities, 1465–1634', *Agricultural History Review*, XIX, 1971

Heal, thesis: F. Heal, 'The Bishops of Ely and their Diocese during the Reformation Period: ca. 1515–1600', unpublished Cambridge Ph.D. thesis, 1972

Hoskins, 'Harvest Fluctuations, 1480–1619': W. G. Hoskins, 'Harvest Fluctuations and English Economic History, 1480–1619', *Agricultural History Review*, XII, 1964.

Hoskins, 'Harvest Fluctuations, 1620–1759': W. G. Hoskins, 'Harvest Fluctuations and English Economic History, 1620–1759', *Agricultural History Review*, XVI, 1968.

Lyon Turner: G. Lyon Turner, *Original Records of Early Nonconformity under Persecution and Indulgence*, 3 vols, London 1911–14

Lysons, *Magna Britannia:* D. and S. Lysons, *Magna Britannia*, vol. II i, Cambridge 1808

P.C.C.: Prerogative Court at Canterbury

P.R.O.: Public Record Office, London

Proc. Cambs. Ant. Soc.: Proceedings of the Cambridge Antiquarian Society

Ravensdale, thesis: J. F. Ravensdale, 'The Historical Evolution of the Landscape of three North Cambridgeshire Villages, Landbeach, Cottenham and Waterbeach (A.D. 450–1850)', unpublished Leicester Ph.D. thesis, 1972

R.C.H.M.: Royal Commission on Historical Monuments

Sheail, thesis: J. Sheail, 'The Regional Distribution of Lay Wealth in England as indicated in the 1524/5 Lay Subsidy Returns', unpublished London Ph.D. thesis, 1968

Spufford, *Chippenham*: M. Spufford, *A Cambridgeshire Community: Chippenham from Settlement to Enclosure*, Department of English Local History, University of Leicester, Occasional Papers vol. 20, 1968

Spufford, 'Dissenting Churches': M. Spufford, 'The Dissenting Churches in Cambridgeshire from 1660 to 1700', *Proc. Cambs. Ant. Soc.*, LXI, 1968

Spufford, 'Note on Compton Census': M. Spufford, 'A Note on the Compton Census', *Proc. Cambs. Ant. Soc.*, LXI, 1968

Spufford, 'Rural Cambridgeshire': M. Spufford, 'Rural Cambridgeshire 1520–1680', unpublished Leicester M.A. thesis, 1962

Spufford, 'Significance of Hearth Tax': M. Spufford, 'The Significance of the Cambridgeshire Hearth Tax', *Proc. Cambs. Ant. Soc.*, LV, 1962

Stone, 'Educational Revolution, 1560–1640': L. Stone, 'The Educational Revolution in England 1560–1640', *Past and Present*, 28, 1964

Stone, 'Literacy and Education, 1640–1900': L. Stone, 'Literacy and Education in England, 1640–1900', *Past and Present*, 42, 1969

Thirsk, *Agrarian History*, IV: J. Thirsk (ed.), *The Agrarian History of England and Wales*, vol. IV: *1500–1640*, Cambridge 1967

Trans. Cong. Hist. Soc.: *Transactions of the Congregational History Society*

V.C.H.: Victoria County Histories of England and Wales

Walker Revised: A. G. Matthews, *Walker Revised, being a Revision of J. Walker's Sufferings of the Clergy during the Grand Rebellion, 1642–60*, Oxford 1948

Acknowledgements

This book owes so much to the help of so many people, in various spheres, that it is almost invidious to single out any by name. I do, however, stand particularly indebted to five groups of people.

My research has been mainly done while I have been immobilised for one reason or another at Keele. The materials for it are in Cambridge and London. Without the unending patience of the Cambridgeshire County Archivist, Mr J. M. Farrar and the Archivist to the University of Keele, Mr Ian Fraser, who were always willing to transfer documents between them, frequently with the help of Mr Stitt, the Staffordshire County Archivist, it would have been quite impossible to complete it. Mrs Dorothy Owen, Archivist to the Bishop of Ely, has shown similar patience, and spent a very considerable amount of time advising me, and xeroxing documents for me. None of these people is in any way to blame for the, no doubt, frequently erroneous use of the materials with which they have kept me supplied. Miss Rosemary Graham has spent a great deal of time checking on my references. Many friends, and students at Keele, have spent time collecting or perusing documents I would not have been able to examine by any other means. Amongst them, I would particularly like to thank Mrs Elizabeth Key.

I have been almost overwhelmed by the kindness of nonconformist historians. Dr G. F. Nuttall has spent much time looking out references for me, not all of which I have been able to follow up, unfortunately. The local historians of the different Cambridgeshire churches have been amazingly willing to share both their bibliographies and their private information with me, and to rescue me from many pitfalls. I should like particularly to mention Mr Kenneth Parsons, who has given me much Baptist material, and Mr Andrew Smith, who steered me through much Congregationalist information.

Financial help for a married woman with a young family, who remains bent on doing part-time research, is never easy to obtain. Without the help of the Covenantors' Educational Trust, and of a grant from

The Eileen Power Fund, I would certainly not have got far enough to be appointed to a Calouste Gulbenkian Research Fellowship of Lucy Cavendish College, Cambridge, from 1969 to 1972. The depth and warmth of support I have received from my college in this time has meant a very great deal to me.

Personally, my debts range from the frankly bizarre onwards. The technicians of the Keele University Workshop took apparent pleasure, in 1967, in spending much time designing a piece of apparatus which enabled me to compare three different copies of documents, and write at a suitable angle, whilst lying flat on my back. It saved me six months, which would have otherwise been academically wasted. This book's existence also owes much to Mrs Elizabeth Jepson, Kirsten Carlsen, Gertrud Reiter, Birgit Rasmussen and Susan Le-Pla, who all aided me superbly in times of particular domestic stress. I am also very grateful to Sally Daunt and Susan Paine. My friends Dennis Jeeps and Jack Ravensdale have spent time which they could ill afford discussing the text, and reading it. So has Dorothy Owen. Ione Shaw helped with corrections which would never otherwise have been completed. I would also like to thank Roger Schofield and Tony Wrigley, who have read and commented on parts of my work, and patiently assisted me, particularly in my statistical worries.

I owe all the training in my craft which I possess to my Professor, H. P. R. Finberg, formerly Head of the Department of English Local History of the University of Leicester. I wish I had a better thank-offering to make.

I have also been greatly helped by the Department of History of the University of Keele; the members of which under successive heads, and most recently under Professor Rolo, have tolerated my presence working under their roof these last ten years, with a hospitality and lack of questioning which is typical of the Department. Mrs Carolyn Busfield, the Departmental Secretary, typed my manuscript. Only my friends will recognise, in that statement, the acknowledgement that she possesses palaeographic powers which are quite out of the common.

I would like to thank Wing-Commander R. F. Pemberton for compiling the indexes. I have also much appreciated the courtesy and consideration for my wishes shown by Mrs Christine Linehan and Mr Robert Seal of Cambridge University Press, who have done a great deal more for this text than their official positions demanded.

Finally, it is customary to thank one's wife, both for her patience, and for compiling the index. In my case, it is more appropriate for me to thank my husband, who did much of the arithmetic, and checked the

Acknowledgements

tables. Much more, he has been, for nearly ten years, the only person fully aware of what I was attempting to do, who continued to encourage me to do it, however adverse the external circumstances. Only someone placed in a similar position could appreciate what that has meant.

Lucy Cavendish College, Cambridge   Margaret Spufford
St Mary's Abbey, Malling
Epiphany, 1973

Publisher's Note

The author and publisher are grateful to the following for permission to reproduce extracts from copyright material held by them: Faber and Faber Ltd, for T. S. Eliot, 'East Coker', in *Four Quartets*, published in *Collected Poems, 1909–1962*; Oxford University Press, for Flora Thompson, *Lark Rise to Candleford*; Penguin Books Ltd, for Leo Tolstoy, *Anna Karenin*, translated by Rosemary Edmonds (Penguin Classics 1954), copyright © Rosemary Edmonds, 1954.

In that open field
If you do not come too close, if you do not come too close,
On a summer midnight, you can hear the music
Of the weak pipe and the little drum
And see them dancing around the bonfire
The association of man and woman
In daunsinge, signifying matrimonie –
A dignified and commodious sacrament.
Two and two, necessarye coniunction,
Holding eche other by the hand or the arm
Whiche betokeneth concorde. Round and round the fire
Leaping through the flames, or joined in circles,
Rustically solemn or in rustic laughter
Lifting heavy feet in clumsy shoes,
Earth feet, loam feet, lifted in country mirth
Mirth of those long since under earth
Nourishing the corn. Keeping time,
Keeping the rhythm in their dancing
As in their living in the living seasons
The time of the seasons and the constellations
The time of milking and the time of harvest
The time of the coupling of man and woman
And that of beasts . . .

The dancers are all gone under the hill.

> T. S. Eliot, 'East Coker', in *Four Quartets*,
> quoting from Sir Thomas Elyot, *The boke named the
> Gouvernour*, Bk I, Ch. XXI (1531)

For Francis and Bridget, and principally for Peter,

who helped me find the excavation of the graveyard of one of the lost villages of Cambridgeshire and who discovered, with me, that the bones of the long-dead, whose lives I have here partially tried to reconstruct, lie very peacefully below the fields they tilled.

Also for the other local historians of Cambridgeshire

above all

Dennis Jeeps and Jack Ravensdale.

Introduction

J'avais commencé, tout au début, par additioner les hectares et les unités cadastrales; j'aboutissais, en fin de recherche, à regarder agir, lutter, penser les hommes vivants.[1]

In general, local historians have confined themselves, since the discipline became respectable, to the economic setting in which local communities, at the village level at least, lived their lives. In a famous inaugural lecture, the study of local history was defined as that of the 'origin, growth, decline, and fall of a local community'.[2] Professor Finberg in that definition did not intend only economic historians to fasten onto the magic words 'growth' and 'decline'. Indeed, he intended local history to develop as a discipline which prevented the tendency of the national historian 'to lose sight of the human person', and even quoted Chesterton on Notting Hill, to defend the local historian from the obvious charge of only chronicling small beer: 'Notting Hill . . . is a rise or high ground of the common earth, on which men have built houses to live, in which they are born, fall in love, pray, marry, and die. Why should I think it absurd?' It has therefore been a source of surprise to me that local historians have almost always interpreted that initial brief in economic terms. We have many studies now of the gentry, landowners, tenants, village economies, open fields, of the way, in fact that most ordinary people, in ordinary villages before enclosure earned their bread-and-butter, or rather lard. What we have not got are studies of the way the ordinary villager before enclosure thought and felt. We do not know much about the religious opinions of the laity, the common people of God, or even whether they had any. We do not know what was argued about, except for crops and boundary stones, or how far the village was open to debate and influence from the outside world. The cynic, or realist, can easily dismiss the notion that the mass of villagers, in the days before the 1870 education act, and of

[1] Emmanuel Le Roy Ladurie, *Les Paysans de Languedoc*, Flammarion edition, Collection 'Science' (Paris 1969), p. 10.

[2] H. P. R. Finberg and V. H. T. Skipp, *Local History: Objective and Pursuit* (Newton Abbot 1967), p. 10; and cf. *ibid*. p. 38.

newspapers, had much time for developing any opinions at all. The life of the ordinary villager has been pictured as, and probably was, a struggle with his environment, and with hard labour, from dawn until dark. Some evidence has been produced that the villager's life was short;[3] there is plenty of other evidence that it was often nasty and brutish. Surely the 'intellectual' life of such people, caught in a ceaseless web of sowing and procreation, harvest and reproduction, ploughing and death, in their fields and their homes, can safely be neglected?

The greatest single piece of evidence that even the mass of common folk in the countryside did not live by bread alone, and that therefore studies of their communal life should not be confined to the way they grew their corn to make their bread, is the way the parish church, and sometimes the dissenting chapel, are, with the manor house, the monuments which dominate the village layout. Furthermore, even the most cursory study of the episcopal records dealing with the bishop's work of visitation and correction in his diocese, shows the amount of constant pressure, usually moral, but occasionally doctrinal, to which the parishioners were subjected.

I have therefore tried to portray the villager in this period, not merely as an economic animal, an item on a rent-roll, or even a man whose moveable assests were conveniently listed and priced at his death, but also as a sentient human being, who could possibly read and even write, and who might be expected to have some reactions to the successive changes in his parish church. As I have done so, my sympathies have increasingly gone out to those who have avoided this very nearly impossible exercise, and the reasons why it has been avoided have become increasingly plain.

There are obvious and glaring omissions in this work. I have, purposely, avoided any consideration of the gentry and parochial clergy whose influence on their tenants and parishioners could obviously be an overriding one, even though Bunyan himself saw it as only one of many.[4] I think myself the docility of tenants to both their lords and their priests can be overstated.[5]

I have also, more seriously, from my point of view, avoided any consideration of the villager as a political animal. I have not the slightest doubt that, particularly in the seventeenth century, he was one, and the consideration of religious opinions without politics, when the

---

[3] Peter Laslett, *The World We Have Lost*, University Paperback (London 1965), pp. 93–4.
[4] See below, pp. 306–7.
[5] See below, pp. 64 (Chippenham), 97–8 (Orwell), 121–4 (Willingham) for action by tenants against their lords; pp. 273–4 and 315–17 for action against the clergy, and 234–7 for general complaints by the laity against 'scandalous ministers'.

Introduction

two were so closely linked as to be almost synonymous, is inexcusable. When an ex-corporal of Cromwell's Ironsides formed one of the first General Baptist churches in Cambridgeshire, at the same time as an ex-cornet was 'preaching the Gospel to every creature',[6] in the Baptist version, and when all three of the lords of the villages which I have used for special case-studies were on the committee of the Eastern Association,[7] I have no doubt that the peasantry in these villages were as actively involved in politics as they were in religion. The loving care and pride with which the 'sword and bandoliers' of one of the yeomen of these villages were recorded in his, and his son's, inventories is proof enough.[8]

Cambridgeshire was one of the areas of recruitment of the Eastern Association. The army was based on Saffron Walden, fourteen miles from Cambridge, when it revolted in 1647[9] and campaigned for public support linking peasant grievances with those of the soldiery. There were organised Leveller groups in the next county of Hertfordshire.[10] It is impossible to believe that Leveller ideas did not spread into Cambridgeshire. Newmarket, half in the county, and Hitchin and Ware in Hertfordshire, all within easy striking distance of Cambridge, were at various times important sites for meetings and demonstrations. Overton's pamphlet *The Hunting of Foxes from Newmarket and Triploe Heaths to Whitehall by five small Beagles (late of the army)* written in 1649 showed that the whole area was one in which both the Levellers and the army were active.[11] Thriplow in Cambridgeshire was later a centre of Independence. Positive proof that the peasantry had religious opinions, and that once these had manifested themselves as a political menace, they were of importance, is to be found in the episcopal records after the Restoration, which suddenly focused, not on the moral state of the parishioners, but on their attendance at 'seditious conventicles'.

However, although I have no doubt that the political bias and actions of the villagers could be traced, at least in part, here courage and time have failed me. I have not, therefore, written a complete local study. What I have done has also suffered from being done in the interstices of domestic life and above all, from lack of time to read comparative

[6] See index of names for Benjamin Metcalfe and Henry Denne.
[7] Neville Butler of Orwell, Sir Francis Russell of Chippenham (R. B. Barber, *An East Anglian Village; or epochs in the history of Chippenham* [Bury St Edmunds 1897], pp. 22 and 24), Sir Miles Sandys of Willingham. A. Kingston, *East Anglia and the Great Civil War* (London 1897), p. 384.
[8] Robert Tebutt of Chippenham, see index of names.
[9] Howard Shaw, *The Levellers* (London 1968), pp. 50–1.
[10] *Ibid.* pp. 67–8.
[11] *Ibid.* p. 80.

Introduction

matter, and put my work in a general context. For instance, Le Roy Ladurie's superb work on the peasantry of Languedoc came out in an available form in 1969, too late for me to reshape the work that I had already done. In many ways he walked the same road before me, as the only reference to his work that I have made, standing at the head of this introduction shows. I also began by counting acres, roods, perches and some thousands of strips, and have ended here by considering the peasant as a human being, as fully as I could. Yet I have not been able to make allusions to the work of the Sixième section, or Ladurie, even though it is so relevant, simply for lack of time. Certainly it is true of all of us that 'One always writes too soon,' but it is truer of me than most of us that if 'One puts it off, one may not write at all.'[12]

What I have attempted to do is to give some kind of general survey of the population of the whole county of Cambridge, excluding the Isle of Ely, and another survey of that part of the Diocese of Ely which lay within southern Cambridgeshire and impinged on the parishioners' lives, morally, doctrinally, and in its ratification of the work of school-masters.

Even within the limited compass of the county, there is enough regional diversification to provide very great economic contrast, from the villages of the chalk uplands, to those of the clays, those of the heavily settled river valleys, those of the fen-edge which run down to the fens and included a comparatively small area of fen common, to the comparatively small number of true fen villages, lying along the old course of the Ouse. Against this general description of the county, the education available within it, and the pastoral work of the diocese, which formed the backdrop to the lives of the commonalty, I have attempted to set detailed studies of the economy, social structure, opportunities for elementary schooling, and religious beliefs of three contrasting villages: Chippenham, which lies on the chalk, but has a couple of hundred acres of fen common; Orwell, which lies on the spring line at the edge of the western clay uplands, but runs down to the river valley below; and Willingham, which was a true fen settlement.

This book therefore represents an attempt not merely to give an account of the way the villager lived his life in the sixteenth and seventeenth centuries, but also his literacy and religious attitudes, his reactions and beliefs, if not his morals. In part the task is impossible, because the source material simply does not exist. However, I hope that I have collected enough divers fragments of material to show that even if a complete picture cannot be drawn, the microcosm of the village

[12] Quoted by H. P. R. Finberg, in 'Preface' to the *Agrarian History of England and Wales, IV, 1500–1640*, ed. Joan Thirsk (Cambridge 1967), p. vii.

reflected, and often interpreted after its own fashion, intellectual and doctrinal movements higher in society. The villager was indeed a sentient reflecting being, with opinions of his own, and he should be treated as such, even if the nature of his opinions can only occasionally be established.

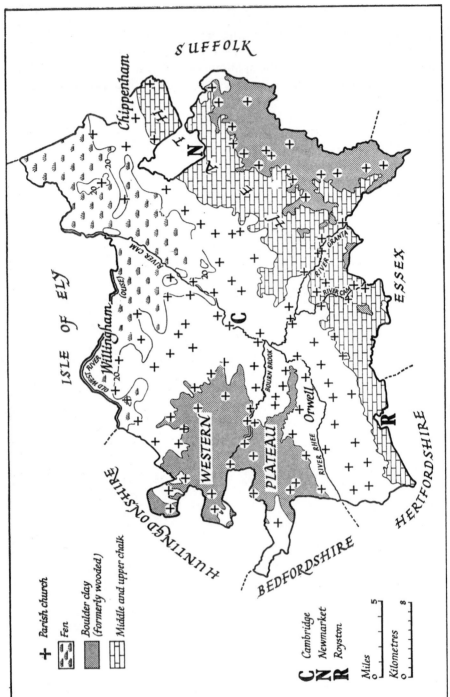

Map 1 Cambridgeshire: natural boundaries and soil types

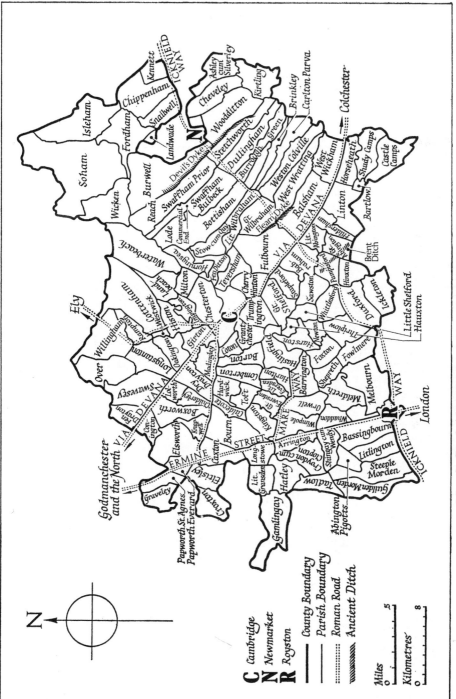

Map 2 Cambridgeshire: county and parish boundaries

PART 1

People, Families and Land

1

The peopling of a county

It is said that the foolish curiosity of Elagabalus attempted to discover from the quantity of spiders' webs, the number of inhabitants of Rome.

Edward Gibbon, *The History of the Decline and Fall of the Roman Empire*, Ch. XXXI.

Until very recently Cambridgeshire has been ill-served by the local historian. The reasons for this are to be found partly in its ancient history. It lay in the disputed land between the Saxon kingdoms of East Anglia and Mercia. The great parallel series of war-ditches that run from the fens on the one hand, up over the gentle rise of the chalk and across the great traffic artery of the Icknield Way to the woods on the boulder clay above it, bear witness to this. From before the Conquest to the present day, Cambridgeshire has belonged fully neither to East Anglia nor to the East Midlands. A certain hesitation about its regional classification has frequently, and unhappily, been resolved by leaving out the mention of it altogether. Since the beginnings of regional studies made by Maitland and Cunningham, little research has been done on the county until very recently, except by archaeologists. A full-time archivist was not appointed to the Record Office until the 1950s, and a record society was not formed until 1972. As a result of this dearth of published materials on the county, a recent thesis on the Eastern Association, in which the first fifty pages or more are dedicated to a discussion of society, religion and politics in the period of personal rule in the eastern counties, includes one single page on Cambridgeshire, although a part of the argument is devoted to the essential unity of interests in the counties concerned.[1]

A second handicap from which the county has suffered is the way it has frequently been treated together with the Isle of Ely. When Cambridgeshire is included in any investigation, the densely settled county and the sparsely settled fens of the Isle are usually lumped together. Dr Glasscock chose Cambridgeshire as the most obvious example of the

[1] C. A. Holmes, 'The Eastern Association', unpublished Cambridge Ph.D. thesis (1969). The author's book based on his thesis, *The Eastern Association and the Civil War* (Cambridge 1974), appeared after the present work went to the press.

3

way in which a county, although the easiest unit on which to base analysis, can also be most misleading, when he examined the taxation returns of 1334. Cambridgeshire ranks eleventh in prosperity on his list of counties, in terms of goods taxed by area, but, as he wrote, this position represents 'a median between the extremes of its various parts, for the valuation of the movable goods on the upland of the county would be right at the top of the list, whereas that on the peat fen would be right as the bottom'.[2] Cambridgeshire was among the most densely settled areas in the south-east. In the late thirteenth century, Cambridgeshire, judging from the degree of fragmentation of its holding, was the most thickly populated of the counties covered by the hundred rolls.[3]

Large parts of the Isle, on the other hand, might well still have been recognised in the sixteenth century, before the great fen-drainage schemes of the next hundred years, by St Guthlac, who had sought complete and utter solitude there in the eighth century, even though it must be admitted that he was disturbed by 'Welsh-speaking devils' marching to war against the Mercian kings, as well as by a stream of more conventional visitors.[4]

If the union of these unnatural partners is taken to be a true marriage, some curious conclusions can, and have been, drawn about its progeny. When, only two years after Dr Glasscock's work was completed, Dr Schofield discussed the distribution of wealth in England between 1334 and 1649, the Isle and the county were taken together.[5] As Schofield said himself, 'This had the effect of cancelling out two rather extreme values and putting Cambridgeshire in the middle of the rank order of Counties,'[6] but . . . 'the line had to be drawn somewhere'.

Similarly, in the relevant volume of the *Agrarian History of England and Wales*, Cambridgeshire appears with the Isle on the key map of farming regions in England[7] as principally a stock-rearing fen county,

---

[2] R. E. Glasscock, 'The Distribution of Lay Wealth in South East England in the Early Fourteenth Century', unpublished London Ph.D. thesis (1963), I, pp. 67–9. I would like to thank Dr Glasscock for generously allowing me to use, and quote from, his thesis.

[3] E. A. Kosminsky, *Studies in the Agrarian History of England in the Thirteenth Century* (Oxford 1956), pp. 216–17.

[4] C. W. Goodwin, *The Anglo-Saxon Life of St Guthlac* (London 1848), pp. 43–67.

[5] R. S. Schofield, 'The Geographical Distribution of Wealth in England, 1334–1649', *Economic History Review*, 2nd ser., 18 (1965), pp. 483–510, particularly pp. 499ff. Glasscock's and Schofield's tables are not comparable; Glasscock gives his counties in the order of tax actually raised from them, while Schofield lists counties in order of their taxable capacity.

[6] By personal communication.

[7] *The Agrarian History of England and Wales*, IV, *1500–1640*, ed. Joan Thirsk (Cambridge 1967) [henceforth Thirsk, *Agrarian History*, IV], p. 4. The county was more sensitively divided by Eric Kerridge, *The Agricultural Revolution* (London

although a small part of it is shown in the Norfolk sheep–corn region. There is patently something wrong here. Cambridgeshire was already producing a considerable surplus of corn for export through King's Lynn in the fourteenth century. 'If any district in medieval times were able to ship corn in a continuous stream to feed the population of other districts, it was this Cambridge area,' Gras wrote.[8] My intention is therefore to dismiss the Isle of Ely from my calculations, whilst still recognising the very real regional diversification within the county.

MEDIEVAL OVERPOPULATION AND THE GREAT DECLINE

Cambridgeshire still seems to have been thickly populated in the 1330s. Even though it is impossible to establish any relationship between the taxable capacity of a county and the size of its population in 1334,[9] the high capacity of the county in the early fourteenth century, even after floods[10] and famine had begun to have their effect, does suggest that a large number of people were taxable in the villages.[11] Central Cambridgeshire was as wealthy as any region in south-eastern England in 1334, including Norfolk and Suffolk with high assessments of forty to fifty shillings per square mile.[12] Some of the fen-edge villages, including Over, Swavesey and Cottenham, had relatively high quotas, of at least twenty shillings per square mile compared with only nine shillings

1967), than in the *Agrarian History*. He shows the clay uplands as part of the 'Midland Plain', the chalk uplands as the 'Chiltern country', the boundaries of the fenland are accurately depicted, and the extreme north-east of the county fringes into the 'Breckland'.

[8] N. S. B. Gras, *The Evolution of the English Corn Market from the Twelfth to the Eighteenth Century* (Cambridge, Mass. 1915), p. 104, n. 3.

[9] Glasscock, thesis, p. 15.

[10] J. R. Ravensdale, 'The Historical Evolution of the Landscape of Three North Cambridgeshire Villages, Landbeach, Cottenham and Waterbeach (A.D. 450–1850)', unpublished Leicester Ph.D. thesis (1972), pp. 126–7. I am much indebted to Dr Ravensdale for allowing me to quote from, and use, his thesis, as well as for his help with my text. Dr Ravensdale's book, *Liable to Floods, Village Landscape on the Edge of the Fens, A.D. 450–1850* (Cambridge 1974) appeared when the present work was in the press.

[11] Particularly if Dr Glasscock is right in suggesting that, even though the 1334 plan of assessment did not provide for the exemption of the poor, 'the 1334 quotas . . . took no account of the moveable property in the hands of a large number of people in every township . . . whose goods amounted to less than the minimum value'. Glasscock, thesis, p. 24.

[12] Only five small areas had assessments higher than this, of over 50*s* per square mile. The map of Cambridgeshire assessments is in Glasscock, *ibid.* I, 114, and should be compared with the complete map of south-eastern England produced by him in I, 64. (The comparer should notice that the shadings on the two maps do not represent the same values.) Dr Glasscock discussed the county in detail in his thesis, I, 108–15; I am very grateful to him for allowing me to quote him and use his work so extensively.

over the whole Isle of Ely. The western clay villages had uniform assessments of thirty to forty shillings a square mile, but the eastern chalk ridge, capped with its boulder clay, was poor in the fourteenth century, as later. Over the country as a whole, the corn-producing areas like Cambridgeshire were wealthy, whereas wool and forest regions were not. By 1341, a shrinkage in the cultivated area had already begun in the county, and a reversion to waste was in progress.[13] Nevertheless it was still comparatively densely populated according to the poll tax returns of 1377, although Norfolk and Suffolk, with Leicestershire and Northamptonshire, were more thickly settled.[14]

Facts like this are apt to appear bleak, and to need translation into human terms before their true meaning is apparent. 'Population movements' in real village life are not generalised characteristics, but hard, and often brutal facts. 'Population rises' mean the physical extension of village streets, the physical extension of the fields round them, and eventually the fragmentation of the villagers' holdings when the fields can be expanded no longer. Ultimately, they mean famine and death. 'Population falls' mean the shrinkage of village streets, tumbling houses, the extension of the waste area round the arable fields, and the gradual build-up of large farms as land becomes available for the greedy, or the far-sighted, to collect. All this is true, not only in the 'lost village' sites which we tend to think of as 'abnormal' and out of the common way; but almost everywhere, in the 'normal' villages.

On average, in England as a whole, there was probably an expansion by something like two and a half times in the number of mouths to feed in the couple of hundred years between Domesday Book and the hundred rolls.[15] The villages in which I have taken a special interest expanded faster than this. In 1279, at Chippenham 143 tenants were cultivating an area occupied by only thirty-two families at Domesday. Of these extra tenants, only four had as much as twenty acres of land. Just over half of the Chippenham farmers had between twelve and fifteen acres, which was the size of holding considered the minimum adequate to support a family. The rest had less than this; they were

[13] *Ibid.* pp. 71–5 and 115.
[14] R. A. Pelham, 'Fourteenth-Century England', *An Historical Geography of England before A.D. 1800*, ed. H. C. Darby (Cambridge 1936), map, p. 232. The drawing of this map together with n. 4, p. 231, strongly suggests, however, that Ely and Cambridgeshire were treated together in it, and that therefore the density in southern Cambridgeshire might have been higher.
[15] M. M. Postan, 'Medieval Agrarian Society in its Prime: England', *Cambridge Economic History of Europe*, I, 2nd ed. (Cambridge 1966), 561–3, and J. C. Russell, *British Medieval Population* (Albuquerque, New Mexico 1948), p. 80 give radically different figures for the total population of England, but very roughly agree on the overall rate of expansion.

cottagers with less than enough to support themselves on, dependent on their ability to hire themselves out as wage-labourers.[16] A similar situation, with a large proportion of the village existing, or failing to exist, under the bread-line, was already established by 1222 at Great Shelford, when the township was surveyed for the bishop of Ely.[17] Already, fifty years before the compilation of the hundred rolls, the population had nearly doubled since Domesday. The size of the average holding of the better-off fell by nearly a half; and at the same time the number of smallholders with too little land to support a family nearly trebled.

Orwell more than quadrupled in size between 1086, when there were twenty tenants there, and 1279, when there were about eighty-nine, including at least seventeen at the hamlet of Malton, which had not been separately listed at Domesday. This rate of growth was not typical of the villages on the difficult soils of the clay uplands, which generally only doubled in size in this period of acute population pressure. Orwell's rapid increase was probably accounted for by its proximity to the valley of the Cam, which both then and later remained the most heavily settled area of the county.[18] In 1342, however, the parishioners were explaining that the value of a ninth of their corn, wool, and lambs had dropped to £8 3s 4d in the preceding agricultural year, from £16 3s 4d in 1291, because land had fallen out of cultivation on account of the great sterility of the soil in the parish.[19]

Bourn, which was already large at Domesday, had a minimum of 183 families in 1279, or at least 900 people. The layout of the village of Bourn today is a puzzle, made up of a chequerboard of half-empty lanes. The number of houses there in 1279 makes sense of the puzzle.[20]

---

[16] Margaret Spufford, *A Cambridgeshire Community: Chippenham from Settlement to Enclosure*, Leicester Occasional Papers, vol. 20 (Leicester 1968), pp. 28–30 [henceforth *Chippenham*].

[17] E. Miller, *The Abbey and Bishopric of Ely* (Cambridge 1951), p. 11.

[18] Margaret Spufford, 'Rural Cambridgeshire 1520–1680', Leicester M.A. thesis (1962) [henceforth 'Rural Cambridgeshire'], pp. 51–7, C. T. Smith, 'Settlement and Population', in *The Cambridge Region 1965*, ed. J. A. Steers (Cambridge 1965), p. 138ff.

[19] *Nonarum Inquisitiones in Curia Scaccari*, ed. G. Vanderzee (Record Commissioners, 1807), p. 210, and A. R. H. Baker, 'Evidence in the "Nonarum Inquisitiones" of Contracting Arable Lands in England during the Early Fourteenth Century', *Econ. Hist. Rev.*, 2nd ser. XIX (1966), 526.

[20] Great attention to village layout is paid in the *Inventory of Historical Monuments in the County of Cambridge, I, West Cambridgeshire* (Royal Commission on Historical Monuments London 1968) [henceforth R.C.H.M.]. It frequently notices vestiges of house-platforms and earlier lanes, as at Bourn (p. 18), Boxworth (p. 28) and Grantchester (pp. 112–13). It is a pity that the vital hundred rolls were not used as a source, as Domesday was, and later documents were, to interpret these patterns, since in many cases the degree of expansion by 1279 makes immediate sense of the abandoned streets and houses.

It is no wonder that this extent of population growth led to the sort of distress that we are accustomed today to associate with posters for the relief of underdeveloped countries. It may, from the degree of fragmentation of holdings, have been unequalled in Cambridgeshire, but it certainly took place elsewhere.[21] In the winter of 1257 such numbers died from starvation by the roadsides that the murder fine, which had hitherto been taken for accidental death as well as murder, was abolished.[22] Cambridgeshire may have been one of the richest areas in England in 1334, but even there the population rise was already being checked. The villager in the late thirteenth century was most commonly a man leading an extremely precarious existence on an inadequate farm, with death by the roadsides a very real risk if the crops failed.

The familiar late medieval slump, which had already begun by 1341 in Cambridgeshire, took place sometime between 1334 and 1524–5, when the next attempts at a 'realistic' taxation, this time listing individual taxpayers, were made. Again, bold statements can best be translated into human terms by concrete examples.

The fifteenth-century history of Chippenham is a reflection of its altered fortunes.[23] The overpeopled village of 1279 had disappeared. The poll tax records only 204 adults over the age of fourteen.[24] There cannot have been more than three hundred inhabitants in the village, at the most.[25] Even at a conservative estimate the population must have fallen by over a half in the century between 1279 and 1377. The extent of late medieval population fall is well-known, so that such figures tend to be taken for granted; but when, as at Chippenham, a later source exists describing whole streets as 'clere decaied' and every other house as missing, they renew their power to shock. When the jury went its rounds surveying the manor in 1544, sixty village houses were still standing, together with the manor, parsonage, and vicarage. The jurors were able to describe another sixty-four crofts as sites where houses had once stood, thus accounting for all but about twenty of the

---

[21] See, for instance, M. M. Morgan (Mrs M. Chibnall), *The English Lands of the Abbey of Bec* (London 1946), E. M. Carus-Wilson, 'The First Half-Century of the Borough of Stratford-upon-Avon', *Econ. Hist. Rev.*, 2nd ser., XVIII (1965), 46–53, M. M. Postan and J. Titow, 'Heriots and Prices on Winchester Manors', *Econ. Hist. Rev.*, 2nd ser., XI (1958–9), 392–411 and J. Z. Titow, *English Rural Society 1200–1350* (London 1969), for effects of population growth.
[22] A. L. Poole, *From Domesday Book to Magna Carta, 1087–1216* (Oxford 1955), p. 393.
[23] M. Spufford, *Chippenham*, pp. 31–2.
[24] I have taken the figures from *Cambridgeshire Subsidy Rolls, 1250–1695*, ed. W. M. Palmer (Norwich 1912).
[25] If a very rough adjustment is made for children under fourteen. M. W. Beresford, 'The Poll Taxes of 1377, 1379, and 1381', *The Amateur Historian*, III (1958), 275.

households in the village in 1279. Over half the village was still missing in 1544. The empty crofts and shrunken streets all emphasised the severity of the decline and make it appear catastrophic to a reader of the survey. The village was a shadow of the community it had been in the thirteenth century. The survey gives a dismal picture of decay, but examination of the fifteenth-century reliefs on taxation assessments made for distress caused by poverty for the rest of Cambridgeshire suggests the degree of shrinkage found at Chippenham was not in the least unusual, and that the effects of the fourteenth- and fifteenth-century slump had probably led to this amount of physical dereliction and reduction in the size of villages in the county everywhere.

The reliefs for poverty treat Chippenham as if it had not suffered at all badly. In 1432–3, Chippenham was relieved only of ten shillings, or six per cent, of its assessment of 1334.[26] In 1489–90, even after a fire sufficiently disastrous to linger on in folk memory, the relief rose only to fifteen shillings, or nine per cent.[27] These percentages are low by Cambridgeshire standards. Reliefs of twenty per cent were reasonably common and in some parishes they rose to over thirty per cent. The hamlet of Badlingham, under half a mile away, was relieved of nineteen per cent of its tax burden in 1432–3 and twenty-eight per cent in 1489–1490. If the judgement of the assessors of the reliefs is to be trusted, the disappearance of half a village was so commonplace an affair in an area as thickly populated as Cambridgeshire had been in the thirteenth century that it called for no special action and indeed earned only a low relief. If the 'normal' village had shrunk to half its medieval size,[28] this is to be borne in mind when the fifteenth-century reliefs are used to judge the effects of depopulation. In them, a village which would appear from a full description as catastrophically reduced as Chippenham would scarcely appear affected at all, and even less as a candidate for 'lost village' status.

The timing of the shrinkage varied from village to village. The population of Orwell-cum-Malton seems to have shrunk by only a quarter by the time of the poll tax,[29] whereas many other settlements, like Chippenham, were already reduced to half their former size. The

---

[26] Public Record Office, London [henceforth P.R.O.], E179/81/80.
[27] P.R.O., E179/81/120.
[28] Miss Davenport's sixteenth-century evidence on Forncett seems to point to a similar degree of shrinkage. F. G. Davenport, *The Economic Development of a Norfolk Manor 1086 to 1565* (Cambridge 1906; reprinted London 1967), pp. 98–105, particularly pp. 102, 105.
[29] The conclusion is based on a comparison of the number of tenants in Orwell in 1279 (*Rotuli Hundredorum*, II [Record Commission, London 1818], pp. 558–9) and those taxed there in the poll tax of 1377 (figures printed by Palmer, *Cambridgeshire Subsidy Rolls, 1250–1695*).

9

fourteenth-century beginnings of contraction in Orwell must in any case have been fairly recent by the time it was complained of in 1342, because the village was prosperous enough to add north and south arcades, and probably the tower as well, to the twelfth-century nave of its parish church at the end of the thirteenth and beginning of the fourteenth century.[30] On the other hand, the decline at Orwell continued during the fifteenth century. The heavy clay was obviously not attractive to those who tilled it. The village was granted a tax relief of twenty-two per cent in 1489–90,[31] which was higher than normal. The numbers taxed in the great subsidy of 1524 showed that there had been a further decline of a quarter in the population, to fifty-two taxable individuals.[32] The subsidiary settlement of Malton had become a lost village represented by a single farm.

Despite this catastrophic shrinkage, Cambridgeshire, with its immediate neighbours to the east and south, all of which also had the climate and communications to supply the corn-market, was one of those counties with fewest deserted villages.[33]

POPULATION CHANGES, 1524, 1563, 1664

In 1524, Cambridgeshire was still one of the most densely populated areas in the country, judging from the number of people able to pay tax within it. Lowland England as a whole had between eight and sixteen taxpayers per thousand acres, but the more densely settled regions, principally East Anglia, had between sixteen and twenty-three taxpayers per thousand acres, with smaller areas within them which had over twenty-three taxpayers per thousand acres.[34]

In the early sixteenth century the villages south of Cambridge in the valley of the Cam were generally medium-sized, with between fifty and a hundred taxable persons, but the small size of their parishes meant that the densities were generally the highest in the county and, indeed, among the highest in the country. A sprinkling of them, like Shepreth, the Shelfords or Sawston contained over twenty-eight, or even over thirty-five persons assessed per thousand acres. This area had been the richest, and by inference, the most thickly-settled part of the county in 1334.

[30] *R.C.H.M.*, p. 189.   [31] P.R.O., E179/81/120.   [32] P.R.O., E179/81/130.
[33] *Deserted Medieval Villages, studies*, ed. M. Beresford and J. G. Hurst (London 1971), map, p. 66, showing sites located up to the end of 1968.
[34] John Sheail, 'The Regional Distribution of Wealth in England as indicated in the 1524/5 Lay Subsidy Returns', unpublished London Ph.D. thesis (1968). I am most grateful to Dr Sheail and the University of London for generously allowing me to use his material.

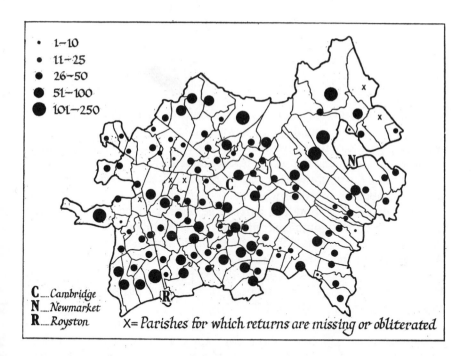

- • 1–10
- • 11–25
- • 26–50
- • 51–100
- • 101–250

C....Cambridge
N....Newmarket
R....Royston

X= Parishes for which returns are missing or obliterated

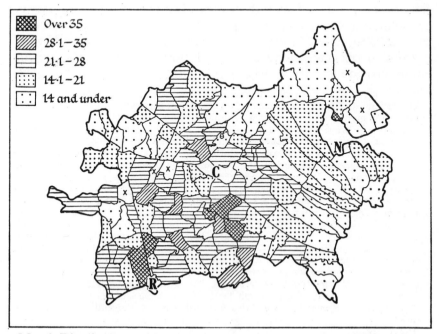

- Over 35
- 28·1–35
- 21·1–28
- 14·1–21
- 14 and under

Map 3 Distribution and density of population in Cambridgeshire in 1524–5

In Cambridgeshire, the larger villages – of over a hundred taxable people – were mostly to be found on the fen-edge and in the fen itself. The parish acreages there, however, were so much larger that the population density was relatively low, at under twenty-one, or even under fourteen, taxable persons per thousand acres, except in a few villages. In general, small villages, with under fifty people assessed, lay on the clay plateau to the west, and on the chalk ridge to the south-east, and it is not surprising that those few settlements which had disappeared in the county lay on these heavy clays. Nevertheless, the western uplands had a number of parishes with between twenty-one and twenty-eight taxable persons per thousand acres. The density of population on the chalk ridge to the south-east was far lower than on the western uplands. Indeed the chalk ridge was not much more heavily settled than the fen-edge to the north of the county, or even the fens of the Isle of Ely. However, even these areas of lowest population density, by Cambridgeshire standards, were of normal, or above normal, density for lowland England as a whole.[35]

One of the biggest gaps in the armoury of the agricultural historian will at last have been filled, when the Cambridge Group for the History of Population and Social Structure produces its aggregative analysis of a wide sample of parish registers from their inception until the census returns of the early nineteenth century. The reasons for the prices of agricultural products moving upwards, steeply though not steadily, from 1500 to the 1650s with a total increase over the whole period of nearly 550 per cent,[36] have exercised historians ever since a contemporary first commented on the beginning of the movement in the discus-

[35] I made my own analysis of the returns for 1524 and 1525 in 1961, and general descriptions of Cambridgeshire based on these are my own, and not Dr Sheail's, just as the maps are my own. They are drawn up on a parochial basis, in the hope that this will prove of most use to the local historian interested in an individual parish. It seems from Dr Roger Schofield's work that the lay subsidies of 1544/6 were probably superior and covered more taxpayers than those of the 1520s. However, large parts of the documents for these later subsidies are defective or lost (Sheail, thesis, p. 12) and so those of 1524/5 give a wider cross-section of the county. I worked out the detailed figures in terms of taxable persons per thousand acres to make them comparable with those of Professor C. T. Smith on Leicestershire and Dr Joan Thirsk on Lincolnshire. It is unfortunate for me that Dr Sheail worked out his figures on the basis of square miles to be comparable with Dr Glasscock's thesis on the 1334 returns. It is therefore not immediately easy to compare his figures with Professor Smith's, Dr Thirsk's or my own. I have, however, counted his figures, above p. 10, on the basis that persons per square mile is approximately 23 per thousand acres.

[36] E. H. Phelps-Brown and S. V. Hopkins, 'Wage-Rates and Prices: Evidence for Population Pressure in the Sixteenth Century', *Economica*, n.s., xxiv (1957), 289–305. Ingrid Hammerstrom, 'The Price Revolution in the Sixteenth Century: Some Swedish Evidence', *Scandinavian Economic History Review*, v (1957), 118–54; Thirsk, *Agrarian History*, iv, 594–5; Y. S. Brenner, 'The Inflation of Prices in Early Sixteenth Century England', *Econ Hist. Rev.*, xiv (1961). See also the summary by R. B. Outhwaite, *Inflation in Tudor and Early Stuart England* (London 1959).

sion in the *Commonweal of this Realm of England*. Once the old favourites, debasement of the coinage and influx of bullion from over-seas in the sixteenth century, have been dismissed as insufficient causes for the rise, the historian searching for an explanation has had to fall back on the assumption that the fundamental cause of the rise must have been a sharp increase in the number of mouths to feed, coupled with inadequate application of new agricultural techniques to push up production so that it kept pace with demand. Until now, this reasoning has been mostly supposition, and lack of detailed and proven knowledge of population movements has hamstrung historians discussing agrarian changes in the sixteenth century, from the undergraduate level upwards. The meticulous discussion of agricultural prices and farm profits in the Tudor and Stuart volume of the *Agrarian History of England and Wales* could only be underpinned by the bleak restatement of Sir John Clapham's estimate that the population of England and Wales nearly doubled in the period between 1500 and 1700.[37]

There have, of course, been attempts to establish population movements in various counties from the central taxation material readily available to the historian, which covers the sixteenth and seventeenth centuries. These unsatisfactory attempts must serve until a large-scale general analysis of population movement from the early parish registers is available.

The numbers of people assessed in the 'great subsidy' of 1524–5 can be compared with the number of households in each parish in the episcopal returns of 1563, with the number of communicants in the episcopal returns of 1603, and with the numbers of people assessed in one of the hearth taxes of the 1660s and 1670s. There are obvious disadvantages to this. The episcopal returns of 1563 are most easily interpreted in terms of population, dealing specifically as they do with 'households'. The hearth tax returns are comparable with them insofar as each person assessed on a certain number of hearths is likely to be head of one household,[38] which would presumably include, like the 1563 returns, servants and others resident within it. The 1524 returns deal, however, with all persons of the age of sixteen and upwards

---

[37] Thirsk, *Agrarian History*, IV, 596–7. By 1978, the initial work of the Cambridge Group to appear in print showed that the rise in population from 1550 to 1650 was one of just over 3 million to nearly 5.5 million, R. M. Smith, 'Population and its Geography in England 1550–1730' in R. A. Dodgshon and R. A. Butlin, eds., *Historical Geography of England and Wales* (1978), pp. 204–8. The percentage increase in population per decade between 1570 and 1630 was as much as 5.6 or 5.5, *Introduction to the Sources of European Economic History 1500–1800*, ed. C. Wilson and G. Parker (1978) pp. 116–17.

[38] Margaret Spufford, 'The Significance of the Cambridgeshire Hearth Tax', *Proceedings of the Cambridge Antiquarian Society*, LV (1962), 60, which shows that multiple occupation, although it existed, was not very common in the county in 1664.

assessed on wages down to a yearly value of £1 and on goods down to a yearly value of £2, and so must include as individual entries a number of younger sons living at home, and servants,[39] who would quite possibly not be included thereafter if they were resident within their employers' houses. The 1524 figures are therefore bound to be proportionately larger than those for 1563 and the 1660s. It is impossible to calculate the degree of difference without knowing what proportion of wage-labourers 'lived in' in the sixteenth century, or moreover, whether there was any change in social habits, and therefore a change in this proportion during the period. If there was no such change in social habits, it must be assumed that since there would be a drop in the numbers returned between 1524 and 1563, any rise in population then would tend to be concealed or minimised.

The work so far done by historians from these, admittedly unsatisfactory, sources includes studies of Leicestershire and Hertfordshire. In Leicestershire the results obtained from this inadequate demographic material were checked by Professor Smith by examination of the birth and death rates given in the parish registers of certain key villages over ten-year periods. The dates between which the main expansion of population took place were thereby pinpointed.[40] His results show that the recorded population of that county, which was admittedly at a very low ebb at the end of the fifteenth century, may have increased by up to thirty-one per cent between 1524 and 1563, and by a further fifty-eight per cent between 1563 and 1603, when the rise was checked. It then remained static, or crept up slowly, and was perhaps only five per cent higher in 1670 than in 1603. Over the whole period, therefore, the population of Leicestershire may have doubled.

In Hertfordshire, there was a similar rise of fifty-eight per cent between 1563 and 1603.[41] Mr Cornwall tentatively estimates a rise of sixty-three per cent for the country as a whole between 1522–5 and 1603.[42]

In Cambridgeshire the picture is rather different. The total numbers assessed in the county not only did not rise between 1524 and 1563,

[39] 'Servant' is taken hereafter to mean an in-servant, as opposed to a labourer with his own cottage. Laslett, *The World We Have Lost*, pp. 14–15. See also Laslett's introductory chapter in *Household and Family in Past Time*, ed. P. Laslett and R. Wall (Cambridge 1972).

[40] C. T. Smith, in *V.C.H. Leicestershire*, III, 137–45.

[41] L. M. Munby, *Hertfordshire Population Statistics, 1563–1801* (Hertfordshire Local History Council, Hitchin 1964), p. 21.

[42] From 2,300,000 in 1522–5 to 3,750,000 in 1603. Julian Cornwall, 'English Population in the Early Sixteenth Century', *Econ. Hist. Rev.*, 2nd ser., XXIII (1970), 44, criticised by R. S. Schofield, 'Historical Demography: Some Possibilities and some Limitations', *Transactions of the Royal Historical Society*, 5th ser., XXI (1971), 125.

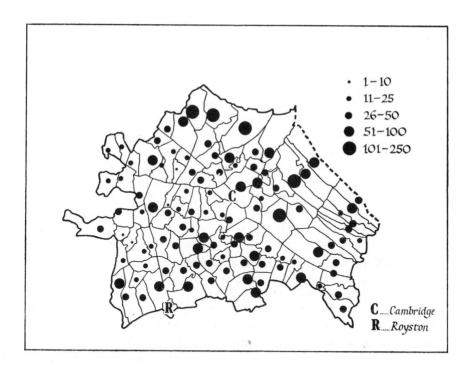

1 – 10
11 – 25
26 – 50
51 – 100
101 – 250

C .....Cambridge
R .....Royston

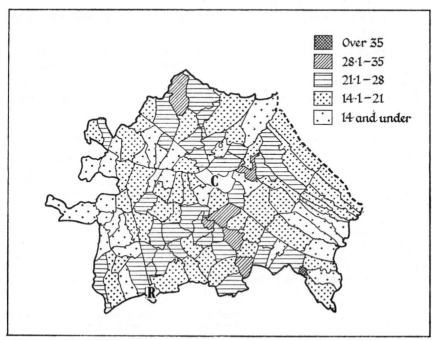

Over 35
28·1 – 35
21·1 – 28
14·1 – 21
14 and under

Map 4 Distribution and density of population in Cambridgeshire in 1563

but actually fell by six per cent.[43] Despite this comparable rise of thirty-one per cent in Leicestershire during this period, the density of households in Cambridgeshire in 1563 was still higher, at eighteen per thousand acres, than it was in Leicestershire where there were only sixteen households per thousand acres.[44] The river valleys of the Cam and the Granta were as thickly peopled as those of the Welland and the Soar, and of the most heavily settled parts of Lincolnshire at the same date.[45] This gives even more force and vividness to my description of the choked conditions in the county in the late thirteenth century. If my deductions (from the fifteenth-century tax reliefs, and later surveys, combined with the visual evidence of the surviving layout of many villages today) that the settlements of Cambridgeshire had commonly shrunk by half in the later middle ages, while remaining mainly immune from wholesale depopulation, are correct, it is remarkable that a large part of the county still fell within the group of south-eastern counties with more taxpayers per square mile in 1524 than any others.[46] It must indeed have been congested in the 1290s. Numbers did rise after 1563, but not at the same rate in this already heavily settled area as in Leicestershire and Hertfordshire. In the whole century from 1563 to 1664, they only rose by thirty-four per cent, as opposed to a rise of fifty-eight per cent in the other counties.

The changes in the pattern of settlement within the county brought about in the sixteenth and seventeenth centuries were considerable. The maps of population in the 1520s and 1563 show little general change; it was the change between 1563 and the hearth tax that was dramatic. The true fen villages along the Ouse, and the fen-edge villages with two or three hundred acres of fen, had been, with the chalk ridge, the emptiest parts of the county in 1524 and 1525.[47]

[43] These figures only cover the area of the county included in the diocese of Ely, for which there is a return of 1563. Two of the fourteen hundreds of the county, Staplehoe and Cheveley, which lie outside the diocese, are therefore omitted from the analysis of the returns for 1524–5 and 1664. The village of Chippenham, which is one of my detailed case-studies, unfortunately lies in the hundred of Staplehoe. Cambridge and the parts of Newmarket and Royston which lie within the shire are omitted from all three sets of figures, as are four small villages for which one or another of the returns is obliterated or missing. I have discussed these figures and the sources from which they are taken fully in 'Rural Cambridgeshire', pp. 44–58, 121–2.

[44] This suggests that the density in Leicestershire in 1524–5, which Professor Smith does not give, must have been something of the order of 12.3 per 1,000 acres, compared with 19.2 in Cambridgeshire.

[45] Joan Thirsk, *English Peasant Farming: The Agrarian History of Lincolnshire from Tudor to Recent Times* (London 1957), pp. 10–11.

[46] Sheail, thesis, general map, p. 129.

[47] Compare maps 3, 4, and 5. The actual figures, according to me (calculated as I have described in n. 43 above), were 4,555 taxpayers assessed in 1524–5; 4,281 households in the same area in 1563; 5,723 taxable persons in 1664.

16

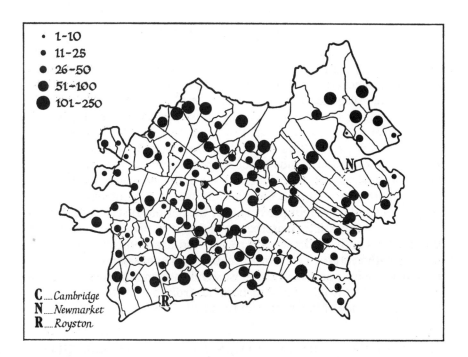

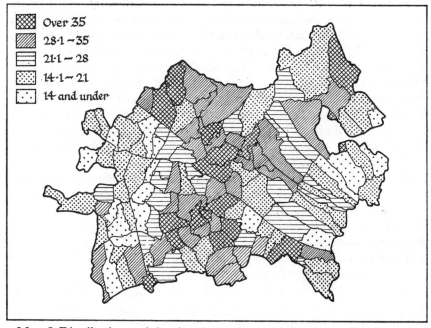

Map 5 Distribution and density of population in Cambridgeshire in 1664

It was these two areas, the fen-edge and the chalk ridge, lying north and east of the old Roman road from Colchester to Huntingdon, which showed the steepest rise in population over the period. The extent of it varied from village to village, from seventeen per cent at Stetchworth to 125 per cent àt Cottenham. Usually, dramatic increases of over 100 per cent were found in the fens or on the fen-edge, but a few upland villages like West Wratting, which had twenty-seven people assessed in 1524, forty-seven households in 1563, and seventy-six persons separately taxed in 1664, could match them. Even parishes which were already densely settled in 1524, like Over and Swavesey, had increases of sixty-six per cent and forty-four per cent over the period. Just as the resources of the fen parishes like Waterbeach had earlier provided a livelihood for squatters and smallholders,[48] so they did again in the expansion of the sixteenth century. The transformation and expansion of the fen and fen-edge villages was one of the most significant and marked changes in the county. The neighbourhood became, from one of the most empty in the county, one of the most thickly settled.

RAPID POPULATION GROWTH IN THE FENS – WILLINGHAM

In a third of the villages of the fen and fen-edge the whole of the rise in population took place after 1563; but it was the only part of the county in which the numbers assessed did not generally fall between 1524 and 1563. Indeed, in almost a third of the remaining villages half, or over half, the total rise took place between 1524 and 1563. Willingham was one of the latter. Only sixty-eight taxpayers were recorded there in 1525. But there were 105 households by 1563 – a rise of fifty-four per cent. There was a further rise of twenty-nine per cent, from 105 to 135 households taxed on their hearths in 1664. The rise was so marked in Willingham that despite the size of the parish it had become one of the most densely populated in the county, with over thirty households per thousand acres.

Because I have made a special study of Willingham, I have also analysed its parish register in some detail. The registers do not, unfortunately, open until 1559, and so they miss almost all the early, and steeper, part of the rise. They show an excess of baptisms over burials from their inception until 1656, apart from the crisis year of 1617 and a few years in the late 1620s. From 1656 onwards to the 1690s, on the other hand, burial figures were generally slightly above baptisms. This trend was reversed for a brief period from 1692 until 1708, but from

---

[48] Ravensdale, thesis, pp. 206–7, when he describes the expansion of Waterbeach into 'Newerowe' as 'the building of a medieval slum for fenmen'.

18

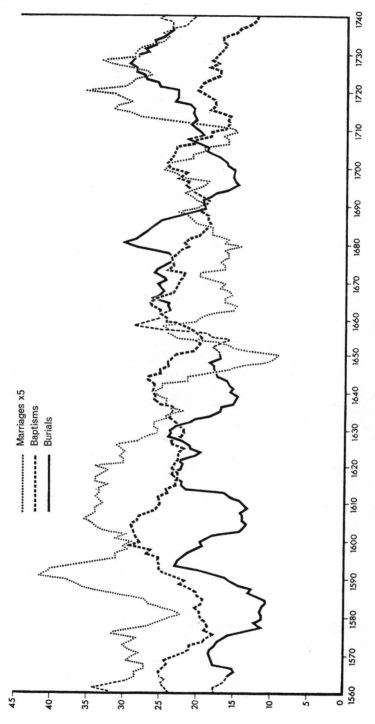

Graph 1 Nine-year moving averages of Willingham population, 1560–1740

Marriages x5
Baptisms
Burials

then until the 1740s, burials again greatly exceeded baptisms, despite a peak number of marriages between 1715 and 1730. There may have been considerable under-registration, particularly of baptisms, because of nonconformity, since Willingham was a stronghold of Congregationalism from the 1660s, and had a flourishing Quaker group as well. Unfortunately no numerical estimate of the number of dissenters there is available, for the figures for Willingham are missing in the Compton Census of 1676. Nathaniel Bradshaw, rector of Willingham, who was deprived of the living in 1662, but continued to preach there after the toleration act, claimed that he left 'fourscore and ten praying families in Willingham' at his ejection.[49] If this were true, it would mean that nearly three-quarters of Willingham people were inclined towards Congregationalism. Registration may therefore well have been affected by the end of the 1650s. Burial figures should have fallen as well as baptismal figures however, particularly in view of the Congregational buryingground within five miles at Oakington, and the Quaker habit of using unconsecrated ground for burials. There is a comment in the Willingham register in 1697, 'Note that Some Dissenters fanatically intered are not taken notice of here.'

The whole question becomes very much more complex when any attempt is made to relate the increases, or decreases, shown in the registers to the number of people who were apparently able to take up land and farm it, and so to the real changing size of the village.

The number of tenants given in the surveys of Willingham made in 1575, 1603, and the 1720s corresponds fairly closely with estimates of the size of the place made from general sources.[50] In 1575, there was a

[49] A. G. Matthews, *Calamy Revised, being a Revision of E. Calamy's Account of the Ministers and others ejected and silenced, 1660–2* (Oxford 1934), pp. 69–70. [Henceforth *Calamy Revised*.] Calamy's account is taken from the First Church Book of Willingham Old Meeting, pp. 40–1. I am very grateful to Mr Dennis Jeeps for gaining access to this for me. See also below, pp. 245–8, 302–6 and 334–7.

[50] It must be admitted that surveys are never satisfactory for this purpose, for several tenants commonly hold more than one house apiece. It is impossible to know how many of these houses are actually occupied by nameless sub-tenants, and this confuses the issue, especially if there is also the contradictory problem of holders of land who do not hold houses. The wills of Willingham men provide ample evidence of sub-tenancies (see, for instance, below, p. 144) and were also sometimes made by men who appeared to be houseless (see, for instance, below, pp. 142–4). The field books of Willingham (as summarised in Cambridge Record Office [henceforth C.R.O.], C.R.O., R59/14/5/8 (b)) in fact provide a kind of model booby-trap for the researcher trying to gain an impression of the size of a place from a survey, because, although they list houses with common rights but no land, they do not pay any attention to houses without common rights, until the 1720s. It is pure chance that a town survey of 1603 and the 1720s survives [C.R.O., R59/14/5/8 (d); I was only rescued from this particular booby-trap by the intervention of Dennis Jeeps, who mentioned this town survey to me] and acts as a corrective to the field survey, since it does include non-commonable cottages (see Table 11, below).

20

minimum of 100 tenants in Willingham, compared with the bishop's estimate of 105 households there twelve years earlier.[51] By 1603, the rise in population shown in the registers had had its effect. There were 125 houses in the town then, and eighteen of these were cottages without common rights, squeezed in on the green by the pond, or built on the croft of a relation, like Robert Clark's non-commonable cottage by William Clark's commonable house, or perhaps built for subletting. The two Henry Ellises, junior and senior, both substantial men, both had cottages at the end of their crofts,[52] listed under their own names as 'owners'. The 1664 hearth tax recorded a total of 135 houses in the village. In the 1720s, there were 153 tenants associated with the place. There were twenty-eight more buildings without common rights than there had been in 1603.[53] At least six more were squashed in round the village pond, and others were on strips which had been specifically described in 1603 as 'lands' or 'leys of grovage'.[54]

There was much mobility among the people of Willingham in these six generations from 1575 to the 1720s. Comparison of the family names given in the surveys of 1575 and 1720s shows the amount of movement into, and out of, the parish. Fifty-eight separate surnames were

[51] No town survey survives as a corrective for this date, however.

[52] C.R.O., R59/14/5/8 (d), plot numbers 27, 28, 75, 88. These may be identified on the map preserved in the C.R.O. unindexed survey of 1793.

[53] Including the almshouse and a meeting-house. It is extremely unfortunate that Willingham has suffered so badly from fires since 1700. Two investigators of the R.C.H.M., Robert Taylor and Tony Baggs, looked at the place for me in 1970, although it was nowhere near the area they were then working in. They estimated that only thirteen buildings then standing dated from before 1700. These represent such a small proportion of the original buildings of the seventeenth-century village that they cannot help reconstruct the dates at which the village expanded, as the far higher proportion of surviving sixteenth- and seventeenth-century buildings at Orwell so usefully can (see below, pp. 25-6). It is still interesting that two out of the thirteen survivors were cottages built on leys, between 1603 and the 1720s (38 High Street, single-storied house with attics, built on leys of grovage between plots number 105 and 104 of the town plan of 1603, and 68-70 High Street, which the investigators suggest was originally a small seventeenth-century house. It was built on plot number 107 of 1603, 'a holt', and there were two small cottages there in the 1720s.)

It is even more interesting that five out of the thirteen surviving seventeenth-century houses were held in 1603 by men, or women, with at least a half-yardland. This suggests strongly that such houses were better built and therefore more likely to survive, than those of the less prosperous. In the case of the house of Henry Graves, senior, who inherited the main holding of a half-yardland from his father, the reason for the survival is obvious. He lived in what is now 'Osborn House', 47 Church Street (plot 68 on town map), which is a timber-framed house which was encased in protective red brick in the very early eighteenth century. Naturally, the spending power for such improvements led to more immunity from fire. I am very grateful to Tony Baggs and Robert Taylor for going to so much trouble for me, and to Dennis Jeeps, who identified the houses they inspected on the 1603 plan.

[54] C.R.O., R59/14/5/8 (d), plot numbers 28, 36, 107.

represented in the place in 1575. The number had risen to ninety by the 1720s, but only a hard core of twenty-two families remained. There had certainly been emigration; thirty-six, or over two-thirds, of the families of the tenants of 1575, went or disappeared because they had only female heirs, or died out. The degree of mobility of a family was strongly related to the amount of land it held, and to the numbers of landholding members within it. Eleven families had more than one member holding land in 1575 in Willingham, and no less than nine of these were still represented in the village in the eighteenth century. On the other hand, all but one of eighteen cottagers who had common rights but no land[55] disappeared completely and left no trace in the surnames of the tenants. They were equally certainly replaced by others, however. Sixty-eight of the ninety names represented in the 1720s, or seventy-six per cent, were those of incomers. Obviously immigration exceeded emigration, and the evidence for growth which the survey made in the 1720s presents seems conclusive.

One village near the Ouse, therefore, expanded so rapidly between 1524 and 1664 that its fens supported one of the highest densities of households in the county. This detailed example helps to explain the differences which developed in the distribution of families and the size of villages in the county between the 1520s and the hearth tax. Other differences also developed, however. The fens and the fen-edge now supported more people, and the river valleys of central Cambridgeshire were, as they had always been, the most heavily settled parts of the county. Settlement might be thicker on the chalk ridge to the south-east, but it was still relatively very sparse.[56]

STAGNANT POPULATION ON THE CLAY – ORWELL

The villages on the western clay plateau, which was more thickly settled than the fens at the beginning of the sixteenth century, were

---

[55] This analysis is based solely on the tenants named in the field book, C.R.O., R59/14/5/8 (b) and does not include the occupants of the extra cottages without common rights shown in the town survey, many of whose names are irrecoverable, because the owner was simply 'the lord' or a landed tenant. It is obvious that, if there was more movement the further down the social scale one went, there must have been much more than I have described, since I have omitted non-commoners and sub-tenants. This may partly explain why, despite the amount of mobility I have described, Willingham appeared to my husband as a relatively static community. Peter Spufford, 'Population Movement in Seventeenth-Century England', *Local Population Studies*, IV (1970), 46.
[56] Compare maps 3, 4 and 5, showing distribution of population and its density in 1524–5, 1563 and 1664.

shrinking. A core of nine villages here and in the upper Rhee valley west of Melbourn had drops in numbers assessed, spread over the whole period from 1525 to 1664, which ranged from thirteen per cent at Orwell to fifty-three per cent at Kingston, to judge from the central government returns alone. In another eighteen villages by the upper waters of the Rhee, or on the clay plateau and its gault periphery, the rise in the number of households between 1563 and 1664 was not adequate, or was barely adequate, to offset the fall in the numbers taxed in the early part of the sixteenth century. The village of Orwell is a community which made a very pleasing contrast, as a special study, to Willingham. It was even more pleasing that, despite the way they were totally contrasted economically and socially, they shared their nonconformity. The difficulties presented by their registers were therefore identical.

Detailed examination of the evidence available on the size of Orwell shows just how misleading subsidy returns can be. There were fifty-two taxable individuals there in 1524, and forty-six households, according to the bishop, in 1563. This difference is probably accounted for by the changed basis of assessment,[57] rather than by any real change. Only forty-five houses were recorded by the hearth tax assessors of 1664, however. This was certainly an underestimate, for the names of all the tenants of the manor, both freeholders and copyholders, were listed in 1649, 1650 and 1672. The numbers recorded were both fairly consistent and static, between fifty-four in 1650 and fifty in 1670. The map made in the 1670s shows fifty-five houses.[58] There may therefore have been an increase of about a fifth in the number of households between the bishop's estimate in 1563, and the 1670s, always provided that the bishop's figure was accurate. The baptism trends from the parish registers suggest fewer families in Orwell in the 1660s than in the 1570s.[59] However, despite the proven inaccuracy of the hearth tax in this instance, the picture of the overall size of Orwell remains a fairly static one with its fifty-two taxable adults in the 1520s, and its fifty to fifty-four tenants in the 1670s.[60]

The entries for both burials and marriages in the parish registers of Orwell begin in 1560, and those for baptisms in 1569.[61] They show

[57] See above, p. 13. On the other hand contrast Willingham, above, p. 18, where the rise must have been even steeper than the figures indicate.
[58] Including the almshouse; excluding the town house and the church.
[59] But see below, p. 27, for possible underregistration.
[60] This latter figure did not include living-in servants, however, as the former did.
[61] *The Register of the Parish of Orwell, Cambs., 1560–1653*, transcr. and ed. R. W. Whiston (Sedbergh 1912). This is a very careful transcript, which has had any extra matter from the bishops' transcripts added.

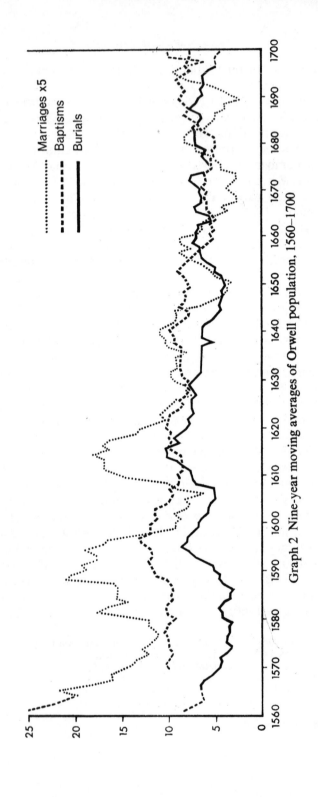

Graph 2 Nine-year moving averages of Orwell population, 1560–1700

Marriages x5
Baptisms
Burials

that there was a continuous excess of baptisms over burials from the 1570s until the late 1650s, with the exception of the second decade of the seventeenth century, when the high number of deaths in the crisis years of 1612 and 1617 brought the average number of burials higher than that of baptisms. Despite crises, there was a natural increase of just over three hundred between 1574–5 and 1635–6. From the late 1650s to the mid-1680s, the number of deaths exceeded the number of births. A recovery then began.

Taking this evidence from the registers alone, Orwell should have been a rapidly growing community in the late sixteenth century, and should have continued to grow, although more slowly, until the mid-seventeenth century. The possible rise of a fifth in the number of households between 1563 and the 1670s is evidence of some increase. There is a certain amount of evidence of new building in Orwell which tallies with this. The infilling of the common green with houses and crofts, and the appearance of tiny intakes of less than a rood within these crofts on the map made in the 1670s is extremely suggestive. The parish register suggests that these extra houses are most likely to have been built at least before the 1650s. There are a few indications which suggest the dates at which building took place. The survey of 1607, as well as mentioning empty tofts which were probably relics of the late medieval decline in population, also mentioned three cottages built on the waste, all granted since 1581. The surveyor commented in 1627 that there was little timber about the town, and that the tenants 'pretended' they had a right to it. He added acidly, 'and out of that small quantity . . . there is much fallen lately and lyeth about their houses which they pretend they had else wheare but the stockes of the treese appeareth in many places upon their owne backsides'. It is perhaps not without significance that Mathew Jeep mentioned his 'new' parlour in his will of 1617. It is certainly not without significance that the recent survey of Orwell carried out by the Royal Commission for Historical Monuments shows that of thirty-five houses still standing in Orwell today which are classifiable as monuments, only two were certainly built in the sixeeenth century or before. Another five were built in the sixteenth century and extended in the seventeenth, or might have been built in either century. Seven were definitely built after 1700. Most of the remaining twenty-one were built in the seventeenth century.[62] This building boom might be interpreted as evidence of great prosperity in the seventeenth century, but on the other hand,

[62] It is impossible to be precise; fifteen houses are lumped together by the Commission in their survey as probably seventeenth-century, but in a few cases eighteenth-century. *R.C.H.M.*, p. 195 (nos 25–39).

a fairly high proportion of these houses were built of a single storey with an attic. The houses in small intakes were of this type.[63] In many cases, it is possible to discover the rent paid by the tenant of a particular house shown on the map of the mid-1670s, and so the probable size of his farm.[64] The most substantial men, like William Fairchild and John Godfrey, who were paying copyhold rents of £3 5s 11d and £2 4s 10d were living in substantial houses of two storeys, built in the sixteenth century and extended in the seventeenth century,[65] or perhaps built entirely in the seventeenth century.[66] Some families which had previously been of substance were hanging on in similar houses, although they were now in very much reduced circumstances.[67] Half-yardlanders were usually content with single-storey houses with attics, however.[68] The few identifiable tenants of the small houses of this type, which were lumped together by the Commission, all held under twelve acres in the 1670s. Clement Godfrey, who paid a rent of 6s 3d and farmed eight and a half acres[69] of copyhold, lived in a cottage on the High Street[70] of this kind. The evidence of the surviving Orwell houses suggests, on the whole, not a wave of seventeenth-century prosperity and a 'Great Rebuilding', but a big increase in the number of smaller houses being built to accommodate the growing population. The evidence of the registers suggests that this building must have taken place very early in the century.[71]

However, the registers also show that Orwell was shrinking, despite the natural increase in the population there. From the 1570s until just before 1600, the numbers of baptisms were rising, whereas between 1600 and 1665 they were falling. This fall began in the late 1590s, even though it had been preceded by a record number of marriages in the preceding decade, which should, if the newly established couples had remained in Orwell, have pushed the number of births up still higher. The combination of a natural increase in the population of Orwell and the tendency for the number of recorded baptisms to fall, argues strongly for a decrease in the number of childbearing couples living there, and so for emigration from the village from the late sixteenth century. Considering the proven mobility of population in the

---

[63] Cf. numbers 31 and 32 on the Commission plan of Orwell, *ibid.* p. 188.
[64] By comparing the tenants on the map with those in the rental made between 1675 and 1682. See below, pp. 102–4.
[65] John Godfrey, monument (7), *R.C.H.M.*, p. 192.
[66] William Fairchild, monument (12), *ibid.* p. 193.
[67] Jeapes, monument (17), *ibid.* p. 193.
[68] Wid. Adams, monument (8) and Adams, monument (11), *ibid.* pp. 192–3.
[69] C.R.O., L63/48/1.   [70] Monument (35), *R.C.H.M.*, p. 195.
[71] If indeed it cannot be backdated to the late sixteenth century, which is the period the registers indicate.

period, it is probably more accurate to suggest that emigration out-weighed immigration. It seems likely that the picture given by the Orwell registers of emigration was even more marked in the other upland villages on the clays, where the returns of 1524–5, 1563 and 1664 indicate a much greater drop in the number of inhabitants.

Late in the seventeenth century, Orwell was one of the strongholds of dissent in Cambridgeshire. It had considerable numbers of both Congregationalists and Muggletonians. According to the Compton Census of 1676, which gave it 58 nonconformists, it had more dis-senters than any other place in the county.[72] The strength of noncon-formity may well have affected registration from the 1650s onwards. Yet the clerk appears to have been meticulous in noting the burials of dissenters. Several were buried in closes, or in their own orchards – like Mary Cundy, widow, a Muggletonian, who died excommunicated and was buried in the close next to the churchyard in 1686, 'with the burial of an asse', according to the disgruntled scribe. There was also a note on one Congregationalist, Margaret Fordham, who died on 1 July 1674 and on 2 July 'was carted to the burying place of the seditious conventiclers at Hogginton', the official Congregational burial ground at Oakington, ten or eleven miles away. There seems little reason therefore to doubt the accuracy of the registration of the burials. Marriages, on the other hand, certainly went unregistered. In 1669 there was a note, 'wee know not whether wee have any. Some wee have who say they are marryed, by Lawlesse ministers, att Law-lesse Churches, as they call them.' The registration of baptisms will almost inevitably have suffered as well. It is just possible, therefore, that the excess of deaths over births recorded from the late 1650s to the mid-1680s is a mere reflection of deficient registration. If this was so, however, the recovery beginning in the mid-1680s, round about the time that toleration effectively started, is difficult to account for, con-sidering that Orwell remained one of the focal points of Congregational-ism in southern Cambridgeshire. In any case, nonconformity there can-not have affected the vital points illustrated by the registers before 1650: the decline of the population, despite the continual natural increase in the parish, and the way in which its people emigrated, from the beginning of the seventeenth century. Detailed examination of the registers here, then, reinforces the general picture given by the subsidies of a shrinkage of settlement on the western clays and their edges, even though it may also correct particular figures drawn from subsidies to more accurate ones.

[72] Margaret Spufford, 'The Dissenting Churches in Cambridgeshire from 1600 to 1700', *Proc. Cambs. Ant. Soc.*, LXI (1968), 75, 79.

Density maps of settlement in the county therefore show that between 1524 and 1664 there was an intensification of settlement on the chalk ridge, which still, however, remained comparatively lightly peopled. There was a corresponding swing away from settlement on the western clays. The villages south of Cambridge increased their size, and their already high parish densities, while the villages on the fen-edge had in some cases doubled in size, and their neighbourhood had changed from one of the most empty in the country to one of the most thickly settled.

No general comparisons between the density of settlement in Cambridgeshire and the rest of the country in the period of the hearth taxes can be made until someone has undertaken an analysis of one of the hearth taxes[73] for the whole of the country, in the way that the taxations of 1334 and 1524–5 have already been analysed. I suspect that when such an analysis is made Cambridgeshire will still appear thickly populated, but that its overall prosperity will appear lower than other parts of the south-east, because of the social structure of its villages.

PROSPERITY AND SOCIAL STRUCTURE IN THE 1520s

Cambridgeshire has never been a 'gentle' county, far less a 'noble' one. The degree of manorial fragmentation found there from the Conquest did not encourage strong lordship. With a few notable exceptions, like the Norths of Kirtling, whose gatehouse still stands in the woods by a moated farm, the Huddlestones of Sawston whose superb sixteenth-century house only left the family hands in the second half of the twentieth century, and perhaps above all the Chicheleys of Wimpole Hall, which is Cambridgeshire's only surviving grandiose

---

[73] The hearth tax return of Michaelmas 1664 (P.R.O., E179/84/437) was chosen for detailed analysis, since it is an extremely thorough revision of the return of Michaelmas 1662 (E179/84/436) which includes frequent corrections of concealments, and comments which were obviously, in some cases, based on personal inspection. For this reason it seemed likely to be the most accurate of the series, and the most suitable for my purposes. The return for Lady Day 1674 would have been even more suitable, being the fullest. However, in 1961, when I was working on the taxes, I was told that Mr Meekings was in the process of completing work on the latter for a forthcoming table in the next general *V.C.H.* for Cambridgeshire and the Isle of Ely and duplication seemed absurd. Analysis of the wrong return is not likely to have mattered very much. Mr Meekings calculated in an earlier volume that a net total of only 191 more entries were given for the Isle of Ely in 1674 than in 1664, which represents an increase of only four per cent and may be thought to be negligible. (C.A.F. Meekings, *V.C.H. Cambs. and the Isle of Ely*, IV, 273.)

mansion, the gentry in the county were minor, and their pretensions were not encouraged by their tenants. Nor were these tenants over-prosperous, by the standards of the south-east. Dr Sheail has analysed the returns of the subsidies of 1524 and 1525 in terms both of numbers of taxpayers and of the amount of tax raised per square mile.[74] In terms of numbers of taxpayers a large part of the county formed part of the heavily settled East Anglian region.[75] In terms of taxation raised only the river valley immediately south of Cambridgeshire main-tained the predominance it has always had, and raised more than fifty shillings per square mile, like parts of Norfolk, large areas of Essex, Kent and Middlesex. By far the largest part of the county only raised between twenty and thirty shillings a square mile for the Exchequer, and was relatively poor.[76]

The reason is not difficult to determine. Men whose wealth was assessed at £20 or more paid tax at the rate of 1s in the pound; men assessed at under £20 paid only 6d in the £1.[77] If an area had a large number of 'wealthy' taxpayers assessed at £20 or more, the sur-tax they paid increased the sums raised in that area, whilst it in no way reflected the general number of those paying tax. Dr Sheail's maps show both that Cambridgeshire was as prosperous as the rest of the south-east, if those paying surtax were excluded, and indeed more prosperous than Essex.[78] If men paying only on assessments of £20 or more were considered,[79] however, it had fewer of them than most of the south-east including, certainly, just those parts of Norfolk, Essex, Kent and Middlesex which appeared most rewarding to the Exchequer in general. In Dr Sheail's words, 'There was a relatively high yield from those assessed for less than £20 in parts of East Anglia, where the map of the distribution of taxpayers suggested a denser population than average. The wealth of the coast of Essex and parts of Kent and Sussex largely rested on the richer section of the population.' His own maps show that the first part of this statement was truer of Cam-bridgeshire than most of the rest of the south-east. Cambridgeshire's relative lack of prosperity in the 1520s, considering the part of the country in which it lay, was therefore accounted for, not because it was thinly peopled, but because it had few gentlemen, and, indeed, few really wealthy yeomen.

More detailed analysis of the subsidy confirms this interpretation.

[74] See above, p. 12, n. 35.
[75] Sheail, thesis, I, 129, and see above, p. 10.
[76] *Ibid.* I, 116.
[77] *Ibid.* I, 131.
[78] *Ibid.* I, general map, p. 133, and county map, p. 159.
[79] *Ibid.* I, general map, p. 134.

The outstandingly wealthy were those who paid on £20 or more; but men who paid on £10 or more were sufficiently exceptional to their contemporaries to be chosen as collectors of the subsidy along with their richer neighbours. Henry Norman of Madingley, who had £10 in goods, was high collector of North Stowe hundred along with Robert Stewkyn of Lolworth who had £40;[80] and he was by no means exceptional. Such men were not, in this rural area, 'lesser yeomen', forming an appendage to the 'yeomen' proper with over £20; it might be more accurate to say that a man with £10 was almost invariably a yeoman, and a man with over £20 was a highly exceptional yeoman. Martin Folkes of Westley Waterless paid on £10 in 1524; under Elizabeth, a Martin Folkes was farmer of the site and demesne of the priory of Swaffham Bulbeck,[81] and in 1662 William Folkes of Westly Waterless died leaving £324 7s 6d.[82] Such a case-history shows no meteoric change, but rather the comfortable maintenance and improvement of a position already occupied at the beginning of the period.

Only just over eight per cent of the taxpayers of the county had £10 or more in 1524–5, and only three and a half per cent altogether had more than £20. This proportion of the really wealthy is much the same as the average in the Lincolnshire fens,[83] and is just under that for Leicestershire,[84] but is of course completely different from that of any urban area,[85] and indeed, most rural areas. For the country as a whole just under ten per cent of the people in the subsidy lists were worth £20 and more.[86]

The group assessed on over £20 included the big landowners and gentry, the Huddlestones and Allingtons with over £100 in lands; although there were only six families who achieved this eminence, and no individual paid on more than £120 and rivalled Sir Thomas Pulteney of Misterton in Leicestershire with his £160,[87] or Sir John Hussey of Old Sleaford in Lincolnshire with his £500.[88] The group also included wealthy yeoman, although nothing is known of the most outstanding, Richard Morgan of Guilden Morden, who paid on £200 in goods. Lesser men are more easily traced and, in fact, more typical, since the vast majority who paid on over £20 paid on between £20 and £60.

[80] E179/81/126.　　　　[81] E134/44/45, Eliz./Mich.7.
[82] Cambridge University Library [C.U.L.], Consistory Court Probate Inventories, bundled under years. See below, p. 38, for the median wealth of yeomen.
[83] Thirsk, *English Peasant Farming*, p. 46.
[84] W. G. Hoskins, *Essays in Leicestershire History* (Liverpool 1950), pp. 129–30.
[85] Cornwall, *art. cit.* p. 63.
[86] Sheail, thesis, p. 131.
[87] Hoskins, *Essays in Leics. History*, p. 128.
[88] Thirsk, *English Peasant Farming*, pp. 46–7.

William Baron of Comberton, who was assessed at £56, left five or six tenements to the use of his grandchildren and nephews, as well as providing for 'all free lands in my hands'.[89] His three sons were all apparently already provided for; one was himself assessed at over £10. William Sweyn of Chesterton, collector of a hundred, left all his lands and tenements, including freehold, copyhold and 'ancient demesne' to his wife, but except 'the Taberd that I now dwell in, the Cheker, and five small tenements or cottages'. He was assessed at £40.

Possibly the greatest importance of the great subsidy of 1524–5 to the historian is that it is the only taxation return made during the century for which most of the returns survive,[90] which is also sufficiently comprehensive to cover many of the poorest members of society as well as the most prosperous. It therefore provides the best opportunity of examining the whole structure of rural society. The men assessed at £20 or more formed the highest pinnacle of the iceberg; from many points of view the lowest examinable part of the same iceberg, the wage-earners, are the most interesting.

The act passed in 1523 for the levying of the subsidy[91] provided for the taxation of those over the age of sixteen with goods to the value of £2 a year and upwards, and those with wages to the value of £1 a year 'having none other substance'. It is therefore possible to discover what proportion of those taxed were wage-earners. Work already done in other counties shows that the proportion varied widely from an average of twenty-two per cent in Leicestershire[92] and thirty-six per cent in Devon,[93] to go between twenty-eight per cent and forty-one per cent in Lincolnshire,[94] although these average figures concealed much higher proportions in individual villages. In the most recent consideration of this evidence, it is suggested that between a quarter and a third of the entire population in rural areas were wage-labourers.[95]

In spite of the assumption of the act of 1523 that those taxed on wages would have no other means of livelihood, the existence of a class of people taxed on 'goods' to the value of £1 has been noticed in various places, and Cambridgeshire is no exception. The collectors of Radfield hundred, which lay on the chalk ridge to the south-east, did not tax a single inhabitant on wages, although between twenty-four per cent and fifty-seven per cent of them paid on £1 worth of substance.

[89] C.U.L. Registered Wills, vol. J, fo. 104.
[90] See above, p. 12, n. 35, on the subsidies of 1544–6.
[91] *Statutes of the Realm*, III, 231.
[92] Hoskins, *Essays in Leics. History*, p. 129.
[93] H. P. R. Finberg and W. G. Hoskins, *Devonshire Studies* (London 1952), p. 419.
[94] Thirsk, *English Peasant Farming*, p. 83.
[95] A. M. Everitt, 'Farm Labourers', in Thirsk, *Agrarian History*, IV, 396–400.

This looks like a collector's foible; and yet the same men, in the neighbouring hundred of Chilford, carefully taxed seven out of sixty-seven men with a pound's worth of substance on wages, although the rest were all taxed on goods. In Cheveley hundred, at the other end of the chalk ridge, nearly half those taxed on a pound were taxed on goods; and elsewhere in the county, a sprinkling, and sometimes more than a sprinkling, of similar cases existed. The link between the two classes of those taxed on a pound is provided by an entry in the list for the village of Teversham, which assessed William Fairman and Nicolas Yugram, both described as 'labourer', on goods to the value of a pound.

There must have been a valid distinction to the collectors between men taxed on goods and on wages. I suggest that the distinction was in part between the labourer, with his own cottage, who was also dependent on earning some wages to keep himself and his family above the bread-line; and the resident in-servant. In the former case, the goods of the man concerned made up more of his livelihood than his wages, and he was therefore much less dependent on wages than his contemporary taxed on them. This situation is more likely because the two hundreds where the distinction is most apparent, Chilford and Radfield, cover the chalk ridge and its boulder clay, which had a different settlement pattern from the rest of the county, and was also much poorer than the rest of the county in every period I have examined in detail.[96] It is also the only area in which, in the revision of the 1662 hearth tax made in 1664, I have found an entry which reads, opposite an assessment on one hearth, made two years before, 'Not Chargeable. The house blown downe.' It is easy to forget that those sixteenth- and seventeenth-century houses and cottages which survive in relatively large numbers now, represent a heavily weighted sample of the better-built, more prosperous village houses, and that an unknown number of people must have lived in shacks like the one so briefly, yet vividly, described in the roll, liable to fall down in a hearty gust of wind. It does seem very likely that the chalk ridge was settled by a higher number of labourers living in poverty-stricken hovels, particularly in the woodland clearings on the upper clays, than the rest of the county.

Although the labourer living in his cottage and earning wages, and the in-servant in his garret must be lumped together as wage-earning, to do so is to some extent to oversimplify the position at the bottom of the social scale. There seems to have been a complete spectrum ranging from the man entirely dependent on wages, through

[96] See, for instance, above, pp. 5, 14–16, 27–8, and below, p. 44.

the man whose labour brought in less of his annual income than his goods, to the one who possibly had only goods, but whose small-holding brought him in no more than a servant's wages, and who, indeed, was worse off than an exceptional servant who was paid £2 a year, like Laurence Waller of Steeple Morden, or the fortunate John Ewen, who worked for an alien in the port of Reach and was paid £3.

Details of the lives of such men are hard to come by. Simon Hullocke of Thriplow, who paid on wages to the value of 30s, left a will[97] which showed him clearly as a man with other resources as well. He left his son 'my place with appurtenances' in Fulbourn, with directions that his mother was to be paid 10s a year out of it. He was also in a position to leave little bequests of 8d or 12d not only to Thriplow parish church, but to both the churches in Fulbourn, and to Little Wilbraham.

It is impossible to estimate how many labourers had, like Simon Hullocke, 'places with appurtenances' and how many, like the five wage-earners who were described by the chantry priest of Clopton as 'servants in my mastres house'[98] were servants resident with their employers. Some distinction could probably be made between labourers with their own cottages and in-servants, on the basis of the number of wage-earners' names which follow those of men of substance in the returns compared with those which come together in a group, but it would be most unreliable, since the lists sometimes suggest that the most prominent villagers were taxed first, and sometimes the list is so jumbled that it might well be taken in the order in which the houses stood. For what it is worth, the servants who appeared to live in were still in a fairly small minority.

The really important conclusion to be drawn from all this is that the proportion of the wage-earning population in Cambridgeshire in 1524–5 was astonishingly high, compared with other counties. In eleven out of the fourteen hundreds of the county, an average of fifty-three per cent of those assessed paid on 30s or less. This very high proportion was probably partly accounted for by the relatively high population density of the county, and partly by the amount of seasonal labour a corn-growing region demanded. Even so, it is amazing that over half the inhabitants of a rural area should already be dependent on wages to bring their livelihood up to a minimum standard, a proportion not quite reached in England as a whole even at the end of the seventeeth century.[99]

[97] C.U.L., Cambridgeshire Wills, vol. J, fo. 95.
[98] *Ibid.* fo. 98v.
[99] Everitt, in Thirsk, *Agrarian History*, IV, 399.

In an article on the subsidy Mr Cornwall has suggested that in market towns,

Assessments at £2 represent a class of small craftsmen and husbandmen partially independent but needing to work for day wages from time to time in order to make ends meet. Above them was a kind of lower-middle class fairly well established, especially those in the upper bracket assessed at £6–9. Worth from £10–19 was a substantial middle class of richer tradesmen and husbandmen and lesser yeomen. Above £20 were those fortunate few ... including prosperous master craftsmen and merchants, yeomen and gentlemen.[100]

These criteria are much too high for a rural area, particularly one with a high proportion of the poor. It is difficult to obtain enough evidence on the size of individual farms that connects with entries in the subsidy lists to give a firm idea of the kind of social standing and prosperity that any particular assessment involves. However, two years after the return was made for Longstowe hundred,[101] Edward Chamberlayne held his first court as lord of the manor of Kingston Wood, and his tenants came into court to acknowledge the fact. As a result, the court roll recited an apparent complete list of their holdings,[102] and in half a dozen cases the entries coincide with those of the subsidy. With this direct evidence, and an assortment of fragments of information gleaned from elsewhere, it is possible to gain some inkling of what a particular assessment meant. It is, however, only an inkling, and is only intended as a suggestion to be explored by further research.

Robert Wright *alias* Ewer, and Robert Bryan, of Kingston were assessed at £2 and £2 13s 4d in 1525. In 1527, Robert Wright held a cottage, a close and seventeen and three-quarter acres of land and pasture; Robert Bryan a messuage and nineteen acres of customary land. Thomas Higney, who had paid on £3 in goods in 1525, also farmed just over seventeen acres of customary land, but had a tenement and five acres of free land as well. Nicholas Garden, or Gardner, who paid on £4 13s 4d, held a messuage, forty-five acres of customary land and a close.

The Cambridgeshire yardland in the sixteenth and seventeenth centuries seems to have varied between thirty and forty acres, with a half-yardland which could in practice be anything from fourteen

---

[100] Julian Cornwall, 'English Country Towns in the Fifteen Twenties', *Econ. Hist. Rev.*, 2nd ser., xv (1962), 63.
[101] P.R.O., E179/81/161.
[102] C.R.O., R52/12/1/7.

to eighteen acres in the former case, to over twenty in the latter.[103] If a half-yardland was widely accepted in the medieval period as the minimum farm on which a family could support itself without other employment, it begins to seem significant that the two men assessed on £2 or £2 13s 4d in Kingston held an acreage appropriate to half-yardlanders, and that £2 was the minimum sum, according to the act of 1523, on which a man should pay on goods. It is possible that men taxed on £2 in goods were paying on the saleable surplus produce of a half-yardland, and that men taxed on £4 held a full yardland? The quantity of moveables a man possessed must have varied very widely, and led to much blurring between categories in the assessments. Yet common sense suggests that the assessors must have had some sort of rule-of-thumb basis of assessment, even though they may have modified it conscientiously by looking into the contents of a good many larders and cheese chambers in Cambridgeshire. The suggestion can only be extremely tentative since it is based on such a minute amount of evidence; but if it were true, it would explain why there is such an abrupt drop in the number of men assessed on more than £4; for such men would hold more than one yardland. Nicolas Garden, who paid on £4 13s 4d held over a yardland. John King of Kingston held three acres of free land, a yardland of customary land, and various pieces, and paid on £5. John Lete, who paid on £6 held 125 acres of customary land, as well as two closes, and eight acres 'de firma' which was presumably demesne. His whole farm was therefore just over 130 acres.

The supporting evidence tends to suggest that men taxed on between £6 and £10 might well hold more than one tenement, and form much more than 'a kind of lower-middle class' in their own villages.

---

[103] One of the questions put to deponents in Exchequer in a case on the demesne of Little Gransden concerned the size of the yardland there. The witnesses were with one exception unanimous that the yardland was forty acres. John Disborough, yeoman, said that he was at a manor court there in the 1580s, and 'being desirous to know how much a yardland contained, the then steward and some of the tenants did say a yardland contained forty acres and half a yardland twenty acres'. The only dissentient was Christopher Meade, gentleman, who was called for the plaintiffs to give evidence on the records of this episcopal manor, and reported that a 'quarter' land had equalled five acres, not ten acres, in the reeves' accounts from Richard II's reign onwards. (P.R.O., E134/5, Jas. I/Hil. 26.)

There is no direct evidence for the size of the yardland at Kingston, but it may also have been forty acres, for in the seventeenth century the stint was fixed on a twenty-acre basis (C.R.O., R52/12/1/10). At Chippenham, in Cambridgeshire, the yardland was thirty acres, as appears from a rental of 1560, drawn up in terms of yardlands, which was annotated in the seventeenth century with the exact acreages involved. In practice, the yardland ranged from twenty-eight to thirty-six acres, and the half-yardland from fourteen to eighteen acres (C.R.O., R55/7/5/1 (1)).

John Wiskin of West Wickham, who, like John Lete, paid on £6, left his son 'all my housses and my lands in fee symple'. In the village of Longstanton, apart from two men paying on over £20, under a quarter of the inhabitants paid on over £4, and the richest of them, Thomas Boston, paid on £8. The Bostons stood out as one of the most prosperous families in the village throughout the sixteenth century, since they held one of the two freeholds of any size.

Whether or not it can be maintained that men taxed on over £4 held more than a yardland of customary land, or rather less free land, the number of men assessed above this figure certainly drops abruptly, and demands separate treatment on that score. Whereas twenty-seven per cent of villagers paid on between over 30s and £4, only ten per cent paid on over £4 and under £10; and they might be, like the Bostons, the highest-assessed in their community.

The picture of Cambridgeshire that the subsidy of 1524–5 gives is of a county in which over half the inhabitants were dependent on wages, and more than another quarter had between £2 and £4 in goods. It is suggested that these last may perhaps have held tenements of up to a yardland in size. Above them, only a tenth of those assessed had from £5 to £10. Men taxed on this sum might have farmed over fifty to sixty acres, and have been among the most prosperous in their villages. Only eight per cent of those assessed had over £10, and the really wealthy worth over £20 were much less common than elsewhere. The high proportion of labourers was in no way compensated for by the outstanding prosperity of the upper yeomanry and gentry.

PROSPERITY AND SOCIAL STRUCTURE IN THE 1660s

The century and a half which followed the 'great subsidy' was the age of the engrosser on the corn-growing uplands,[104] and the age of fragmentation in the stock-rearing fens, where every holding broke down into the smallest fragments that could support a family under the pressure of population growth.[105] Analysis of the hearth tax therefore illustrates the very different ways in which different regions of the county had developed in this time, the polarisation of village society into a group of yeomen and labourers on the one hand, and the much more egalitarian communities of the fens on the other.

The hearth taxes can be used as general guides to wealth.[106] During

---

[104] See below, Chippenham, pp. 66, 70 and Orwell, pp. 99–104.
[105] See below, Willingham, pp. 144–50.
[106] For a full account of this, M. Spufford, 'Significance of Hearth Tax', pp. 53–64.

the course of working on inventories made for Cambridgeshire in the decade 1661 to 1670,[107] it proved possible to relate a hundred of them to the appropriate hearth tax entries to see whether a correlation existed between a man's wealth at his death, and the size of the house he lived in during his life, indicated by the number of hearths it contained.

By the 1660s a very considerable economic division existed between the wealth owned, and the acreages farmed, by men described by their neighbours at their deaths as 'yeomen', 'husbandmen' and 'labourers'.

There are about a hundred and fifty inventories amongst those made for the decade in which the local appraisers described the dead man's position among them. There seems no reason to doubt these descriptions. A man's description of himself in his will as a 'yeoman' may be suspect and include an element of wishful thinking; his neighbours, when they draw up his inventory, are unlikely to make the same mistake. There is no reason to suppose that the inhabitants of small communities have become more critical with time, and a modern survey of a Cumberland village shows the acute sensitivity felt by the inhabitants towards matters of social degree.[108]

Inevitably, the more substantial members of society were more strongly represented amongst the inventories. Only eighteen men were called 'labourers' and twenty-four 'husbandmen', although there were fifty-eight yeomen, and fifty-five assorted craftsmen. There was still enough material to give a vivid picture of the material benefits enjoyed by each.

Over half the labourers appear to have been landless, and to have had perhaps 'an ould kowe and a heffer' like Thomas Willobys of Harston. Edward Jacob of Whittlesford had a small parcel of wheat, rye and barley in his 'chamber above' which was 'all of them gleaned corne', not corn grown on his own land. On the other hand, the better-off had a little land. John Ison of Whittlesford had three acres, one and a half roods of wheat, rye and barley sown when his inventory was taken in May 1666. Edward Curtis, who lived in Lode Street, Bottisham, had 'in the field Swaffarn[109] growndes and heads' worth £8 3s 4d, which were of much greater value than any other labourers' arable crop. Altogether, the labourers' goods were appraised at sums of up to £80, but the median was £15.

Few of the husbandmen's inventories gave a clear picture of the

---

[107] Some 340 inventories survive for the decade.
[108] W. W. Williams, *The Sociology of an English Village: Gosforth* (London 1956).
[109] Saffron.

size of their farms, but those which did divided into two sharply
defined groups. Half of these men farmed under ten acres of arable,
and judging from their farms alone, can have been scarcely distinguish-
able from the better sort of labourer, although their household goods
were usually worth much more. Thomas Baron of Hardwick had an
acre of wheat and rye sown, and an acre of tilth to sow with winter
corn in December 1662, as well as two acres of stubble to sow, presumably with spring corn. His land and his crops and fodder in store
were worth only £8 3s 4d, and his three cows, six sheep and single pig
another £10, yet his household furnishings brought his estate up to the
value of £42 0s 8d.

In contrast to these men with their surprisingly tiny farms, husbandmen like John Affield of Harston, who farmed twenty-one acres in all,
or Thomas Peck of Barnwell, who had twenty-one acres sown, and
must have farmed over thirty, formed a middle group with traditional
holdings of from twenty-one to forty acres, or between a half-yardland
and a yardland. William Cokaine of Fenditton had a crop of over
forty-two acres in his barn in November 1666, and may well have
farmed over sixty acres in all, but he was exceptional. It is surprising,
and perhaps very significant, that the inventories show that only half
the husbandmen occupied traditional holdings, and half had been
reduced. The amount of personal wealth left by them ranged from
£10 to £250, and a quarter of them left over £70, but the median was
£30, or double that of a labourer.

Among the yeomen's inventories were fifteen which gave the
acreage of the whole farm. Just as the husbandmen's and labourers'
inventories embraced wide extremes, so those of the yeomen began at
one end, with John Pratt of Stetchworth who cultivated a total area of
four acres and left goods to the value of £11 15s, and ended at the
other with Thomas Edwards of Longstanton, who had 177 acres sown,
apart from the fallow, 113 acres of meadow and pasture, and left
goods to the value of £1131 18s 8d. However, the John Pratts were
rare; a yeoman might, and many did, farm only a yardland and a half,
but the median yeoman farm was ninety-two acres, and the median
yeoman wealth £180. The eighty-five-acre farm of William Folkes of
Westley Waterless was not far removed from the typical. The largest
group of yeomen were those farming 85 to 100 acres. There were as
many big farms of over 130 acres as small ones of under 40 acres,
although they usually only ran up to 200 acres, and William Salt of
Chesterton, who farmed 320 acres of arable, was exceptional.

Economically, therefore, the distinctions between men described
as yeomen, husbandmen and labourers were pronounced, and the

38

division between yeomen and others particularly so, as the medians of their wealth show. The median wealth of a labourer was £15, that of a husbandman £30, that of a craftsman £40, and that of a yeoman £180. But it would be wrong to categorise too much. Each group contained members who could well, judging from the value of their goods, be fitted into the next. The possessions of two labourers were appraised at over £30, and one of them, Thomas Doggett of Over, held bonds to the value of £77 10s. A quarter of the husbandmen had over £70, and men like Thomas Peck of Barnwell, with his comfortable house, his twenty-one sown acres and his goods worth £200 13s 4d, were far better-off than nearly a third of the yeomen, who had goods worth under £100, and perhaps, like William Howling of Shelford, a typical five-roomed cottage and only thirteen and a half acres in the open fields. It is perhaps easy to overstress economic criteria as being the main ones dividing social groups, simply for reasons of convenience. However, if it is borne in mind that the edges of each group blur indistinguishably into the next,[110] it is certainly safe to say that the 'average' yeoman was an entirely distinct being from his fictional neighbour, the 'average' husbandman, who could still not be confused with the 'average' labourer in the same village.

Just over a third of the hundred inventories which could be definitely related to a particular hearth tax assessment proved to be those of householders taxed on one hearth, just under a third of those taxed on two hearths, and the remaining third of those taxed on three and more hearths.

In each case, the relationship of inventory and assessment proved that just as groups of labourers, husbandmen and yeomen included people with widely varied ranges of goods, land and wealth, but were very distinct from each other in general terms, so also houses with different numbers of hearths might each shelter an assorted body of people ranging from rich to poor, and yet, in general, an incontrovertible association existed between wealth and house size.

Over four-fifths of the occupants of houses with one hearth had under £50, and their median wealth was £25, between that of a labourer and a husbandman. The hearth in a single-hearthed house was in the hall, or its variant, so that the hall was still used for cooking, despite the fact that almost half the service rooms in three- and four-roomed houses were known as 'kitchens'. The usual pattern was for

---

[110] The way in which inheritance customs in Cambridgeshire caused families to sprawl right across the economic divisions within a village was partially responsible for this blurring. See the discussion on the Butler family, below, pp. 108–11, for instance. I am therefore extremely reluctant to use the word 'class' to describe these different economic groups.

spare utensils to be banished to the kitchen, which held, like the kitchen of William Tilbrooke of West Wratting, kettles, and pewter, and dairy equipment. There were no utensils in his hall except those which belonged to the fireplace itself; the bellows, tongs, firepan and cob-irons.

Three-quarters of the occupants of houses with two hearths had between £10 and £100, and their median wealth rose to £60, or double that of the average husbandman. When there was more than one hearth, probate inventories cannot be trusted to indicate the position of the additional ones, for they usually give only the position of the main cooking hearth. In most two-hearthed houses the cooking was done in the kitchen, and so the kitchen hearth was given; occasionally it was still done in the hall, and so a hearth in the hall was given. Only in one two-hearth house did the inventory give both hearths, and they were in kitchen and hall. There is not a single example of a house with two hearths in which a heated parlour or chamber was indicated.

The median wealth of the occupants of houses with three hearths rose again to £141, a figure just under that which yeomen might be appraised. A house with three hearths might have from six to eleven rooms, but over three-quarters had six or eight rooms. They were occupied by people with personal wealth of from just under £30 to over £500, but the vast majority had from just under £30 to £200. The biggest single group of Cambridgeshire yeomen lived in eight-roomed houses.

The position of the third hearth varied considerably, according to the information given in the inventories. The hearth most commonly supplied with fire-irons was in the kitchen still, with the hall hearth mentioned next. But the parlour was sometimes heated in a house of this size; Henry Sell, yeoman of Gamlingay, had a hearth in his 'chamber below' judging from the 'iron grate' listed there, although he does not seem to have had one in his parlour. Richard Wootton of Ickleton had hearths in his parlour and hall. Moreover, one hearth was sometimes upstairs in a three-hearth house. Thomas Alban, blacksmith of Shepreth, who had seven rooms and three hearths, had a hearth in his hall, which he used for cooking, having no kitchen, and another in the chamber over the parlour, for five chests and six chairs, a little pair of cob-irons and a fire-shovel were listed there along with his bedstead. There were no fire-irons in his parlour, where the third hearth presumably was. Samuel Mortlock of Whittlesford had a hearth in his hall, and the only other implements connected with fires were in the chamber over his buttery, where he had two pairs of cob-irons.

The median wealth of the occupant of a house with four or more hearths shot up to £360, the wealth of a very substantial man indeed. A house with four hearths or more had from six to fourteen rooms, and might be occupied by a person with from £34 to £1,132. Five-eighths of these people had over £300. Only very considerable yeomen or prosperous shopkeepers occupied such houses in general. The house of John Mickelly of West Wickham, who left £546 12s 2d is a good example of these outstanding houses. It had thirteen rooms. Not all their positions are known, but downstairs he had a hall, and a parlour, which contained amongst other things a long table and eighteen leather chairs, kitchen, dairy, brewhouse and cellar. Upstairs he had chambers over the hall, the parlour, the dairy and the porch. The positions of his own bedchamber and of the chamber for storing cheese are not stated, nor was that of his 'round' chamber, which contained a bed with curtains, had hangings on the walls, and contained plate and linen which brought the value of the contents of the room up to £25. The house had five hearths, and it is the only large house in which the inventory gives the position of all five. There were fire-irons, cob-irons and tongs in the hall, the parlour, the kitchen, the chamber over the parlour, and John Mickelly's own bedchamber.

It is therefore clear that the hearth tax can be used as an economic guide, and also as a social guide in the sense that all persons with three or more hearths are likely to be yeomen, just as labourers are very unlikely to occupy a house with more than one hearth. But the extent of economic and social overlap shown by the inventories, and the blurring of economic and social divisions caused by inheritance and personal preference, mean that although the tax may be used as a guide to status and wealth in general, it may not safely be used in any individual example. The case of Richard London, husbandman of Hinxton, who have five hearths and only £34 to his name, and conversely, of Thomas Amey, husbandman of Harston, who had a two-roomed cottage with one hearth and left £119 15s 6d, are instructive examples of the dangers of oversimplification.

When an analysis of one of the hearth tax returns for Cambridgeshire was made and the results were mapped, it showed conclusively in some cases, and merely suggestive in others, the results which the economic processes at work in the last hundred and fifty years had had.[111]

Parishes with over fifty per cent of houses with one hearth, whose inmates were likely to have had the worldly goods appropriate to labourers, were scattered all over the county, with the single exception of the group of parishes to the north of the county, bordering on the

---

[111] The return of Michaelmas 1664 was chosen for this purpose. See p. 28, n. 73.

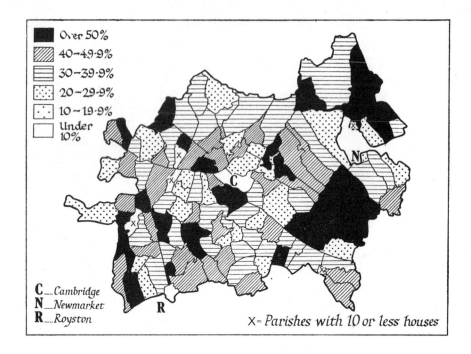

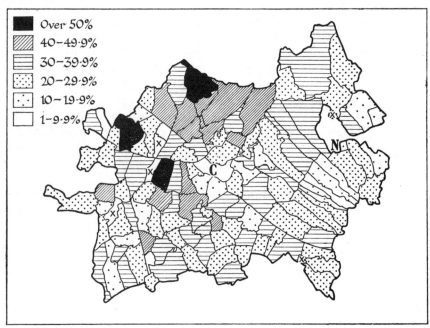

Map 6 Percentages of houses with one or two hearths in
Cambridgeshire in 1664

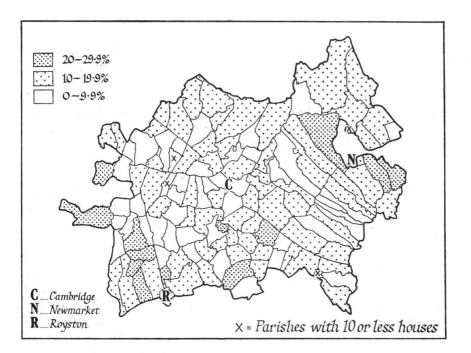

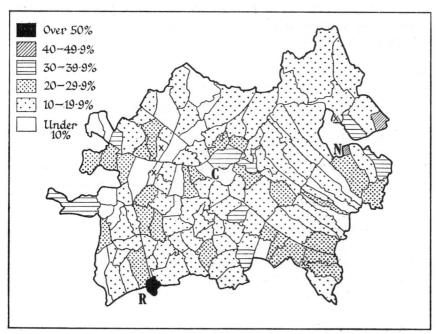

Map 7 Percentages of houses with three, and four-and-more hearths in Cambridgeshire in 1664

Ouse, running from Swavesey, through Willingham and Cottenham, to Waterbeach. There, the percentage was uniformly lower, just as the percentage of houses with two hearths was uniformly higher, than elsewhere. In most cases it was over forty per cent, and in the case of Willingham it was over fifty per cent. Nor did a single one of these parishes have more than twenty per cent of houses with three or more hearths. Swavesey and Willingham in particular were noticeably short of really prosperous houses with four or more hearths. Here, then, in the northern fens and on their edges, was a group of parishes which had clearly developed differently, economically, from those in the rest of the county.[112] Its dominant characteristic was an abnormally high proportion of the middlingly-prosperous, in village terms, paying tax on two hearths.

The opposing characteristics of the uplands where polarisation had taken place, are not proved by the hearth tax analysis, but suggested by it. There was a really noticeable band of parishes with over fifty per cent of houses with one hearth on the chalk ridge, running from Balsham to Woodditton. The poverty of this area has been stressed again and again.[113] There was apparently no general compensating development of the large farming unit here, however, for the percentages of houses with three and more hearths were also low.

There are indications that polarisation was taking place in the numbers of parishes with fairly high proportions of forty per cent or more of 'labourers' houses with one hearth, combined with over twenty per cent or even up to forty per cent of houses with three and four hearths. These were only found in the area south of Cambridge and the subsidiary river valleys to the west and the east. But they were only hints; and it is obvious that the hearth tax is a more accurate guide to the developments in economically egalitarian communities than to polarised ones. Just as Thomas Amey living in his two-roomed cottage, taxed on one hearth, and leaving £120, formed an instructive example of the dangers of oversimplification in interpreting hearth tax returns in individual cases, so also can the village of Chippenham be taken as an instructive example of the danger of taking it as an accurate guide to the situation in even a whole parish. Very properly, Chippenham does appear on the maps as a village with more than fifty per cent of cottagers. It also, very properly, appears on the maps as possessing a low number of inhabitants living in houses with two hearths, who might be expected to own around £60. We know, therefore, that Chippenham had cottages fit for labourers in abundance, and very few husbandmen. Unfortunately,

[112] The reasons for this are discussed below, pp. 137–41.
[113] See above, p. 32 and 32, n. 96.

what is not apparent on the maps is the predominance of the large yeoman farmer, for Chippenham did not possess a high percentage of men with either three, or four-and-more hearths. Yet Chippenham has emerged from my investigations as the parish which provides the most definite and striking evidence of the early emergence of the large yeoman. Chippenham was a paradise for the engrosser.

From the picture of Cambridgeshire, its population, and its people's wealth, it is now time to turn to the general reasons for change in the structure of English rural society in the sixteenth and seventeenth centuries, and then to the ultimate love of the local historian, the particular case-histories of particular communities which prove the general point.

2

The problem: the disappearance of the small landowner

The importance of mounting population pressure, and therefore of the upward movement of food prices between 1500 and 1650, lies in the profound effect these changes had on the whole structure of rural society, and on the distribution of its land. It is necessary to glance back at the medieval distribution of land before appreciating the magnitude of the changes which took place in the sixteenth and seventeenth centuries.

Admittedly, the somewhat egalitarian picture of medieval manorial society that emerges from the great surveys of the thirteenth century, taken when pressure on land and seigneurial power was at its height, is probably partly the result of the need of estate-owners to maintain the integrity of holdings for administrative purposes. The neat tenements of half a yardland, which form the holdings of such a large proportion of the unfree tenants who were lucky enough to have land at all, on the open-field manors of eastern England[1] may not have been in reality nearly such tidy units as they appeared in the hundred rolls. However, even if the true state of affairs was complicated by subletting amongst the unfree tenants, it probably remains true that only a small minority of villeins held as much as thirty acres of land at the end of the thirteenth century. In all, exactly six villein tenants in the four eastern counties surveyed in 1297 had over thirty acres. The uncontrolled market in land amongst the free tenantry tended on the whole to lead to fragmentation of freeholds even below the villein level. Still, rare though he was, the tenant who held an acreage well above average, and even employed labourers to farm it, did exist even in the thirteenth century in eastern England.[2] Fixed rents gave him the opportunity to benefit whenever bad harvest years drove up the value of his surplus produce. The fall in population which took place even before the Black Death gave such men an opportunity to consolidate and expand, and

---

[1] E. A. Kosminsky, *Studies in the Agrarian History of England in the Thirteenth Century*, ed. R. H. Hilton (Oxford 1946), p. 216.
[2] R. H. Hilton, 'Peasant Movements in England before 1381', reprinted in *Essays in Economic History*, ed. E. M. Carus-Wilson, II (1962), 85–6.

the emergence of the capitalist farmer, who had perhaps acquired as much as 300 acres,[3] and disliked legislation which prevented him from bidding for the necessary wage labour to run his holding,[4] was a fourteenth-century phenomenon. The slump after the Black Death, and the slack land market of the fifteenth century made it possible for the enterprising man to enlarge his holding further, as well as for the wage-labourer to acquire one. Whenever the pattern of land distribution has been compared at different dates in the earlier middle ages and in the fourteenth and early fifteenth centuries, whether in the villages of Leicestershire,[5] Northampton,[6] Norfolk[7] and Cambridgeshire,[8] the same tendency has been observed towards the emergence of a group of men distinguished socially from their fellow villagers by the greater size of their farms.

The most complete study of the results in the sixteenth century of this growing differentiation in rural society was made by Tawney in 1912. He pinpointed with unerring instinct both the growth of the medieval land market amongst the peasantry, and the diversity which this had led to by the sixteenth century,[9] despite the fact that the background of medieval population movements which had made the situation possible was unknown to him. Tawney's survey showed that in the more densely populated south and eastern parts of the country, uniformity amongst the size of the copyhold tenants' holdings had almost disappeared.[10] Norfolk and Suffolk, which had been the most heavily settled counties in England at Domesday, still had the highest proportion of holdings under subsistence size in the sixteenth and early seventeenth centuries. No less than fifty-four per cent of copyholders on the manors Tawney examined there, *excluding* the cottagers, had under ten acres.[11] On the other hand, over eight per cent of the tenants had over

[3] Ten virgates at thirty acres to the virgate in 1394. F. M. Page, *The Estates of Crowland Abbey: A Study in Manorial Organisation* (Cambridge 1934), pp. 81, 152–3.
[4] Hilton, 'Peasant Movements', pp. 88–9.
[5] R. H. Hilton, *The Economic Development of Some Leicestershire Estates in the 14th and 15th Centuries* (London 1947), pp. 91, 100, 105.
[6] Morgan, *The Abbey of Bec*, p. 111.
[7] Davenport, *A Norfolk Manor, 1086–1565*, pp. 81–3.
[8] Page, *The Estates of Crowland Abbey*, and M. Spufford, *Chippenham*, pp. 37–8, 39–41.
[9] R. H. Tawney, *The Agrarian Problem in the Sixteenth Century* (London 1912), pp. 72–97 and 59–72.
[10] *Ibid.* pp. 63–6. The table from which these conclusions are drawn is constructed from material of various dates from the reigns of Henry VIII to James I.
[11] I have followed Kosminsky (*Studies in Agrarian History*, pp. 216–17) in assuming that less than a half-yardland, or about ten acres, is inadequate for subsistence in the arable uplands, where the additional resources of fen or woodland were not available.

fifty acres even in these counties. These figures could scarcely have been matched at the end of the thirteenth century.[12]

What, then, was the likely effect of a renewed growth in population and a rapid increase in the price of foodstuffs in the sixteenth century on this already diversified society? It is self-evident, in the first place, that the farmer with a holding above the average size benefited. He was farming for the market. If he was a barley producer the value of his produce rose eightfold between the mid-fifteenth century and the mid-seventeenth century.[13] At the steepest period of rise, between the 1540s and the 1590s, the market value of all agricultural foodstuffs rose by 167 per cent.[14] Assuming – and it is a major and key assumption – that this surplus was not being transferred to a landlord in the form of increased rent,[15] the yeoman farmer with a freehold or copyhold on a fixed customary rent could not fail to prosper in sixteenth-century conditions, even without any effort to improve his husbandry and thereby increase his marketable yields. There is ample proof that he did so, from William Harrison's comments on the new luxuries of pewter, glass and feather beds to be seen in farmhouses in the 1580s, to the evidence of the physical rebuilding and expansion of these farmhouses themselves.[16]

It is equally self-evident that the agricultural labourer, who had been better-off in the fifteenth century than ever before, suffered as much in the sixteenth century as the yeoman prospered. The purchasing power of wages sank, as prices rose. Despite rises in the actual wages paid, the real value of an agricultural labourer's wages, was, at the lowest point in the second decade of the seventeenth century, only forty-four per cent of its fifteenth-century value.[17] It is also likely that as population rose and pressure on the supply of land increased the proportion of landless labourers in society increased too. Provision made for cottages

---

[12] No direct proof is possible. The hundred rolls did not cover Norfolk and Suffolk. However, the four other counties grouped together by Kosminsky to form his heavily settled eastern region, in which the degree of fragmentation of holdings was greatest in 1279, had between them exactly six holdings of over one virgate of land out of 8,891 unfree tenements enumerated in the rolls. Since none of these counties had been as heavily settled in 1086 as Norfolk and Suffolk, it is highly unlikely that the latter had a higher proportion of holdings of over a virgate. *Ibid.*

[13] Thirsk, *Agrarian History*, IV, 602.

[14] *Ibid.* p. 605.

[15] Fines were not apparently raised at Orwell in a period of engrossing between 1607 and 1627 (see below, pp. 100–1), nor were uncertain fines responsible for the breakdown of holdings at Willingham, since the freeholds there were equally vulnerable.

[16] W. G. Hoskins, 'The Rebuilding of Rural England, 1570–1640', *Past and Present*, 4 (1953), *passim*.

[17] Thirsk, *Agrarian History*, IV, 600.

to be built on the waste by the 1550s,[18] and the actual surviving examples of these cottages in gravel pits, and on improvised sites of the kind,[19] show the effect general economic changes were having. As the number of wage-labourers rose, the amount of work available for them in areas of enclosure decreased.[20] Moreover the simplest economy for the larger farmer in times of economic pressure was to lay off men.[21] Hence the Elizabethan problem of the wandering, unemployed and able-bodied poor.

The key question to be answered is not how the economic changes of the sixteenth century affected the yeoman, or the agricultural labourers, but how they affected that considerable section of the rural population which held, at the beginning or in the middle of the sixteenth century, an 'average' holding which was still recognisably a lineal descendant of the 'typical' medieval holding, that is, one obviously composed of a half-yardland, or even a couple of half-yardlands. How was the tenant or owner of fifteen, twenty-four, or even thirty acres affected by the economic situation? Was there a natural tendency for rural society to be still further polarised not only by the big farmer waxing fatter, and the labourer correspondingly thinner, but by the tenants of medium-sized farms getting elbowed out? When Johnson wrote on *The Disappearance of the Small Landowner* in 1909, he concluded, to his own great surprise, that the most critical period for the small owner was the end of the seventeenth century and the first half of the eighteenth century.[22] Johnson's work has not been followed up by the detailed regional studies which alone could prove his thesis; but modern scholars are agreed that the class of small owners was certainly very much reduced before 1760.[23] The theoretical reasons why this should have been so fall into two completely distinct categories.

The first, the traditional villain of the piece, lies in seigneurial attempts in the sixteenth and seventeenth centuries to undermine the legal position of the large class of copyholders of inheritance, or copyholders for years with rights of renewal, by replacing their secure customary

[18] *Ibid.* pp. 224–5.

[19] For instance Ashley, in Cambridgeshire near Newmarket, where an example of a labourer's cottage constructed of poles literally tied together with string still survives. I am indebted to Dr Peter Eden for this information, given verbally.

[20] A good concrete example of the effect of an influx of wage-labourers into an open-field village in the seventeenth century from the ring of enclosed villages which surrounded it is given by A. C. Chibnall, *Sherington: Fiefs and Fields of a Buckinghamshire Village* (Cambridge 1965), pp. 200–4.

[21] Thirsk, *Agrarian History*, IV, 232.

[22] A. H. Johnson, *The Disappearance of the Small Landowner* (Oxford 1909; reprinted London 1963), pp. 132–47.

[23] Bibliography and critical summary by Dr Joan Thirsk in 'Introduction' to *ibid.* (1963 edn.), p. xii.

tenancies with tenancies for life or for years. They thus transferred the profits of the price rise from their tenants' pockets to their own. The extent of this sort of effort by manorial lords anxious to extend their demesnes and sustain the sinking value of their rent rolls is unknown. It probably never will be known, or capable of expression in measurable terms. Tawney reckoned that almost as many copyholders in the sixteenth century were only tenants for life, or for years with no right of renewal, as were secure.[24] From this it follows that determined and successful action by estate-owners might well have had a most important part to play in the decline of the 'median' farmer. Professor Habbakuk has suggested, however, that twenty-five per cent of the farming population were freeholders, and that almost half of the rest, or only about thirty-five per cent of the peasantry as a whole, risked exploitation by legal means. The word 'only' may perhaps be questioned; one third of rural society is a proportion to be reckoned with. Professor Habbakuk uses Gregory King's estimates, made in 1688, that there were 180,000 families of freeholders (including copyholders) in the country, against only 150,000 families of leaseholders, to support his contention that the larger part of the peasantry must have been dispossessed between the 1680s and the 1780s. By the 1780s, ninety per cent of the land was leasehold. This use of King's figures certainly shows that there must have been an escalation in the dispossession of the small owner during the following century. But they also suggest that the small farmer had already suffered considerably by 1688, and that a proportion of the peasantry 'at risk' had in fact succumbed. Whether this proportion had succumbed from direct exploitation, or for other causes, can only be tested by the local historian from village to village and manor to manor. No doubt the results of such examinations will vary widely from place to place. By no means all villages had twenty-five per cent of freeholders, and a handful of villages chosen for detailed study may well have more, or less, than half their copyholders on insecure tenures. The historian of particular settlements, working with too small a sample, is unlikely to add anything to the statistical answer to this problem. He can only be aware that the legal situation of the villagers and the action the lord chose to take on it is one of the factors in his problem, and add concrete examples of what, in actual places, and at actual times, really happened.

The second, and more potent, set of reasons why the smaller farmer might perhaps have succumbed during the price rise lies in purely

---

[24] Tawney, *Agrarian Problem*, p. 300. The whole of the following argument is taken from H. J. Habbakuk, 'La disparition du paysan anglais', *Annales*, XX (Paris 1969), 649–63.

economic causes. The rise, I have said, was not steady. The force behind it may have been population growth, but some of the violent fluctuations within it were caused by the groups of bad harvest years which occurred during the period, in the 1550s, the last fifteen years of the sixteenth century, and the crisis of the 1620s,[25] as well as in the mid-1640s and late 1650s, 1670s and the bad years of the 1690s.[26] Each of these dearths drove up the price of grain.

The lean period before the bad harvest of 1549 coincided with the great agrarian risings.[27] Many of the other harvest crises also coincided with outcries and legislation against enclosures, pastoral husbandry, and the engrossing of farms. In the abundant harvest year of 1593, all legislation against the conversion of arable to pasture was repealed, but new acts against enclosure and engrossing followed in 1597 after the severe crop failures of the next four years.[28] Governmental action of this kind is sufficient evidence of the agrarian distress which followed dearth. A vivid example of the way the poor were affected is given in the life of Richard Greenham, who was minister of the first model Puritan parish in the country, Dry Drayton in Cambridgeshire, between 1571 and 1591. It is recorded that

In a time of scarcity, when Barley was at ten groats the bushel, (which in those days was an extraordinary price) he by his prudence brought it to passe, that the poor had it sold them for four groats the bushel of every husbandman in the Town; and thus he effected it. There were about twenty Plough-holders in the Town, all which he by his holy perswasions drew to an agreement amongst themselves, to hire a common granary, and therein to lay up corne for the poor, some more, some lesse, every man according to his ability; so that some laid up one Coom, some a quarter, some three Cooms, and Master *Greenham* himself laid in five Cooms, all of which was delivered out to the poor at a groat a peck . . . So that in that dear time all

---

[25] Thirsk, *Agrarian History*, IV, 632. General climatic deterioration may well have been responsible for many of these bad harvest years. The period 1550–1850 has been called a 'Little Ice Age' (H. H. Lamb, *The Changing Climate* (London 1966), pp. 10–11) and from this point of view perhaps the most important feature of the climatic deterioration was that not only was the weather colder, but from 1550 onwards to about 1680, nearly twenty per cent of the annual rainfall was in July and August. (Lamb, pp. 186–8.) These were, of course, the months when the harvest would have been most vulnerable.

[26] Christopher Hill, *The Century of Revolution 1603–1714* (Edinburgh 1961), p. 321. The harvests of the sixteenth and seventeenth century have been examined in two papers by W. G. Hoskins, 'Harvest Fluctuations and English Economic History, 1480–1619', and 'Harvest Fluctuations and English Economic History, 1620–1759', *Agric. Hist. Rev.*, XII (1964), 28–46, and XVI (1968), 15–31. C. J. Harrison, 'Grain Price Analysis and Harvest Qualities, 1465–1634', *Agric. Hist. Rev.*, XIX (1971), 135–55, investigates the harvests of all grains, not only wheat.

[27] Thirsk, *Agrarian History*, IV, 222–4.

[28] *Ibid.* pp. 228–9, 231. Hoskins, 'Harvest Fluctuations, 1480–1619', p. 38.

the poor in the Parish had been well neer famished, had it not been for his prudence, and liberalitie, which he also continued, until the price of corn abated, which was suddenly, and extraordinarily; for that corn which was sold for a noble the Bushel, was within one moneth after sold for fourteen pence the bushel.

But during the forementioned dearth, by publike Order, the bushels were cut, and made lesse; This Master *Greenham* preached much against, and publikely reproved wheresoever he came, and withall gave his man a charge, that if the Clerk of the Market sent for his bushel to cut it, he should not carrie it in, which was done accordingly, for which he came into trouble but the Lord delivered him out of the same.

Also at this time though his bushel was bigger than other mens, yet he would often charge his man not to strike off all the corn. He used not to trouble himself with reckonings and accounts, but would sometimes ask his man when he came from the Market, how he sold corn? and if it was dear, he would say '*I Pray God bring downe the price of it*' and if it was cheap, he would heartily blesse God for it.[29]

Who were the poor in Dry Drayton? A purely theoretical reconstruction of farm accounts on a thirty-acre holding in the first twenty years of the seventeenth century shows that the farmer of such a tenement in a time of poor harvests might well be poverty-stricken. During fair years when grain was selling cheaply, the net profit on a thirty-acre farm was perhaps just over £14, leaving a surplus of only between £3 and £5 after essential foodstuffs were bought.[30] In bad years, despite the fact that any available surplus sold at much higher prices, the scarcity of the crop reduced overall profits so much that the next year's farm expenses and essential outgoings could no longer be met. A run of years of this kind would drive such farmers out of business. This statement is highly significant because it is questionable whether, even at the beginning of the seventeenth century, the majority of farmers, as opposed to cottagers, held as much as thirty acres in the more densely populated arable areas of England. If they did not, it is easy to see that a far higher proportion of small farmers risked failure for purely economic causes, than risked exploitation because of their legal situation.

The larger farmer was not only immune from the effects of harvest

[29] Samuel Clarke, *A Generall Martyrologie, containing a Collection of all the greatest Persecutions which have befallen the Church of Christ from the Creation to our present Times, whereunto are added the Lives of Sundry Modern Divines* . . . (1651). Professor Hoskins has kindly suggested to me that the harvest year concerned was 1586–7 – unless Richard Greenham stayed long enough in Dry Drayton to witness the effects of the harvest year of 1590.

[30] The whole of this discussion is based on Thirsk, *Agrarian History*, IV, 650–8, particularly pp. 653, 657 and 658.

failures, and short-term crises, but was actually in a position to profit from them. Even though he had a larger labour bill to meet, the man with between fifty and one hundred acres increased his income in a time of crop failure, since he inevitably had a relatively bigger marketable surplus than his neighbour with a smaller acreage.[31] He did so whether or not he made any effort to improve his husbandry, and so increase his yields even further.

It is impossible to judge how far the smaller farmer was further penalised, in the period before 1650, by his inability to lay out cash on technical improvements. The general deficiency of farm accounts makes it impossible to judge how much effort even the larger arable farmer was making in this direction, not to mention the small one. There is a certain amount of evidence for increasing yields over the period 1450 to 1650,[32] which suggests that an effort was being made. The biggest single factor in this in the sixteenth and seventeenth centuries, as it had been in the thirteenth century, was probably the mere extension of the cultivated area by the clearance or reclamation of new land. Fen drainage schemes were the most striking example, both of this process, and also of the type of improvement which demanded capital outlay. The other striking innovation demanding considerable expenditure beyond the reach of the smaller man was the floating of water meadows which helped to increase general fertility by making it possible to winter more stock. But most of the improvements possible before 1650, at least in the light land areas of sheep–corn husbandry, where enclosures and conversion to pasture were not alternatives, simply consisted of better and more careful husbandry – extra ploughings, extra attention to manuring and marling, extra effort to obtain seed and stock for breeding from other localities. There is simply no means of knowing how standards of husbandry rose in general, especially among the farms of a yardland or so in the open-field area. It is a fair guess that here again the small man tended to suffer. He could scarcely afford a bill for additional labour as well as the upkeep of his household, and ultimately these practices demanded more labour as well as more cash.

Conditions changed after 1650. There was probably a halt in population growth, and from 1650 to 1672 there was a fall in the average prices of agricultural produce.[33] Although this was then arrested, there was a further fall from a new high level in the 1680s. The over-

---

[31] *Ibid.* pp. 650–63, particularly p. 659.
[32] *Ibid.* pp. 606 and 652.
[33] Hill, *The Century of Revolution*, pp. 318–19. Hoskins, 'Harvest Fluctuations, 1620–1759', pp. 20–1.

all tendency for food prices to rise, which had been so noticeable a feature from 1500 to perhaps the 1630s,[34] was significantly missing in the second half of the seventeenth century. The factor which had led to the enrichment of the farmer producing for the market on a large scale had disappeared. Moreover, the violent price fluctuations which were so disruptive to the economy of the smaller farm continued. Meanwhile there was an increase of central and local taxation on the peasantry from the civil war onwards. These are some of the reasons which led Professor Habbakuk to characterise the period from 1660 to 1740 as one in which the peasant owner, whether freeholder or copyholder, was likely to be forced to sell, and the area of demesne land to expand. King's figures for the 1680s show that the movement was then already well under way. Local examples in print show that the yeomanry suffered considerably in some places between 1650 and 1700. At Sherington, in Buckinghamshire, for instance, owner-occupiers and local gentry held eighty-eight per cent of the land in 1650. By 1700, the number of farmers tilling their own land was only half what it had been fifty years before,[35] and some prominent yeomen families were forced to leave, to become London craftsmen. In 1750, only about a third of the land was owned by farmers and gentry, and the rest by non-residents.

There was one possible means of escape from these economic pressures of the second half of the seventeenth century which was open at least to the farmers of light soils. The years after 1650 saw the adoption, on a really significant scale, of the new fodder crops, turnips, clover and sainfoin, which transformed farming rotations on sands and chalks.[36] Before 1650, the only new fodder crop which had gained a considerable footing in East Anglia was coleseed, or rape.[37] Despite improved techniques, crops which could really improve the fertility of the soil were lacking.[38] After 1650, they came in. There is a certain amount of evidence to show that the farmer of light soils withstood the pressures of the mid-seventeenth to mid-eighteenth centuries better than the clay-land farmer, precisely because he could make a genuine increase in productivity by introducing new crops. It seems reasonable to assume,

[34] E. H. Phelps Brown and Sheila V. Hopkins, 'Seven Centuries of the prices of Consumables, Compared with Builders' Wage Rates', in *Essays in Economic History*, ed. Carus-Wilson, II, 183.

[35] Chibnall, *Sherington*, pp. 204–7, 236–7.

[36] E. L. Jones, 'Agriculture and Economic Growth in England, 1660–1750: Agricultural Change', *Journal of Economic History*, XXV (1965), 2–5.

[37] Thirsk, *Agrarian History*, IV, 173–4.

[38] Jones dismisses the widespread introduction of ley farming, which constituted a major improvement in sixteenth-century agricultural technique in both Dr Thirsk and Dr Kerridge's view as unlikely to have any real effect on soil fertility, *art. cit.* pp. 4–5.

though, that even in the arable regions of lighter soil the smaller farmer was handicapped as against the larger by his comparative inability to invest cash sums in experimental crops after 1650, even if he was not so handicapped before 1650.[39] When the peasant was not forced to sell, therefore, as a result of changed economic circumstances, it seems likely that the trend towards the amalgamation of farms, which I have suggested was likely as a result of the economic situation up to 1650, may well have continued, and indeed accelerated, after that date, with the additional reason that the survival of the independent farmer now demanded more cash to invest in improvements.

The object of the following chapters is to examine the actual changes in the distribution of land in a selection of Cambridgeshire villages between the mid-sixteenth and the early eighteenth centuries, and to see how far these changes correspond in reality with those which the theoretical reconstruction of the probable fortunes of the yeomen, the average farmers and the landless, given above, suggests.

The information which must be obtained for each community to do this satisfactorily begins with the extent to which population did rise or fall during the period, and so the degree to which there was pressure on the available supply of holdings. This can only be done by analysis of a series of good and full parish registers. The essential framework of the investigation is a comparison of farm sizes in each village at the beginning and end of the period. For this, not one, but two, estate surveys, field books, or maps which list each tenant's holdings in detail are indispensable. These should ideally also contain sufficient detail to show the legal position of the various tenants, so that any change which had taken place in their tenures, and the extent to which they were vulnerable to direct exploitation, is evident. So also is any expansion which had taken place in the area of the demesne. In order to test the hypothesis that economic causes rather than legal ones might well have been responsible for the demise of many a medium-sized farm,[40] a good series of court rolls is necessary, to examine the extent to which the crisis years, of, for instance, the 1550s and 1560s and the 1590s actually coincided with a larger increase in the turnover of holdings. The distress of the small farmer would thus be patent. It also seems desirable to clothe this statistical skeleton with flesh by using the materials contained in wills. They are the most personal of all records, and often

---

[39] *Ibid.* pp. 9–15. Certainly it is very noticeable that only one man, one of the very considerable demesne farmers, was shown on the map of Chippenham made in 1712 as a grower of sainfoin. See below, p. 63.
[40] See above, pp. 50–2.

the only personal record any individual villager ever left behind him. They are therefore the only source from which his private life can ever be reconstructed. Wills are largely unused by local historians, compared with the almost too well-known probate inventories which should accompany them.[41] They tend to be thought of as the province of the genealogist. However, they provide a mass of information which is not obtainable elsewhere. Quite apart from giving almost the only slender information which exists on the personal religious beliefs of the ordinary man behind the plough, a dying man in his will makes provision for his widow, gives dowries to his daughters, and provides for his sons. In the process, he usually states whether his land is copyhold, freehold or leasehold, and therefore gives much more comprehensive information than, say, a court roll entry, to which a will often acts as a corrective.

As well as providing economic information, wills also provide a mass of social detail, down to rare glimpses of domestic tension and feeling which are really all we have to give any impression of the way the villager thought and reacted, and the way his family group worked. For present purposes, they give invaluable information on the extent to which inheritance customs contributed, by primogeniture, to the accumulation of land in the hands of individuals, or by partible inheritance, to the redistribution of holdings amongst the members of the family concerned, and so to a constant levelling-down of farm size.

It goes without saying that a village which has a sixteenth- and a seventeenth-century field book, good parish registers, a continuous series of court rolls, and a plentiful supply of inhabitants' wills made at the right dates, would represent a local historian's paradise. As such, it is rarely found. Even if it were, and all these conditions were fulfilled, it must still be said that reliable answers might not be obtained. Subtenancies are not recorded in field books and estate surveys.[42] In the sixteenth century, as in the thirteenth, a painstaking reconstruction of the distribution of land made from these sources reflects only the official view of the lord of the manor, not the view of the actual tenants. Furthermore, only parishes which contain one manor can be worked on, if the estate surveys are to give the complete size of farm each tenant held within the community. This limitation in itself means that in a county like Cambridgeshire, where manorial subdivisions were the rule,

---

[41] This piece of special pleading for the use of wills was written before I found the plea for the use of wills made by Dr Joan Thirsk in 'Unexplored Sources in Local Records', printed with *Sources of Information on Population 1500–1760* (Canterbury 1965), pp. 16–17. I appear to have inadvertently answering many of the questions she proposed there.

[42] See below, pp. 61 n. 8, 67 (Table 1) n., 142–4, 148–9 for the seriousness of this. It is

exceptional parishes have been chosen for study. These disadvantages seem unavoidable, but should be stated.

In practice, field books are the rarest, and least dispensable, of these various sources. They are so rare that I have not found it possible to avoid working on a parish with two of them, even where the registers, or some other equally fundamental piece of evidence, have proved too defective to provide the other necessary information. The parishes examined here are therefore far from the ideally documented communities which I have suggested are desirable. Moreover, to take individual communities and their lands, which comprise at the same time single parishes and single manors, is to falsify the past in yet another way. If the documentation permitted, the local historian ought to take a 'neighbourhood' or contingent group of communities. The dealings of men like Warren of Snailwell,[43] Dillamore of Chippenham,[44] and Butler of Orwell,[45] who all began as yeomen, all extended over several neighbouring parishes. The activities of lesser men also extended, in a more limited way, over more than one parish, but the historian remains ignorant of the extent of their doings because of the parochial limitations of his or her work. The historian is therefore getting a very false impression by taking single communities and limiting the analysis made by his, or her, microscope to them. Professor W. M. Williams, in his study of nineteenth- and twentieth-century 'Ashworthy' in Devon was confronted by the same problem. He found that 'Ashworthy' was part of a 'social area' much larger than itself. He established that the limits of this area were not fixed, but varied considerably in different contexts.[46] The ideal basis for a study of this kind would not be a number of contrasting village communities, but a number of contrasting 'neighbourhoods' or 'social areas', each extending over a group of parishes within approximately an eight-mile radius of a focal village centre. Such an ideal study was quite unrealistic for me because of the limitations both of documentation and time.

emphasized by C. J. Harrison, 'Elizabethan Village Surveys: A Comment', *Agric. Hist. Rev.*, xxvii (1979), Pt. II.

[43] See below, pp. 80–1.
[44] See below, pp. 86–7.
[45] See below, pp. 108–10.
[46] W. M. Williams, *A West Country Village, Ashworthy; Family, Kinship and Land* (London 1963), pp. 38–41.

3

The reality: the small landholder on the chalk: Chippenham

SOURCES, POPULATION CHANGES, FIELDS, CROPS AND STOCK

The parish of Chippenham lies right out in the north-east of Cambridge-shire, near Newmarket and the Suffolk border. Its hamlet of Badling-ham, which formed a separate manor, bordered on the river Kennet, across which Neolithic man had found his most hospitable environment on the sandy soils of the Breckland. Chippenham comes close to a local historian's paradise though even there the documentation is incomplete. The manor was monastic, and had served as the Infirmary of the Hospitallers in England. The village itself lay immediately south of an inlet of the fen. The High Street stretched from the parish church, down to the village green, where South Street crossed the High Street. On the way, it passed the manor house and infirmary buildings with their chapel, where convalescent brethren had once strolled in the three courtyards and the great garden within the moat, before returning to the heat of Rhodes.

The manor of Chippenham was one of the pieces of property in Cambridgeshire acquired by Sir Edward North from the court of Aug-mentations. Sir Edward had it surveyed in October 1544, and the docu-ment which was the result of this survey ran to seventy-nine folios.[1] It listed every one of the sixty-three messuages and cottages which still stood there, every croft or enclosure where there had ever been a mes-suage or cottage, every single strip in the open fields and its abutments, and the commons and common rights. In all, it covered 1,964 acres of open-field arable alone, acre by acre, rood by rood, and sometimes perch by perch. The manor did not remain in North's hands; it was sold to Sir Thomas Rivet, who lived in the manor until he died in 1582, and left it to his daughter Alice. She married Sir Thomas Gerrard, one of the Gerrards of Gerrard's Bromley in Staffordshire. By 1626, the manor had come in marriage to the Russell family, who were again resident lords. One of them married Cromwell's daughter. They, in turn, sold the manor in 1688 to another Russell, Edward, later Lord Orford.

[1] C.R.O., R55/7/5/1 (15).

The small landholder on the chalk: Chippenham

Various stages in the evolution of the landscape and in the holdings of the manor can be anatomised during this time. In 1560, a full rental was drawn up[2] which would seem a very informative document if it did not pale in significance beside the survey made sixteen years before. As it is, it illustrates the changes over this brief period. In 1636, both the survey of 1544 and the rental of 1560 were annotated with great care, with the names of the present tenants. An analysis of these annotations gives a new survey of the tenurial situation in 1636, and the way in which the distribution of holdings had changed over the last hundred years. In 1712, Lord Orford celebrated his creation of Chippenham Park, which had swept away half the village layout, by commissioning a magnificent estate map,[3] which not only shows the village site with such clarity that the 1544 survey can be mapped on the eighteenth-century base,[4] but also names and gives an acreage to every single strip in the open fields. Another analysis of the tenurial situation in the early eighteenth century can therefore be made.

The court rolls of Chippenham run from the late fourteenth century onwards. From the time when the first survey was made in 1544, until it was annotated in 1636, the rolls are almost continuous,[5] with only a ten-year gap from 1547 to 1557 and a two-year gap from 1624 to 1626. The condition of the 1602–24 roll is very poor, however, and parts of it appear to be a rough draft only.

Only a thin series of wills made by the inhabitants of the village survive up to the date of the second survey. Only thirty-five were registered before 1636. On the other hand, there is more information on the farming practices of Chippenham than on those of the villages of southern Cambridgeshire which lie within the diocese of Ely, for the inventories of Ely do not survive before 1662. Chippenham has an odd inventory dating from 1576, and a series beginning in 1647.[6]

The serious gap in the Chippenham evidence is that of the parish registers, which have been mutilated. The baptisms survive from the end of 1559, with a break for the civil war from 1646 which continues to 1664, since some pages have been torn out. Unfortunately the burials are completely missing until 1654. The marriages survive from 1569 until 1593, when a group of pages have been cut out, and then run from 1653 onwards. No bishop's or archdeacon's transcripts have

[2] C.R.O., R55/7/1 (1).   [3] C.R.O., R58/16/1.
[4] See Map 8.
[5] C.R.O., R55/7/1, f (1509–47), g (1557–1601), h (1602–24), i (1626–38).
[6] The wills and inventories for the deanery of Fordham are in the Bury St Edmunds and West Suffolk Record Office, whose former archivist, Mr Statham, I have to thank for much kindly and persistent help. Unfortunately the original wills were still unrepaired, and therefore inaccessible when this was written.

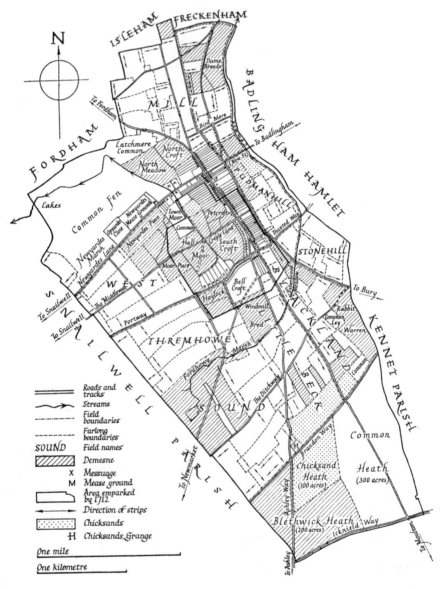

Map 8 The Lordship of Chippenham in 1544 (based on the map of 1712)

survived,[7] so the missing evidence is irreplaceable. It is all the more serious in that the subsidy returns for 1524 and 1525 for Chippenham are missing, obliterated beyond recall. The demographic evidence on the size and growth of Chippenham is therefore very scanty indeed. The sixty-three houses standing in 1544 argue for a resident population of between 250 and 300.[8] The record of baptisms from 1559 onwards would indicate a population of between 300 and 360 for the whole parish, including the hamlet of Badlingham, which is consistent with this 1544 evidence.[9] A nine-year moving average of baptisms suggests a fluctuating birth rate in a population of round about the same size until the 1630s.[10] After an increase in the 1630s, the population again remained more or less static in size until the end of the century. There were probably about sixty-seven houses in Chippenham in 1664, although even the hearth tax is difficult to use for Chippenham.[11] If this were so, the resident population of the village now stood at between 270 and 330, and that of the whole parish, including Badlingham, at between 310 and 380. There had been no real change in the size of the village since 1544, despite the heightened level of births since the 1630s.

[7] Chippenham lies in the deanery of Fordham in the diocese of Norwich, not in Ely, and transcripts which do survive are therefore in the Norfolk and Norwich Record Office in the Central Library, Norwich.

[8] Reckoning on between four and five people to each house. But there were so many tenants without houses and, alternatively, tenants holding two or more houses, that all arguments from the number of standing houses are inevitably shaky, since some tenants may have been non-resident, and some houses vacant.

[9] There were 111 baptisms in the first decade for which the registers survive.

[10] From 1567, the number of births fell, until a renewed rise to a peak in 1581, followed by a further fall to 1595. There was then a slow recovery until just after 1600, and an equally slow overall drop until after the bad years of the early 1620s. A further recovery then began. A return of the number of communicants in 1603 survives for the diocese of Norwich, but the figure it gives for Chippenham was so improbable that it in no way made up for the lack of the episcopal return of the number of households in 1563, which survives for the diocese of Ely, but not for that of Norwich. The Chippenham figure of communicants in 1603 was only sixty-six, which gives a ludicrously low total of well under 200 inhabitants in the parish. (Using the multiplier of 2.8 established by C. T. Smith for the Compton Census in *V.C.H. Leceistershire*, III, 140–3 and tentatively adopted by him when using the communicants' return of 1603 as a basis for population figures.) It fits none of the other available information, and is possibly incorrect, for although the printed edition reads 'cxxvi' this is an error in transcription from the manuscript, in which 'clxxvi' has been implausibly altered to 'lxvi'. I am much indebted to Mr A. R. Allan, formerly of the Bury St Edmunds and West Suffolk Record Office, who gave me this information from his private research.

[11] Because the hearth tax figures for the parish give no separate total for the hamlet of Badlingham. Seventy-six houses in all were taxed in Chippenham, probably including those in Badlingham. When Badlingham was mapped only five years earlier, there had been at least nine houses there. If all seventy-six houses were in Chippenham, the rise in the number of houses, and presumably families, would still have been only just over twenty per cent since 1544. M. Spufford, *Chippenham*, pp. 44–5.

The registers, which from the 1660s contain burials as well as baptisms, show that, overall, baptisms just exceed burials from 1666 to 1700.[12] The map of 1712, however, shows only a maximum of fifty houses in Chippenham, as against at least sixty-seven in the mid-1660s. But in 1702 Lord Orford had created his park and had previously removed at least twenty-five houses which had been standing within the emparked area.[13] The row of new cottages of uniform plan along the lane to Badlingham which he built in the late seventeenth century in partial compensation must represent one of the earliest pieces of estate architecture in existence. All the same there must have been considerable compulsory migration away because of the emparking. The stable size of the community from 1544 to 1664, in a time of general population increase, suggests that even before the emparking, emigration from Chippenham had exceeded immigration, and people had been forced off the land there.

The fragments of information which are available on the size of Chippenham suggest a relatively stable community apart from a short period of growth in 1630s. Its growth was, however, interfered with by the landscaping ambitions of the lord of the manor, and some of its people were forced to leave the village at the end of the seventeenth century.

The territory of the village of Chippenham lies on the gentle slope of the chalk which here stretches almost imperceptibly down from the main traffic artery of the Icknield Way at the south, to an inlet of peat fen at the north. The fields of the parish are all on freely drained, light soils, which were mainly derived from chalk, but also contain patches of sands and gravels.[14] The field system was highly complex. There were no less than eight fields there in 1544,[15] but despite this complexity, the inventories show that the rotation was a classically simple one. Eight inventories made between 1576 and 1670 give acreages of land sown with different grains before harvest, or details of the crops in the barns after harvest.[16] In general, these inventories give a reasonably uniform impression. However many fields there were, almost exactly half a

---

12 The registers show a natural increase in the population from 1666 to just before 1680. The number of burials rose steeply from 1677 onwards, and exceeded baptisms for more than half the decade 1680–90. After that a renewed increase began and continued until 1770.
13 M. Spufford, *Chippenham*, pp. 46–7.
14 Soil Survey of England and Wales, Sheet 188.   15 See Map 8.
16 Inventories made in June, before the harvest, seem likely to be complete, and so, probably, do those made in September, immediately afterwards. The risk that some grain may be have been sold or used for food so that the picture of the harvest is distorted, increases as time wears on. Inventories made in November, and still worse in January, are less reliable.

man's sown acreage was down to winter corn, of which an overwhelmingly large proportion was rye, which was ideally suited to the light sandy soils to the south of Chippenham. The other half was down to spring corn, which was almost entirely barley. There were small patches of wheat, oats, and peas, but in general they appeared negligible. The practices of the yeomen farming large acreages, and those of men who still held traditional holdings were identical. In September 1647, inventories were made for John Hodgkin, a yeoman lessee, who had 129 acres under the plough that year, and John Bentley, who had the crop of fifteen acres and one rood in his barn. Hodgkin had forty-six per cent of his land down to rye, and fifty-four per cent down to barley. Bentley had had forty-four per cent down to rye and fifty-two per cent to barley. He also had one rood, or two per cent, down to wheat, and two per cent to peas. The inventories give practically no information on any fodder crop or legumes. There is no mention of clover in them, although a yeoman of Badlingham, and Robert Tebbutt of Chippenham, both possessed 'mustard quarnes' in 1688. Sanfoin appears on the map of 1712 in the closes of one of the demesne lessees. There seems, from the inventories, to have been very little innovation or improvement.

Apart from the open fields, there were two large areas of common in Chippenham. To the south, by Icknield Way, is a considerable area where the grassland only forms a shallow skin over the chalk. Nowadays, the trainers of Newmarket exercise their gallops over this grassland by the beech trees on the hill; in the sixteenth and seventeenth centuries, this was the much-prized 'heath' of Chippenham, as it was of the adjoining parish of Snailwell, and indeed of every parish in this area of Cambridgeshire since they all run from the fen on the one hand to the Icknield Way on the other. The heath was partially common and partially demesne; in 1544, there were 600 acres of it. Long before, in the twelfth century, the inducements of population pressure had led to attempts to cultivate the heath. But the twelfth-century enterprise was doomed to failure, and the heath was not successfully farmed until methods of cultivating light soils were introduced here in the eighteenth century. Indeed, without the heath as grazing land, it would have been difficult to maintain the fertility of Chippenham. Lord Orford's map of 1712 shows a charming pastoral scene of a shepherd sitting cross-legged playing his pipe to his sheep on Chippenham Heath. Chippenham, like many other parts of Cambridgeshire, belonged to the fold-course area, where the arable was kept in good heart for corn by folding sheep flocks on it.[17] In 1544, the farmer of the demesne and the parsonage was

[17] K. J. Allison, 'The Sheep–Corn Husbandry of Norfolk in the Sixteenth and Seventeenth Centuries', *Agricultural History Review*, v (1957).

running a minimum of 2,000 sheep in Chippenham, and was also trying to deny the tenants the right to common their own sheep.[18] An attempt was also made by Sir Thomas Rivet in 1565 to enclose the 200 acres of peat fen which lay immediately north of the village, and formed the other principal area of pasture, as well as a source of fuel, for peat digging was carried on there. It was partially flooded and contained two lakes, according to the 1544 survey. Arthur Young thought very little of the purposes to which this fen was put in the late eighteenth century. He wrote that it 'was constantly flooded; when fed it was with cows and young stock, but to little profit . . . cows and horses mired and lost, and their skeletons found when the drains were cut'.[19] The inhabitants of Chippenham thought a great deal of the fen, however. They fought Sir Thomas Rivet's attempt to enclose the common in the sixteenth century, and caused trouble in 1630 when Sir William Russell tried to cut a new river to drain the fen. He eventually petitioned the Privy Council, because not only did 'divers ill-disposed persons in a riotous manner . . . disturb his said workmen by interrupting his proceedings' but also, 'some . . . of them who have beene sett on worke this winter in the making of the New Ryver have . . . indeavoured to fill up the said River againe by flinging in the earth which they were paid for to fling out'.[20]

It looks as though, despite the nuisance they managed to make of themselves, the tenants lost their fight to retain the right of folding their own sheep in the sixteenth and seventeenth centuries, for one of the concessions made by Lord Orford to get the agreement of the principal tenants to his proposals for emparking in 1702 was to re-grant them rights of common for cattle over the part of the fen in the occupation of the demesne lessee, and over lammas land in Chippenham. Sheep were specifically excluded.[21] Not a single sheep appeared in the inventories made of the crops and stock of Chippenham before 1700. The sheep flocks which kept the corn land of Chippenham in good heart must then have become a manorial monopoly, and the attempt made to deny the tenants the right to participate in the fold-course which was noted in 1544 had been successful.

The inventories showed that the farmers of Chippenham did, however, keep cattle and pigs, for which they still had common rights. No one could equal the yeomen like the two Hodgkins, father and son, who had seventeen and sixteen cattle apiece, or the Tebbutts, father

18 M. Spufford, *Chippenham*, pp. 20, 44.
19 *Ibid.* p. 54.
20 *Acts of the Privy Council, 1630–1*, pp. 158–9, no. 445. I am indebted to Dr Joan Thirsk for this reference.
21 M. Spufford, *Chippenham*, p. 47.

and son, who had ten and thirteen. These were usually cows and calves and the emphasis was obviously on milk production, not fattening. Even the smaller men like the shoemaker, James Harley, who only had three acres of copyhold, had a couple of cows. It must have been cow manure which was so carefully appraised in the yards. Cheese was obviously a staple in the diet. Almost every dairy had a cheese press in it, although only Lawrence Briant of Badlingham had a pair of butter scales, which perhaps argues that he was producing butter for the market. Again, only the most substantial yeoman had as many as a dozen pigs, but even the smallest landholder usually had one or two. At least five of the inventories were those of cottagers, or widows, living on their rights of common, like Walter Gill who had no land or stock in April 1665, when his goods were appraised at £14, but who had three cows, which had already been sold by his widow when the inventory was drawn up. John Aves's two cows and three pigs were his only link with the land in 1696. A widow, Mary Kent, whose goods were worth £9 in 1680, had one cow and one pig in the yard.

Horses were used in Chippenham for ploughing but they were not kept by everyone with land. The more substantial yeomen had them, and men like Robert Tebbutt with his 104 sown acres, two ploughs and four carts, and John Hodgkin with his 129 sown acres, three ploughs, and two carts, had seven and ten apiece. A smaller yeoman worth only £70 or so, like Edward Mason, who must have held a little over a traditional thirty-acre holding, judging from his sown acreage of twenty-three and a half acres, also had horses, but lesser men on the whole did not, and must have borrowed them when necessary. There was little sign of innovation in farm tools either, but a couple of the outstanding yeomen had rollers, as well as the more usual ploughs, harrows, rakes and carts.

LAND DISTRIBUTION

The history of the changing size in holdings in Chippenham during this period is a fascinating one, which can be traced in great detail. In medieval Chippenham, the standard holding was the half-yardland, and in 1279 almost half the tenants held between twelve and fifteen acres. No villein held more. Only ten per cent of the land was freehold, and four freehold tenants held more than a half-yardland.

In the slump of the next two centuries, the gradual build-up of holdings began, as the pressure on land relaxed, and the ambitious saw their way to increasing the size of their farms. By 1544, the ambitions of successful demesne farmers had seen to it that such freeholds as there were had disappeared; only ten acres of free land remained in peasant hands by that year. From that time onwards, only copyhold tenures were of any importance in Chippenham.

Amongst the copyholds, a great change had taken place. Since the 1470s[22] tenements changing hands in the manor court had much more commonly been full yardlands than before. By the time the survey of 1544 was made the effect of this could be seen (see Table 1). There were forty-five landholding tenants in that year, and ten of them held two yardlands or more of copyhold land. The largest copyholder had 101 acres. Another eleven men held a yardland, or a yardland and a half. Nearly half the landholders held more than the medieval standard subsistence holding.[23] The old middle rank of the peasantry with subsistence tenements had almost disappeared. Only six men held a half-yardland now, instead of seventy-three, and half the inhabitants of the village held a house and croft only, or a house and up to two acres of arable. So the proportion of wage-labourers, as well of the prosperous, was much increased.

Some change in the distribution of land took place in the next twelve years, as the rental of 1560 shows (see Tables 2 and 5). Only twenty-nine tenants appeared to hold land instead of forty-five.[24] The number of those holding very small acreages had apparently fallen sharply, and the number of those holding houses with no land at all had risen slightly, which suggests a further increase in the number of labourers. The most significant change was perhaps the inclusion in the rental of a section headed 'in the hands of the lord' which was mainly let to farm, or held 'at will'. This covered 126 acres, admittedly against over a thousand acres of free and copyhold. It included a half-yardland 'sometime holden by court roll' at 8s a year and now 'letten to farm', at 20s a year.

When, on 22 September 1636, the survey of Chippenham made just under a hundred years before was painstakingly annotated, the way in which land was distributed had changed radically (see Tables 3, 5 and 6). There had been two major changes. Over five hundred acres of land had been converted from copyhold to leasehold since 1560. As well, the sizes of the remaining copyhold farms had changed dramatically. The larger copyholds of two yardlands and upwards were not affected; nor were the minute holdings of less than six acres which helped to support the more fortunate cottagers. But the middle

[22] M. Spufford, *Chippenham*, p. 38.
[23] *Ibid.* pp. 39ff.
[24] This is almost certainly a defect in the rental, which probably ignored the tenants of small acreages.

TABLE 1 *Tenants and farm size in Chippenham, 1544 survey*
(Customary measurements corrected to nearest acre)

Range of size	Occupant	Free tenure	Copyholds (*seized* asterisked)	Total
90 acres and over	Late Moss		111a.*	111a.
	Thomas Rawlings		101a.	101a.
5 half-yardlands	Late Wm Hadenham		83a.	83a.
	James Roger		76a.	76a.
	Robert Clement		74a.	74a.
4 half-yardlands	Late John Clement		62a.	62a.
	Robert Norman		61a.	61a.
	John Kydd		56a.	56a.
	William Kirke		56a.	56a.
	Late James Clement		53a.	53a.
3 half-yardlands	Thomas Deresley		51a.	51a.
	Thomas Fryer		48a.	48a.
	John Mountford		43a.	43a.
	William Norman		42a.	42a.
	Nicholas Gee		41a.	41a.
2 half-yardlands	William Taylor		36a.	36a.
	Late Akes		36a.*	36a.
	John Dix Senior	2a.	32a.	34a.
	William Clerke		30a.	30a.
	Mr Myrphrim		30a.	30a.
	Richard Taylor		28a.	28a.
1 half-yardland	Anthony Hills		19a.	19a.
	Late Porters		18a.*	18a.
	William Chapman		16a.	16a.
	Harry Shelley		14a.	14a.
	John Thurstan		13a.	13a.
	John Cater		13a.	13a.
Under half-yardland	Late Jervis		9a.*	9a.
	Thomas Kynwardine		7a.	7a.
	T. Pleasaunt		4a.	4a.
	The Lord of Fordham	3a.		3a.
	William Clement	2a.		2a.
	William Death		2a.	2a.
	John Ball		2a.	2a.
	Stephen Cole	2a.		2a.
	Late John Taylor		2a.	2a.
	Laurence Mather		1a.	1a.
2 acres and under	William Cater		1a.	1a.
	William Cayler		1a.	1a.
	Robert Bell		1a.	1a.
	John Kyrke		1a.	1a.
	John Barrett junior	1a.		1a.
	Joan Taylor	½a.		½a.
	James Scott		½a.	½a.
	Robert Bet		½a.	½a.
Total		10a.	1276a. (237a. *seized*)	1286a.
Messuage only		3 (+1)	11 (+1)	15 (+6)

NOTES: Holdings are grouped in terms of half-yardlands, which here nominally contained fifteen customary acres, as these were the basic units from which they were normally built up. The plus signs in the 'messuage only' column represent surplus houses in the hands of tenants, which were presumably available for subletting. There were also five houses of unknown tenure.

TABLE 2   *Tenants and farm size in Chippenham, 1560 rental*
(Customary measurements)

Range of size	Occupant	Free tenure	Let to farm	Customary tenure (*at will* asterisked)	Total
90 acres and over	Robert Gill			200a.	200a.
	William Taylor	1a.	46a.	88a.	135a.
	Thomas Norman		38a.	½y.* } 1½y.	c. 99a.
5 half-yardlands	Richard Kent			78a.	78a.
	Widow Haylock			2½y.	76a.
	Edmund Francis			74a.	74a.
4 half-yardlands	Steven Taylor			2y.*	66a.
	Thomas Deresley			2y.	c. 60a.
	William Kynwardine			2y.	c. 60a.
3 half-yardlands	Roger Ware		½a.	1½y.	50½a.
	Robert Norman			1½y.*	46a.
	Robert Shene			1½y.	c. 45a.
	Robert Corder			1y. 9a.	41a.
2 half-yardlands	Nicholas Cheesewright			30a.	30a.
	Edward Sherlock			30a.	30a.
	Henry Wixe		27a.		27a.
1 half-yardland	Margaret Blythe			½y. 3a.	c. 18a.
	John Clement			18a.	18a.
	Thomas Clark	1a.		16a.	17a.
	Robert Scott			½y. ½a.	c. 15½a.
	Thomas Clement		15a.		15a.
	William Harley			14a.	14a.
Under half-yardland	Thomas Kynwardine	7a.		1a.	8a.
	Simon Wixe			8a.	8a.
	John Wixe			8a.	8a.
	William Clements	3¼a.		3a.	6¼a.
	Mark Webber	3a.		1a.	4a.
	Richard Walden			4a.	4a.
2 acres and under	John Cap			1¼a.	1¼a.
Total		15¼a.	126½a.	17y. 586¾a. (4y. 200a. *at will*)	c. 1255½a.
Messuage only			3	9	12 (+12)

NOTES: If the acreage of the holding is given in the 1560 rental itself, this is given in the relevant column. Otherwise the size is expressed in yardlands. Where an exact acreage was given by the 1636 annotator for the latter holdings this is entered in the 'Total' column. Where no such acreage was given, an approximate conversion has been made on the basis that a half-yardland nominally contained fifteen customary acres.

TABLE 3   *Tenants and farm size in Chippenham, 1636 reconstructed* (Customary measurements)

Range of size	Occupant	Leasehold tenure	Customary tenure	Total
90 acres and over	Thomas Dillamore	8a.	199a. 2r.	207a. 2r.
	Blackelys	200a.		200a.
	John Hodgkin	104a.	50a. 2½r.	154a. 2½r.
	John Cheesewright	73a.	30a. 1½r.	103a. 1½r.
	Tebbutt	94a.	2r.	94a. 2r.
	John Francis		94a. 1½r.	94a. 1½r.
5 half-yardlands	John Kent		83a. 2½r.	83a. 2½r.
4 half-yardlands	Edward Hawes	62a.		62a.
3 half-yardlands	J. Turner		51a. 3r.	51a. 3r.
	John Taylor	50a.	2r.	50a. 2r.
	John Tetsal	42a.	2a.	44a.
2 half-yardlands	John Bentley	31a.	6a. 2½r.	37a. 2½r.
	Edward Cheesewright	30a.		30a.
1 half-yardland	No tenant in this range			
Under half-yardland	John Harley		10a.	10a.
	William Dawbery		6a. 1r.	6a. 1r.
	Unknown tenant	4a.		4a.
2 acres and under	Martin Hills	2a.		2a.
	Tolworthy		1a. 2r.	1a. 2r.
	Hadenham		1a.	1a.
	Timothy (?) Hall		1a.	1a.
	Ambrose Clement		3½r.	3½r.
	Ger. Scott		3r.	3r.
	Barrett		1½r.	1½r.
	Widow Ames		2 twelve feet	2 twelve feet
Total		700a.	541a. 2½r.	1241a. 2½r.

'Messuage only' not possible to reconstruct at this date

NOTES: The leasehold column has been reconstructed from the annotations made in 1636 on the rental of 1560. The customary column has been reconstructed from the annotations made on 22 September 1636 on the survey of 1544.

range of sixteenth-century holdings, from a half-yardland, or approximately fifteen acres, to one and a half yardlands, or forty-five odd acres, had, with one single exception, disappeared completely. In 1544 and 1560 there had been half a dozen half-yardlands; in 1636 there were none. In 1544 and 1560 there had been first six, then three yardlands; in 1636, the only remaining conventional holding was the yardland of thirty acres which Nicholas Cheesewright had held in 1560, and which his descendant John still retained, although he also had over seventy acres of leasehold. In 1544 and 1560, there had been five and four holdings of one and a half yardlands; in 1636 there were only two, and both of these were fragments of larger holdings which had been over sixty acres in 1560. Instead of the thirteen holdings of fourteen to fifty-one acres which had existed in 1560, under eighty years later there were only three. Of these only John Cheesewright's thirty-acre holding was a medieval unit which survived as a reminder of the past.

In Chippenham, then, the most critical period for the small owner was not the first half of the eighteenth century, as Johnson, or more lately, Professor Habbakuk, have supposed.[25] The small farmers of Chippenham had already suffered by 1636, and they had been forced out at some point between 1560 and 1636. Certainly, the process continued after 1636. It was completed by Lord Orford's actions in 1696, when he bought up most of the remaining copyhold land in the village. But this remainder was all concentrated into the hands of five men, and the three holdings which were described in detail in the court rolls were between 120 acres and 155 acres each.[26] A reconstruction of land-holding in Chippenham from the map of 1712[27] (see Table 4) is in many ways simply a further proof that changes had already taken place by 1636. It adds nothing new. The small farmer had long gone out of business in 1712, and he had not reappeared in Chippenham, nor was he ever to do so again.

The same tendency towards the disappearance of the small farmer was apparent in the tiny adjacent parish of Snailwell. Only twenty-six people were assessed there in 1525[28] and exactly the same number paid hearth tax in 1664. If anything, then, the settlement dwindled in between. There were twelve freeholders and copyholders in the village according to a survey made in 1560.[29] The large farms there were much bigger than those at Chippenham. Three of them were already over 130 acres, three were of sixty-one to ninety-one acres and only three were of the size at risk, eighteen to twenty-five acres. Three were under ten acres. It is not possible to trace land distribution at Snailwell as it is at Chippenham, but five of these farms had entirely disappeared, including all three of the half-yardlands, and two of those of over 130

[25] A. H. Johnson, *Disappearance of the Small Landowner*, H. J. Habbakuk, 'La disparition du paysan anglais'.
[26] M. Spufford, *Chippenham*, p. 46.
[27] *Ibid.* p. 48.
[28] P.R.O., E179/81/137. See M. Spufford, 'Rural Cambridgeshire', pp. 105–8, for Snailwell at more length.
[29] C.R.O., R55/7/43/2.

TABLE 4   *Tenants and farm size in Chippenham, 1712 map*
(Statute measurement, with approximate customary equivalent. No
distinction in the type of tenure is indicated)

Range of size (customary)	Occupant	Holding in statute acres	Customary equivalent
Over 250 acres	John Tetsal	392a. 3r. 15p.	472a.
	Ambrose Davy	384a. 0r. 10p.	461a.
	Thomas Elliott	244a. 2r. 33p.	294a.
90–250 acres	John Godfrey	122a. 2r. 10p.	147a.
	Robert Howes	103a. 2r. 1p.	124a.
	William Delamore	103a. 1r. 3p.	124a.
	Robert Seeker	97a. 3r. 27p.	118a.
4 half-yardlands	William Harwell	56a. 0r. 12p.	67a.
	Robert Hawes	43a. 0r. 8p.	52a.
3 half-yardlands	No tenant in this range		
2 half-yardlands	No tenant in this range		
1 half-yardland	George Abbott	12a. 1r. 14p.	15a.
Under half-yardland	Edward Hawes	3a. 3r.	5a.
	William Burroughs	3a. 1r. 13p.	4a.
	'Cadmans'	3a.	4a.
2 acres and under	Thomas Kent	1a. 2r. 35p.	2a.
	William Delamore, gardner	1a. 1r. 30p.	2a.
	Thomas Tolworthy	1a. 0r. 35p.	1a.
	John Crane	1a. 0r. 17p.	1a.
	Richard Hawes	2r.	1a.

NOTE: The conversion from statute to customary measure has been made on the basis
of 100 statute acres being equal to 120 customary acres.

acres, in a further survey made over a hundred years later, in 1684.[30]
Instead, there was one large farm of 348 acres of customary and free
land of open-field arable held by Martin Warren.

The social effects of the disappearance of the middle-sized tenement
of the sixteenth century can be misinterpreted. It is possible to assume,
without really examining the evidence, that the conversion of the
majority of the copyholders to leasehold by 1636 must have led to a
fall in the prosperity of the yeomen holding the large leaseholds. It
certainly did mean that when, in the late seventeenth century, an occasion arose when the lord of the manor wanted land in hand, most of
his tenants, however considerable they were, were in no position to
fight. Legally, they were weak. But the evidence of the inventories,
which with a few exceptions start in 1647 after the conversion to leasehold, show that although they might be legally weak for a large part at

[30] C.R.O., R55/7/43/5.

least of the seventeenth century, leaseholding yeomen could flourish economically.

The Chippenham surveys show quite clearly that the community had become increasingly polarised economically between 1544 and 1712. In 1544, over half the tenants held a house only, or a house and up to two acres of land. In 1664, half the houses in Chippenham had only one hearth. The occupancy of such a house often indicated status and wealth not much higher than that of the average labourer.[31] By 1712, three-quarters of the inhabitants had a house and a couple of acres at most.

The surviving inventories would be extremely misleading if this general context was not known. Over a third[32] of them were stated to be the inventories of yeomen or gentlemen, and some of the remainder, in which the social status of the dead man was not given, were almost certainly also those of yeomen. A large number of the inventories were made in the 1660s. In this decade the median wealth of those appraised in the 340 inventories which survive for the Consistory Court of Ely was £40. The median in Chippenham was £76. The median wealth of Cambridgeshire yeomen in general was £180, whereas in Chippenham it was £299. The median wealth of the three men who were specifically described as husbandmen in Chippenham was the same as in the rest of the county, at £33. That of craftsmen was lower, at £24 against £40. It is obvious that the inventories which survive for Chippenham are a thoroughly unrepresentative sample of the village community in general, although Chippenham yeomen may in reality have been better-off than many in the county. The greater wealth of the yeomen of Chippenham at their deaths than Cambridgeshire yeomen in general suggests that engrossing had by that time proceeded further than in most places.[33]

The prosperity of the leaseholders can be illustrated from the history of the Tebbutt family. In 1636, Robert Tebbutt held only two roods of copyhold, against ninety-four acres of leasehold land, which were made up of holdings of three yardlands converted since 1560. A list of farmers made in 1664[34] shows that by then Robert Tebbutt was paying

---

[31] M. Spufford, *Chippenham*, p. 46. See above, pp. 38–9.

[32] Nine out of thirty-one usable inventories.

[33] Yet see above, pp. 44–5, for the failure of an analysis of the hearth tax to indicate this clearly.

[34] Abstract of Title to the Manor, C.R.O., R55/7/7/88. It is not clear to me whether the list of rents in 1664 is a list of rents from customary or leasehold land; it includes men like Tebbutt and Tetsal whose families were certainly farming only leaseholds thirty years before (Table 3), but it also includes Dillamore, whose father was equally certainly farming only copyhold. The main point remains valid; that men like Tebbutt, whose family started by leaseholding, were prosperous enough to extend their farms, and perhaps acquire considerable copies as well.

TABLE 5 *Landholding in Chippenham, thirteenth to eighteenth centuries*
(Number of tenants)

Range of size	1279 Hundred Rolls, free and unfree	1544 Survey free and copyhold	1560 Rental freehold let to farm customary	1636 Leasehold and customary tenure	1712 Map all tenures
250 acres and over	0	0	0	0	3
90–250 acres	0	2	3	6	4
5 half-yardlands	0	3	3	1	0
4 half-yardlands	0	5	3	1	2
3 half-yardlands	0	5	4	3	0
2 half-yardlands	4	6	3	2	0
1 half-yardland	73	6	6	0	1
Under half-yardland	7	4	6	3	3
Total (over 2 acres)	84	31	28	16	13
2 acres and under	54	14	1*	8	5
Landless householders	5	21	24	†	31

* Possible defect in rental.
† Not discoverable.
Half-yardland here nominally contained 15 customary acres.

TABLE 6 *Landholding in Chippenham, sixteenth and seventeenth centuries*
(Number of tenants by copyhold and customary tenures only)

Range of size	1544	1560	1636
90 acres and over	2	2	2
5 half-yardlands	3	3	1
4 half-yardlands	5	4	0
3 half-yardlands	5	4	2*
2 half-yardlands	6	2	1
1 half-yardland	6	5	0
Under half-yardland	3	4	3
2 acres and under†	10	3	10
Total customary tenants	40	27	19

* Although falling just within this range of size, these were not traditional medium-sized holdings. John Hodgkin held 50a. 2½r. of customary land, but these three apparent half-yardlands had not been accumulated in the period 1560–1636, since they had already been part of two conglomerate holdings, both of which were over sixty acres, in 1560. John Turner held 51a. 3r., but these three half-yard lands did not represent the survival of a holding of this size since 1560, since they had also been part of a larger holding at that date.
† Excluding tenants of copyhold messuages only.

the most substantial rent on the manor, of £35 a year, and was also farming the tithes of part of the rectory at an annual rent of £70. At his death in 1668 his inventory showed that he had 104 acres sown, and so must have been farming at least 150 acres. He also had four ploughs and four carts. Some of this land was copyhold by now, because he provided for his widow's relations to pay for his debts by selling sixty acres of copyhold which he had bought from John Francis. This was not his entire copyhold, however, because he described it as the 'firstlands' bought from John Francis. His house was extremely comfortable. He had a hall and parlour downstairs, a dairy, buttery, backhouse, and cellars, as well. The hall and parlour both had fireplaces, and although he was not particularly modern in his notions and still used his parlour for sleeping as well as for sitting, and his hall for cooking as well as for living, they were both fairly well furnished, with leather chairs in the parlour, and framed chairs and joined stools in the hall. The hall fireplace had two muskets and a fowling-piece as well as a sword and bandoliers hanging over it; these were very rare in an inventory, and it sounds as if he may have been out in the civil war.[35]

Upstairs, there were chambers over the hall and parlour, and a cheese chamber, as well as garrets. It is possible that the house was the parsonage farm; a third storey was very rare in Cambridgeshire, judging from the inventories. In all, his goods were appraised at £258 19s 8d. He left everything to his widow, and it sounds from his will as if he was childless; in fact he left a son and a daughter.

The son, another Robert, died in 1682. He was umarried, and left everything to his sister Jane. It is impossible to make out the acreage of his farm, since he died after harvest. The crop in his barn was appraised at a lump sum very near that of his father's, before the harvest fourteen years before. There was no great change in his stock, either. He had inherited a considerable sum from a childless uncle, and his 'debts in the Booke' were worth £121, whereas his father's were unappraised. His whole personal estate was therefore appraised much more highly than his father's, at £412, although the size of his farm may not have changed very much.

He lived in the same house as his father, and the downstairs was

---

[35] Sir William Russell of Chippenham had been a friend of Charles I, who repeatedly visited him there to play a game of bowls, as a distraction after the beginning of the civil war. (D. and S. Lysons, *Magna Britannia* (London 1808), ii, 166.) His heir, Sir Francis, became a colonel in the parliamentary army in 1643, however, and two of his children married Cromwell's children. He ended as a peer in Cromwell's House of Lords (*The Complete Peerage*, new ed. by Vicar Gibbs, iv [London 1916]). The Chippenham tenantry may well have been involved, although Sir Francis did not succeed his father until 1654. See Introduction.

much the same, except that he had moved his father's sword to the parlour, and added six more leather chairs. He was literate, and acted as one of Chippenham's chief appraisers after deaths. Upstairs, in the closet next to the parlour chamber, which was a comfortable bedroom with two chairs, there was a silver tankard, two tumblers, two wine cups, seven silver spoons and a 'parcel of books'. It sounds as though he spent his evenings pleasantly.

At the end of the century, when Orford was buying out his copyholders, he bought up the land formerly in the occupation of Robert Tebbutt at £35 a year, for £700.[36] Possibly as well as this, he bought from Henry Branch and his wife Jane, formerly Jane Tebbutt, the 150 acres of copyhold that they held.[37] Leaseholding in the seventeenth century did not necessarily lead to penury.

Indeed, even the humblest of those for whom inventories were made had goods which in the sixteenth century had been regarded by William Harrison as remarkable. Feather beds, pewter, and napkins had percolated a long way down the social scale. Even the husbandman who died in 1669, owning goods worth only £5 5s 0d, had a couple of chairs in his chamber and two in his hall, and two pewter dishes, although his bed was admittedly flock, not feather. Henry Lane, of Badlingham, who had goods worth £24 in 1675, had a house and pightle only. His entire harvest in September was 'a little parcell of wheat and barley and hay' worth £3. But he still had a feather bed, and brass and pewter worth £1 12s 0d, including three kettles, a skillet, a warming pan, five pewter dishes, a basin and three porringers. The 'luxury goods' of a century before had reached the poor.

When the period when the small owner was forced off the land is established, it then becomes possible to consider the reasons for his vulnerability.

The first, and most obvious, explanation at Chippenham is the traditional one – seigneurial action. The conversion of 585 acres to leasehold between 1560 and 1636 is proof of exactly the sort of activity which Tawney thought was one of the main causes of the agrarian problem of the sixteenth century.[38] There is no doubt that Sir Thomas Rivet was buying copyholders out. There is a great deal of doubt, however, as to whether this is a complete explanation. In the first place, with a very few exceptions, copyholds at Chippenham were copyholds of inheritance, in which the tenant was admitted to hold 'to him and to his heirs'. As recent work has shown, the possession of this type of copyhold gave the

---

[36] Abstract of Title of the Manor, C.R.O., R55/7/7/88, pp. 26–7.
[37] C.R.O., R55/7/1 (cc) (1694–9).
[38] See above, pp. 49–50.

tenant a considerable amount of legal security.[39] Certainly, there was some land, which even by 1560 was customary but held 'at will', as the rental noted,[40] and this was invariably leasehold by 1636. Yet it formed only a small proportion of the customary land which had been converted. If Dr Kerridge is right in his assertions of the legal security of the copyhold of inheritance, action taken by the lórd to convert customary land could not have succeeded in Chippenham, unless some factor other than the purely legal one of tenure acted as a powerful incentive on the tenants to sell.

Secondly, and much more tellingly, the tenants of medium-sized holdings did not only fall victim to action by their lord. They also fell victim to the actions of their more successful engrossing peers. Twelve holdings of between a half-yardland and one and a half yardlands disappeared between 1560 and 1636. Seven of them had come into the hands of the lord and were farmed out; of these, two had already been let to farm, and one was held at will in 1560. The other five were still customary holdings in 1636; but they had lost their separate identities and fallen into the hands of the engrossing yeomen of Chippenham. In 1636, five men still held copyholds of over fifty acres in the village. They were headed by Thomas Dillamore, who had 199 acres and 2 roods of customary land. On his death bed he very properly inserted in his will a passage, which was not common form, thanking God 'for my worldly state wherewith it hath pleased God to blesse me'.

These farmers of large copyholds had all collected fragments of other holdings. Dillamore held land which had been in the possession of no less than fifteen men in 1544; his nearest rival, John Francis, had pieces of holdings which had been in seven tenants' separate possession. If nearly half the middle-sized holdings which had disappeared between 1560 and 1636 had fallen into the hands of fellow copyholders, farming on a larger scale, the reasons forcing their occupants in this direction cannot have been legal. They must have been economic.

A wholesale analysis of the transactions in the court rolls between the rental of 1560 and the reconstructed survey of 1636 should, in theory, show whether transfers which appear to be sales coincided with and followed closely on bad harvest years. It also seemed worthwhile attempting to trace the dates, according to the court rolls, at which the tenants of the conventionally-sized tenements which appeared so particularly vulnerable were fragmented. An effort was also made to try to trace the dates at which men like Dillamore and Francis accumulated

[39] Eric Kerridge, *Agrarian Problems in the Sixteenth Century and After* (London 1969), pp. 37–41.
[40] Asterisked on Table 2.

their holdings, and see if these dates happen to coincide with or follow on the dates of bad harvests.

In fact, a blanket analysis of the court roll transactions proved unsatisfactory. The manor court was extremely busy in the sixteenth century, compared with a large part of the century before when there had been an average of only one transaction of any magnitude in a year.[41] Even so, when the court business was divided up into normal transfers following deaths, family gifts and exchanges, and what appear to be genuine sales, there were still so few of the latter that a year in which there were more than two sales stood out. These numbers, like much historical evidence, are too slim to carry the weight of an argument, and should not be given much importance.

Since they are the evidence that exists, however, they must be used. The inventories show quite convincingly[42] that barley and rye were the only grain crops of any great importance in Chippenham. Between 1576 and 1670 wheat never amounted to more than four per cent, and oats and peas together to more than six per cent of the acreage.[43] An examination of the effects of bad harvests in Chippenham should therefore only take account of the prices of barley and rye, since failures in the harvests of these staple grains would be the ones which would affect the tenants severely. The series of rye prices between 1540 and 1640 is defective, but enough material exists to show that, on the whole, bad years for barley were also bad years for rye, and that therefore the tenants of Chippenham were doubly vulnerable.[44]

The really bad years, when the prices of grains rose very steeply above the normal fluctuations, were the mid-1550s, the terrible years of 1595–7, 1622, 1630 and 1637. There were less drastic, but still sharp, price rises in 1572 and 1573, 1585 and 1586, 1590 and 1600. For what it is worth, the sales in the manor court of Chippenham rose above the normal two in the mid-1560s, and in 1596 and 1597. The peak in the mid-1560s might well reflect the long-term effects of the dearth of 1555 and 1556, combined with the poor harvests of 1558 and 1563.[45] The

---

[41] M. Spufford, *Chippenham*, pp. 34–5.

[42] See above, pp. 62–3.

[43] On the eight farms for which such calculations could be made.

[44] See Note to Graphs 3 and 5, Appendix 1.

[45] I have usually used only the data for barley and rye where it is available, to assess the harvest quality, although I have sometimes had recourse to the harvest designations of Professor Hoskins in his 'Harvest Fluctuations, 1480–1619', pp. 28–46. These have been discussed and sometimes corrected by C. J. Harrison, 'Grain Price Analysis', pp. 135–55, which uses the same materials as Professor Hoskins but bases them on a thirty-one-year moving average of the prices of all grains, not only wheat. This leads to some interesting differences, and where it is appropriate, I have chosen the designations based on all grains, rather than those of Professor Hoskins. I have described the harvests of 1558 and 1563 as 'poor', however, solely

peak in 1596 and 1597, when there were four and five sales, does follow the deficient harvests of 1594 and 1595, the terrible dearth of 1596 and the bad harvest of 1597. It is extremely unfortunate that the state of the court rolls between 1602 and 1624 is so poor, because the evidence suggests that these years may well have been crucial.[46]

A wholesale analysis of manor court transactions of this type is unsatisfactory for two reasons, apart from the smallness of the numbers involved. First, the rolls do not appear to record all the purchases of copyholds made by the lord of the manor for conversion to leasehold. In other ways, however, they appear fairly full and satisfactory. The descent of most holdings can be traced through the rolls if necessary. This is not generally true of those holdings which were bought in for leasehold. Of the seven holdings of the size that were 'at risk', of between a half-yardland and one and a half yardlands,[47] the two which were let to farm and the one held customarily at will in 1560 naturally never appeared in the rolls at all. The purchase of only one of the remaining four was recorded, when Edward Sherlock, holder of one customary yardland in 1560, surrendered it to the use of Sir Thomas Rivet, in that year. Robert Corder, customary holder of one and a half yardlands in 1560, only appeared in the rolls when his widow entered a close of four acres of copyhold after his death in 1574. It must have been the only remaining copyhold he held, but there is no record of the previous sales which had reduced his forty-five acre farm to this state. The rolls do record the purchase of at least 230 acres of land by Sir Thomas between 1562 and 1580, but there are no notes on any purchases of copyholds by the Gerrards or the Russells, and 230 acres alone does not account for the whole acreage of new leasehold by 1636. It is interesting, though, that the bulk of Rivet's purchases which are recorded fall in just those years in 1564, 1566 and 1567, when there was also a record number of sales between tenants. The idea that economic distress lay behind the sales is strengthened.

The second reason for finding a blanket analysis of the rolls unsatisfactory is that a crude comparison of the number of recorded sales with harvest years is unlikely to correlate, because, except in cases where a run of really bad harvests followed each other (like those of the mid-1590s), the effects on the tenants were probably delayed. The general existence of a money-lending system in rural society, which permitted a man to stave off the immediate effect of a bad harvest, and to prevent

on the basis of the rises in the prices of barley for those years (Thirsk, *Agrarian History*, IV, 818–19). In both Hoskins' and Harrison's calculations, omitting barley, these years are 'average' or even 'abundant'.

[46] See below, pp. 83–4.
[47] See above, pp. 69–70, 76.

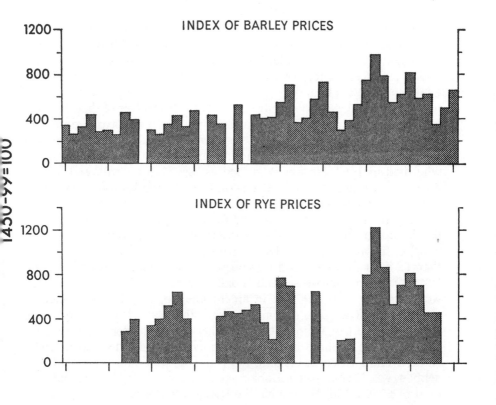

INDEX OF BARLEY PRICES

1450-99=100

INDEX OF RYE PRICES

TRANSACTIONS IN MANOR COURT

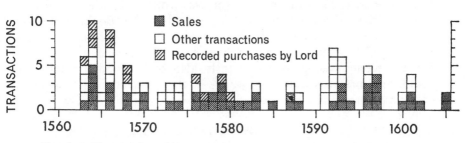

TRANSACTIONS

■ Sales
□ Other transactions
▨ Recorded purchases by Lord

1560   1570   1580   1590   1600

Graph 3 Transactions in the manor court of Willingham, 1560–1605

a foreclosure on his holding when he was unable to pay the rent, by borrowing makes a neat correlation between years of bad harvest and court surrenders impossible.[48] Borrowing and credit appear to have underpinned the whole of rural society. The wills and inventories of Chippenham people make it plain that it was normal practice for retiring yeomen and even husbandmen to divest themselves of their farming goods and stock and then lay out their money on loans and mortgages and, it is fair to assume, live off the interest. The clearest case was that of James Cooke, a yeoman of Badlingham, the hamlet of Chippenham, who died in 1667. He was described as 'aged' in his will, and had no farm goods at all, though he lived comfortably and his rooms were well furnished. His estate was valued at the very large sum of £404 13s 10d, and of this 'good' debts accounted for no less than £336. He also had the large sum of £55 14s 8d in ready money in the house. It was most unusual for anyone, even the most prosperous yeoman, to have more than £5 or at the most £10 in his purse at his death. James Cooke's will left his residuary legatees all his 'bonds, leases and mortgages' and they were certainly bringing him in an income, for he left his brother an annuity of £8 a year, amongst many other cash sums to kinsmen. Joseph Tebbutt of Chippenham, brother of a considerable yeoman,[49] had limited household goods worth only £13 when he died in 1675. Apart from £75 worth of malt, the principal inheritance he left to his nephew was 'Debts in his Booke, good and bad' worth £211 out of a total of £299 8s 0d. Even men like Richard Turner, who died in 1668, and was described as a husbandman although he retained only two pigs and the fowls in his yard, had over half of his £75 in bonds. It was apparently much more unusual for active farmers to engage in money lending. Robert Tebbutt, the younger, was worth £412 when he died in 1682. Of this £121 was accounted for in debts in the 'Booke' but some of these may well have been inherited from his uncle Joseph. Robert was the only yeoman still farming who was owed considerable sums.[50] However, enterprising men obviously also built up their estates by acquiring mortgages while they were still alive. The engrossing yeomen of Chippenham had parallels in every corn-growing village I have looked at.

In 1600, a yeoman, Martin Warren of Snailwell, who was presumably an ancestor of the highly successful Martin Warren of 1684 who farmed

---

[48] Forthcoming article by J. R. Ravensdale and Margaret Spufford, 'Money lending in Rural Society'.
[49] See above, pp. 72, 74.
[50] Although admittedly when the appraisers had priced Robert's own father's goods in 1668, they had admitted to ignorance of anything he was owed.

nearly 350 acres of open-field arable,[51] made his will.[52] He was pros-perous enough himself; he desired to be buried within the parish church, which was always a telling sign of status within a community. His career can only be guessed at. He had a house 'in Ludgate', and referred to Sir John Cotton of Landwade, to whom he left a bequest, as 'my old master'. He had six sons, one of whom was called Erasmus. One of them seemed already established. Three of the rest he set up on land he had acquired from six different men, in Snailwell, and in three other parishes. The two remaining sons, and an unmarried daughter, he estab-lished with £100 apiece, which was a still very substantial sum in yeo-man circles in 1600. The youngest son, William, was left an annuity, as well as his £100, 'towards the bringeing upp of the same William in learning'. Martin Warren left his wife not only all the normal house-hold goods, and pewter, but all his silver plate and pots 'except one Cuppe or goblett guylte with goulde' which he gave to his son and namesake, Martin. Martin Warren of Snailwell, who died in 1600, and old Nicholas Butler of Orwell, the other side of the county, who died in the following year,[53] sound as if they were in very similar positions, and had very similar ambitions.

It does not come entirely as a shock to the reader, although it is a delightfully logical surprise, that one of Martin Warren's daughters had married Thomas Dillamore of Chippenham, judging from the reference to 'my son Thomas Dillamore'.

Thomas Dillamore, the arch-engrosser, who in 1636 farmed the land which had been farmed by fifteen other men in 1544, described himself as 'aged' when he made his will in 1638. He provided for one of his seven sons by leaving him the reversion of all the copyhold lands in Woodditton which had been Thomas Collen's, after the death of Collen's widow, as well as a mortgage on another sixteen acres of Thomas Collen's, which Dillamore obviously expected would be for-feited. Unfortunately, Dillamore's inventory does not survive, but the cash bequests made in his will alone amounted to the enormous sum of £450, and the size of the residue is, of course, unknown.

Men like James Cooke and Thomas Dillamore must often have pro-vided a short-term solution to farmers embarrassed by bad harvests. Tenements must have been in some cases mortgaged to these enterpris-ing yeomen with cash to spare, years before they came up officially for transfer in the manor court. Thomas Dillamore actually left the cash for

[51] See above, p. 71.
[52] Bury St Edmunds and West Suffolk R.O., Will Register Coppinge. See also below, p. 340.
[53] See below, p. 109.

the entry fine on the lands mortgaged to him in Woodditton to the son he chose to inherit them. If this sort of transaction often took place, as the evidence suggests that it did, any picture of the effects of bad harvests which can be obtained from a general analysis of manorial transactions must inevitably be a blurred one. Indebtedness was also the lever by which small peasants in the Beauvaisis were forced off the land after 1647. It has led Professor Goubert to speak of the 'endemic burden of peasant debt'.[54]

It therefore seems that individual case-studies of the group of five holdings of between a half-yardland and a yardland-and-a-half in 1560,[55] which were no longer in existence by 1636, are the most likely way of discovering why and exactly when they disappeared. A sixth holding, which was to become leasehold, remained a copyhold for a large part of the sixteenth century and its descent too can be traced.

Not a single one of these tenements at risk disappeared before 1598. The half-yardland which Thomas Clarke held in 1560, described in the rolls as a pightle and sixteen acres, was split between John Francis and Thomas Dillamore in 1636. Thomas Clarke died in 1563 or 1564, and his son, another Thomas, who was under age, was admitted with his mother. In 1578, he was readmitted in his own right. He had no heirs, and in 1592 his brother was admitted. Two years later he too was dead, and his son, another William, was admitted. But William also, was short-lived. In 1597, his widowed aunt, the only remaining member of the family, daughter of the original tenant of 1560, was admitted in her turn. She surrendered the tenement in the next year, 1598, to the use of John Francis, and so it disappeared.[56]

Here, the demise of the holding might be taken to be very much a matter of demographic misfortune. It is perhaps pure fluke that the final surrender into the hands of one of the engrossing copyholders took place in 1598, the year immediately following four bad harvests, which marked the peak of sales in Chippenham. But it is extremely striking that parts, at least, of two of the other half-yardlands were also sold

---

[54] Professor Goubert's findings in *Beauvais et le Beauvaisis de 1600 à 1730* (Paris 1960) were translated and compressed into 'The French Peasantry of the Seventeenth Century: A Regional Example', in *Crisis in Europe 1560–1600*, ed. T. Aston (London 1970), pp. 163, 165.

[55] See above, pp. 76 and 78. These were thirteen holdings of between fifteen and fifty-one acres in 1560. One of them survived. Seven fell to the lord, and the dates of their purchase cannot all be traced. Five, here studied in detail, fell to the engrossing yeomen.

[56] It is interesting that the only piece of Thomas Clarke's holding to find its way into the lord's hand, and to be converted to leasehold, was the single acre of freehold which he held in 1560. The type of tenure seems to have had very little to do with the fate of the holding.

in 1598. The tenement croft and half-yardland which Anthony Hills held in 1544, together with an odd three acres of customary land, were held by his wife, who had remarried and was Margaret Blythe by 1560. In 1593, she died, and Thomas Hills, Anthony's nearest heir, was admitted. But he did not keep it. In 1598, he surrendered part of the holding to Thomas Dillamore. There was no demographic mishap here; the holding had not had to withstand repeated fines[57] and Thomas Hills was probably a youngish man himself, because he had only inherited his own father's smallholding in 1592.

The last of the half-yardlands to be sold, or at least fragmented, in 1598 was that of John Clements. After his death in 1566, his widow Alice held his eighteen acres until she surrendered it to her son, another John, in 1591. He must have been at least twenty-four.[58] In 1598, John surrendered the holding to the use of Thomas Cheesewright. It seems to have become a leasehold between 1598 and 1636.

Not a single one of the tenements at risk disappeared before 1598. It was, then, possible for the half-yardlander to survive the main part of the price rise of the sixteenth century. It may be true to say, not that the half-yardlander could not make ends meet during the price rise, but that the man with fifty acres or more was doing so well that he was in a position to snap up the smaller holdings when they did come on to the market. Whether the sales of 1598 were really related to the harvest situation, with which they coincide so neatly, or whether this was indeed pure coincidence, it is impossible to tell. Perhaps these holdings fell in 1598 because their tenants had already become indebted, or had mortgaged them in the preceding years. But it is at least possible to narrow down the crucial years at Chippenham still further than the period 1560–1636 as a whole, and to say that the holdings at risk there were actually fragmented between 1598 and 1636. It is also possible to say that the initial sales followed the highest grain prices ever yet recorded.

The gaps in the court rolls from 1602 on make it difficult to be precise about the dates at which the remaining holdings fell. Two of them were apparently mortgaged between 1598 and 1633.

One of these, the Scott half-yardland, had supported Robert Scott from at least the time his name was recorded in the rental of 1560 for thirty-seven years until his death in 1597, although he did sell, in 1580, one surplus tenement and croft he had held in 1560. In 1624, Augustus Scott surrendered his cottage and half-yardland to the use of his son

---

[57] The only one levied on it in thirty-three years was £3 on the death of Margaret Blythe, which seemed to be fairly typical of the general level of fines at that date.
[58] See below, p. 89.

Francis and his daughter-in-law Francesca. But, in the manor court of 1628, it was learnt that Augustus Scott had surrendered his holding to the use of John Kent, who had died, and whose son, another John Kent, was admitted. The elder John Kent had died in 1625–6 so the final surrender in the manor court therefore followed a mortgage by at least three years. This surrender in 1628 represents the final disappearance of the Scott half-yardland. John Kent, junior, held eighty-four acres of customary land in the survey of 1636.

Robert Shene's holding disappeared even later. He had held one and a half yardlands in 1560. In 1584, his son Thomas was admitted. By the time of the court of 1632 he had died, and his eldest son, another Thomas, inherited. But in 1633, it was learnt that Thomas Shene, deceased, had surrendered what was described as a 'messuage and all lands belonging thereto' to Thomas Dillamore, who entered it. The survey of 1636 showed Thomas Dillamore in possession of all the lands which had been Robert Shene's in 1560, except four acres which John Bentley had acquired. The history of the last of the holdings at risk to pass through the court rolls is incomplete; William Harley held a half-yardland in 1560, but no Harley was recorded in the rolls until 1602, when a Walter Harley sold a fragment of a holding amounting to six acres to John Francis. For what it is worth, the legible transactions in the rolls for 1602 onwards give an impression of sales of more fragments like this than do the previous rolls. The lack of information on the dates when Thomas Dillamore built up his copyhold of two hundred acres also makes one feel that the key period was probably this one from 1600 on when the rolls became defective, since in general they seem fairly reliable. Thomas Dillamore's only acquisitions recorded in the rolls before 1602 were one of about seventy-four acres in 1588, which was probably mostly made up of copyholds which had been seized, and were in the hands of the demesne farmer, in 1544. He had also bought part of Anthony Hills's half-yardland, and an odd three acres, in 1598. The bulk of John Francis's holding of ninety-four acres was inherited from his father, Edmund, who appears to have profited from the earlier wave of sales in the 1560s. He had accumulated two yardlands and a tenement of fourteen acres, all in 1564.

One more factor which might affect the way holdings were built up, or diminished, remains to be considered. This is the provision made for younger sons. That made for widows is also of general social interest. Even though it is not necessarily so strictly relevant, the provision made for a widow could, of course, and often did, place an additional burden on a holding, which must be considered.

The effect that even semi-partible inheritance could have is illustrated clearly by an entry in the court rolls of 1632, dealing with the Shene holding. This was the tenement of one and a half yardlands which eventually fell to Thomas Dillamore. In 1636, the annotations on the survey made it plain that Dillamore and John Bentley had both acquired parts of the holding. The court rolls explained the reason. After the turn of the century, wills were regularly read in the court and often quoted. In April 1632, John and Thomas Shene, sons of Thomas Shene who had died since the last court, came and read his will. He had left four acres of arable to John, who was admitted for an 8s 4d fine, and 'my house and all the rest of my lands' to Thomas, who paid the steep fine of £12. The history of the main holding has already been told; but in 1634, John Shene surrendered his four-acre inheritance to John Bentley, who thus acquired his interest in the holding.

INHERITANCE CUSTOMS

The granting of a portion of land, which was not in itself adequate for support, to a younger son, merely weakened the main holding and made the engrosser's task easier. An examination of the wills of Chippenham men which survive makes it possible to see how common such inheritance customs were.

A dozen men who died leaving wills in Chippenham between 1520 and 1680[59] provided in them for more than one son, and therefore give some opportunity for examining the way in which the pattern of land distribution was affected by inheritance. Only two of the twelve men left their holdings outright to one son, and made no attempt to set other sons up with any toehold on the land at all. The remaining seven either attempted a true division of land amongst their sons, or handed on the bulk of the holding to one, and attempted to provide small tenements for the others, sometimes by deliberate purchase. The men who attempted to set up their younger sons on smallholdings were usually of some substance, like Edmund Francis, who left his son John a messuage of sixty acres in 1570, but a house and fourteen acres to his other son George, after his mother had died. Both were purchases he had made in 1564. John Hodgkin, a very considerable yeoman and demesne lessee, was worth £552 when he died in 1647. He farmed over one hundred acres of leasehold as well as at least forty acres of customary land. His

[59] The sample of wills I have worked from is oddly made up. It consists of the thirty-seven which survive from the earliest in 1520 to 1640, together with another fifteen which accompany the surviving inventories. Many more wills do survive for the period 1640–1700, which I have not been able to see.

eldest son, Martin, whose inventory also survives was joint residuary legatee and held his father's farm and house virtually unchanged, except that he added the gracious touch of a pair of virginals in the hall. The second son was apprenticed and was left £120 as well, presumably to set him up in whatever craft he had chosen. The youngest son was left a freehold house sublet by his father, and 'the land, meadow and pasture which descended to me from my father, and ten acres of copy which I bought of old John Turner'. 'Old John Turner' had been admitted to his father's yardland in 1602, and sold ten acres to John Hodgkin, which he had already sublet to him, in the court of 1623.

William Clarke was one of the men who held a yardland in the 1544 survey, who attempted to divide his land up more equally among his five sons rather than provide a smallholding for the younger. Martin was left a house that his father had sublet, and barley to sow the land; Thomas and Nicholas were to share the house that Thomas was already dwelling in, and also to have barley to sow the land. The last two sons could only be left cash sums of £2 each. The yardland which William Clarke occupied himself he left his wife for life and then to their infant yet unborn. If it failed to survive, the holding was to pass to one of the two sons who were left only cash. So one way and another William Clarke set up four children with land.

The most interesting case of the subdivision of a holding was that of Thomas Dillamore, the arch-engrosser who died in 1637. His inventory unfortunately does not survive, but his will is in itself most revealing. He died as his will stated 'not sick, but aged in body'. He had married twice, and had had one son, another Thomas, by his first wife, and six by his second, as well as four daughters, who were left dowries of £100 apiece, huge by the current standards. Thomas Dillamore had not only engrossed holdings in Chippenham, but had also acquired by mortgage a holding in Woodditton which must have been very considerable since he expected the fine on it to be as much as £40.[60] He had also bought a house and at least a half-yardland in the nearby parish of Fordham, and another acre or so in Freckenham. His dealings thus covered at least four parishes. The most considerable part of the holding went to Thomas, the eldest son by his first marriage, who got all the land in Chippenham. Some of it, indeed, had been transferred to him already; one of the few entries in the Chippenham court rolls which throw any light on Thomas Dillamore's business transactions show him acquiring part of the Hills's half-yardland and an odd five acres in 1598, and immediately transferring it to his son. In the following year he

[60] The fine he paid on 74 acres in Chippenham in 1599 was only £13 6s 8d although obviously one would not expect consistency from manor to manor.

transferred seventy-four acres and various odd messuages which he had acquired in 1588 to Thomas, junior, who by then was married, forty years before his father's death. As well as all the Dillamore acquisitions in Chippenham, Thomas also got a part of the land his father had acquired in Woodditton, although the bulk of this went to another son, Robert. The land in Fordham and the residue went to a third son, Colin, who was executor with his mother, and was to inherit after her death. On the whole, then, although Thomas Dillamore divided up his land, he did so on a parochial basis, and established three sons on adequate holdings. The provision made for two of the others was a mystery; they were either established elsewhere, or were out of favour with their father, for they were fobbed off with 5s and 10s apiece. Another was left £10, and the last, obviously still a very small child, an annuity of £4 during his mother's life. Even so, the total cash bequests which the widow and one son were responsible for paying out amounted to over £450, and since none of the Chippenham land was in their hands, the residue must have been extremely large in contemporary terms.

In Chippenham, therefore, a great effort was made to establish younger sons with land. Where holdings like the yardlands of William Clarke were concerned, the tendency must have been to weaken farming units and make them less capable of weathering bad harvests and surviving as viable economic units. Even when there was no attempt to provide younger sons with land, the effort to provide them with a cash sum to start them off in life often had a weakening effect on the holding.[61] Sometimes the burden placed on a tenement was obviously preposterous in economic terms. Henry Lane of Badlingham, who only had a house and pightle with it, provided in his will in 1669 that his eldest son, when he inherited, should pay legacies of £5 a year for four years to his brother and sister. The constant social effort to provide some at least of younger members of the family with land must in the end have given more opportunities to the engrossers whether they were lords of the manor or larger copyholders. On the other hand, the very same care shown by the more substantial yeomen, and the willingness of men like Thomas Dillamore and John Hodgkin to subdivide their holdings, must have acted as a brake on the development of the really large farms. There is no doubt, however, from the proven disappearance of the middle-sized farms, that the economic forces pressing such people off the land into the increasing ranks of wage-labourers were stronger than the constant endeavours made by the community to provide land for as many of its sons as possible.

[61] See below, pp. 106–8 for similar customs at Orwell.

PROVISION FOR WIDOWS

The way in which men provided for their widows in Chippenham was very different from that in which they provided for them at Orwell. Twenty-two men left both widows and sons capable of inheriting at Chippenham. While it was normal at Orwell to leave the widow the holding only until the son was twenty-one, and carefully specified house-room after that,[62] only one woman in the parish of Chippenham was left rights of board with her eldest son. Not every testator went to the extreme of Robert Gyll, who died in 1590, and 'dyd before honeste wytnesses saye he wolde geve nothinge of his goodes to ainy of his Children but that his wiefe shoulde have all his goodes'. A Robert Gyll had held 200 acres of leasehold and customary land held at will in 1560, so if this was the same man, he was probably still prosperous. James Clement, who died earlier in the century, leaving three sons and five daughters, trusted his wife as much as Robert Gyll, for he left the residue to her sole discretion, partly to lay out 'to the pleasure of God and welthe of my sowle'. But the norm in Chippenham according to the wills was to leave the widow a life interest in the house and land. Three-quarters of the wills[63] did just this. Admittedly, some of these women were the widows of the very prosperous, who at Orwell too were on the whole the only widows to be left life interests. Edmund Francis, who died between May and October 1570, still holding the two copyhold messuages with sixty and fourteen acres apiece which he had held in the rental of 1560, left his son John the messuage and sixty acres, and his wife Margaret the fourteen-acre holding, with the remainder to the other son George. At the court on 14 October 1570, Margaret and George were admitted to the fourteen acres and John to the sixty acres. Margaret Francis probably died in 1582, when George was readmitted to the same holding. Thomas Dillamore's wife Frances was left a house and land in Fordham for life and was also residuary legatee with one of her sons. John Hodgkin, who was worth £552 when his goods were appraised in 1647, left his wife Anne all his copy and freelands in Chippenham and elsewhere in the counties of Cambridge and Suffolk for life, and also made her joint residuary legatee with her eldest son, Martin.

But the wealthy were not the only men who left their wives a life interest. Robert Clement, who died between 1552 and 1554 had an adult son John, who was overseer of his will, but he left his house to his wife Margaret for life, and then to John and his heirs. Still humbler

---

[62] See below, pp. 112–15, for a general discussion of the 'normal' provision for widows.
[63] Fifteen out of twenty-two.

men pursued the same policy. John Rowninge, who was a labourer in Badlingham, left his house to his widow Anne for her life in 1609, and laid down that it should be sold after her death, and half the proceeds go to his son, the other half to his two daughters.

The court rolls multiply examples of cases in which the widow was left a life interest. It was the common procedure for a man, on entering a holding, to surrender it at once and re-enter it with his wife, thus presumably giving her such an interest. In this way, in 1597, Augustus Scott inherited his father's half-yardland and at once surrendered it, and was readmitted with Katherine, his wife. In 1564 Thomas Clarke died, and left his widow Margaret and her son and heir, Thomas, sixteen acres of arable and a pightle. Fourteen years later Thomas was admitted in his own right, presumably after his mother's death.

This picture is no doubt overstated. There are examples amongst the wills of widows being granted an interest only during the minority of their sons, like the will of William Haylock, who left his house and land in Chippenham to his widow only until his son John was twenty-one, in 1566. There are also numerous examples in the court rolls of widows, like Maria Stubbings, in 1589, being admitted to their husband's holdings only until the heir reached the age of twenty or twenty-one. It seems likely, though, that the widow in Chippenham must usually have had considerable rights in the holding, and that she may frequently have had a legal interest after her son's majority. In practice, the widow must frequently and willingly have relinquished the management of the holding when her son came of age, whether or not she legally retained a share in it. Sometimes she gave up any legal right; in 1591, Alice Dayrell, who had been the wife of John Clement, surrendered the messuage of eighteen acres to which she had been admitted after his death in 1567. There had been no mention of any heir on her admission; but she surrendered to her son and heir, John Clement. Twenty-four years had elapsed since her own admission, and there was no question of a forced surrender when her son reached legal age. She must have chosen to relinquish her rights.

One of the nicest examples of the power which was unobtrusively wielded by widows in Chippenham is that of Philippa Tebbutt. She was the 'loveing wife' of Robert Tebbutt, yeoman, who died in 1668.[64] He left her all the residue of his considerable estate except sixty acres of copyhold, which he left to his wife's father to sell for paying off his debts. There was no mention of any son or daughter in Robert's will and he gave the impression of dying childless. Yet when his son, another Robert, died in 1682, unmarried, he was able to devise all his

[64] See above, p. 74.

Chippenham estate to his sister, including the sixty acres his father had intended to be sold, for, as he said 'the debts of my said father were since otherwise paid by my late deare Mother deceased'. Such women were obviously powerful.

If widows commonly held life interests in their husband's holdings in Chippenham, one would expect this to be reflected demographically. Remarriage must have been frequent among widows, while it is just possible that their sons married somewhat later, rather than following the usually assumed pattern of marrying almost at once after the death of the father. A general slight lowering of the birth rate might well have been the result, and it is just possible that the relatively stable size of the community in the sixteenth century[65] may be related to these social customs. These points would certainly repay demographic investigation if only the material existed.

CONCLUSION

At Chippenham between 1560 and 1636 holdings of fifteen to forty or forty-five acres, made up of recognisable medieval units, disappeared. The unchanging size of the population suggests that men were forced by the situation to emigrate. There was a growth in the proportion of people holding fifty acres or more, and in the proportion of cottagers. Detailed examination of the court rolls show that the tenements in question disappeared between 1598 and 1636.[66] Although there was a considerable conversion of copyhold to leasehold on the manor, the number of copyholders whose land was engrossed simply to be added to the copies of their more prosperous brethren suggests that vulnerability to seigneurial action and legal factors did not underlie the change.[67] No definite proof can be brought forward to show that the smaller farmer was obliged to sell because bad harvests forced him out,[68] but the disappearance of holdings at risk in Chippenham started in 1598, in an exceptionally bad period. It is equally true that examples have been cited showing that men managed to live on holdings of fifteen or eighteen acres for thirty years or more during the very worst of the price rise, up to the 1590s, even though additional burdens were placed on these holdings, in an area of nominally impartible inheritance, by the care taken to provide for all the sons of a marriage, and by the interest of widows. It is still possible to argue that the larger yeomen were doing so well that by the end of the sixteenth century they were in a position to buy up smaller holdings whenever they came on the

---

65 See above, p. 61.
67 See above, pp. 75ff.
66 See above, pp. 82–4.
68 See above, pp. 50–2.

market, rather than that the smaller man was forced to sell. Even so, however the facts are interpreted, it remains true that economic factors rather than legal ones underlie the disappearance of the smaller farmer in Chippenham, and the period in which the smaller farmer disappeared was a very brief one, a mere thirty years at the beginning of the seventeenth century. In one Cambridgeshire village at least, we must re-date *The Disappearance of the Small Landowner*[69] by at least a century.

When he examined the economic position of peasants in the corn-growing north of the Beauvaisis,[70] the limitations of his material allowed Professor Goubert to work in great detail only on the period after 1660. He found exactly the type of polarisation I have described here, and described the corn-growing plateau of Picardy as a 'bleak countryside, with a monotonous type of farming, [where] peasant society appeared only in brutal contrasts. At the social peak was the large farmer, flanked by five or six *laboureurs*; down below was the wretched mass of *manœuvriers*; between them, nothing.' By inference Professor Goubert deduced, although he was not able to prove, that these contrasts between social groups were not so marked in exactly that period between 1600 and 1635[71] when I have shown the pace of polarisation was probably highest in Chippenham. The crucial years for the peasants in the cereal-growing part of the Beauvaisis were between 1647 and 1653, in years of bad harvest, when exactly the same thing happened as I have demonstrated for Chippenham in the bad harvest years of the 1590s and thereafter. In Professor Goubert's words, 'Crushed by debt, the small peasants had to give up a large part of their land to their creditors.'[72]

The timing then, was different, but exactly the same machinery was at work: 'The more substantial *laboureurs*, those who had surplus crops to sell, sold them at considerable profit since the prices of cereals had risen two, three or even four times. Thus enriched they bought up lands from their debtors among the small peasants.'[73]

It must be admitted that cereal-growers all over Europe found themselves in trouble from the 1650s onwards.[74] The price of rye, an index to the fortunes of arable farmers, declined far more than the price of livestock. In the whole century after 1650 it averaged only sixty-five per cent of its value from 1600 to 1650. The events which brought misery and starvation to many of the inhabitants of the Beauvaisis fit

[69] See above, p. 49.
[70] Goubert, 'The French Peasantry of the Seventeenth Century', pp. 141–65.
[71] *Ibid.* pp. 161–2.
[72] *Ibid* p. 163.
[73] *Ibid.*
[74] H. Slicher van Bath, *The Agrarian History of Western Europe A.D. 500–1850* (1959; Engl. tr. London 1963), pp. 206–12, particularly pp. 208–10.

better into this European chronology than the misfortunes of those men at Chippenham with medium-sized farms who were forced off the land between 1597 and 1636. Yet however tempting it is to slot the small misadventures at Chippenham, which were nonetheless momentous to those who suffered them, into a general pattern called 'The Crisis of the Seventeenth Century'[75] it remains only a temptation. These specific examples of small cereal-growers being forced off the land well before the 1650s do much to substantiate my suggestion that men holding medieval standard holdings of a half-yardland, a yardland, or even a yardland-and-a-half, found themselves in trouble in bad harvest years during the price rise, long before the general down-turn of the economy in the seventeenth century. Where the particularisation does not fit the generalisation, it is surely the generalisation that has to be modified, not the other way round.

[75] The opening essay by E. J. Hobsbawm in *Crisis in Europe 1560–1660*, ed. T. Aston, pp. 5–58. When Mr Hobsbawn wrote, in 1954, he was – as he said himself in his 'Postscript' written in 1965 (pp. 54ff.) to the reprinted article – attempting an early synthesis towards the beginning of a historical debate. But his remarks on the English agrarian situation do seem to have been somewhat simplified and removed from the social realities. He suggested that 'the price-rise, the upheavals in landownership, and the growth of demand for agrarian produce might well have led to the emergence of capitalist farming by gentlemen and the kulak-type of peasant on a greater scale than appear have occurred'. He found no evidence for this. He might have been cheered by the examples of men like Thomas Dillamore, John Francis, Martin Warren of Snailwell and the Butler family of Orwell, who presumably represent 'kulak peasants' (p. 24). It is similarly impossible to regard all peasants as 'miserable' (p. 34). It is unlikely that Sir Miles Sandys (see below, pp. 120–7) saw his peasants in such a light. Any detailed study of any area, in England at least, is likely to lead to modifications of generalisations of this type.

Map 9   Orwell in the 1670s

Key to Map of Orwell

1 Butlers New Close.   2 Mortlocks Close.   3 Vicarage.   4 Parsonage.   5 Town House.   6 Fairchild.   7 Godfrey.   8 Almshouse.   9 Caldecut.   10 W. Johnson   11 Spring.   12 Butlers Nooke.   13 Spring.   14 Ladies Yard (Ley strips divided amongst tenants c. 1682).   15 Butlers Lady Close.   16 Lordship.   17 Richard Barnard, Dissenter.   18 Butlers House.   19 Camping Close or Orchard.   20 17th-century cottages.   21 Demesne pasture divided amongst all tenants, 1627.   22 Johnson.   23 Ambrose Benning, will writer.   24 Caldecut, Dissenter?   25 John Godfrey.   26 The Green.   27 Widow Adams, Dissenter.   28 John Adams, Dissenter.   29 The Outward Marsh Demesne, divided amongst all tenants, 1627.

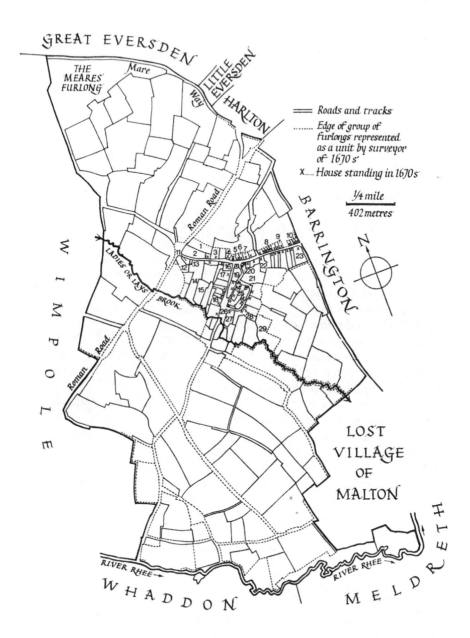

GREAT EVERSDEN

THE MEARES FURLONG

Mare Way

LITTLE EVERSDEN

HARLTON

BARRINGTON

Roman Road

LADIES OR LAYS

BROOK

WIMPOLE

Roman Road

N

= = Roads and tracks

.... Edge of group of furlongs represented as a unit by surveyor of 1670's

x ...... House standing in 1670's

¼ mile

402 metres

LOST VILLAGE OF MALTON

RIVER RHEE

RIVER RHEE

MELDRETH

WHADDON

4

The reality: the small landholder on the clay: Orwell

SOURCES, FIELDS, CROPS AND STOCK

Orwell lies to the south-west of Cambridge. The parish now includes the territory of the lost village of Malton, which was ecclesiastically separate in the middle ages, and remained a separate manor outside the scope of this survey. Both geographically and socially, Orwell is strongly contrasted with Chippenham. The parish boundaries are formed on the south by the river Rhee, the western branch of the Cam, and on the north by the Mare Way, a prehistoric route which runs along the top of a steep ridge of boulder clay which projects here from the main boulder clay plateau to the west of the county. The village itself lies tucked away just under this ridge, off the main Roman road linking Cambridge with the Ermine Street, on the spring line and on the chalk which underlies it and which formed its building material. The chalk outcrop is relatively narrow here, however, and the soil south of the village down to the river alluvium is heavy and ill-drained, over gault clay.[1] On the whole, therefore, the village is more geographically akin to those on the clay uplands than to those on the edge of the fens.

It is Orwell's situation which makes it worth investigation. The population history of the clay villages was very different from those on the fen-edge, and many, though not all, of them shrank during the sixteenth and seventeenth centuries.[2] An examination of land distribution in one of them therefore seems particularly important. Otherwise, Orwell would not be singled out for special attention, for the documentary sources are incomplete. Orwell had been a royal manor since it came to the crown from the inheritance of Margaret, countess of Richmond.[3] The demesne was leased, but was surveyed in 1601,[4] and

---

[1] John Jones, *A Human Geography of Cambridgeshire: A Suggested Method of Studying the Home Area* (London 1924), pp. 54–5, and *The Cambridge Region, 1965*, ed. Steers, map facing p. 84.

[2] C. T. Smith, 'Settlement and Population', in *The Cambridge Region, 1965*, ed. Steers, pp. 150–1. See above for a detailed discussion of Orwell's population, pp. 23ff.

[3] Lysons, *Magna Britannia*, II, 243.

[4] P.R.O., E178/485, 43 Eliz. Partially defective, but a contemporary copy exists in the C.R.O., L63/57/5.

a series of disputes over the demesne leases were investigated in the court of Exchequer in 1605.[5] The copyholds alone were surveyed in 1607 by an Exchequer Commission,[6] and again as a preliminary to the sale of the manor in 1627.[7] The change in the distribution of the copyhold holdings can therefore be examined over this single generation, which lived through a time of acute harvest-failure and distress in Cambridgeshire. The disadvantage is that Orwell, unlike Chippenham and Snailwell, had a considerable area of freehold land, and the distribution of this is unknown, except at the beginning of the century. An examination of farm size which disregards the freeholds is admittedly inadequate, although the deficiency is not as serious as might be supposed, from the common error of treating freeholders, copyholders and leaseholders as three distinct groups of tenants. In fact, a yeoman of any pretensions probably held land by all three tenures. It is extremely unfortunate, however, that the magnificent map of Orwell, probably made in the mid-1670s,[8] after the manor had come into the hands of the Chicheley family, has lost its accompanying terrier, and that only a fragment survives of a full survey of both freeholds and copyholds with notes on their recent history, made some time after 1682.[9] It is not therefore possible to examine the way land distribution continued to change after 1627, although a rental made between 1675 and 1682[10] and a series of notes on the demesne and demesne leases made in the early eighteenth century[11] do provide some clues. The registers are good, beginning in 1560,[12] but the court rolls are unfortunately missing for the period between the two surveys of 1607 and 1627. Only a fragmentary sketch can therefore be attempted to the seventeenth-century tenurial situation in Orwell, and the reasons for the changes there.

In 1627, the surveyor of Orwell wrote,

The manor of Orwell is entire and situate within five miles of the University of Cambridge and within four miles of Royston which is a great Market Town for Corn and Cattle and lyeth against a hill side upon the same in the open fields but not any wood nor Cole neer unto yett. The Land is most field grown arable except some few pastures about the towne and the soyle is rich *and the sole Comodity is Corne*[13] and some small parcells of Saffron grounde. The soyle naturally doth cast Clover grass which beinge Suffered to grow until it bee almost ripe and then Cut is the Choycest provender for horses ... The Royalties of the Manor are but usual and the benefitt small

[5] P.R.O., E134/3, Jas.I/East.18.   [6] C.R.O., L63/49.   [7] C.R.O., L63/58/2.
[8] Map in C.U.L., on which the present Map 9 is based.   [9] C.R.O., L63/58/1.
[10] C.R.O., L1/130, pp. 23–5.   [11] C.R.O., L63/58/3.
[12] *The Register of the Parish of Orwell, 1560–1653*, ed. Whiston.   [13] My italics.

and the rather because the game of huntinge hawkinge and fowlinge is there preserved for the Kinges pleasure when he lays at Royston. The Fishing of a small river of about a rood and a half over belonges to the Manor for half a Mile in length.[14]

Although the field layout at Orwell was of the complicated type typical of Cambridgeshire[15] and the mapmaker of the 1670s divided the furlongs into no less than eleven different groups of widely varying acreage, there was apparently some kind of two-course system run there at the beginning of the century. The arable of the tenements listed in 1607 was divided simply between the 'High' and the 'Low' field. By the beginning of the eighteenth century there was a three-course system, and the arable of the demesne farms was divided between 'River, Oat land and High Fields'.

In discussing an area he calls the 'Midland Plain' Dr Kerridge says that the 'inflexible, uniform, three-field course of (1) tilth (2) breach (3) fallow, may be seen throughout the length and breadth of the plain'.[16] Orwell lies at the eastern edge of Dr Kerridge's 'Midland Plain', and the inventories of Orwell men from the late seventeenth century confirm that such a system was then followed. The two sown courses were known as the tilth field and the brokeland. The tilth field was the one that had been fallow in the previous year and had been brought to a fine tilth in the summer. It was used in general for autumn sowing, with wheat, meslin, rye and better quality barley. The broke-land was the land that had been the tilth field in the previous year and was rough ploughed or 'broken' in the autumn and sown in the spring with barley, oats or peas.[17]

Only one of the inventories gives any clear indication of the proportions of crops sown, since the others which do give acreages were taken at harvest time when part of the crop was in the field, and part in the barn. The inventory of Christopher Adams in 1686 indicates that he had twenty-two acres of tilth, of which eight had been sown with wheat and meslin, and fourteen remained to be sown, presumably with barley. He also had thirty acres of brokeland ready to be sown with oats and peas. The amounts of various grain in three barns appraised during the winter months can give only an impression of what was grown, but suggest that, as everywhere else in the county, barley was the most important single crop. Barley was followed fairly closely by

[14] C.R.O., L63/58/2, dated by me from internal evidence to 1627–8.
[15] M. R. Postgate, 'The Open Fields of Cambridgeshire', unpublished Cambridge Ph.D. thesis (1964). See also Postgate's chapter on 'The Field Systems of East Anglia', in A. R. H. Baker and R. Butlin, *Studies in Field Systems of the British Isles* (Cambridge 1973).
[16] Kerridge, *The Agricultural Revolution*, p. 93.   [17] *Ibid.*

oats, and the name 'Oat field' presumably derives from this speciality, which distinguishes the arable crops of Orwell from those of Chippenham or Willingham.[18] Just under a quarter of the grain in stock was wheat, and there were also small amounts of peas in store.

Although the surveyor of 1627 went on to say that there were about two hundred acres of meadow and pasture in Orwell which was lammas ground and commonable to all the tenants of the manor, the late seventeenth-century map of Orwell shows no trace of any extensive common. The open-field furlongs continued right up to the Mare Way on the north,[19] and down to the river Rhee on the south. The only meadow and pasture shown on the map fringed the little brook which ran through the village itself, 'Ladies' brook, or 'Lays' brook, and also fringed the river.

From the squabble over the demesne leases, which came to a head in 1605 it is plain that there was a chronic shortage of meadow and pasture in Orwell. There had certainly not been a resident lord of the manor at least since before Sir Simon Burley, who had held it in Richard II's reign.[20] The motte sketched on the seventeenth-century map on the toft called 'lordship' on the High Street had never been replaced by a building in a more modern idiom. It is not surprising that, even if the demesne was leased by the crown to an intermediary before the tenants themselves, they had got into the way of thinking of the demesne very much as a permanently available supply of leasehold land. It is significant that a copy of the survey of the demesne made in 1601 was headed 'Townlands alias Burylands'.[21] It had probably been farmed by the town ever since the fourteenth century, and seems never to have been sublet to one demesne farmer but to have been divided up amongst the more prosperous tenants.[22] The villagers of Orwell seem also to have had a tradition of taking communal action over obtaining this extra land. When the queen leased the demesne arable to a Mrs Jean Audley sometime in the early 1590s, some of the tenants approached her 'in the behalf of all the tenants to have compounded with her for the same'. There were 240 acres of demesne arable, against only just over thirty-four acres of demesne meadow and pasture. It was the struggle to obtain this meadow and pasture which brought many of the Orwell tenants to give evidence in Exchequer in

---

[18] See above, pp. 62–3, and below, pp. 128–9.
[19] Some of their names are suggestive of clearance, but they may of course have been thirteenth-century survivals rather than the product of new sixteenth-century pressures. The largest of all, next to Mare Way, had the look of a remaining piece of waste, now under cultivation.
[20] Lysons, *Magna Britannia*, II. [21] C.R.O. version, L63/57/5.
[22] See below, pp. 101–2.

1605. The negotiators had had trouble in obtaining their lease from Mrs Audley in the 1590s. She made what they considered unreasonable demands for the arable of 6s 8d an acre, as well as a fine of £100, for an eighteen- or nineteen-year lease. The negotiators decided that her demands were so large because she claimed that the demesne meadow and pasture were demised to her. The eldest son of a yeoman of Orwell, Thomas Butler, who was studying at Gray's Inn, and was only in his twenties, offered his aid at a public indignation meeting of the tenants, held in traditional fashion in the church chancel. He suggested that he should obtain a separate lease of the demesne meadow and pasture direct from the queen, if the tenants would either pay him the cost of any suit Mrs Audley brought against him, or pay him a yearly rent for the land. They chose to pay him a rent, and in addition, to let him enclose and hold in severalty the acre and a quarter which was all that was left of the common green[23] for his trouble. All went well for some years, but then Mrs Audley obtained an order that the tenants should take sub-leases of the meadow and pasture directly from her. Butler unwisely tried to keep his new close, and a band of the more important tenants, enraged at being mulcted on every side, tore down the hedges and put in the majority of the town herd of cattle. There is of course no record of the judgement given on this case in the depositions which survive, but Butler must have won. In 1627, the surveyor noted before writing out his terrier of the demesne pasture 'in lease to Mr Butler . . . and got in by Mr Butler who was the Bailiff, and shared amongst the tenants and soe they now hold it, only the heirs of Mr Butler have the greatest part'. And so indeed they did: five-and-a-half of the thirty-four acres were held personally by Thomas Butler's widow, a considerable quantity of the rest was sublet by the Butler family, and only ten acres were specifically said to be 'divided amongst the tenants' or 'in the possession of all the tenants'.

The dispute over the demesne grassland illustrates two points, apart from the way one yeoman rose to prosperity: the villagers' capacity for communal action; and the shortage of pasture which obviously caused much anxiety. Since the court rolls are missing for the preceding period, there is no means of knowing whether the stint had dropped when the surveyor noted in 1627 that it stood at one cow for every house and one for every twenty acres of land.[24] The whole town herd contained between 140 and 160 beasts, or about three to a house, when it was put into Thomas Butler's close early in the century. The arable

---

[23] The Orchard or Camping Close.
[24] Although the villagers might put as many as they could upon the common, which seems to have disappeared during the century.

was mainly kept in good heart by the fold-course system which extended over much of Cambridgeshire as well as Norfolk. Sheep were stinted at the rate of two a house and twenty for every fourteen or twenty acres of land in 1627, and the flock was divided into two. Every copyholder had rights of foldage, which were carefully listed in the survey of 1607. Even so, the inventories which survive from 1662 on show that by the end of the century nearly half those for whom inventories were made were not keeping sheep.[25] The eleven people who kept sheep kept between one and sixty-one, but the median was ten. Only two men kept over twenty, and they were both very considerable yeomen: Christopher Adams, who had forty, and William Swann, who had sixty-one sheep. The general picture fits in with the polarisation of landholding I have postulated for Orwell. Even at the end of the century, after the great expansion of the demesne, and the reorganisation of the village arable from a two- to a three-course system, the lack of pasture kept the numbers of cattle very low. One of the demesne farmers who held 270 acres of arable in the early eighteenth century[26] ran 160 sheep and had the right of foldage for 156 nights, but had only twenty cattle in all. The largest herd mentioned in the inventories was only seven, and the median was only two.

LAND DISTRIBUTION

The material illustrating the land distribution at Orwell is deficient since it mainly consists of two surveys of the copyholds made in 1607 and 1627. The lack of information on the freehold land is serious, because, of all the villages included in this study, Orwell was socially distinguished by the amount of its freehold land.

Orwell was, to Maitland, the supreme example of the free Saxon village, where the Normans had reduced the sokemen to villeinage, and no freemen survived by 1086.[27] By the end of the thirteenth century, however, there was again a considerable amount of freehold, which survived for several centuries. The seventeenth-century map of Orwell covered just over 1,450 acres of open-field arable in the manor, and the surveys made at the beginning of the century covered 240 acres of demesne arable, about 200 acres of common and 600 acres of copyhold. There must therefore have been about 400 acres of freehold in the manor then.

[25] I have been able to obtain copies of nineteen inventories proved between 1662 and 1700. Eight did not mention sheep. Unfortunately the inventories for the Diocese of Ely were partially inaccessible to me.   [26] C.R.O., L63/58/6.
[27] F. W. Maitland, *Domesday Book and Beyond: Three Essays in the Early History of England* (1897; paperback edn, London 1960), pp. 91, 172, 179, 186.

TABLE 7   *Landholding in Orwell, seventeenth century*
(Number of tenants by copyhold tenure alone)

Arable acreage	1607	1627	1670s (probable from rent paid)
90 acres and over	0	1	4
Over 3 half-yardlands	0	1	
3 half-yardlands (44–51a.)	3	2	
1 yardland (25–37a.)	7	5	3
1 half-yardland (13–22a.)	12	9	5
Under a half-yardland	7	8	21
2 acres and under*	7	22	
Total copyhold tenants	36	48	33

* Includes tenants without copyhold arable, but with copyhold cottages, and small closes of pasture, meadow or orchard.

Between 1607 and 1627, a period which included the crisis years of 1612, 1618 and 1627 – three of the eight years at Orwell between 1560 and 1700 when the number of deaths rose to at least fifteen – a very noticeable change in the distribution of the copyhold land took place. With the exception of the crisis years themselves, baptisms were still outnumbering burials, and the number of copyholders increased from thirty-six in 1607 to forty-eight in 1627 (see Table 7). Most of this increase was accounted for by a rise in the number of cottagers with two acres or under, from seven in 1607 to twenty-two in 1627. In 1607, there had been twelve standard holdings corresponding to a half-yard-land, which was normally of fourteen acres[28] but could in fact be any-thing from thirteen to twenty-three acres. There had also been seven holders of yardlands of between twenty-five and thirty-seven acres. By 1627, there were only nine half-yardlanders, and five yardlanders. The men holding over forty acres had benefited, however. In 1607, there had been three holdings of over forty acres, running up from forty-five to just over fifty. In 1627, there were four of these holdings, but two of them were much larger. Richard Fairchild held nearly seventy acres, and Mary Butler, widow of Thomas, held ninety acres of arable during the minority of her son Neville.

It is obvious that the changes in the distribution of land which took place at Chippenham also took place at Orwell, and that there, too, although to a lesser extent, holders of traditional farms of a half-yardland or a yardland were squeezed out, whilst the number of

[28] There is a hint in the survey of 1627 (C.R.O., L63/58/2) that the half-yardland had once contained twenty acres, since stints were organised on a twenty-acre basis; yet if a man held only fourteen acres he might run the same number of sheep on the common as if he held twenty acres.

cottagers increased radically, and the men with an acreage larger than normal profited. It is infuriating that the Orwell court rolls do not exist for this period, and it is therefore impossible to see whether the larger farms were built up, and the traditional medieval holdings diminished, in bad harvest years. Certainly this change cannot be attributed to legal action on the part of the lord. Copyholds were stated in the 1627 survey to be copyhold of inheritance, and the tenants were therefore relatively secure, and could not be ousted from their farms without considerable effort. A comparison of the two surveys made in 1607 and 1627 showed there had been no rise in rents. It is true that fines both for alienation and on descent were at will, but the surveyor noted in 1627 'they pretend they may let estates by deeds for three years without licence', and by virtue of that custom, 'they let leases from three years to three years *ad infinitum*'. It does not sound as though fines had been exploited either.[29] Despite this lack of seigneurial intervention, the amount of change in these twenty years shows that the larger copyholders were engaged in swallowing up their neighbours, just as they had been at Chippenham. Economic pressures on the smaller farmer, combined with a slight rise in population, and so an increase in the number of cottagers, must therefore, have made this engrossing possible.

This account based on the distribution of copyhold land alone, which disregards both 400 acres of freehold and 240 acres of demesne leasehold, is inevitably incomplete. An undated list of lessees of the demesne exists,[30] which must have been made before Nicholas Johnson *alias* Butler died in 1601, for on it he appears as the tenant of thirty acres of demesne. The demesne was then divided up into holdings of between five and thirty acres, although most of them were of ten or twenty acres. The majority of these demesne tenants were still alive when the copyholds were surveyed in 1607. All but one of them were men who already held a yardland or more of copyhold land. All those holding over forty acres of copyhold also held twenty acres of demesne on lease.

A survey was made in 1602 or 1603 of both the freeholds and the copyholds of the manor.[31] It is manifestly unreliable as far as the copyholds are concerned, since it omits important tenants like the Butlers,

---

[29] They may well have been exploited later in the century, judging from a comparison of the fines taken at a few courts copied out in the late 1580s and 1590s with the profits of court obtained after the purchase of the manor by four citizens of London early in the reign of Charles I. But this profiteering could not have been responsible for the changes noted in the early seventeenth century. Orwell Memorandum Book, C.R.O., L1/130, pp. 9–15.

[30] C.R.O., L1/130, p. 8.   [31] C.R.O.,L1/130, pp. 5–7.

and only covers about 350 out of 600 acres of copyhold land. It seems to be more reliable on the freehold, however, since it covers 390 out of the known total of 400 acres of arable.[32] The lord of the manor of Malton held nearly 150 acres of this freehold and another fifty acres were accounted for by the glebe and the townland of Orwell. One of the Cambridge colleges, Peterhouse, had another twenty-five acres. A good deal of this 225 acres of freehold land was therefore presumably available as leasehold, to lesser tenants, to change the pattern of holdings revealed by the copyhold surveys of 1607 and 1627. The inadequacy of the information on the copyholds in 1602 and 1603 makes it impossible to see clearly how the freehold was distributed amongst the copyholders even then, but only one of the copyholders, Thomas Holder, who was listed as holding a yardland of twenty-eight acres, also held thirty-two acres of freehold arable. One half-yardlander, Mathew Jeep, who held fourteen acres of copyhold, also held eighteen acres of freehold. Apart from these two men, there were five tenants who only held freehold land, according to the survey. Three had the equivalent of a yardland, of between twenty-five and thirty-seven acres, one the equivalent of a half-yardland, and one held ten acres. It is not possible to trace changes in the distribution of the freeholds later in the century. There is a rental of 1649, which is incomplete since it only included twenty-two copyhold tenants, but it did include twelve freeholders. Seven of these held copies as well as freeholds, and of these seven, at least three, and probably four, already held copyholds of thirty acres or more, like Neville Butler, eldest son and heir of Thomas Butler whose legal talents had been so usefully employed at the turn of the century. A quarter at least of the freehold in the hands of villagers therefore went to enlarge the acreages of copyholders who were already well-off by Orwell standards, but this is as far as the evidence will stretch. On the whole it seems to indicate that both demesne leasehold and freehold land tended to swell the farms of those copyholders who were already more than usually prosperous.

The later seventeenth-century surveys which followed up those of 1607 and 1627, and must have showed whether the polarisation of holdings continued at Orwell, are irreplaceable. There is, however, a certain amount of indirect evidence which shows the way things developed. A rental, which from internal evidence can be dated to between 1675 and 1682,[33] lists tenants paying between them £25 5s 2½d

---

[32] Admittedly this included some meadow and pasture, and some land in Wimpole, but there were also two arable holdings of unknown size to counterbalance this defect.

[33] C.R.O., L1/130, pp. 23–5. It is headed 'Quit rents' but the term was used loosely at Orwell, and included both freehold and copyhold rents.

for their copyholds. In 1627, the copyhold rents had amounted to £24 10s 0d and in 1607 to £28 11s 2½d. There was not much change in the copyhold rents, therefore. There was, however, a marked change in the distribution of the rents amongst the tenants. In 1607, the three tenants holding between forty-five and fifty acres had paid rents of between £2 0s 5d and £2 8s 2d. Yardland holders paid between 25s and 37s 8d. Half-yardland holders paid between 12s 6d and 21s 8d. The increase in the size of the largest holdings was reflected in the rents in 1627, when two of the four men holding between forty-four and ninety acres were paying rents of over £3. In the late 1670s, as in 1627, there were still four men who stood out from their fellows because of the size of the rents they paid, but judging from their rents alone, the size of their farms had not increased much since 1627. Two of them still paid well over £3 rather than £2, and the third nearly £3. The rental indicated that they had all acquired fragments of land from between two and six men as well as their own. There may not have been much change in the size of the largest farms, but the ranks of the farmers who held average-sized holdings continued to thin. Whereas in 1607, there had been seven men holding yardlands, and five in 1627, there were only three tenants paying a rent appropriate to such an acreage in the 1670s. Whereas in 1607 there had been twelve tenants holding half-yardlands and nine tenants in 1627, there were only five paying an appropriate rent in the 1670s. There had clearly been a further diminution in the number of men holding traditional yardland and half-yardland holdings.

It is rather more difficult to reach any conclusion on changes amongst the tenants holding less than a half-yardland from the rental, because once the traditional holdings had been fragmented, the rent paid by the tenants was not necessarily nearly so clearly related to the acreage which he held. In 1607, for example, the rents of those holding between twelve and four acres varied from 11s 8d to 4s 0d. There was an overlap with the cottagers holding under four acres, who paid between 6s 4d and 10¾d, although most of them paid under 2s 0d. In 1607, there were fourteen men holding under twelve acres. In 1627, the number had risen to twenty-eight. By the 1670s, however, only twenty-one men were paying rents of under 11s 8d. If the inference is to be trusted, there were fewer fardel holders and cottagers later in the century than in 1627, and there had been emigration from this group between 1627 and the 1670s. There may also have been emigration from amongst the holders of half-yardlands and yardlands.

Although engrossing had obviously started as a spontaneous process in Orwell, and was not brought about by seigneurial intervention, the lords of the manor intervened later in the seventeenth century and hastened the process, just as they had done at Chippenham. It is impossible to tell at what point this intervention took place. It looks, from the shaky evidence of the rental of the 1670s alone, as if the holders of traditional tenements were by then losing their land, not to the larger farmers, whose farms had not expanded much since 1627, but to the lord of the manor. It is equally impossible to discover what form this seigneurial intervention took, and whether the freeholders had remained immune from ill effects, and the copyholders alone had suffered. It is only possible to state that by 1707 the leasehold acreage had swollen by over 300 acres, from 240 to about 575 acres. The leasehold rents brought in £256 3s 4d,[34] instead of £12 1s 6d, as they had done a century earlier. Even though it is impossible to discover how far the process of spontaneous amalgamation of farms went during the seventeenth century before the lords of the manor started to profit from it, in a sense it is more important to establish that the economic polarisation at Orwell began as a spontaneous process and preceded the build-up of the demesne, than to establish exactly how the lord took advantage of the existing state of affairs.

INHERITANCE CUSTOMS

The wills of the villagers of Orwell do something to transform the somewhat bleak figures setting out the distribution of land in the early seventeenth century, and to interpret the economic framework of their lives in personal terms. Unfortunately they are not in themselves an impeccable source. Half a dozen of the men who left wills before the 1630s had married sons, for whom they usually made no provision. Edmund Barnard, who died in 1575, provided for his sons, Hugh, and Robert his youngest, but John, who already had four children, got only a relatively small bequest of grain. Frequently these men were widowers. If one or more of their sons had been able to marry, the implication is that a proportion of older men had already divested themselves of parts of their holdings before they came to make their wills. The only alternative is that these were men who had lived to such an

---

[34] C.R.O., L63/58/3. The quit rents of the manor still stood very near their old total, in 1707, at £26 1s 6d, and the profits of court at £30 a year, which is puzzling if the copyholders rather than the freeholders had suffered from the conversion to leasehold. There are other rentals giving particulars of farms dated *c.* 1708 (L63/58/2), between 1708 and 1720 (L63/58/7), and 1720 (L63/58/5). In the last of these the quit rents are said to have been paid by the copyholders. It is possible that the bulk of the increase in the acreage of the demesne leasehold was accounted for by the enclosure of the 200 acres of common mentioned in 1627, which did not appear on the map made in the 1670s.

age that their sons had in some cases managed to establish themselves, perhaps by going into service, and then becoming labourers. But it is extremely significant that it was possible for a son to set himself up, and marry, before his father's death. In Chippenham, of course, there were examples of 'retired' yeomen making a living out of moneylending.[35] In Willingham, the court rolls actually illustrate such retirements when a holding was transferred from a living father to a son.[36] The only explicit statement I have ever yet found on the retirement of such a man is made in the deposition of William King, a yeoman of Little Gransden, who was aged, he reckoned, about 'Fourscore and Twelve years, or thereabouts' in 1648/9, when his evidence was taken in a suit,[37] obviously as the oldest inhabitant. He had been bailiff and rent-collector and lived there for sixty years. He retained a phenomenally clear memory. He was said to be neither a freeholder, nor a copyholder, in Little Gransden. He had been, in his time, farmer of four different farms there, but, it was explained, 'his wife being dead, and his Children growen upp, he now liveth as a sojourner with one of his sonnes'. The word 'sojourner' was an emotive one. It was used by the translators of the Authorized Version of the Bible, who included Jeremiah Radcliffe, D.D., rector of Orwell itself, who was buried there, and John Richardson, inheritor of a half-yardland at Linton, regius professor of divinity in the University of Cambridge.[38] The bishop of Ely, Lancelot Andrewes, was another. These were men who knew their Cambridgeshire well although, of course, the word was common currency in the rest of the country as well. They used *sojourner* to cover the wandering and rootless, and classed them with the fatherless.

In the Authorized Version of the Old Testament, King David used the term to cover the spiritual condition of all his people – 'We are strangers before Thee, and sojourners, as were all our fathers. Our days on the earth are as a shadow, and there is none abiding.'[39] Once a man had retired and given up all his land, in seventeenth-century Cambridgeshire, he was a sojourner, although he might live in the house that had once been his own. There he had, by right, no abiding place.[40]

Without the Orwell court rolls, it is impossible to discover the background of these married sons. It is also impossible to be certain that a testator who appeared to be leaving all his land to one son on his deathbed, had not previously divided his holding between his offspring in the

---

[35] See above, pp. 78, 80.   [36] See below, p. 162.   [37] P.R.O., E134/24, Car.I/Hil. 2.
[38] See below, p. 179, for Richardson.   [39] 1 Chron. 29:10, 14.
[40] See below, p. 182, for a retired man living with his son and daughter-in-law in the 'low chamber' off the hall.

manor court. Despite these drawbacks, the wills provide some very interesting information.

The first fifty original wills which survive for Orwell are dated between 1543 and 1630. They therefore cover the period between the two surveys of 1607 and 1627, as well as the fifty years which preceded them, and with all their limitations they give some indications of the kind of provision that men tried to make for their families. Only thirty-seven of the fifty were relevant; the rest were the wills of widows, landless craftsmen, or clergy with no land to leave. Another fifteen of the thirty-seven men who left bequests of land were childless, had only daughters, or had only one son. Their bequests were therefore of little interest.[41]

The twenty-two wills which really were of interest were those of the men who had more than one son to provide for. The provisions in these showed quite clearly that the farmers of Orwell were almost equally divided on the issue of whether to leave all their land to one son or not. Ten of the twenty-two did so, and tried to provide for the others with cash sums, and often with bequests of stock and grain as well. The other twelve tried to give their younger sons at least a toehold on the land, by leaving them a small part of their holdings.

Even where primogeniture was the rule, as much as possible seems to have been done for the other children. Some of the wills show how the cash to set them up in life was provided, and incidentally gives some idea of the degree of financial strain that must have been placed on the family holding by this provision. Richard Kettle, yeoman, made his will in 1560. One of his sons, Arthur, was already married, and his father merely cancelled his debts to him. Richard Kettle had two other sons, John and William. He left his copyhold to his son John, but only on condition that John paid William a sum of £9 15s 0d out of the profits of the holding at the rate of 30s 0d a year. If he failed to keep up these payments, the holding was to pass to William 'according to ye Lawdable custome of Orwell aforesaid'. It is obvious from similar detailed directions given in the wills that it was indeed the custom of Orwell that the tenement, not the father's savings, if any, usually bore the weight of providing for the younger children. William Griggs, who made his will in 1613, was probably the only son of John Griggs who died in 1588. John Griggs had been a substantial man, and when he died William, his residuary legatee, was married already. John Griggs was one of the two men in the sample who had a son, but still left land, as opposed to cash, to his two daughters. He was able to leave them each a cottage which he had previously sublet to different tenants. William Griggs held

[41] I have taken as a sample the first fifty original wills surviving.

106

ten and a half acres of copyhold land, according to the survey of 1607, although his will makes it plain that he held freehold as well. In 1613, he provided for three sons, whose order in the family he specified. The youngest, Edward, simply got a cottage and three roods which had been the dower of one of his aunts in 1588, and £8 in cash. But William thought of an ingenious method of making sure that his second son, John, got his share of the profits of the main holding. He laid down that although his eldest, another William, was eventually to get all his copyhold and freehold except his youngest brother's three roods, John was to hold it all for six years, including six harvests, and then to receive a lump sum of £8 as well. If William refused to pay John and Edward their cash bequests, the freehold land owned by their father in the next parish of Barrington was to be divided between them. The result of this particular provision was that the second son seems to have flourished more than the first. John Griggs held seventeen acres and three roods, or a full half-yardland of copyhold in 1627, so the profits of his six harvests plus his £8 must have stood him in good stead. William, the eldest, had eleven acres of copyhold, which was probably the same holding that his father had had in 1607. Edward, the cottager, was still in the village, although he seems to have had only one of his original three roods.

This sort of provision went right down through the lower strata of Orwell society. William Sampfield, labourer, started life as a servant in the household of William Higney, a yeoman who died in 1558. Higney left 26s 8d to William Sampfield, on condition that he stayed with his widow for one more year. When William Sampfield made his own will thirty years later, he left his cottage, garden and orchard to his only son, who was, however, to pay 13s 4d a year out of the holding for four years after he reached the age of twenty-two, to be divided equally between his two sisters. He was to give house-room to his mother as well.[42] It is difficult to conceive how a labourer's cottage could bear such an annual burden on top of the rent when the wages of agricultural labourers were steadily losing purchasing power.[43]

The most extreme example of such a procedure was provided by Robert Barnard, a labourer who died in 1615, in the middle of the decade when wages were at their lowest, in real terms, between 1450 and 1649. He was probably the youngest son of Hugh Barnard, a husbandman who had left his youngest son Robert half his saffron ground in 1575. If so, he had been comparatively successful, because as well as a cottage and croft, he had acquired three acres of arable to dispose of at the end of his life. He left this holding to one of his sons, who was

[42] See below, p. 113.   [43] Thirsk, *Agrarian History*, IV, 865.

not, according to his will, the eldest. The condition on which it was left was that a portion of £2 a year should be paid out of the holding to each of Robert's other six sons and single daughter in a specified order.

The burdens placed on holdings which were negligible by Midland standards, by such provisions, and which in any case can only have made a marginal yearly profit[44] must have been immense. It is difficult to escape the conclusion that the anxiety shown by fathers to provide for all their sons, whether they actually practised primogeniture or not, must have been one more factor which put the smaller holdings at risk in crisis years.

When partible inheritance was practised, of course, the tendency towards polarisation was inevitably increased. Some examples have already been given. There was no social difference which dictated the way land was left. William Higney, John Holder and Robert Greville, who made their wills in 1558, 1559 and 1560, were all prosperous men, judging by their bequests. They all had more than one son. They might all have been supposed to have a feeling for the family land.[45] But William Higney and Robert Greville left all their land to one son. John Holder left his eldest son three copyhold tenements and a lease, but his second got a house and land, his third two and a quarter acres and cash, and even his fourth son got an acre of land with his cash. Such examples can be multiplied from the wills and the surveys, even without looking at extreme cases like John and Thomas Woodward, who were presumably brothers, and who each held two bays of the same house in 1607 and three and a half roods of land apiece.

The Butler *alias* Johnson family is the most interesting example of a group of kin which tried to set up all its members with land, since despite the inbred tendency for the family holdings to break down, it also produced an engrosser. The family can be traced back only to the beginning of the register in the 1560s (see Appendix 1). There seem to have been three brothers called Butler *alias* Johnson originally, John, Henry and Nicholas. From John descended a branch of the family which was eventually simply surnamed 'Johnson'. Their first cousins, descended from Nicholas, were simply known as 'Butler'. Nicholas, who died last, may have been the eldest. He was certainly much the most successful. The family must have been more than usually important in sixteenth-century Orwell. Henry and Nicholas expressed a wish in their wills to be buried in the north aisle of the parish church, near their parents,

---

[44] See above, p. 52.
[45] Such a thing did exist; the 1607 survey contains statements describing tenements like that of Nicholas Johnson, 'formerly John Johnsons, before Richard Greville, before Robert Greville, and Grevilles *ex antiquo*'.

rather than in the churchyard, which was the normal thing to do.[46] Burial within the church always argued unusual standing in the community.

The will of Nicholas Butler made in 1601 describes him as a yeoman,[47] and provided no less than five sons with land, in four different villages. His attitude seems to have been very similar to that of Thomas Dillamore in Chippenham. The eldest son, Thomas, got all his father's free and copyhold land in Orwell and Wimpole, as well as his 'great gilt silver cup and two silver spoons'. William received all his father's land in Great and Little Eversden, and George all his copyhold and closes in the next village of Barrington, except Barrington windmill, which Thomas, as the eldest, kept. Laurence and Peter were both provided with holdings just over the Huntingdonshire border at Great Gransden. It is impossible to tell how much of this land Nicholas had bought himself, and how much he had inherited from his father, who had certainly been an Orwell man. The two Gransden holdings at least had been bought by Nicholas. He had obviously got himself into financial difficulties at some point, because his brother Henry, who had died nine years earlier, had remitted all the debts Nicholas owed him, and had also left Nicholas's son, Thomas, two houses and seven acres of freehold and fourteen acres of copyhold which he had bought from Nicholas. It looks as if Nicholas had been over-ambitious. However, he could still set his five sons up on the land, he had sent the eldest of them up to Gray's Inn to study law, he had married his two daughters off to yeomen in Little Eversden, and Clavering in Essex, and he lived in some comfort, with the great gilt cup and two silver spoons that were such objects of pride. He was definitely known in the village as a yeoman,[48] however, and despite his obvious satisfaction with his eldest son, he still dispersed his land, whether inherited or purchased, amongst all his sons.

By the time Thomas, the eldest son, died in 1622 he was self-styled 'gentleman'.[49] He seems to have done much to increase the family importance, quite apart from the brisk business sense he had shown in acquiring the lease of the demesne pasture in Orwell when he was a very young man.[50] In the 1607 survey, he apparently held only a yard-

---

[46] There is no surviving monument or slab in the north aisle today.
[47] It is not surprising that Nicholas Butler *alias* Johnson's will was proved in the Prerogative Court of Canterbury (henceforth P.C.C.), Wills, 74 Woodhall. There seems to have been no reason why his brother Henry's will was proved there, however; he left no land outside Orwell, P.C.C., Wills, 32 Dixy.
[48] This emerged in the Exchequer depositions of 1605 (P.R.O., E134/3, Jas I/East.18) where he was mentioned, although he was by then dead.
[49] P.C.C., Wills, 18 Savile.   [50] See above, p. 98.

land of twenty-five acres. His stepmother had another twenty-one acres for life, but it was to go to another brother after her death. Between 1607 and his death in 1622, Thomas acquired the ninety acres of copyhold which his own widow was to hold with her son Neville in 1627. There is, of course, no information on the amount of freehold he held, or acquired. Thomas left all his land entirely to his son Neville in 1622, together with 'all my books whatsoever'. He probably did not split it because of a dynastic accident, for his other son had died in early childhood. He also was prosperous, for apart from sending Neville up to college he was able to leave his three daughters dowries of £100 apiece.

Neville turned the title of gentleman claimed by his father into an economic reality. He married the heiress to whom Orwell Manor had come,[51] and eventually sold all his Orwell land to Sir Thomas Chicheley, whose seat was at Wimpole in the next parish, and he bought the lands of the dissolved priory at Barnwell. Neville and Cecily had twelve children, two of whom were educated at Cambridge University. When Neville died in 1673,[52] he was able to leave his 'dear and loving wife' a jointure of no less than £80 a year, and his unmarried daughters £500 or the equivalent, each. He did not leave a mere silver cup and spoons like his grandfather; he left his wife 'all the plate' instead. Moreover, he was able to add to the usual admonition to his executor to pay his debts, the highly unusual words '(these) being very small and to perform this my last will as he will answer for the same at the dreadful day of Judgement for I certainly know there is sufficient to perform the same'. The family held the Barnwell estate until the death of the last eccentric male heir in 1765.[53]

The Butler side of the family showed considerable business sense and acumen, but until Thomas Butler's death in 1622, they remained, in reality, substantial yeomen. If Thomas Butler had had two sons to divide his land between they might well have remained so.

John Johnson, one of the three original brothers, behaved exactly like his brother Nicholas. John died over twenty years before either of his brothers, and must have been a young man with a very young family. The first of his five children did not marry for fifteen years after their father's death. John styled himself as a 'husbandman' simply. He had four sons, and provided land for three of them. This land was specifically purchased for two of them. John acquired a tenement and

[51] Lysons, *Magna Britannia*, II, 243. Neville's wife Cecily was Cecily Aglionby. The Aglionbys were free tenants of the manor in the rentals of the 1670s. The marriage did not take place in the parish, so they cannot have been a resident family.
[52] P.C.C., Wills, 1675, fo. 42   [53] Lysons, *Magna Britannia*, II, 147.

110

sixteen acres of land which had been Grevilles *ex antiquo* to set up his son, another Nicholas, who was later churchwarden and village scribe, and a cottage and five acres of land for his son Richard. Another son, Laurence, who was a maltster, got his father's own house and two closes which had also been bought. He, in turn, carefully divided what he had between two of his sons at his death. All four of John Johnson's sons had been further enriched by the land of their childless uncle Henry, the third of the Johnson *alias* Butler brothers. Henry's widow enjoyed his forty-four acres of copyhold and ten and a half acres of freehold land for life, but the copyhold was split into three holdings of between twelve and fourteen acres, each of which went to a Johnson nephew. Yet none of the Johnson side of the family held more than thirty-five acres.

The family history is interesting both because it illustrates the way land was often distributed amongst all the sons of the family, and because it shows the way in which family links were maintained between the relatively humble and the very prosperous sides of the family. Nicholas Johnson the churchwarden who died in 1627, could identify the handwriting of his cousin, George Butler. He acted as rent-collector for his highly successful cousin Thomas Butler, the lawyer, and witnessed his will. Nicholas's brother Richard's son, another Nicholas, in turn acted as a witness to wills with his cousin Neville Butler. Neville, another highly successful man, witnessed Nicholas's own will when he died in 1649. He probably wrote a few of the Orwell wills himself, and one of those he bestirred himself to write was that of old Richard Johnson, his father's cousin, in 1638. The connection was maintained, therefore, from the time John Johnson died leaving his brother Nicholas Butler overseer of his will and young children in 1568, right through until 1649, and probably until Neville bought the priory lands of Barnwell, and removed from Orwell. There seems to have been a close family network, and a remarkably unexclusive amount of give-and-take between cousins, one group of which were acquiring plate, books, university education, and ex-monastic lands, and the other group of which were continuing to live in Orwell on between fourteen and thirty-five acres apiece.

PROVISION FOR WOMEN

It was not common for women to inherit land, although they did so when there was no son, or occasionally at the whim of an eccentric father, or even grandmother. John Holder, who had four daughters and five sons living when he made his will in 1558, passed the bulk of it on to his son Thomas.[54] Thomas's daughter Beatrix inherited the holding from him, and held a full yardland of twenty-eight acres in 1607. She was the only unmarried woman holding land in Orwell at that date, although several men held in the right of their wives. Dowries were very important, and they were specified with as much care in the wills as the inheritances for the sons, but they usually consisted of a cash sum, stock, grain and furnishings. John Holder left his two unmarried daughters £3 6s 8d, six sheep, one cow, and six quarters of barley and malt apiece in 1558, as well as various cupboards, hutches, bedsteads, linen and half-dozens of pewter dishes. This sort of bequest was fairly typical, although the size of the cash sum varied, of course, according to the status of the dying man. The age at which daughters inherited was normally eighteen, or on their marriage, although it occasionally rose to between nineteen and twenty-one. Sons got their inheritances later on the whole, usually at twenty-one, although again there were exceptions when some inherited earlier or a little later.

The amount of dower received by a daughter on her marriage was strongly related to the provision a husband later made for his wife. Sometimes the relationship was directly stated. In 1591, John Skinner, who had eight children in all, left his wife her original dower to bring up the two youngest children, who were probably the only children of the marriage.

Wills usually provide for the widow with extreme care, and in great detail. Much more is known about the provision made for widows than about the way in which their aged husbands were catered for after they became incapable of farming the family holding, for the simple reason that on the death of a householder the land usually passed to the heir if he was of age, or a statement was made of how it should be disposed of during the minority if he was not. In both cases, the rights of the widow were affected. A householder's will therefore usually contains some explicit information on the way his wife is to be supported after his death. A married woman's will gives no such indication, unless she held land in her own right, since her husband in any case continued in the undisturbed occupation of his holding. The way in which the retired yeoman or labourer was looked after is much more of a mystery, although enough evidence survives to suggest that retired yeomen 'sojourning' by their son's fires did exist.[55] The number of men with some sons established on the land by the time they died suggests that such semi-retired men were not at all rare.

Very frequently, the children of a man on his death-bed were, like the daughter of Thomas Brocke, who died in 1597, of 'younge and

[54] See above, p. 108.   [55] See above, p. 105.

tender age'. In this case, the normal pattern was for the widow to be left her husband's holding or holdings, on which to rear them. After the majority of the eldest son, she was usually given house-room, and a small acreage on which to support herself. This was to be tilled for her by her son. The amount of house-room was, again, carefully defined. Grace Meade was left the right to use the little parlour in the house inherited by her son in 1585, 'with free egresse and regresse to the same',[56] and furnishings for it, including bed and bedding. She was also left four acres of land which her son was to plough for her, and a load of hay a year. Her husband left her sheep, cows, and a yoke of steers for ploughing as well. All these provisions only held, of course, so long as she remained unmarried. Maintenance of the widow almost always ceased on her remarriage, and sometimes the feelings of the dead husband seem to lie behind this cessation, as well as the purely practical consideration that her new husband, and his land, should support her. Something of the kind seems to underlie the phraseology of John Adams, who stipulated in 1592 that Alice, his wife, 'shall have the Chamber that I lye in . . . so long as she shalbe unmaryed and to like to lye therin and kepe the same to hir selff'.

Just the same type of provision for the widow seems to have been made at all social levels. William Sampfield, the labourer who died in 1586,[57] had acquired a cottage with a garden and an orchard by the time he died. There was, of course, no question of his leaving his wife an acreage of land for her sole use. However, he provided for her with as much care as any yeoman. She was to have the whole tenement until her son was twenty-two, and then the 'chamber that I lye in' with the right of entrance and egress both to it and to the fire in the hall. She was also to have one white apple tree and one 'sweting' tree in the orchard, and 'roome upon the said ground to harbour one bullock', on condition that she made no other claim on the holding.

If the children were already of an age to inherit the holding when their father died, the widow was almost always given house-room and maintenance at once, like Margery Greville, who in 1560 was left a 'Chamber . . . to hir owne use during hir naturall Liffe And also two Acres wheate and iij Acres barley to take them at hir owne Choyse out of my sone Rychardes croppe yerely during hir said liffe.' It was very rare in Orwell for a widow not to be left maintenance and house-room. Richard Jeap left his wife Alice a cow, a sheep and a lump sum of 40s

---

[56] Rights of 'Egresse and regresse' given in a will in no way imply a separate entrance for the widow, and a separate dwelling. They merely lay down that she is to be allowed access to her room, and to the fire to cook, undisturbed.
[57] See above, p. 107.

in 1562, instead of house-room, and there were also a couple of cases of widows who were left their husbands' holdings during the minority of their children, but were not specifically provided for after their sons came of age. These were quite exceptional, however. There seems to be no doubt that the widow was generally provided with rights to bed and board in her son's house for life, in this village. Even when a tenement was sold, the seller might retain some interest in it to support his wife. John Johnson had purchased a house from Richard Greville, which he bequeathed to his own son in 1568. He stipulated, however, that when his son came into the property, he was to 'discharge my wife against mother greville for all the things she may claim of the said house and land yerely during her natural life'. In this case, a widow had been 'sold' with the house.

The frequency of the provision made in wills for widows to live with the inheriting son makes a sharp contrast with the impression gained from seventeenth-century censuses that households were invariably composed of a married couple, and their children or servants, and only very rarely included the older generation.[58] In Mr Laslett's words, 'living with in-laws can only have been very occasionally in the world we have lost. It is impossible that it can have been the ordinary expected thing to do.' Mr Laslett has restated this thesis even more strongly: 'Our ancestors do not seem to have had much truck with resident mothers-in-law, a feature of their lives which marks them out as being very different from the lives of the Chinese or the Japanese.' He points out the comparative rarity of the family containing three generations, that is, the family with a resident grandparent. Indeed, the figures he gives, based on an analysis of no less than a hundred English communities between 1574 and 1821, show a remarkable drop from 70.4 per cent of households containing two generations, that is, a couple and their children, to only 5.8 per cent of families containing a grandparent as well as children.[59] There seems to be a flat contradiction here between Mr Laslett's general figures, and the impressions gained from wills. The wills, on the contrary, suggest that living with in-laws, or rather, having a widowed parent to live with one, when one was of an age to inherit the farm, was very much the ordinary, expected thing to do. According to the wills, a household should very frequently have contained the older generation. But the contradiction can be resolved. In the first place, Mr Laslett shows himself that even if the proportion of houses

[58] Laslett, *The World We Have Lost*, p. 91.
[59] Peter I .slett, 'Size and Structure of the Household in England Over Three Centuries', *Population Studies*, XXIII (1969), 219–20 and Table 14, p. 219. The figures are commented on at length in various chapters of Laslett and Wall, *Household and Family in Past Time* (1972).

in which the senior generation lived with its active sons and daughters was as low as 5.8 per cent, the overall proportion of widows and widowers in society was low too, and included only 6.2 per cent of the population.[60] If the two figures are compared it suggests that by far the largest proportion of the few widows and widowers in society did indeed live with their grown-up descendants.

A more subtle resolution of the apparent contradiction is also possible. The will-making population was weighted by men leaving at least some children under age. If a man died leaving children who had to be provided for until they reached maturity, he was naturally strongly influenced into making his own, often individual, notions of proper provision for them legal. This is why very few wills survive made by retired men who had established all their sons on the land, or with some sort of stock or trade, and married off all their daughters. Old men were not driven by the corresponding feminine inclination of old ladies to apportion their remaining kerchiefs fairly amongst their favourite daughters and granddaughters.

It naturally followed that if most wills were made by men with at least some children under age, the widow, on whom the burden of carrying out these provisions fell,[61] was in her turn, provided for, after she had fulfilled her obligations, and all the children had reached maturity. The emphasis on provision for widows in wills is therefore explained.

Detailed examination of the eight earliest suitable censuses[62] shows that by far the largest category of households containing widowers or widows held no married offspring. They were headed by the remaining parent. Over fifty per cent of households containing a widowed parent was also headed by it. The slant of the wills more commonly

---

[60] *Ibid.* Table 7, p. 215, no. 3.   [61] Together with her eldest son if he was of age.
[62] I have taken the positions of widowed people within the households listed in eight of the censuses the analyses of which Mr Laslett has kindly let me have copies. They are: Cogenhoe, Northants., 1624; Clayworth, Notts., 1676; Chilvers Coton, War., 1684; Clayworth (second census), 1688; Lichfield, Staffs., 1695; Harefield, Msx., 1699; Stoke-on-Trent, Staffs. 1701; Puddletown, Dorset, 1724. I have rejected any census after 1724 on the grounds that social custom might change. I have also excluded Dersingham, 1692, which had only four widowed persons, as unrepresentative, and both the parishes of St Michaels Poultry, London, 1695, and St Peter Mancroft, Norwich, 1694, as showing a different urban pattern. This may appear inconsistent, and possibly is. Stoke-on-Trent in 1701 was a complex of industrial villages, and I have no qualms about including it. Lichfield I have included to give weight to the number; it followed the general patterns of the other seven censuses, with the exception of having a far higher proportion of widowed persons in households headed by a non-relation than country parishes.

I am very grateful to Mr Laslett for allowing me access to his tables, and debating the point raised with me, and to Dr Tony Wrigley for encouraging me to set my findings on the provisions made for widows in wills in a general context.

made by people leaving children under age than by those with grown families, is reflected in the censuses, with their preponderance of households of unmarried children, under the guidance of one parent.

Secondly, the censuses show that there were two ways, which were more common than the rest, of providing for the parent who had successfully brought all the children of a family to maturity. Either the widow or widower lived with a married son or daughter, as at Orwell;[63] or he or she lived alone, in a separate cottage.[64] Individual settlements adopted different solutions, but these were the most popular. The charitable foundation of almshouses could and did provide another solution as did lodgings frequently with another widowed person. The normality of the provision made in the wills for widows of both Orwell and Willingham is brought home. It is not in conflict with the analyses of the places occupied by widowed people in early censuses. On the other hand, comparison of the position of widows at Chippenham, who usually had a life interest in the house and land,[65] with those in the censuses shows that this was a highly unusual village custom. Presumably such women could and sometimes did live alone, in which case they would be classified in a census in the common category of 'solitaries'. But they might well also have fallen into the comparatively unusual categories of becoming heads of households which included a married son or daughter. At the most, only three per cent of widowed people could be classified thus.

The problem of remarriage enters into this. It is, in fact, highly unlikely in a period of rising population that a widow with a life interest in land, as at Chippenham, or even during a lengthy minority, if she was left land until a young family came of age, as at Willingham, would not remarry. I can produce examples to show that such remarriage actually took place, but not figures to show how often it did so.[66] Grace Caldecot of Orwell married Edmund Barton in 1564. He was burried in February 1579, leaving her with two young sons. She married Roger Davies *alias* Fludd, the vicar, who was himself a

---

[63] I have lumped together the figures for widowed people living in houses headed by a son, and by a daughter (son-in-law), categories 6 and 7, on the analyses of the census on Mr Laslett's unpublished Table 30, which deals with the position of widowed people, since it does not appear to me a very important one.

[64] As at Willingham, see below, pp. 163–4, although the first solution was adopted there too. [65] See above, p. 88.

[66] See above and below, pp. 89, 161–2 for other examples from Chippenham and Willingham. Mr Laslett suggests that remarriage was commoner for widowers than for widows (*The World We Have Lost*, p. 99), and his figures that show a higher number of widows than widowers in the community (*art. cit.* p. 215) seem to bear this out, although they must also reflect different expectation of life for men and women. Nevertheless, I have the impression that remarriage was extremely common amongst widows with even the slightest interest in land.

widower, in July that year, after five months of widowhood. He, in his turn, was buried in October of the next year, and she married her third husband, Robert Adam, another widower, only three months after her second husband's death. She had better luck with him, and they had twenty years of marriage and at least one child together before he died in 1602, leaving her as well as house-room and an annual supply of food, 'the bed and bedding wherein I and the said Grace my wife commonly lyeth uppon'.

A widow with young children, and a holding on which to bring them up, probably found a husband essential for the working of the tenement. From the prospective husband's point of view, a widow with land, even held during her children's minority only, was probably a good match in a time of rising population and land shortage. Thomas Adam, who died in 1592, certainly thought his wife Margaret might be an attractive proposition, even though he left her his house, and free-hold, copyhold and leasehold land only until his son John was twenty-one. His will laid down that if she remarried 'he that shall mary hyr, before he dothe contracte matrimony with hir shalbe bounde to my . . . Brother Robert Adam to perform . . . all such legacyes as she is charged with by . . . this my wyll, And if he shall refuse so to do, then I wyll she shall have no benefytt by this my wyll.' If a widow with an interest in land only during her children's minority was a draw to suitors, one with a life interest was, of course, even more eligible. Widows with a life interest were not all that common, but they were probably snapped up after a decent, or indecent, interval when they came on the market. In the survey of 1607, for example, two men appeared who had married the widows of the Butler brothers.[67] Richard Fairchild had married the widow of old Nicholas Butler, with her life interest of twenty-one acres. He held no other land in 1607, but his marriage probably gave him a start, for in 1627 he held sixty-eight acres in his own right, and his farm was only surpassed in size by that of his stepson Thomas's widow. Thomas Mortlock had married the widow of the childless Henry Butler in 1594, within four months of Henry's death. He held forty-four acres of copyhold and ten and a half acres of freehold in her name in 1607, although all of it was to revert to nephews and great-nephews on her death.

Even if remarriage was extremely common, it still remains true that in general widows were expected to find shelter with their inheriting sons,[68] and that some of them did in fact do so. The same Thomas

---

[67] See above, pp. 109–10, 111.
[68] Fourteen of the thirty-two landed men leaving widows provided them with house-room with their sons.

117

Adam who in 1592 safeguarded his sons' inheritance if his wife re-married, also provided for his wife's maintenance if she did not do so. He laid down 'she shall have the chamber in my house and also one Acre of Tylthe and one half acre of brokeland next the best to be tylled yerely for hir, as my said mother-in-lawe nowe hathe . . . and if my said mother-in-lawe be then lyvinge, then I wyll my said wyffe shall have hir dwelling in my kechinge.' John Adam junior, inheritor of the holding, was to support and give house-room to both his mother and his grandmother, if need be, one in the chamber and one in the kitchen. The John Adams, senior and junior, of Orwell seem to have shown quite as much sense of responsibility to the older generation as any Oriental.

CONCLUSION

The evidence on the distribution of land at Orwell is much less com-plete than for Chippenham, but it does show that in the first thirty years of the seventeenth century there was a noticeable diminution in the number of customary tenants holding half-yardlands and yardlands, and a corresponding increase in the size of the larger holdings, and in the number of cottagers. This economic polarisation probably con-tinued during the century, and there was at the same time a tremendous expansion of the demesne, which may have absorbed the commons, as well as the arable of some of the tenants. Meanwhile, there was a con-tinuous increase in the population at least from 1570 to 1650, but since the community remained approximately the same size, there was obviously emigration. The very fact of population pressure did nothing to halt the attrition of the middle-sized holdings. Unfortunately, in the absence of the court rolls for the early years of the century, there is no way at all of discovering whether this attrition coincided in any way with bad harvest years. It was taking place at exactly the period from 1598 to 1636 when it was most marked at Chippenham. This may, of course, have been mere coincidence.

The wills of Orwell men are particularly informative, and rich in illustrations of the way in which inheritance customs tended to put additional strains on tenements. Even when impartible inheritance was practised in the sense of at least the main part of the holding going to one son, small acreages frequently went to others. When this did not happen, the holding was responsible, according to the custom of the manor, for providing cash bequests to other sons, as well as dowries for daughters, and maintenance for the widow. The widow was rarely given a life interest in the holding, as she was so often at Chippenham, but she was almost always given support for the rest of her life.

118

The community of Orwell was close-knit, attempting to support all its offspring and its widows in reasonable security. This very tendency to try and make provision for all its sons in the seventeenth century seems to have been partly responsible for the economic divisions which became increasingly apparent within it.

Map 10 Willingham in about 1603

This map is constructed from two nineteenth-century copies both of which purport to be of the map made of Willingham in 1603, recording the Agreement between Sir Miles Sandys and his tenants. The original map does not survive. The tofts and crofts of the settlement itself, and the open-field furlongs, are recorded in the copy made in 1793 (C.R.O., Willingham Parish Deposit 1965, unindexed). This does not cover the meadows or fens. Some of the meadows and the allotments made under the 1602 Agreement are recorded in the 'Plan of the lands of Jesus College' (C.U.L., Ms Plans 253 (R)). Mr Jeeps has worked out the boundaries of the remaining fen commons and meadows in detail.

119

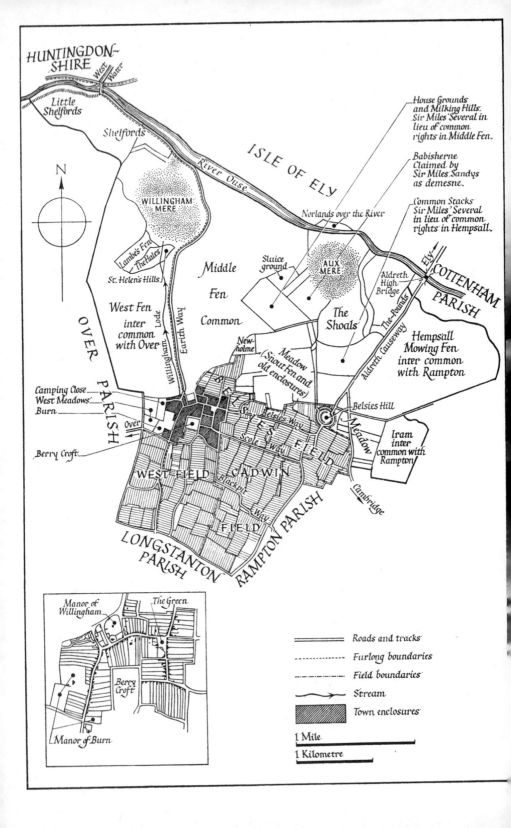

HUNTINGDON-
SHIRE

West Water

Little
Shelfords

Shelfords

River Ouse

ISLE OF ELY

N

WILLINGHAM
MERE

House Grounds
and Milking Hills.
Sir Miles' Several in
lieu of common
rights in Middle Fen.

Babisherne
Claimed by
Sir Miles Sandys
as demesne.

Norlands over the River

Common Stacks
Sir Miles' Several
in lieu of common
rights in Hempsall.

Lambe's Fen
The Hales

St. Helen's Hills

Middle

Fen

Common

Sluice
ground

AUX
MERE

The
Shoals

Aldreth
High
Bridge

The Pounds

Ely

COTTENHAM
PARISH

West Fen
inter
common
with Over

Willingham Lode

Earith Way

Newholme

Meadow
(Snout Fen and
old enclosures)

Aldreth Causeway

Hempsall
Mowing Fen
inter common
with Rampton

OVER PARISH

Camping Close
West Meadows
Burn

Over

Berry Croft

BELSIES WAY

Belsies Way

Scole Way

Belsies Hill

Meadow

Iram
inter
common with
Rampton

WEST FIELD

CADWIN

Blackpit Way

FIELD

FIELD

Cambridge

LONGSTANTON
PARISH

RAMPTON PARISH

Manor of
Willingham

The Green

Berry
Croft

Manor of Burn

Roads and tracks

Furlong boundaries

Field boundaries

Stream

Town enclosures

1 Mile

1 Kilometre

5

The reality: the small landholder in the fens: Willingham

SOURCES, FIELDS, CROPS AND STOCK

The parish of Willingham presents a complete and valuable contrast, both physically, and in the way it developed, to both Chippenham with its couple of hundred acres of fen, and the upland village of Orwell. Willingham had over 4,500 acres of territory, of which the arable of the three open fields took up only between 1,000 and 1,200 acres. This was less even than Orwell, which was a community under half the size of Willingham in 1563, and had over 1,400 acres of open-field arable. The territory of Willingham included one of the minor fen meres, of at least eighty acres, and part of a major one,[1] and also had nearly 3,000 acres of fen. The village economy was therefore totally different from that based on arable farming in the other communities chosen for special study here.

The bishop of Ely had held the principal manor, which shortly after alienation from the see in 1600 came into the hands of Sir Miles Sandys. This corresponded with the parish, with the exception of the minute sub-manor of Burne, which contained only about a hundred acres of demesne and sixty acres of copyhold land.[2] Sir Miles, who was knighted by James I and obtained a baronetcy in 1612, was one of the co-adventurers heavily involved with Francis, fourth earl of Bedford, in the draining of the Great Level.[3] He had been engaged in private improve-

[1] A. K. Astbury, *The Black Fens* (Cambridge 1958), p. 39. Sir Miles Sandys in 1621 mentioned his 'fishing called Milfords' and estimated the adjacent demesne fen called Axmeare at 300 acres. Mr Dennis Jeeps tells me that in a P.R.O. survey of Over, which I have not seen, the 'Great Mere' was said to cover 380 acres. P.R.O. E134/ 17–18, Eliz. 1. It will be obvious to any reader of this text that I owe a great deal to Dennis Jeeps. I am particularly grateful to him for his generosity in allowing me to investigate superficially here his own village, Willingham, which he knows so well. Some points I have deliberately left out, as I hope that he will write a proper study of Willingham himself. Any errors, as apart from omissions, are in no way his responsibility, since he has tried so hard and so kindly to improve the accuracy of this work. [2] Lysons, *Magna Britannia*, II, 285.
[3] For a general history of the drainage, H. C. Darby, *The Draining of the Fens*, 2nd edn (Cambridge 1956), pp. 40–8, 58–77, and for the extent of the Sandys' involvement in the drainage, n. 6, p. 58. For Sir Miles Sandys' part in committee in 1649 and 1650 in the renewed Bedford drainage undertaking see L. E. Harris, *Vermuyden and the Fens* (London 1953), pp. 94, 98–9, 102, 110.

ments on his own estates long before this major enterprise began in 1630. He was heavily involved, like his neighbours, the Hindes of Madingley and Cottenham, in a general movement to enclose fen commons in the area in the late sixteenth century. These improving gentry inevitably became involved in disputes over commoners' rights.[4] Sir Miles had already fallen out with his tenants at the manor of Stretham[5] by 1597 over common rights, the exaction of labour services, and uncertain fines. A series of disputes with his Willingham tenants began very soon after his purchase of the manor in 1601. His situation there was not easy, for like some of the other men who bought in the episcopal sales late in Elizabeth's reign, he found himself in the unhappy position of being unable to find part of the demesne. The purchaser at Little Gransden who hired an antiquarian to search the bishop's records and identify the demesne strips did better than Sir Miles, who was reduced in 1621[6] to petitioning Chancery to subpoena his own tenants to help him identify his demesne lands, which he accused them of laying to their own copyholds to increase, he said, the size of the half-yardland from fifteen to twenty acres.[7] He had earlier admitted himself that the demesne had been leased to the tenants since at least the reign of Henry VI. He was caught, in fact, in the general difficulties of men who were trying to resume direct demesne farming now that the price rise had made it profitable for them to do so, after the demesne had been leased to the tenants possibly ever since the beginning of the fourteenth-century slump.

He may also have had particular difficulties of his own. The Willingham documents give a strong sense of a community accustomed to self-government and directing its own life,[8] because the management of the fen commons called for considerable organisation. To meddle in the affairs of a village of this kind, which had never had a resident landlord, was to stir up a hornet's nest. The tenants, understandably, had acquired a sense of right over the demesne. The tell-tale name of 'Bury alias Townlands' which the Orwell tenants used shows[9] that this happened elsewhere. What did not necessarily happen elsewhere were the determined efforts made by the tenants of Willingham themselves,

[4] The movement made by local gentry in the late sixteenth century to profit from the fen pastures, and to reduce their tenants' common rights was written up by Archdeacon Cunningham, who published the lengthy orders governing common rights at Cottenham in 1596, and various documents illustrating the disputes at Cottenham and Stretham. W. Cunningham, 'Common Rights at Cottenham and Stretham in Cambridgeshire', *The Camden Miscellany*, XII (1910), 173–287.
[5] *Ibid.* p. 184.   [6] P.R.O., C.2. Jas. I, S.19/64.   [7] See below, p. 126.
[8] This is well illustrated in the way the villagers set about obtaining arbitration on a dispute over stocking the commons in 1655 (C.R.O., R59/14/5/9 (b)) and an agreement on common rights in 1677/8 (C.R.O., R59/14/5/9 (f)).   [9] See above, p. 97.

which was revealed by Sir Miles in a 'Complaint to the Queen',[10] first to purchase the manor themselves and then, when that failed, so to obstruct and harry the successful purchaser that he was unable either to identify or to enter into his property. The means used were those the Willingham community had already successfully adopted to establish their school;[11] they simply passed the hat round. Sir Miles wrote in his Complaint:

Richard Peereson George Frogge Thomas Brazier and others the saide late farmors of the ... demesne landes ... havinge alsoe formerlie bene suitors to your hignes Comissioners appoynted for the sale of the said Mannor and for the purchaseinge [thereof] ... and havinge bene denyed the same for that they woulde not give soe muche for the same as your subiecte paied, they the saide Richard Pereson George Frogge and Thomas Brasier associatinge themselves with one ——[12] Frogge who heretofore hathe bene an Attorney at the lawe and for his lewde behaviour and badde carriage dismissed from the practise thereof ... beinge discontented that they could not obtayne the purchase of the saide Mannor at their owne rates and prices ... They raised and collected great somes of money amongst themselves by rate or taxe and Contribucion not onelie to mainteyne all suite whatsoever whiche shoulde be commenced by your subiecte for and concerninge the said Mannor or anye part thereof which soe was ... withholden from them. But also to vexe molest and wearie out your said subiecte by prosecution of actions and suites againste him for enteringe ... the saide demeasne landes.

They were very successful. The ringleaders had been identified by Sir Miles, but the whole community was involved, and large and repetitive sections of his 'Complaint' read like an early draft of 'Widecombe Fair'. Sir Miles most unwisely enclosed closes of meadow and fen which he believed to be several, free from tenants' right of common, soon after his purchase of the manor, and trouble really broke out in April 1602, when

the said Richard Pereson George Frogge Thomas Brasier [13] Frogge Henry Ellis th'elder Henry Greve Henry Pereson John Scratche Alexander Bowles William Marshall Giles Nightingale Robert Butterie William Asheman Henry Fromente William Brasyer th'elder William Crispe Henry Townsende Robert Few Jonas Crowche John Brasier William Brasier the younger

[10] This draft Complaint is in the Willingham Parish Council deposit (unindexed) of 1965 in the C.R.O., but it has at present been mislaid. I am very grateful to Mr Hill of the Record Office who searched for it at some length for me, and even more grateful to Mr Jeeps, who has allowed me to quote both from a xerox copy in his possession, and also from a lecture given by him in Willingham in 1971, which makes sense of the document (parts of which are missing) and sets it in its proper context in the dispute. Without their help I would have been unable to make even a simple reconstruction of the quarrel.
[11] See below, pp. 193–5.   [12] Name blank in text.   [13] Space left in text.

123

Thomas Hallywell Edward Hallywell William Love John Ragge John Greene William Gunnell John Bedell Henry Ellis the younger John Ratbye John Button and divers others the Tennantes of the saide Mannor whose names your subiecte as yett knoweth not,[14] beinge all armed with swordes staves daggers pitchforks mattocks spades shovells and other weapons ... did in a verey ryotous rowteous and forceible manner enter into the foresaid parcell of meadow grounde ... Your subiect did to his uttermost indeavoure perswade the saide ryotous and disordered persons unto peace ... and used manye meanes by arbitrary Course and otherwise ... But they Contynewinge in their malicious humor aforesaid, and beinge eagerlie and furiouslye bente againste your Subiecte to vexe molest and trouble him with multiplicitie of suites at the Common lawe have not onelie refused all good offers of peace and quietnes But that which is more ... did ... enter into Certen parcells of meadowe ... being parcell of the demeasne landes ... and ... did putt into the same above fortie head of Cattell and with the saide Cattell did ... consume the grasse of your subiect then there growinge ... which unlawfull Acte Alexander Bowlles your subiectes Bailie of the ... Manner John Cole Thomas Page William Sawforde and William Steckarde ... having notice they ... the xxvij daie of Aprill in verey quiett and peaceable Manner ... did take and distreyne the saide fortie heide of cattell ... and ... did drive them towards the Common pounde But as your subiectes Bailie and the others were drivinge them ... [divers named tenants and others, all armed] in forceible manner assembled themselves together and then and there did assault ... the said John Cole [etc.] ... and take awaie the saide fortie heade of cattel ... and did also beate wounde and evill intreate the said John Cole that he was thereby in greate perill of deathe and not therewith Contented ... did then and there use Speeches in disgrace of your subiecte askinge what your subiect was and withall affirminge that they had dealt with a better man than your subiect was And further willed your subiectes servauntes then to require your subiecte to drive theire cattell to the pounde and then he shoulde be well-handled for his paynes.

Sir Miles appears to have been helpless in the face of this infuriated assault, and personally stung by the unfavourable comparison between himself and the untraceable labourer John Cole who got beaten up.[15] Whether or not the unknown lawyer who had been barred from practising was as dubious a character as Sir Miles made out, it is easy to believe that his own servants did indeed proceed in a 'very quiett and peaceable Manner' when they attempted to distrain the cattle of

---

[14] He was already well-informed considering he only bought the manor on 8 November 1601, and entered it on the 12th. Compare the list of tenants in the survey of 1603, below, Table 9. Almost all the substantial members of the community were involved. He subpoenaed forty, some of unknown name, in this complaint.
[15] It is noticeable that the only one of the men acting for Sandys to appear on the list of tenants in 1603 was Thomas Page. Cole was not a Willingham man, and neither was Sawforde or Steckarde.

such a united and hostile community. These tenants were not hungry, tractable, or subservient men.

The dispute was initially settled by the arbitration of the bishop of Ely in October 1602.[16] The award was confirmed by decree in Chancery.[17] The agreement reached under the bishop's guidance allowed a considerable amount of enclosure, but laid down that Sir Miles must leave way for 'a great herd of cattle in the same place where formerly the way hath been for the drift of cattle'.[18] In return, Sir Miles's rights of common 'for any manner of cattle whatsoever' were extinguished completely in Hempsall, Middle and Newditch Fens. The changes made as a result of the award appear even on William Haywood's small-scale map of the fens surveyed in 1604, which on the whole includes very little detail. It shows a considerable area of land in the fens between Willingham and Sir Miles Sandys' main seat at Wilburton, across the fen in the Isle of Ely, as 'Sir Miles Sandys Several'.[19]

The award of 1602 satisfied neither tenants nor lord. In 1621, Sir Miles reopened the whole affair in a further plea to Chancery, which showed he was at loggerheads with his tenants on almost every issue, from the sizes of the copyholds and whether they were, or were not, of inheritance, rights of fold-course on the arable fields, common for cattle, down to his and his tenants' rights of pasture on the fens, which fens were demesne and which were not, and the sizes of stints. He stated in his bill that the tenants were not satisfied with the award of 1602, and 'do exclaim against the orator ... for the great gain and profit which the orator doth daily enjoy by the said Award'. He stated his willingness to forgo it, if his rights could be but established in Chancery.[20]

---

[16] Bishop Heton was new to the scene in 1599, but ought, in theory, to have been able to get advice on the customs of the manor, which had been lately in the possession of the bishopric.

[17] Cunningham, 'Common Rights at Cottenham and Stretham', p. 185 said this was not done, but Sir Miles in his Bill to Chancery in 1621 refers to the decree. P.R.O., C.2. Jas. I, S.19/64.

[18] Cunningham quoted from the adjudication, *ibid.* pp. 184–5. There are several copies of it in the C.R.O. The one I have used is R59/4/1/17.

[19] The map is reproduced as Plate 44 in Astbury, *The Black Fens*, facing p. 128. The changes are shown in detail in the University Archives, Book of Sewers, L.80 fo. 18, photostat in C.U.L. Mr Jeeps kindly gave me this reference.

[20] The end of the dispute is not known, but Sir Miles does not seem to have been a tactful or sensible administrator, as his ultimate bankruptcy testifies. He was involved in too much litigation, both at Stretham and Willingham, and some of it gives the impression that he made too great financial demands in his dealings, and then was unable to enforce payment of any of them. He was, for instance, involved in a continued dispute with the Hinde family whom he admitted as copyhold tenants of one of the fens claimed by him to be demesne at Willingham. He tried to claim fines of £100 on this but the land changed hands frequently and he never got a

The superb series of estate surveys which survive for Willingham are partially connected with the sale of the manor in 1601 and the disputes which followed.[21] It begins with one of 1575, which is followed by a terrier taken from a map made in 1603.[22] It seems likely that this terrier is closely linked with the agreement made between Sir Miles and his tenants under the guidance of the bishop of Ely in the previous year. It is a great pity that the demesne fens and enclosures are, like the commons, excluded from its scope. A survey made late in the 1720s forms a convenient method of seeing how Willingham holdings had developed throughout the seventeenth century.

Sir Miles was perfectly right when he complained that his tenants' half-yardlands had been increasing gradually in size. In the thirteenth century, the half-yardland in Willingham had contained fifteen acres.[23] In the eighteenth century the surveyor who so thoughtfully, and unusually, began his book with a page headed 'The Marks and Abbreviations made use of in this and other Books, . . . describ'd and Explain'd as follow' wrote decisively 'The half Yard Land contains of Arrable Land, Meadow and Marsh about 20 acres.' In 1602, the award ordered that the copies

shall not bie adiuged strictlie to conteine but fiveteen acres, but that the . . . Marrishe groundes in great Shelfords and Snowte fenne and other meddowe and marrishe groundes . . . which have been used with their said coppies as

penny. He nevertheless continued, while still arguing the case, to admit new tenants to it. Eventually he took the latest tenants to Chancery for payment of £200 of back fines (P.R.O., C3/324/37). He would have done better to rate his fines less steeply and to get them paid. It is interesting that one of the men who was briefly admitted as tenant of this fen was a member of the Audley family who became so unpopular at Orwell (see above, pp. 97–8). It looks as if a relatively small group of gentle families were attempting to profit from the sales of episcopal property.

[21] C.R.O., R59/14/5/8 (b). The surveys of 1575, 1602 and the 1720s are set out in parallel columns for the purposes of comparison in this master volume in an eighteenth-century hand. I have based my analysis almost entirely on this together with the survey of the town of Willingham itself made in the 1720s which compares the house-sites in 1603 and the 1720s. C.R.O., R59/14/58 (d). There are at least fifteen Willingham surveys and field books made before the end of the eighteenth century alone in the C.R.O., and I make no pretence of having attempted to do more than produce the barest framework of the tenurial situation.

[22] The original map does not survive, but was copied into a detailed survey of the parish made in 1793 (C.R.O., Willingham Parish Council deposit 1965, unindexed). Dr J. R. Ravensdale generously lent me his tracings of these copies.

[23] The entry for Willingham is unfortunately missing from the hundred rolls, but the survey in the Ely Coucher Book of 1251 shows that the typical holding of the medieval landed peasant at Willingham was, as it was at Chippenham, a half-yardland containing fifteen acres (Gonville and Caius College, MS 485/489). I owe my knowledge of this to the kindness of Mr Dennis Jeeps, who lent me his duplicated text, translated by Dr R. C. Smail. I am also indebted to Dr Smail for his help and hospitality.

126

parte of the said messuage and halfe yardland shall still be deemed and taken as part of them.[24]

Whether or not the allotments of meadow and pasture laid to each holding represented a gain to the tenants in the sense of legal recognition of their right to hold the land they had gradually accumulated, the main sacrifice on Sir Miles's part was undoubtedly the extinction of his common rights.[25] The tenants do not seem to have felt, by 1621, that this was adequate recompense for their loss of common rights over the land enclosed by him. The whole topic of fen drainage and enclosure was a matter of hot debate and there was much general protest from the poor over the loss of their commons in the first half of the seventeenth century.[26] Certainly, after the commissioners of sewers had judged in 1637 that Bedford's scheme had so far succeeded that he was entitled to the 95,000 acres of land specified in the original agreement, the villagers of Willingham, with those of Over and Cottenham,[27] were engaged in petitions against the part of this allotment which encroached on their territory.[28]

Sandys' involvement in the drainage schemes in the end brought about his own financial ruin. He was the principal debtor amongst the Adventurers in 1649.[29] His son, who was knighted in his father's lifetime, wrote in the 1640s,'I owe divers sums which my father borrowed at interest when he adventured large sums of money with the Earl of Bedford in the draining of the fens' and by 1645 was saying 'I could not pay £100 now if I had to go to prison. I have had to sell my land to pay my debts.'[30]

Between 1603 and the 1720s, nearly two hundred acres of the demesne arable of Willingham was sold piecemeal to the tenants, mostly in fragments of an acre or so. Under forty acres of demesne was left in hand for the owners of the chief manor in the eighteenth century. The tenants may therefore have lost important common rights in the fen in the Sandys era but, in return, they gained freedom from common by the lord's cattle on considerable other areas of the fen, and a couple of hundred acres of arable which had previously been leased to them, as

[24] There was an escape clause providing that any land which the lord could prove had been absorbed by the tenants in the last fifty years was recoverable by law.
[25] I have no information on the size of the demesne herds and flocks before their abolition; this would undoubtedly be possible to find in the Ely medieval estate records.
[26] Darby, *Draining of the Fens*, pp. 50–8.   [27] *Ibid.* pp. 58–9.
[28] Harris, *Vermuyden and the Fens*, p. 68. Sandys was reporting to his son at court on general rioting in the area in 1638. Darby, *Draining of the Fens*, p. 61.
[29] Harris, *Vermuyden*, p. 102.
[30] Quoted by Darby, *Draining of the Fens*, p. 59.

well, possibly, as the legal title to allotments of meadow and marsh which they had gradually added to their half-yardlands anyway. This exclusion of the lord's cattle from part of the common fits in with the general pattern of division of rights of common between lord and community in the parishes of the fen-edge in the seventeenth century.[31] It opened the way to the development of peasant dairying on a large scale.

The Willingham economy depended a great deal on stock-raising and milk production, fishing and fowling. In the late eighteenth century it was among the villages said to have large herds of cattle and rich pastures as well as very good arable[32] and in 1808 much of the cheese named after the neighbouring village of Cottenham was actually made in Willingham, which had then about 1,200 milk cows.[33]

The nature of the economy of Willingham in the sixteenth and seventeenth centuries is brought out clearly if the jigsaw of small pieces of information on crops and stock provided by the magnificent series of village wills which survive from the sixteenth century, and a few inventories of the late seventeenth century, is put together[34] and combined with the communal rulings on the stocking of the commons made in the second half of the century.

Despite the general complexity of field systems in Cambridgeshire, the system in Willingham was mercifully simple. There were three fields, Cadwin, West and Belsies, and the arable of the holdings appears to have been distributed roughly equally among them. John Ellis, who died in 1586, was one of the Willingham 'aristocracy' who held a half-yardland. He left his wife, Joan, the entire copyhold for twelve years until his eldest son came of age, and after that, three acres for life 'viz. in every field one acre'. Henry Ingle, a husbandman who died four years earlier, holding only a cottage and close, did have a lease and he likewise left his wife three acres of 'ferme land' for the rest of the lease, an acre in each field. William Biddall, another tenant of a half-yardland who died in 1586, left his wife Cecily half an acre in West field, half an acre in Cadwin field and half an acre in Belsies field, with half an acre of marsh in the 'middle snout'.

However, even if the acreage of the holdings was evenly distributed amongst the three fields, the distribution of crops was slightly more

[31] For this development in Cottenham, see Ravensdale, thesis cit. Ch. IV, 'Sheep', pp. 294–324, *passim*.
[32] C. Vancouver, *General View of the Agriculture in the County of Cambridge* (1794), pp. 125–6.
[33] Lysons, *Magna Britannia*, II, 286.
[34] Original Wills proved in the Consistory Court of Ely, bundled under years, *passim*. I have been able to obtain copies of only forty-four of the inventories for Willingham proved between 1662 and 1700, although a minimum of seventy-two certainly survive. See p. 99, n. 25.

complex. The proportion of wheat and meslin sown was generally higher in the fens than elsewhere in the county, and often formed nearly a third of the acreage under cultivation. Willingham was no exception. Almost all of the tenants had at least forty per cent of their land sown with wheat or meslin. Even so, barley, as usual, formed half or nearly half of the sown acreage, and so the winter cornfield also contained barley. The inventory of William Fisher, taken in 1670, was explicit. In the 'wheatfield' he had two acres and one rood of wheat, but it was accompanied by two acres of barley. He had another two acres of barley in the 'broke' field, with two acres and one rood of peas. The emphasis on peas was also typical of the fens, where they generally formed nearly a fifth of the crops in the late seventeenth century, although in southern Cambridgeshire in general they accounted for little more than five per cent of the sown acreage.

The arable was kept in good heart by the normal fold-course system. According to Sir Miles Sandys in 1621[35] the tenants were stinted to thirty sheep for every half-yardland, and these were all to be folded in the lord's fold, whether they belonged to freeholders or copyholders. The stinting regulations were being disregarded. However, sheep were surprisingly unimportant in the inventories of the late seventeenth century.[36] The few men who kept sheep either kept a single one in the yard, or a reasonable flock of ten or more. This was surprising, considering that the rules for stocking the commons, drawn up in 1655[37] and repeated, in essentials, in 1677/8,[38] limited the number of sheep kept to six to each commonable house and ten for every half-yardland, with fragments of holdings stinted accordingly. This gave the town a minimum sheep flock of 1,000 sheep.[39] It was to be divided as nearly as possible in four, one part of which was to be kept from Lady Day to the end of harvest on the fallow field, and the rest on the other commons. It is inexplicable, then, that those whose goods were appraised did not leave at least six sheep, if, of course, they were commoners.

The farmers of Willingham were not in any case principally concerned with their arable and their sheep folds. In his Chancery bill of 1621, Sandys listed fens covering at least 1,880 acres all of which were demesne, let to farm to the tenants, or due to pay agistment. In his

[35] See above, p. 125.
[36] Thirty out of forty-four inventories do not mention sheep. The highest number kept was fifty.
[37] C.R.O., R59/14/5/9 (b).
[38] C.R.O., R59/14/5/9 (f).
[39] There were 107 houses with common rights in Willingham, and twenty-eight original half-yardland units. I have excluded all other land, and the double common rights of the lord of the manor of Burne and the rectory from the estimates of sheep and horses and cattle, so all the estimates are very low indeed.

opinion, the tenants were limited by custom to pasturing only cattle which had been bred within the manor. However, he said, they

> do common with such a multitude of cows, horses, sheep and other cattle there that the orator is debarred of mowing, jeesting, and feeding, as of right the orator ought to do, and they have so surcharged the ... fens called West fen and middle fen and all other the said grounds with their sheep and cattle that whereas the orator ... has heretofore or by his farmer usually kept upon West and middle fen a thousand or more of their own sheep besides a jeesting of other sheep and great cattle, the orator can now make little or no benefit of west and middle fen ... And also (they) do daily keep such great store and abundance of sheep and other cattle *not bred within the same manor*[40] that the orator is wholly deprived of the benefit of keeping any sheep or great cattle or commons on the grounds aforesaid.

It does not sound from this as if, in 1621, there was any sort of stint on 'great cattle'. Sir Miles Sandys' complaint was that beasts bred outside Willingham were being taken in as well. This was not a new source of friction. In 1575, the court rolls[41] record the verdict of the homage that 'none of the inhabitants of this town holding any land if he let it to any other shall not let any grazing in the middle fen and newditch fen with the same land, unless he let the house and the land whole together'. The ruling had obviously been a cause of much friction; there was a memorandum in the roll: 'The cause why this was not ingrossed at the last court was because it was doubtful whether such orders might be made ... and further because ... many controversies have been concerning the said Middlefen.' It sounds as if the tenants had been letting their common rights to outsiders.[42]

By the mid-1650s, however, the growth in the size of Willingham[43] and the breakdown of the traditional tenement[44] had led to trouble. The eight men whom the villagers 'did willingly and freely' choose to settle the controversies, which, they said 'doe frequently and daly ... grow amongst the inhabitants ... by reason of ye unequall useing rateing and feeding of ye commons' could not reach agreement. So, according to the procedure laid down for them by their 'electorate', they in turn chose four non-resident gentlemen to act as arbitrators.[45]

These arbitrators laid down a stint for cattle and horses, apparently for the first time, although the allusion to 'rating' as a cause of friction may mean that some tentative attempt had been made to introduce a

[40] My italics.   [41] C.R.O., L1/118.
[42] Or were engaged in fattening, and taking in for summer pasturage, as well as dairying.
[43] See above, pp. 20-2.   [44] See below, pp. 144, 148-9, 150.
[45] All stated in the preamble of R59/14/5/9 (b).

stint between 1621 and 1655, and had failed. Sheep were stinted at six for a commonable house and ten for a half-yardland, which probably represented no change, except in the precision of the language, from 1621. The stint for cattle and horses was generous, at eight for a house with rights of common on Middle, Newditch, and West Fens, and Clattox,[46] as well as four for a complete half-yardland on Middle and Newditch Fens. The rights of those with smaller acreages were in proportion. Much care was taken over the ratio of mares and geldings to cows; four acres of arable gave a tenant the right to common a cow as against five acres to common a horse. Only a third of the beasts on Middle and Newditch Fens owned by a man with a house and a half-yardland of arable were to be horses. Above this number, a mare or gelding counted as two cows. Willingham farmers today still reckon a horse eats as much as two cattle.

The arbitrators' ruling was virtually confirmed by the short agreement signed or marked by all the commoners in 1677–8,[47] so the stint did not, apparently, drop in the next twenty years. The town of Willingham in the mid-seventeenth century, was therefore running after stinting had been introduced, a herd of cattle and horses which, at an absolute minimum estimate, approached a thousand beasts and must in reality have considerably exceeded it.

One or two men bred horses in a small way. Richard Lypton had four horses and three colts in his yard in 1669, and Henry Crispe and Edward Halliwell also had seven horses apiece. Considering the care given to regulations for stinting horses, it is surprising that more were not appraised in the inventories.[48] The dominance and profitability of keeping cattle are forcibly demonstrated. A couple of pigs were kept by almost everyone, although neither pigs nor geese were allowed on the commons.

The inventories also bring out the importance of cattle. The median herd of cattle owned by the husbandman in the fens in the 1660s was not radically different in size from that of his upland counterpart[49] – the

---

[46] I find the details of the arbitration confusing. Each commonable house had the right to run five 'great cattle' on Middle and Newditch Fens, and, as far as I can make out, the three on West Fen and Clattox were additional.

[47] See below, pp. 195–6 for elementary ability to write at Willingham, and a discussion of this document.

[48] About a third of those whose inventories were examined kept no horses. Twelve of the twenty-nine who did have horses had only one. The median was two. No one had more than seven, except Henry Aspland and Mrs Ann Fuller, who was probably the lessee of the sub-manor of Burne.

[49] M. Spufford, 'Rural Cambridgeshire', pp. 25–7. The figure was eight cattle in the small sample of inventories for the whole fen area, as against six for the whole of southern Cambridgeshire. About a fifth of the Willingham men whose inventories I

difference lay in the amount of arable held by each. A man could be described by his neighbours as a yeoman, as was Thomas Biddall of Willingham by his appraisers after his death in 1660. Yet he had, in the month of July, not a single rood to be harvested on the ground, not a single bushel of grain in stock, and not a single plough or harrow to be priced. He was a landless man. And yet, in his yard he had twelve cattle and in his cheese chamber 120 cheeses worth £6. Another of the numerous Biddall family, a weaver, had three and a quarter acres sown in April. Perhaps he held half a dozen acres in all, with his fallow. Yet he had twelve cattle in the yard, as many as yeoman like one of the Tebbuts at Chippenham, with their farms of a hundred or more acres under the plough.[50] Such examples can be multiplied from the inventories, which provide ample evidence for the predominant role of cattle and cheese-making in the 1660s and 1670s in Willingham. The inventories of two Thomas Biddalls, one a yeoman and the other a weaver, show that cheeses were priced at 1s each in 1670. They weighed about five and a half pounds each.[51] There were references to 'parcels of cheese' scattered throughout the inventories and these 'parcels' were not uncommonly priced quite highly at thirty shillings or more, which means over a hundred and fifty pounds of cheese were often in stock for the market. The knowledge of the amount of cheese involved gives much more conclusive evidence than any other that cheese-making was as important in Willingham in the late seventeenth century as in the early nineteenth century, when Lysons commented on it.

The late sixteenth-century wills provide ample evidence that the emphasis on cattle and on cheese-making was not a new thing in seventeenth-century Willingham. Bequests of stock were important in the wills. Henry Graves, a half-yardland holder who died in 1590,[52] leaving a wife carrying a child, left her 'six milk cows of the best' at her choice outright, and his 'milking yard' along with the rest of his land for twenty-one years until his child came of age. She was also to have the use of all his 'mares foals and colts' for twenty-one years, along with his other chattels. Widows were carefully provided with adequate grazing for a cow or so. Cecily Biddall,[53] along with her acre and a half

examined kept no cows. The median number kept by the thirty-six who did own cattle was nine, but eleven of the thirty-six kept nine to twelve cows.
50 See above, p. 65.
51 By comparison with the inventory of Edward White, made in 1692, who had fourteen stones of cheese, or 196 lb, valued at £1 15s 0d. The price of cheese was very stable in the seventeenth century. Writtle cheeses weighed about 11 lb and were also priced at 2s a cheese in the same period. F. W. Steer, *Farm and Cottage Inventories of Mid-Essex, 1635–1749* (1950), pp. 37–9.
52 See Tables 8 and 9 for the Graves's holdings in 1575 and 1603.
53 See below, pp. 140–1 for the Biddalls.

of land and half an acre of marsh was left four cows and 'one mare called Brigstock'. She was also to have the right of pasturing three milk cows in Middle Fen 'with house room there for their feeding in winter and room for fodder and the yard in summer for them for her widowhood'. Robert Salmon held only a customary cottage with common rights,[54] but when he died in 1586, he provided that his widow should have the pasturing of a beast in the Middle Fen for life, and room for her cattle and fodder in the yard. A man like Matthew Ewsden, who died in 1595, and seems from the surveys to have been landless, carefully divided his cheeses up amongst his children, as well as his cattle.[55]

The fen common meant even more to men like Matthew Ewsden than to the holders of half-yardlands.[56] William Spratforth was one of the few labourers who made a will. He left his brindled cow to one son, his brown cow to the other, and the residue to his wife. Robert Lammas, who held nothing according to the court rolls, went to great pains in his absurdly complex will to provide for his only daughter Mercy, by selling a cow and putting the money out to interest until she was twenty-one.

The fen provided other perquisites than grazing. George Crispe left one of his sons 'three copies at the ponds' in 1577 and this bequest duly appeared in the court rolls as 'three selions and three ponds'. In 1593, a surrender was made in the court rolls of eight ponds in Willingham at a rent of 2s a year. There were men in Willingham who depended totally on the fen, rather than using it to supply the deficiencies of their smallholdings or their earnings as labourers. William Pearson, who died in 1582, had held neither land nor cottage in the survey of 1575, although his brother had held a cottage and half a dozen acres. William left his wife his customary lands in the marsh for life, and one load of willows out of Bostons Holt. She got, in addition, her husband's portion of the lease of the 'fodder ground Reed ground and willowes in the great haills' (sic). She was to pay 6s 8d a year towards the rent of this to Simon, the only child, and was also to let him have '400 of reed' to

---

[54] See below, p. 163 for Salmon's other provisions for his widow.
[55] See below, pp. 141–2 for Matthew Ewsden, and p. 336 for his widow's religious opinions.
[56] The introduction of stinting in the 1650s probably hit cottagers harder than anyone else. A majority of the cottages built to accommodate the increasing population (see above, p. 21), had no common rights. A commoner was perfectly free to sublet his rights. The regulations of 1655 and 1677/8 laid down only that if common rights were sublet, they must be let for the whole year. However, the introduction of stinting presumably increased their value, and the price asked by commoners. The minimum that a commoner would sublet for may be deduced from the regulation, agreed in 1655 and 1677/8, that a commoner who gave due notice that he was unable to take up his rights was entitled from the fen-reeves to the startlingly large sum of 13s 4d per beast not kept.

repair his house 'if it needs so much'. He, in turn, inherited all the rest of 'my boatsgayt with the fishings fenns marryses willowes oziers reed grounds and all other profyttes therein' as well as all the 'customary ponds' in the marsh and the 'pickerills' within them. The will of William Pardye, made in 1593, was more succinct. He was a waterman, and he left his only son John, two cows, 'all my lodge as it standith . . . with the fodder that is upon the same lodge, my boat in the fen, my boots and a pair of high shoes'.

When the changes in the distribution of land which took place in Willingham in the sixteenth and seventeenth centuries are considered, it is therefore essential to bear in mind the existence of men like William Pardye, who held no land and had few goods, but could eke out a living with a boat, a pair of boots, a pair of high shoes, and a couple of cows.

LAND DISTRIBUTION

The way in which land was distributed amongst the Willingham community changed very markedly between 1575 and the early eighteenth century. The pattern which evolved was completely different from that of the other villages examined. In 1575 in Willingham, there were certainly seventy-six tenants of houses, with or without land, with at least another twenty-four houses which may have been sublet (see Table 8). The 'typical' holding was still the half-yardland and its attendant house and croft in the village. Twenty-eight of the forty copyholders on the main manor were holders of half-yardlands. In addition to these forty copyholders, there were thirteen freeholders. There was comparatively little overlap between the tenants of freeholds and copyholds; only three men, including George Crispe, held both in any quantity. George Crispe held nearly ninety-four acres of freehold and copyhold land,[57] and was the only tenant with over a yardland. Another four men who here stood out as unusually prosperous, although they would not have done so elsewhere, held between twenty-seven and forty-four acres of arable. Nearly half of the landholding tenants held a half-yardland which varied in practice between sixteen and twenty-five acres, although it nominally contained twenty acres.[58]

---

[57] I have included acreages of meadow and marsh in this discussion of the size of holdings in 1575, although the meadow and marsh may not, legally at least, have been attached to the holdings until 1603. The inclusion makes the size of holdings in 1575 more comparable with later dates. See above, pp. 126–7.

[58] According to the surveyor who compiled the abstract of the three surveys of 1575. 1603 and the 1720s, C.R.O., R59/14/5/8 (b), on which this whole section is based. See also above, pp. 126–7.

TABLE 8 *Tenants and farm size in Willingham, 1575*
(Figures to nearest acre, including meadow and marsh*)

Range of size		Freehold land	Copyhold land	Leasehold land	Total
Over 1 yardland	George Crispe	56a.	38a.		94a.
Half-yardland to 1 yardland	John Salmon		44a.		44a.
	William Brasier		26a.	4 + a.	30 + a.
	Henry Fromont	11a.	19a.		30a.
	John Lamb		14a.	13 + a.	27 + a.
Half-yardland	John Graves		25a.		25a.
	Robert Peapes	11a.	12a.		23a.
	William Graves		23a.		23a.
	John Brasier		17a.	5 + a.	22 + a.
	John Bowles		22a.		22a.
	William Biddall		22a.		22a.
	William Ashman		22a.		22a.
	Richard Croxon		21a.		21a.
	Abraham Ellis		21a.		21a.
	Thomas Page		21a.		21a.
	John Ingle	19a.	2a.		21a.
	Henry Graves		21a.		21a.
	Henry Orinel		20a.		20a.
	Henry Ellis		20a.		20a.
	Thomas Cranwell		19a.		19a.
	Thomas Bowles		19a.		19a.
	Henry Townsend		19a.		19a.
	John Ellis		19a.		19a.
	Henry Noble		19a.		19a.
	John Ragg		19a.		19a.
	William Jordan		18a.		18a.
	Henry Jordan		18a.		18a.
	Robert Jordan	18a.			18a.
	Thomas Gibson		18a.		18a.
	Thomas Hallywell		17a.		17a.
	John Buttris	16a.			16a.
	Robert Cauket		15a.	1 + a.	16 + a.
	William Ingle		12a. (+ 9 strips)		c. 16a.
2 acres to half-yardland	John Button	12a.			12a.
	Robert Graves	10a.	1a.		11a.
	William Moody		10a.		10a.
	Robert Ellis of Over	9a.			9a.
	Widow Strongman		9a.		9a.
	Robert Buttris		9a.		9a.
	Thomas King		9a.		9a.
	William Love		9a.		9a.
	William Foot	8a.			8a.
	John Radcliffe			5a. (+ 8 strips)	c. 8a.
	Richard Fue			7a.	7a.

135

Range of size		Freehold land	Copyhold land	Leasehold land	Total
2 acres to	John Priest		6a.		6a.
half-yardland	Thomas Pearson of				
(*cont.*)	London	6a.			6a.
	Edward Townsend		6a.		6a.
	Robert Adams		5a.		5a.
	John Barliman	5a.			5a.
	Mathew Benton	4a.			4a.
	T. Adams			4 + a.	4 + a.
	Grace Rose		4a.		4a.
	Henry Slye		3a.		3a.
	William Orinel				
	(? Gunnel)		1a.	1 + a.	2 + a.
2 acres and	John Mady		2a.		2a.
under	John Brown		2 + r.	1 + r.	3 + r.
	Richard Clarke		3 r.		3 r.
	T. Biddall			2 + r.	2 + r.
	J. Biddall			2 + r.	2 + r.
	John Marshall			2 + r.	2 + r.
	Richard Marshall			1 + r.	1 + r.
	William Cranwell			1 + r.	1 + r.

Holders of commonable houses or cottages without any land

John Adams	Thomas Gaylet	Richard Pearson
John Auger	Henry Ingle	The Rectory
William Auger	Lambert	John Ridley
John Blythe	John Loder	Robert Salmon
Henry Carter	Robert Marshall	Starling
Robert Crouch	William Myllis	The Village
Thomas Eggleton	Mr Nightingale	John Wright
Mathew Ewsden	Mary Nightingale	

Totals

Holders of land with commonable houses	53
Holders of commonable houses without land	23
Houses in hands of those with more than one house	24
Total houses in 1575 field survey	100

[This survey takes no account of non-commonable houses]

* It is by no means certain that this meadow and marsh had been legally, at least, added to the holdings by 1575. It has been included to make this table comparable with the others.

+Indicates additional acreage of unknown size, particularly applicable to leaseholds held by Jesus College over which not much care was taken in the surveys.

Between forty and fifty per cent of the villagers of Willingham in 1575 held only a house, or a house and a couple of acres. In all, sixty-seven of the tenants named in the survey held under a half-yardland, and therefore in medieval theory held less than enough land for subsistence. However, the complete geographical distinction between Willingham, with its enormous acreage of fen, and the other open-field communities discussed here, must be remembered. The common rights, which went with all holdings and most landless houses in Willingham in 1575, completely changed the value of the arable holdings which would indeed have been insufficient to provide a living in an upland area. A half-yardlander in Willingham was a wealthy man.

A generation later, in 1603, the signs of change were already apparent. A half-yardland was still recognisably the 'normal' holding in 1603, apart now from the houses with no land attached, but there were only twenty tenants of half-yardlands as against twenty-eight a generation earlier (see Table 9). Henry Ellis, George Frogg and William Love had acquired extra land and moved up to swell the numbers of those with between twenty-six and forty-four acres. There were eight of these more substantial men in 1603.[59] Others, like the Ingles and the Nobles, had lost parts of their land and joined the growing ranks of the cottagers with between two and fourteen acres.[60] In this single generation, over a quarter of the copyholds had been split. Most of these fragmentations were admittedly minor ones of a rood or two, often to another member of the same family. Only four holdings had really been subdivided in a major way, one of them into five parts. In each of these cases the family of the original tenant had held on to a part of the land, which suggests that the fragmentations had been forced on unwilling men by their inability to hold on to their land in the difficult economic circumstances at the end of the sixteenth century. In this generation no less than a quarter of the copyholds completely lost their association with the family which had been holding them in 1575.

The degree of fragmentation was less marked amongst the freeholds than amongst the copyholds at this stage. Only two of them were split, although one of these was in four fragments by 1603. On the other hand the rate of change in the families who occupied the holdings was nearly as high as on the copyholds. Nearly a quarter of the freeholds were in the hands of completely different families. In this single generation, therefore, just under a third of the copyhold and freehold tenements were split, and thirteen of the fifty-three holdings came into the hands of tenants of another family.[61] On the other hand, over half

---

[59] The other extra 'large' holding was formed when George Crispe, who held ninety-four acres in 1575, died and split his holding between his two sons. The younger, William, held thirty-six acres in 1603.

[60] See below, pp. 157–8 for detailed case-studies and analysis of the possible causes of these fragmentations.

[61] This is excluding change of family name through heiresses.

TABLE 9   *Tenants and farm size in Willingham, 1603*
(Figures to nearest acre)

Range of size	Occupant	Freehold land	Copyhold land	Leasehold land	Total
Over 1 yardland	Henry Crispe	56a.	3a.		59a.
Half-yardland to 1 yardland	Henry Fromont	11a.	27a.		38a.
	William Crispe		36a.		36a.
	George Frogg		34a.		34a.
	Henry Ellis, senior	2a.	30a. (+ 1 strip)		*c.* 32a.
	William Love		30 + a.		30 + a.
	John Adams			28 + a.	28 + a.
	Henry Graves, senior		28a.		28a.
	William Brasier, senior		25a.	1 + a.	26 + a.
Half-yardland	Dr William Smith		24a.		24a.
	Henry Graves, junior		23a.		23a.
	Robert Peapes	11a.	12a.		23a.
	Henry Townsend		23a. (+ 1 strip)		*c.* 23a.
	John Graves, senior		23a.		23a.
	John Biddall		22a.		22a.
	William Ashman		22a.		22a.
	Thomas Hallywell	5a.	16a.		21a.
	Thomas Brasier		21a.		21a.
	Robert Buttris		20a.		20a.
	Ellin Salmon		20a.		20a.
	The Lord (in hand)		19a.		19a.
	William Cranwell		19a.		19a.
	Thomas Bowles		19a.		19a.
	Thomas Ingle	19a.			19a.
	Henry Ellis, junior		19a.		19a.
	John Ragg		19a.		19a.
	Alice Jordan	18a.			18a.
	Thomas Gibson		18a.		18a.
	Robert Cauket		15a.	1 + a.	16 + a.
2 acres to half-yardland	Abraham Ellis		14a.		14a.
	Thomas Page		14a.		14a.
	John Button	12a.			12a.
	Robert Graves	11a.			11a.
	Henry Pearson		10a.		10a.
	John Brasier		10a.		10a.
	Robert Fue			10a.	10a.
	William Buttris	10a.			10a.
	John Biswell, in right of his wife	10a.			10a.
	Edward Hallywell	9a.			9a.
	Francis Noble		9a.		9a.
	Richard Pearson		7a.		7a.
	John Priest		6a.		6a.
	Simon Pearson	6a.			6a.
	John Page		6a.		6a.

Range of size	Occupant	Freehold land	Copyhold land	Leasehold land	Total
2 acres to half-yardland	William Ingle		2a. (+ 8 strips)		c. 6a.
	William Brasier, junior	4a.	2a.		6a.
	Edward Townsend		5a.		5a.
	Agnis King		5a.		5a.
	Katherine Malin		5a.		5a.
	Mathew Benton	4a.			4a.
	Henry Biddall		4a.		4a.
	Lawrence Milford		3a.		3a.
	William Carter		3a.		3a.
2 acres and under	William Strongman		2a.		2a.
	Robert Ingle		1a. 3r.		1a. 3r.
	William Gunnell (? Orinel)		1a. 2r.		1a. 2r.
	Robert Clark		3r.		3r.
	William Burwell		1r.		1r.

Commonable houses of cottages without any land

Anthony Adams	Thomas Gaylet	Thomas Ladd
Anthony Archer	Thomas Graves	Thomas Lambert
William Auger	Ingram Haydon	In the hands of the Lord
John Bowles	William Haynes	Henry Marshall
Thomas Bowles, junior	Unnamed tenant of Jesus	John Marshall
William Bowles	College, Cambridge	William Marshall
Unnamed tenant of the	Unnamed tenant of Jesus	The Rectory
manor of Burne	College	William Ridley
William Clarke	Unnamed tenant of Jesus	George Rockley
Joan Dodson	College	Thomas Rooke
Thomas Fromont	Jordan	Starling
Richard Fue	Arthur Jordan	Jos. Starling

Totals

Commonable houses with land (field survey)	54
Commonable houses with no land (field survey)	32
Commonable houses in the hands of those who already had one, presumably sublet (field survey)	18
Commonable houses in town survey, but not in field survey, category not clear	3
Non-commonable houses with land (field and town surveys)	2
Non-commonable houses with no land (town survey)	4
Non-commonable houses in the hands of those who already have a commonable one, presumably sublet (field and town surveys)	12
Total number of houses known for 1603	125

the holdings remained both intact and in the hands of the same family as in 1575.

The economic information contained in the wills made between the two surveys of 1575 and 1603 gives a considerable amount of insight into the way men made a living from such small holdings. Whereas in

Chippenham the tenant of a half-yardland seemed a very humble man by the end of the sixteenth century, cast economically and socially in the shade by the engrossers who held so much more land,[62] the wills of the half-yardlanders of Willingham give an entirely different feel. In Willingham, such men were, comparatively speaking, wealthy. Their personal goods, their stock, the provision they were able to make for their families, and the general attitudes conveyed in their wills suggest prosperity. The history of the Biddall family illustrates the point, as well as demonstrating the ways in which younger sons could eke out a livelihood.

William Biddall left a half-yardland of twenty-one acres of arable and marsh in 1575.[63] He had a fairly big house, for he was able to leave his widow the hall and two chambers as well as the loft on the north-east of the house. Most Willingham wills at this date only mention the hall and kitchen, or a single chamber. William had five sons and a daughter. The daughter was already married, to the tenant of another half-yardland, and one of the sons was established by the time his father died in 1586 and had six children of his own. John Biddall, who inherited the house and half-yardland from his father and was his residuary legatee, was also already married with two children.[64] Henry appears to have been the next son; he was to inherit if John refused to fulfil his father's bequests, and was also to divide the household goods with his mother, to receive £12 within three years, and was set up with three mares and their foals, Star and Conny, an interest in the grain crop of the holding in the next year, and other bequests of grain. The fourth son, Richard, received two and a half acres of freehold his father had bought from one John Loder in Longstanton, together with £3, the white mare called Grubb, and her colt.

Richard died in 1589, before his mother or any of his brothers. He had married, leaving a small son and daughter, and had done astonishingly well from his two and a half acre holding, which he left to his son, for he also left him a bequest of £50 and his daughter a dower of £22. The Biddalls were a strongly united family. Richard's elder brother, Henry, was to manage the two and a half acres for him for half the profits, until his nephew came of age. Richard also left all his brothers' and sisters' numerous children a calf, or at least a bushel of barley apiece, and his widowed mother a mare. Cecily herself left bequests for all her numerous grandchildren.

Richard Biddall was not the only man to do well out of two and a

---

[62] See above, pp. 65–70.
[63] It was family land, for according to a court held after his death his father John had been admitted to it in 1534 or 1535.   [64] See below, p. 162.

half acres of freehold; the will of John Loder, who had sold the land to Richard's father, also survives and also gives a feeling of prosperity. He was able to leave cash bequests of £5 to various people, he had two servants, ample goods, and could afford also to leave his neighbours a flitch of bacon and ten shillings 'to make merry about the feast of Pentecost next'.

The last son of old William Biddall was another William. William was obviously a special case; his father did not expect him to marry, for he left him £12, a bed and bedding and the 'hay house the quantity of two mowsteads to make him a shop'. He also provided for his executor to give him 'meat and drink for life, as I have done'. It seems very likely that William was crippled in some way. He became a shoemaker. Although he needed a sheltered environment, he was obviously not an economic drag on his family, because when he died, unmarried as his father had expected, in 1593, he left numerous small cash bequests to all his nephews, nieces and small cousins, and remitted debts owed to him by both his older brother Henry and by another William Biddall 'the weaver'. He also owned part of a sheep flock in common with Henry and his eldest brother John.

The history of William Biddall and his five sons illustrates several points: the relative prosperity of half-yardland holders in the fens compared with their counterparts in the uplands, the comparative prosperity of men holding very small acreages like John Loder and Richard Biddall, and the frequent adoption of a trade by younger sons like William Biddall to eke out a small living.

All these points are reinforced by other wills left by Willingham men, including those of cottagers, labourers and artisans. There were plenty of testaments of cottagers, or men living on small holdings, like Matthew Ewsden. Matthew Ewsden described himself as a husbandman in 1594, although in 1575 he appeared only as the tenant of a landless cottage with rights of common. He had acquired a lease by the time he died, and went to great trouble to provide for his widow, three sons and two daughters. He had left each two cows at least, and the hay and fodder were left to them 'indifferently for the wintering of the cattle together'. He disposed of nine cows and heifers with four calves, as well as two steers; this was again the kind of herd that only a prosperous yeoman would have had at Chippenham. Matthew's widow, Christian, was left 'the' feather bed, all the pewter, the painted cloths, and the firing. The cottage had two rooms, a hall and a kitchen which served as a bedroom, for it had a bed in it with a 'nethermost' and an 'uppermost' coverlet, which were carefully bequeathed to different children. Each child was also left three or four pairs of sheets and some cheeses. The eldest son, John, was left the residue; his brother William a small lease, the boat and the nets. The two brothers were to share half the main lease for the remainder of the term, and their mother the other half. Matthew left his eight sheep to his two eldest sons 'for the taking of a new lease'. The dying man laid down that the peas should be sold once they were threshed and the money divided equally amongst his wife and children, and so the wheat should be sown 'the four nobles being paid out of it'. The whole picture is of far greater comfort from a cottage holding than could ever be gained in the uplands.

William Fromant was one of the rare men to describe himself as a labourer when he died in 1591. It appears from his will that he held a cottage and half an acre of land.[65] His daughter's dower was only 26s, but all the same, he could dispose of goods which to William Harrison in the 1580s were luxuries – flaxen sheets, three pewter platters of the best, a best candlestick and a new brass pan.

There were wills of artisans in the series as well as those of cottagers and labourers. Robert Ward, who died in 1589, was a weaver, and a landless man. His will mentioned four cows, however, and more significantly, eight men were indebted to him, one at least of whom was a half-yardland holder. His trade brought in enough ready money to make him one of the small village moneylenders who were probably so vital to the community in times of scarcity.[66] John Bowghton who died in 1591 was another man whose family name appeared nowhere in either the surveys of 1575 or 1603 or in the court rolls in between. He seems to have been another landless man. As well as leaving his son his planes and chisel, squares and rule, he was able to leave him £12 and both linen and feather bed. The examples of craftsmen I have used here have all been of landless men, but not all craftsmen were landless,[67] and the exercise of valuable common rights in a pastoral area was the equivalent of land-holding in an arable area. It would be valuable to use the evidence of wills and inventories over a wide area to discover more about the complex, but important, issue, of how far, and for how long, craftsmen continued to draw income from land, and to hold land, not only in the 'industrial' villages that were to become the cities of Stoke or Sheffield, but in areas that were to remain predominantly rural.

[65] He does not appear in the court rolls at all, and was therefore probably one of the elusive group of under-tenants.
[66] See above, p. 80. The wills of Willingham provide just as much evidence of money-lending as those at Chippenham. The most striking example is of course the way in which a young girl would lend her dower out at interest.
[67] See below, p. 157.

For the landless men of Willingham, everything must have depended on whether or not their cottages had common rights. Even after the stinting in the mid-seventeenth century, the allowance for a commonable house was generous.[68] But for those who lived in the new cottages without common rights which had already appeared by 1603, and continued to appear in increasing numbers throughout the century,[69] things cannot have been at all easy. They must have depended on wages, and on subleasing a right of common for one or two beasts from a more fortunate man; and the evidence available shows how expensive this must have been.[70] The tenant of a non-commonable cottage was not necessarily to be pitied. He sometimes held other land as well, like William Love and Thomas Bowles. William Love had two other houses, both with rights of common, and thirty acres of arable. Thomas Bowles also had one commonable house and nineteen acres, and a landless cottage with rights of common. Robert Clark and William Burwell, on the other hand, held three roods and one rood of open-field arable respectively, which cannot have given them much in the way of common rights. The existence of a non-commonable cottage each in the town survey solved the mystery of where they lived, for, according to the field survey, they had no houses. The men who were really to be pitied in 1603 were Charles Fromant, John Barliman and Christopher Parkinson, whose existence would not, were it not for the town survey, be suspected, for they held nothing at all but their non-commonable cottages. They represented, in 1603, the tip of the iceberg of unknown size, which was made up of labourers and sub-tenants.

The wills illustrate this too, for they show the existence of genuine poverty even in parishes like this, where all the resources of the fen common were available. Early in 1589, Roger Biddall died leaving three sons. To one he left 10s and a pair of sheets; to another 'my second table', one sheet and three shillings, and to the third 'my biggest kettle, one pewter dish a pillow and a pair of sheets'. The residue, whatever that was, went to his wife. Despite the proud bequest of one pewter dish and the fact that he had two tables, the whole estate sounds pretty meagre, at a time when dowers for girls were quite often as much as £10.[71] Such examples do not stand alone. No transfers of land or even of landless cottages appear in the court rolls as the result of these men's deaths, any more than the passing of John Bowghton left any record other than his will and an entry in the registers. Since the court rolls do record transfers of very small pieces of land and of cottages, either the recording was sporadic, or it is a mystery where

---

[68] See above, p. 131.
[69] See above, p. 21.
[70] See above, p. 133, n. 56.
[71] See above, pp. 140–1, for the Biddall family.

these men lived. Very probably they formed one of the army of sub-tenants of whose existence the wills give so much proof. Many of the half-yardlanders had bought up one or more apparently landless mes-suages. Henry Graves, who died in 1590, specifically laid down that William Lammas, his sub-tenant, was to have the house he dwelled in for life for 13s 4d a year, which incidentally appears a much higher rent than most of those which are sporadically entered in the court rolls. Robert Lammas, who died in 1603, appeared nowhere in the survey made that year, and he left little but two cows and a calf. He must have been the sub-tenant of a more prosperous man. It is im-possible to judge how many men like this never appeared in the surveys at all, but the wills of such men are fairly numerous. It is extremely sobering to consider the minute size of the will-making population[72] and the fact that however 'poverty' may apparently be illustrated from the wills, the really poor did not make them. The existence of this shadowy army of people must not be forgotten when generalisations are made about the relative prosperity of cottagers and tenants of smallholdings in fenland, or forest, communities. They formed a class which knew real and bitter poverty.

The overall impression left by the wills is of the prosperity and purchasing power wielded by those who held a conventional tenement which by the end of the sixteenth century seemed negligible in the up-lands, the comparative affluence of men who held only a couple of acres, and the frequent adoption of a trade by cottagers and younger sons who depended on the existence of the fen common.[73] Beneath these groups there was a concealed substratum, of unknown size, of under-tenants with no common rights, who were really poor.

In the five generations between 1603 and the survey taken in the 1720s, a tendency towards the breakdown of holdings which was noticeable between 1575 and 1603 continued. The rate of change was no faster,[74] but the end results, over so much longer a period of time, were dramatic. The breakdown of the half-yardland as a recognisable unit was accomplished. There was a rise of twenty-two per cent in the number of tenants, from 125 to 153. The numbers of the 'affluent' by Willingham standards remained roughly constant, although the pro-portion of them fell sharply. Eight men held over a half-yardland in the 1720s, although sixty years before, in the 1660s, the average holding of a self-respecting yeoman was already around eighty acres elsewhere in Cambridgeshire. The majority of these 'large' Willingham holdings were much smaller than that, and contained thirty to forty acres.

[72] See below, p. 197, n. 21. See also M. Spufford, 'Inheritance and Land in Cambridge-shire', *Family and Inheritance*, ed. J. Goody, J. Thirsk and E. P. Thompson (Cambridge, 1976) pp. 169–73.
[73] See the example of the Biddall family, pp. 140–1.   [74] See below, p. 151, n. 82.

144

TABLE 10   *Tenants and farm size in Willingham, 1720s*
(Figures to nearest acre)

Range of size	Occupant	Freehold land	Copyhold land	Leasehold land	Total
Over 1 yardland	Andrew and Elizabeth Meires	21a.	55a.	6a.	82a.
	John Ellis		53a.		53a.
Half-yardland to 1 yardland	Samuel Knight		40a.		40a.
	Thomas Aspland	8a.	30a.		38a.
	William Johnson			37a.	37a.
	Joseph Aspland	13a.	19a.		32a.
	John Pearson of Over	7a.	24a.		31a.
	Heirs of John Butler	4a.	12a.	14a.	30a.
Half-yardland	Jane Nevil	5a.	20a.		25a.
	John White		25a.		25a.
	Heirs of Sayes			25a.	25a.
	John Walman		24a.		24a.
	Heirs of Joseph Sneesby	17a.	5a.	1a.	23a.
	Wiseman	15a.	2a.	6a.	23a.
	Anne Battle		22a.		22a.
	Jeff John Graves		22a.		22a.
	Thomas and Elizabeth Harris		21a.		21a.
	Thomas Pyke		21a.		21a.
	Henry and John Marshall	20a.			20a.
	Levitt	20a.			20a.
	Anne Wiseman	20a.			20a.
	Thomas and Jane Manlove		20a.		20a.
	John and Elizabeth Osborne	2a.	c. 17a.		c. 19a.
	Co-heirs of Elizabeth Crouch		9a.	8a.	17a.
	Thomas Ewing		17a.		17a.
	Deborah Berfoot	10a.	6a.		16a.
	John Graves, senior	16a.			16a.
	John and Anne Ancel		16a.		16a.
2 acres to half-yardland	John and Elizabeth Reed of St Ives	4a.	11a.		15a.
	John Rooke			15a.	15a.
	James Pattison	14a.			14a.
	Henry Onion		11a.	1a.	12a.
	Elizabeth Ingle, widow		12a.		12a.
	Thomas Bacon, Esq.		11a.		11a.
	Jane Aspland	11a.			11a.
	Henry Ingle and William Ingle, junior	11a.			11a.
	Henry Hallywell	2a.	9a.		11a.
	William Fisher	2a.	8a.		10a.
	William Ingle, senior	2a.	8a.		10a.
	Abraham Love	7a.	2a.	1a.	10a.

TABLE 10 (*cont.*)

Range of size	Occupant	Freehold land	Copyhold land	Leasehold land	Total
2 acres to	Susan Neeve	10a.			10a.
half-yardland	Anne Munsey		10a.		10a.
(*cont.*)	Thomas Graves	3a.	6a.		9a.
	John Bodger	9a.			9a.
	Anne Graves	1a.	8a.		9a.
	Francis Wiseman	8a.		1a.	9a.
	John Ingle		9a.		9a.
	Margaret Pyke		9a.		9a.
	Margaret Lack		3a.	6a.	9a.
	Mary Ingle	1a.	7a.		8a.
	Thomas Heard			8a.	8a.
	Sarah Boult	8a.			8a.
	Yates		*c.* 7a.	1a.	*c.* 8a.
	Allin Crispe	5a.	3a.		8a.
	James Rooke	2a.	5a.		*c.* 8a.
			(+ 3 strips)		
	Robert Clark		7a.		7a.
	Anne Harris	5a.	2a.		7a.
	William Stibull	4a.	2a.		6a.
	James Proctor		6a.		6a.
	Heirs of Katherine Collett	1a.	5a.		6a.
	Anne Dodson	3a.	3a.		6a.
	Joseph Richardson		6a.		6a.
	John Reed	2a.	3a.		5a.
	John Jordan, junior	3a.	2a.		5a.
	Mary King		5a.		5a.
	Samuel White	5a.			5a.
	Thomas Biddall of				
	Longstanton		5a.		5a.
	George Reed	4a.	1a.		5a.
	William Fromont		5a.		5a.
	Anne Read		4a.		4a.
	Edward White	1a.	3a.		4a.
	John Newman	1a.	3a.		4a.
	Heirs of John Proctor	4a.			4a.
	Anne Rule, widow		4a.		4a.
	Dingly Askham, junior		4a.		4a.
	Robert Reaper	2a.	2a.		4a.
	John Graves, junior	4a.			4a.
	John Rose	3a.			3a.
	Mark Fisher of Over	3a.			3a.
	Mark Benton	3a.			3a.
	William Clarke	3a.			3a.
	John Oakitt		3a.		3a.
	Thomas Carrington	1a.	2a.		3a.
	John Benton		3a.		3a.
	John Stibull	3a.			3a.
2 acres and	John Berry	1a.	1a.		2a.
under	Edward Chapman		2a.		2a.
	John Crispe	1a.	1a.		2a.

Range of size	Occupant	Freehold land	Copyhold land	Leasehold land	Total
2 acres and	George Lack	2a.			2a.
under	John Fue	1a. 3r.			1a. 3r.
	John Biddall		1a. 2r.		1a. 2r.
	Jane Rooke, widow	1a. 2r.			1a. 2r.
	William Fue, junior,				
	surgeon	1a.			1a.
	Henry Searle	1a.			1a.
	John Wiseman		3r.		3r.
	Mary Finkle		3r.		3r.
	The Lord, in hand				
	Heirs of Thomas				
	Fromont	2r.			2r.
	Keatch	2r.			2r.
	Thomas Lucas		2r.		2r.
	William Wiseman		2r.		2r.
	Sarah Fuller *alias*				
	Aspland		1r.		1r.
	Thomas Pauley		1r.		1r.
	Katherine Sampson		1r.		1r.
	Thomas Cranwell		1r.		1r.

Houses or cottages without any land

Guy Sindry
Dennis King
John Munsey
Gregory Newman
Tobias Norris
Henry Pyke
Joseph Thody
Mary Allen
Thomas Aspland of
  Isleham
Thomas Biddall of London
E. Berfoot and W. Clark
John Buttris
Richard Campes

Edward Clark
Jeremy Crispe
Thomas Duckins
Mark Fisher, son of
  William
John Graves of Oakington
Thomas and Anne Gleaves
William Harris
William Chinery
James Sault
Woodham
Sarah Croxon and
  Elizabeth Mason
Elizabeth Fue

Mathew Love
Anne Hunt
Rebecca Butler and Sarah
  Marshall
Unnamed tenant of
  Burne
Henry Markham
Thomas Munsey of
  Haddenham
Rectory
Matthew Boyden
Richard Fue
William Hamson of
  Haddenham
Elizabeth Graves

Totals

Houses with land (field survey)	67
Houses with no land (field survey)	36
Houses in the hands of those who already have one, presumably sublet (field survey)	29
Houses in town survey, but not in field survey	21
Total number of houses known for 1720s (only 107 of these have common rights)	153

Both the numbers and the proportion of the entirely landless had fallen, from fifty-four per cent in 1603 to thirty-two per cent in the 1720s. In the other villages investigated the rise in the proportion of the landless was one of the most marked phenomena. In Willingham, by contrast, the most striking change was undoubtedly the huge rise over the seventeenth century in both the numbers and proportion of the tenants who were more than cottagers, but still held less than a half-yardland, or between two and sixteen acres. Whereas these tenants made up twenty-one per cent of the community in 1575 and twenty per cent in 1603, in the 1720s they accounted for thirty-seven per cent of the inhabitants. The large farm did not develop in Willingham, therefore; the numbers of landless fell over the seventeenth century, whereas the numbers of those with smallholdings which would have been under subsistence level in the uplands rose steeply. The different economic development here is shown clearly in the analysis of the hearth tax records, which show both a lower proportion of people with one hearth and a much higher proportion of people with two hearths in this region of Cambridgeshire than elsewhere.[75]

Even though the numbers of the landless had fallen by the 1720s there had been a considerable increase in the numbers of people living in houses with no rights of common, from eighteen in 1603 to forty-six in the 1720s, or from fourteen to thirty per cent (see Tables 11 and 12). This figure of thirty per cent of Willingham householders living in cottages with no rights of common may, or may not, coincide with the thirty-two per cent who were landless by the 1720s, but this is impossible to tell. Some people lived in non-commonable houses, but held land, which gave them both something to live off and common rights, if it was as much as three or four acres. Others were tenants of one or even more houses, which gave them rights of common[76] but had no land. The technical situation in the 1720s was too involved to disentangle. It is certainly true that the increase in the number of cottagers without common rights meant that there had also been an increase in poverty and misery in Willingham over the seventeenth century. The size of the iceberg of the poverty-stricken, which represented the labourers, cottagers and sub-tenants without rights of common is even more difficult to estimate in the early eighteenth century than in 1603.[77] It was certainly much larger.

The breakdown of holdings in Willingham involved the fragmentation of three-quarters of the copyholds, and all but one of the freeholds, although in some cases the fragmentation consisted only in the original house belonging to the tenement being detached from it. Well over

[75] See above, maps 5 and 6.   [76] See above, pp. 130–1.   [77] See above, pp. 143–4.

TABLE 11 *Landholding in Willingham, 1575-1720s*
(Numbers of tenants)

Range of size		1575	1603	1720s
Over 90 acres		1	0	0
1 yardland to 90 acres		0	1	2
1 yardland (26–44 acres)		4	8	6
Half-yardland (16–25 acres)		28	20	20
2 acres to half-yardland		21	24	57
2 acres and under		8	5	20
Total tenants of land		62	58	105
With house *and* land in field surveys		53	54	67
Total houses in town surveys	at least	100*	125	153
Landless (assuming that all tenants of land occupy houses)	at least	38	67	48
Without common rights (there were only 107 commonable houses)		not knowable	18	46

* There is no town survey for 1575 and the field survey takes no account of non-commonable houses.

TABLE 12 *Landholding in Willingham, 1575-1720s*
(Percentages)

Range of size	1575	1603	1720s
Over 1 yardland	1	1	1
1 yardland	4	6	4
Half-yardland	28	16	13
2 acres to half-yardland	21	20	37
Total landed (over two acres)	54	43	55
2 acres and under	8	3	13
Landless	38	54	32
Total	100	100	100
Without common rights	not knowable	14	30

half the houses which had been connected with a particular holding
in 1575 had now lost the connection. The original twenty-eight half-
yardlands were divided up amongst no less than seventy-six tenants. It
had now become so common for one man to hold fragments of various
copyholds, bits of freehold, and an acre or two of ex-demesne land, and
perhaps even a small lease as well, that the distinction between copyholders and freeholders was no longer a meaningful one. The integrity
of the half-yardland holding was completely lost.

149

One indication of the break-up of the holdings was found in the stinting regulations of 1655[78] in which it was found necessary to lay down different stints for every three, or four, or five acres of 'odd lands' which a tenant held over and above a half-yardland, from those laid down for tenants who held three, or four, or five acres in all.

There was, in the 1720s, a continuous sequence of holdings of every size from one acre upwards, and the old medieval units could no longer be detected simply from their acreage. The rate of change was as noticeable on the freeholds as on the copyholds. It is therefore clear that legal factors had little or nothing to do with the situation. Indeed, the process of fragmentation is best illustrated by the disintegration of two freeholds. In 1575, George Crispe had held a full yardland of customary land, and over forty acres of free land. He divided this between his two sons.[79] In 1603, Henry Crispe was holding the free land and William Crispe the customary, both halves much increased in size by the addition of meadow and marsh. By the 1720s, the freehold was split amongst fourteen tenants. The freehold of the Buttris family was already disintegrating by 1603. John Buttris had held in all fourteen acres of the arable in 1575. William Buttris had some nine and a half acres of this in 1603, together with the appropriate allotment of meadow and marsh, but Henry Ellis, William Brasier and John Biswell had each acquired small pieces of the original holding ranging from one and a quarter acres to three and a half acres. By the time the holding was surveyed again in the 1720s, it was divided amongst ten tenants, none of whom held more than four acres and most of whom held under one and a half acres of it.

Even in this extraordinary state of flux, some holdings survived intact, although the acreage of the holding alone was no longer sufficient to indicate whether it was newly manufactured or an ancient unit. Eleven of the fifty-three holdings remained intact for the whole 150 years.

A quarter of both the copyholders and the freeholders in the 1720s retained some association with the land held in 1603 by an earlier member of the same family, although it might be only to occupy the house, or a single rood of land. Two holdings remained both intact and in the hands of the family which had farmed the land in 1575. Henry Ellis held a half-yardland of just under sixteen acres of arable in 1575. By 1603, Henry Ellis 'senior' was the tenant of the same holding, augmented by nearly another four acres of meadow and marsh. John Ellis, clerk, in the 1720s held the identical land his forefathers

[78] C.R.O., R59/14/5/9 (b), clauses 8 and 10. See also above, pp. 130–1.
[79] See below, pp. 160, 163.

had held, together with the same house. In the same way, John Graves in the 1720s held the same freehold which Robert Graves had held in 1603 and 1575. The Graves family seems to have been notably less peripatetic and more rooted in the ancestral land than its contemporaries. 'Jeffrey John' Graves was tenant of another copyhold tenement in the 1720s which had been in Graves's hands in 1575, intact but for the house. John Graves of Oakington had retained the house of yet another, although he had lost the land. Thomas Graves still had the same five and a half acres of a fragmented holding held by Henry Graves in 1603, which had apparently been built up from the half-acre held by Robert Graves of the same holding in 1575. The only other example of continuity of family holding in the village was provided by Mark Benton, who in the 1720s still held a part of the freehold land which had been in Matthew Benton's hands in 1575. Apart from these there were no other examples at all of the same family holding the same land right through from the late sixteenth century to the early eighteenth century. Some land may, of course, have passed in the female line, but the situation is reminiscent of nineteenth- and twentieth-century 'Ashworthy' where both mobility within a ten-mile radius of the parish and mobility from holding to holding was normal.[80] As one would expect, emigration in Willingham was most marked amongst the landless labourers holding houses alone,[81] but there certainly seems to have been no tradition of the 'family land' passing from father to son there, with the possible exceptions of the Ellis and Graves holdings.

CAUSES OF THE BREAKDOWN OF HOLDINGS

Since the rate at which holdings fragmented at Willingham was no faster in the five generations or so between the surveys of 1603 and the 1720s than in the generation between 1575 and 1603,[82] it seems reasonable to confine a detailed examination of the possible reasons for the breakdown of holdings to the earlier period only. This policy also has merit, because most of the unrest at Willingham followed the Sandys purchase of the manor, and so the effect of changes made by a new, innovating and greedy landlord should not affect the picture very much.

One possible reason for the breakdown of holdings at Willingham is, of course, the effect of bad harvests. The surveys of 1575 and 1603

[80] W. M. Williams, *A West Country Village, Ashworthy*, pp. 38–41, 53–83.
[81] See above, pp. 21–2.
[82] Thirty-nine out of fifty-three copyholds and freeholds unfragmented after twenty-eight years (1575–1603) is approximately equivalent to eleven out of fifty-three unsplit after 154 years (1575–late 1720s).

were well-timed to throw into relief any changes brought about by harvests because on the whole there were good harvests in the 1570s, but these were followed by severe crop failures in the last fifteen years of the century. The last years of the century, from the mid-1580s on, were in theory a time when 'the subsistence farmer, was reduced to misery, the middling farmer survived, and only the large farmer with a considerable surplus did well'.[83] It is relevant to know how far the existence of extensive fen common cushioned a community against the effects of bad harvest, or how far it was still basically dependent on its arable produce for foodstuffs.[84] It seems from the wills and inventories that a bad harvest would not hit the smallholders of Willingham really hard while they still had their dairy produce and, if need be, their meat, to fall back on. An analysis of the parish registers made on a yearly basis,[85] compared with annual harvest fluctuations, suggests that Willingham people were not vitally affected by bad harvests. There was one exception: deaths soared in 1596 to a peak unmatched since the beginning of the register. Baptisms fell to a new low level at the same time, and the combination of the two may well indicate that there was starvation in Willingham in this year, which was a year of dearth after two deficient harvests.[86] In 1596, the prices of barley and wheat were approximately forty per cent and thirty per cent higher than ever before, and in 1597 were still higher than ever before 1596, although the situation was not quite as bad. This was the year which saw the break-up of the few surviving half-yardlands at Chippenham.[87] It does seem possible that successive harvest failures did lead to deaths in this year at Willingham but, in general, the pattern of the harvests is not reflected in the pattern of births and deaths in the register. There was no echo of the bad or deficient harvests of 1586 or 1590 in the register; nor does the harvest of 1600, when barley prices were higher than any year except 1596, seem to have had any effect. It was a prolific year for the inhabitants of Willingham; baptisms were very high. There was a peak of deaths in 1613, which again came as the second of two successive deficient harvest years. The record number of sixty deaths in 1617 was in no way related to prices, which, for barley at least, were relatively low.

The registers suggest then that Willingham families were only put

---

[83] Thirsk, *Agrarian History*, IV, 228.
[84] For the relatively steady movement of livestock prices compared with grain, see *ibid.* pp. 628–9.
[85] Harvest year.
[86] See Appendix 2, where I have used C. J. Harrison's designations ('Grain Price Analysis') again.
[87] See above, pp. 82–4.

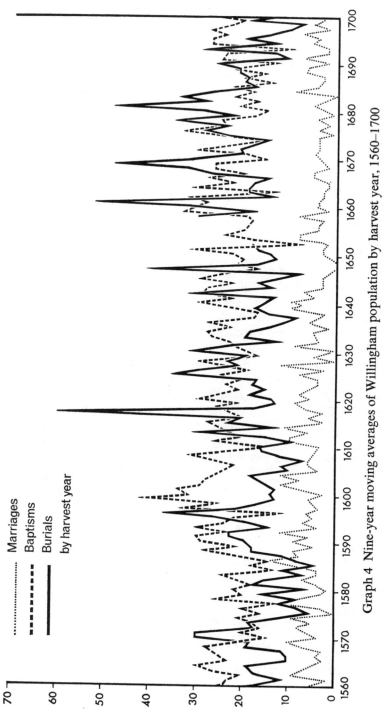

Marriages ....
Baptisms - - - - - -
Burials ————
by harvest year

Graph 4 Nine-year moving averages of Willingham population by harvest year, 1560–1700

in jeopardy by bad harvests when there was a run of two or three, and they had perhaps eaten both seed corn and spare stock. In general their resources of stock saw them through bad years.

An analysis of the transactions in the court rolls from 1575 to 1603 leads to this same conclusion (see Graph 5). Willingham, people were not generally driven to split their holdings by bad harvests, and there is no watertight correlation between bad harvest years and abnormally large numbers of transactions in the courts. Again, the court roll evidence is unsatisfactory.[88] Although Willingham was larger than Chippenham, and therefore more business naturally went through the manor court,[89] there were normally only about four transactions a year, including a couple of sales. A year in which there were more than six transactions in all, or more than three sales, stands out as a peak year. It is impossible to base much of an argument on figures of this order.

Insofar as it is possible to use them at all, the figures suggest that bad harvests did not generally determine the date of land transactions in Willingham. There was sometimes an apparent correlation. The deficient harvest of 1590 did coincide with eight court transactions, and the terrible year of 1596 was marked by four sales. The bad harvest of 1586 had no immediate effect, but there were six transactions, which may have been related, in the court the following year. The deficient harvests of 1575[90] and 1600 were not reflected in the proceedings of the manor court at all. The manor court, on the other hand, was comparatively very busy in years when prices were not high, like the average years of 1577 and 1582, and the abundant year of 1584. Moreover, all the busy years in the Willingham courts fell before 1590, with the

[88] C.R.O., L1/118 (1547–1602). The next roll does not begin until 1623. The roll gives the impression of being generally reliable, but it is incomplete. Most of the descents of the copyholds listed in the survey of 1575 can be traced through the roll to the tenants listed in the survey of 1603. There are omissions of 'large' holdings, like the half-yardland held by Henry Jordan in 1575 which had been surrendered to George Frogg by 1590. The transaction did not appear in the rolls. The descent of only five of the twenty-eight half-yardlands is incomplete. The descent of some of the smaller holdings either did not appear, or was too complex to follow. A disproportionate amount of space was given up to the doings of cottagers and tenants of fragments of land, who often could not be found in the 1575 survey. This may be evidence for the reliability of the rolls rather than the surveys. It of course fits into the evidence that landless men were far more mobile members of the population than others (see above, p. 22). On the other hand, the rolls were certainly untrustworthy guides to the exact dating of some events (which does throw more doubt on the validity of comparing court transactions with harvest years). Some deaths were reported twice, like that of George Crispe, 'who died since the last court' both in 1577 and 1578. Worse still, Simon Lamb appeared, in two admittedly ambiguous entries, to die both in 1591 and 1602. There was some confusion over the dates of sales as well.

[88] See above, p. 77.

[90] This appears as average in the C. J. Harrison classification, but no data for barley are included.

154

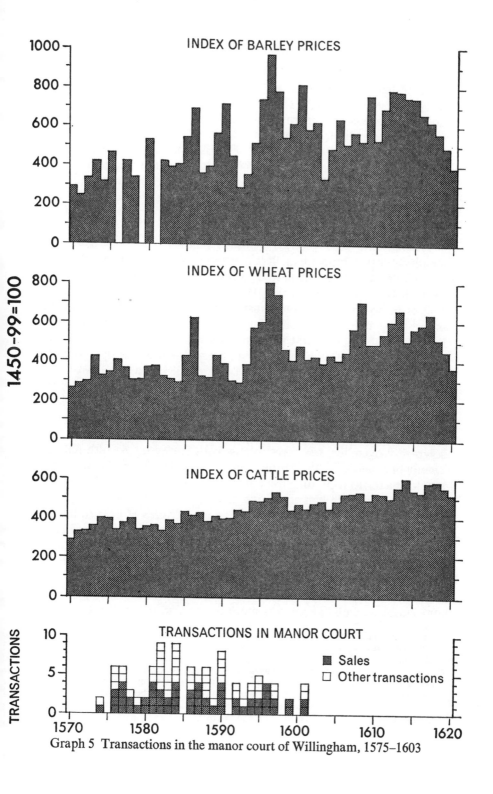

Graph 5 Transactions in the manor court of Willingham, 1575–1603

exception of 1596, although the last decade of the century saw more years of dearth and high prices than the 1580s and was one of the worst decades of the century.[91] The degree of coincidence is in no way convincing, whereas in general, peaks of sales and general transactions at Chippenham did follow bad harvests.[92]

A small group of inventories of Willingham men which survives from between 1660 and 1700 largely bears out the impressions given by the wills of 1575 to 1603, on the way in which men with much smaller holdings than in the uplands could make a better living in Willingham than they could in the uplands.[93] Only forty-four of these inventories were available.

Whereas the nine yeomen whose inventories survived from seventeenth-century Chippenham left a median of £299, and yeomen from the whole county a median of £180, the eleven men described as yeomen by their neighbours in Willingham left a median of only £48. This is in no way surprising considering the relative size of their holdings.[94] The existence of the fen common may have made smaller holdings viable, but it did not lead to great wealth. Only two Willingham yeomen were as prosperous as the yeomen of Chippenham. One was Henry Aspland, appraised at £407 in 1681, the other was Walter Crispe, whose stock and goods were valued at £267 in 1670. He must have been a descendant of George Crispe, yeoman, who had the largest holding in Willingham in 1575.[95] Walter Crispe had thirty-nine and a half acres of arable in all, eight and a half of wheat and meslin already sown in November, ten acres to sow with barley in the tilth field, and twenty-one acres in the 'broke' field. Together with the fallow this would make up a holding very like the fifty-nine acres held by Henry Crispe in 1603. He had the crops of twenty-five acres of barley, seven acres of wheat and meslin, and six and a half acres of peas in his barn, which were valued at £75. He also had a bull, twelve cows and calves, and four bullocks worth £25. His thirty-five loads of hay and fodder in the yard were worth another £12. His was a bigger herd of cattle than any Chippenham yeoman had. There were 105 cheeses in his dairy. He had half a dozen horses worth another £25, and twenty-six sheep and lambs as well. There was more diversification on Walter Crispe's

[91] Harrison, *ibid.*
[92] Compare Graph 3 and Graph 5.
[93] See above, pp. 135ff.   [94] See above, pp. 134–7, 139–40.
[95] See above, pp. 134 and 150. It seems very likely that he was the tenant of the customary half of George Crispe's holding which had passed to his second son, William, and in turn to his eldest son, William, in 1624, since the freehold part of the holding was so subdivided by the end of the seventeenth century that it is difficult to believe that it still contained this acreage in 1670.

farm, which would have been a relatively small one in Chippenham even by the beginning of the sixteenth century, than on any Chippenham farm in the seventeenth century. There was another Crispe inventory amongst those for Willingham, that of George Crispe, who was also described as a 'yeoman'. He was probably given this title by his appraisers because of his family status rather than his prosperity, unless he was a retired man, for his worldly goods were assessed at £24 in all. He had no land or crops in stock at all, although he had a mare, four cows, five sheep and a parcel of 'hay, straw, and stuff' in the yard. He also had eighteen skips of bees in the bee-yard which was an unusual addition.

Apart from Henry Aspland and Walter Crispe, only one other yeoman, Thomas Halliwell, held more than a half-yardland. He was appraised at £145 in 1678. Three men appraised, two yeomen and a ropemaker, had holdings of a size to correspond to the standard half-yardlands. The two yeomen were appraised at £128 and £76.

William Fisher, who had four acres and one rood sown in the wheat or tilth field and the same in the broke field, must have had a dozen acres with his fallow. Eight other men had sown acreages of from one acre three roods up to ten acres, and must clearly represent the occupations and way of life of the farmers of the increasing numbers of small-holdings of between two and sixteen acres who formed thirty-seven per cent of all the Willingham tenants by the early eighteenth century.[96] Only one such man was described as a husbandman but three of them were called yeomen, whilst two of them were weavers and another was a ropemaker. At least fifteen of the men who were appraised in the late seventeenth century at Willingham were landless. They included not only five labourers, as might have been expected, but also two yeomen, as well as a miller, a carpenter, a shoemaker and two victuallers. Social status and indeed economic status no longer depended entirely on land. One of the more prosperous men in the inventories was John Brasier, a fisherman, who held only two roods of land, but left goods worth £84. The inventories bear out the impression that by-employments were becoming extremely important in Willingham. Nearly a third of the inventories were of craftsmen, who left a median wealth of £55. Unlike the yeomen, they were generally more prosperous than their counterparts in Chippenham,[97] or elsewhere in Cambridgeshire,[98] because some of them held up to a half-yardland as well as the

[96] See above, Table 12.
[97] Median wealth £25 of five represented in Chippenham, £40 in Cambridgeshire in the 1660s.
[98] The median wealth of the fifty-five craftsmen whose inventories survive in the Consistory Court for the 1660s is £40. See above, p. 39.

proceeds of their trades, and all but one of them, landless or not, ran cattle on the fen, and were therefore presumably commoners, or sub-tenants of rights of common.

Willingham, then, developed differently from the other villages. The large farm never emerged as the dominant unit, and the numbers of the entirely landless fell rather than rose, whilst holdings in general got smaller and smaller. This difference cannot have been accounted for by types of land tenure. There were freehold tenants in Willingham, but their holdings were as liable to disintegrate as any others.[99] It is obvious that freehold tenure made no difference to the individual tenant's ability or desire to hold on to his land. The forces which made for fragmentation at Willingham were not related to incidents of tenure. Nor were they related to a rise in rents forcing gradual sales upon the tenants. Copyhold rents did not rise between 1575 and the 1720s. Admittedly, entry fines may well have risen,[100] since only a handful of the copyholders were specifically stated to hold by fine certain in the eighteenth century. Their holdings were however no more immune from fragmentation than the freeholds.

Willingham was of course peculiar in another respect. Far from there being any attempt to enlarge the demesne, a step which included, as it did at Chippenham and Orwell, buying out the tenants and amal-gamating their holdings, the collapse of the Sandys fortunes threw their demesne lands on to the market to enlarge the tenants' holdings, and compensated to some extent for the rise in the numbers of the latter. But this in itself does not explain why the economic factors which made for the growth of large farms did not operate in Willingham, since seigneurial enterprise consolidated, rather than initiated, the work of the engrosser at Chippenham and Orwell. Theoretically, the Willing-ham tenants with over fifty acres should have been as well placed to profit from the distress of their neighbours as their brethren in Chippenham and Orwell. In fact, distress only seems to have squeezed the smaller tenants into parting with small pieces of their holdings. It may well be that this was so because the resources of the fen common enabled them to live on smaller and smaller holdings. Men in an upland area in a similar set of circumstances had nothing to fall back on. Professor Goubert found the same distinction between the northern,

---

[99] See above, pp. 137 and 150.

[100] There were not enough entry fines noted in the court rolls, at least between 1575 and 1603, to be sure of this. Sandys' Chancery suits (P.R.O., C3/324/37, for instance), show that he was trying to raise fines, and the signs used by the eighteenth-century surveyor to indicate tenure by fine certain show that it was then, at least, uncommon.

corn-growing Beauvaisis, with its sharp social pyramid, and the southern pastures and woods of the Beauvaisis, where such social distinctions were not so sharp, and manual workers were not only a little less poor, but also far less numerous, and rarely a majority in their village.[101]

INHERITANCE CUSTOMS

Another of the possible causes of the breakdown of holdings over the period is of course inheritance customs. If fathers with more than one son divided their holdings more readily between their heirs in Willingham than in Chippenham or Orwell, one explanation of the Willingham situation would be found.

Fifty-five wills survive made by men from Willingham between the surveys of 1575 and 1603.[102] Fifteen of these were the wills of craftsmen, or of men who seemed to be without any interest in either land or a holding. This was a surprisingly high proportion, and bore out the general impression that there was a large number of men who were either supporting themselves on by-industries, or who were subtenants in Willingham. Another seven wills were made by widows or spinsters. Only thirty-three wills were therefore relevant, since they were those of men with land, or at least a cottage, to leave. Only a dozen of the thirty-three men had more than one son to provide for at their deaths, and these twelve men behaved in exactly the same way as their counterparts in Chippenham and Orwell.[103] Only one of them, Robert Marshall, left his cottage outright to his eldest son, who was still to find cash sums to set up his brother and pay his sister's dower out of the holding. The others either divided their holdings between their sons, or attempted to keep the main holding intact but provide youngers sons with an acre or two or a cottage.

The smaller and more negligible the holding, the more likely the dying man was to divide it between his sons, like Matthew Ewsden, who split his lease between his wife and two eldest sons. John Phew had nothing but an interest in 'the great shoal called Axmeare' which he divided between his two sons. John Buttery had a free cottage which he left to one son when he came of age, and three acres which he left to the other.

The men who held a half-yardland all tried to keep the main holding intact. William Biddall handed his entire tenement to his son John,

---

[101] Goubert, 'The French Peasantry of the Seventeenth Century', pp. 149–50.
[102] Original wills only.
[103] See above, pp. 85–7, 105–8.

but he did divest himself of the two and a half acres of freehold which he had purchased, to establish a second son.[104] John Graves handed on his messuage and half-yardland to one of his sons in 1597, but the other two were established in cottages their father had purchased. The integrity of the holdings was maintained, but they were not built up, although the tenants of half-yardlands in Willingham were in a position to acquire land,[105] simply because these acquisitions went to provide for younger sons, and so to increase the number of smallholders. The prime example of a man who split his tenement between his two sons was of course George Crispe, who left all but three acres of his yard-land of copyhold to his son William, and his fifty-six acres of freehold to his elder son Henry.[106]

Since the main holdings were kept intact, at least in the few wills of half-yardlanders which survived, and since also the number of men leaving more than one son was so small, the tendency to divide holdings can hardly be treated as significant, or as the main cause of fragmenta-tion. Inheritance customs were no different in Willingham from Chip-penham or Orwell. Well-to-do fathers in all three villages tried to set up their younger sons with cottages or fragments of land. The only difference between the villages was that cottagers in Chippenham or Orwell were very much less likely to be able to live on their holdings than they were at Willingham. The well-meaning attempts made by families in these parishes to establish younger sons on the land therefore tended to weaken traditional holdings still further, and provided more opportunity for the engrosser to purchase small parcels of land in bad years. At Willingham, there may not have been very many fathers who had younger sons to establish, but when they did so the smallholdings they created for these purposes were much more likely to be viable economic units. It was more feasible to live on a fragment of land in the fens. Therefore the same tendency of fathers to try and establish younger sons on the land probably had a more lasting effect at Willing-ham than at either Chippenham or Orwell, where it was a positive incentive to the engrossers. It probably encouraged an increase in population in Willingham, at least until the commons were stinted.

This rise in population and immigration from outside indicated by the surveys was almost certainly the other principal reason why the available land was divided into smaller and smaller fragments. The resources of the fen, which made it possible to live off much smaller holdings than the uplands, meant that the normal policy followed by the landholding fathers of Willingham of providing, when they could, cottages and an acre or two for their sons probably encouraged this

[104] See above, p. 140.   [105] See above, pp. 137–40.   [106] See above, p. 150.

tendency; and this was so until the 1650s at least. On the other hand, another factor must have been involved in the breakdown of the half-yardlands. If there were twenty-eight half-yardlands in Willingham in the thirteenth century, and these were maintained as recognisable units until the end of the sixteenth century, there must have been some new reason why these tenurial units which had remained intact for over 300 years disappeared in the seventeenth century. It seems very probable that the bishop of Ely, as manorial lord, had taken good care to maintain his holdings intact even though many of them may well have been sub-tenanted.[107] Fragmentation may well have been the result of the way the Sandys family lost control of their tenants soon after purchasing the manor.

A rise in population, which was perhaps associated with the loss of control by the lord of the manor, seems therefore to have been the principal factor responsible for Willingham's individual pattern of development over the seventeenth century. The pattern of development in which the number of small farms increased over the seventeenth century may in fact have been typical of settlements in fen regions, although it looks highly idiosyncratic, compared with the other upland villages surveyed here. The average size of fenland farms at the beginning of the seventeenth century was very much smaller in the fenland in Lincolnshire, where it has been investigated properly, than in a normal arable region. The vast majority of holdings was certainly under twenty acres and indeed under ten acres. The pattern of land distribution in the fen village, was, and remained, completely different from the pattern of land distribution in upland villages, and the emergence of the large farm as a unit was confined to the latter.[108]

PROVISION FOR WOMEN

The wills of Willingham give a strong impression, which would have to be confirmed by detailed work on the registers, that the demographic structure of the community was very different from that of Chippenham and Orwell.[109] This impression was given partly by the half-dozen landed

[107] The Ely Coucher Book gives the total number of holdings and lays down that each half-yardlander shall come with 'as many men as he has working for him' at harvest time.

[108] Joan Thirsk, *Fenland Farming in the Sixteenth Century*, Leicester Occasional Paper 3 (Leicester 1953), pp. 39–41, particularly Tables 4 and 5.

[109] Since this was written, a family reconstitution of Willingham, by Miss G. Reynolds, has shown that mortality among both children and adults was higher there than in any other community so far studied by the Cambridge Group except Gainsborough. Life expectancy at birth was probably under thirty years. (Personal communication from Dr Wrigley.)

161

men who died childless, or hopefully leaving their tenements, like Henry Graves in 1585, to their widows, and then to 'my child, be it man or woman, if it please god she be with any'. It was strengthened by the fact that of the thirty-seven men who left widows between 1575 and 1603, half also left children who were usually considerably under age. This was so much the case that the widow of a landed man in Willingham was very rarely left a room, a small acreage, and board with her inheriting son, as she normally was at Orwell. Nor was she usually left the holding for life, as she was at Chippenham if she had young children. The norm for a widow of a man with land and young children at Willingham was to be left the copyhold or freehold for the term of years until the eldest son came of age. Often, this was a very considerable time, varying from twenty-one years when the child was unborn, down from seventeen, sixteen, fourteen, twelve to six years. Very frequently no provision was made for the widow after that. William Fromant a labourer who died in 1591, left his wife his cottage and half-acre of land 'for life, viz. for sixteen years' which is perhaps a significant statement, revealing that men did not expect their widows to live long after seeing their children reach adulthood. Alternatively, the remarriage of the widow must have been assumed, as it certainly was by Richard Biddall,[110] who left his land to be supervised by his brother for his infant son, and wrote 'whosoever shall marry my wife hereafter shall be bound by two sureties before the marriage is solemnized to perform my will'. In a time when the population was rising, and there was immigration from outside, a woman left a holding for a lengthy term of years might well expect to remarry. The interest these women had in the land must have provided one more means of making a living to the landless man.

On the very fragmentary evidence of the wills, it does not seem as if men were dying leaving young families because they married much later in Willingham than elsewhere. Half a dozen men died leaving sons already married with children of their own, as William Biddall did.[111] Marriage in Willingham did not in any case have to wait until the family tenement became available on the death of the father. Examples of men who came into court and surrendered holdings to their sons are not uncommon in the court rolls. Half-yardlanders like John Brasier and Thomas Cranwell 'retired' in this way, and so did men like William Jordon and Robert Marshall, who held only a messuage and its appurtenances. Arrangements like this might be made principally to safeguard the inheritance of the holding, but it seems likely that they also gave the sons some rights at least. On commonsense grounds, early

[110] See above, p. 140.   [111] See above, p. 140.

marriage should have been more feasible in a place where a cottage, common rights and a boat could guarantee some kind of living. It looks, therefore as if Willingham men may well have died younger than their contemporaries in the uplands, and that the proximity of the fens did not lead to longevity, whatever other advantages it gave.[112] Early death, rather than late marriage, would account for the numbers of young families left in their mother's keeping.

There were of course exceptions to the rule that the widow was left the holding only until the majority of her eldest son. A handful of men leaving young children did make some provision for their wives after the children's majority, assuming neither her death nor her remarriage. They were usually more prosperous men, like the half-yardlander, John Ellis, who had a free cottage to leave his wife in addition to the main holding, even though she was to hold the latter for twelve years until her son could inherit. Willingham men more commonly left their widows a separate cottage. George Crispe's two sons were three and a half, and one and a half, according to the court rolls, when their father died. They were not to inherit their father's land for eighteen years. His wife Clemency was to hold his land during the nonage of the boys, unless it seemed good to his executors to take it in hand, but if she lived until her eldest son was twenty-one, she was to have 'the little house next to my dwellinghouse, and so to depart out of my dwellinghouse'. Such separations were, apparently, not thought of in either Chippenham or Orwell. She, in fact, remarried a month after the baptism and death of the posthumous child she was carrying.

Robert Salmon, a landless man with a cottage, had an only unmarried daughter of age. He made specific provisions for a separate shack to be built for his wife, with its own fireplace, if domestic tensions mounted. The daughter was to inherit, but Robert left

Rose, my wife, a bedroom in my kitchen with the easement of the fire there ... and if my said wife Rose and Agnes Salmon my daughter cannot agree for the kitchen then I will my said daughter ... at (her) costs and charges shall build her a little house on the backside of the kitchen with a Chimney in it. And if so, my said wife shall depart from the kitchen into the little house before mentioned.

This recognition of the possibility of domestic tension between the generations, and the provision of solitary housing for the widow was found only in Willingham, not in Orwell or Chippenham, although as

[112] One alternative, of course, is that on the whole men with land only made wills if their children were under age; but it is strange, if so, that it was not generally so, and that, for instance, more men with land at Orwell whose children were of age did make wills.

Mr Laslett's analyses of censuses show, it was also found elsewhere in the seventeenth and early eighteenth centuries, and was the main alternative to living in the household of a married son or daughter.[113] William Brasier, who left a half-yardland in 1589, gave his widow house-room in his son's house, but also provided an annuity to give her separate accommodation if this did not work in practice. He laid down that she should be head of the house until his son married, but he further made quite sure that the comparatively rare situation which did occur, according to the census return for Cogenhoe in 1624, Clayworth in 1688 and Lichfield and Stoke-on-Trent in 1695 and 1701, when a widowed parent remained head of a household including a married son, did not happen in his own son's house. His specifications for the avoidance of trouble were unusually full. He left his wife the back chamber next to the malt-house for life, with access to the kitchen fire, but provided that if his son and his wife

cannot agree together in the house, she is to be paid £3 a year for life ... also, if she shall remain in the house with him, I will that my executor shall find her meat and drink sufficiently ... (and) ... permit and suffer my wife quietly and peaceably to enjoy the dwelling in my house at her will and pleasure during her life without any check or taunt and that she shall be ruler and have the government of my house in all things *until my executor shall marry*.[114]

Yet accommodation in the house of a married son was also a normal provision for a widow, so both the main alternative forms of looking after the elderly were found in Willingham – William Biddall left his wife Cecily house-room.[115] So did Henry Angwood, a smith who was the only landless man to make permanent provision for his wife. His only daughter was married, and was left the residue, but Henry Angwood wrote,

my true intent is that my daughter and her husband Pyttes ... shall ... faithfully nourish and maintain my said wife with the sufficient meat and drink and clothing and lodging with all other things necessary and meet for her for the full term of her natural life.

The full range of alternative types of provision for widows which the censuses show were commonly made were therefore to be found in Willingham.

[113] See above, pp. 115–16.
[114] My italics.   [115] See above, p. 140.

General Conclusions to Part One

In a fen parish the resources of stock farming and dairying made it economically feasible for small holdings to survive. Therefore, when manorial control slackened in the seventeenth century, conventional medieval tenements which had maintained their integrity for centuries fragmented and there was a great increase in the number of tenants with small, but viable, holdings of between two and sixteen acres.

The arable acreage was not in any case important here; nor was it comparable with those in the uplands. The tenant of a half-yardland of fifteen acres of meadow and marsh, was, in Willingham, a wealthy yeoman. It was not the acreage of arable but the possession of fen-commons and the stock which went with them, which mattered. The existence of the fens and their grazing rights meant that bequests of fragments of land to younger sons here seem often to have established a new family in the village. Similar bequests which were made to younger sons in Orwell and Chippenham by fathers who nominally also practised impartible inheritance could not usually establish a family. In the fens younger sons could remain and still make a living from their fragments of land, without weakening the main holding, as elsewhere, below a point at which it was no longer a viable unit. In addition, the influx of people from outside who had been displaced elsewhere was probably greater than the small number of men who left such villages. The marked expansion of fen settlements in the sixteenth and seventeenth centuries therefore becomes much more comprehensible.

On the other hand in upland areas, which were primarily arable, the 'typical' medieval holding was no longer a viable economic unit in the price rise of the sixteenth century, as the 200-acre farm is no longer a viable unit today. In two parishes, the engrossing movement and the 'disappearance of the small landowner', have been shown to be phenomena which were accelerated in the late sixteenth and early seventeenth centuries. In one of these, it was possible to show with precision that the last half-yardland unit disappeared in exactly those years of dearth when prices were the highest so far recorded. The general rise in

165

TABLE 13   *Landholding on the chalk and in the fen*
            (Numbers)

Customary acreage of arable	Chippenham		Willingham	
	1544	1712	1575	1720s
250 acres and over	0	3	0	0
90–250 acres	2	4	1	0
74–84 acres*	3	0	0	1
52–68 acres*	5	2	0	1
1½ yardlands	5	0	0	0
1 yardland	6	0	4	6
half-yardland	6	1	28	20
Under half-yardland	4	3	21	57
Total (over 2 acres)	31	13	54	85
2 acres and under	14	5	8	20
Landless households	21	31	at least 38	48
Total tenants	66	49	at least 100	153

* These acreages corresponded to five, and four half-yardlands respectively at Chippenham.

population was probably responsible insofar as it was the motor of the sixteenth-century price rise. The immediate causes were bad harvests, causing sharp annual rises in prices, which forced the farmer of fifteen or thirty arable acres to sell, since his marketable surplus was too small to meet his outgoings. These bad harvests were in turn probably partly caused by the general climatic deterioration of the later sixteenth century, which by a combination of shorter and wetter summers made bad harvests more common. Population movements in the actual parishes surveyed did not seem to be immediately relevant to the state of landholding, and what really mattered was probably the overall number of mouths to feed which affected prices in the whole regional marketing area.

Inheritance customs had little bearing on this movement towards larger farms, except insofar as the common practice of trying to provide the younger son or sons either with a cottage and a couple of acres, or a cash sum, out of the proceeds of the main holding made the latter even more vulnerable. So also did the custom of providing bed and board for life, or even a life interest, for the widow.

Every village studied in depth presents finally more problems than it solves. If the documents are analysed in great detail, it becomes painfully apparent that surveys contain holdings which do not appear in court rolls, that court rolls contain transactions between tenants who

TABLE 14   *Landholding on the chalk and in the fen*
           (Percentages)

Customary acreage of arable	Chippenham		Willingham	
	1544	1712	1575	1720s
250 acres and over	0	6	0	0
90–250 acres	3	8	1	0
74–84 acres	5	0	0 ⎫	
52–68 acres	7	4	0 ⎬	1
1½ yardlands	7	0	0 ⎭	0
1 yardland	9	0	4	4
Half-yardland	9	2	28	13
Under half-yardland	6	6	21	37
Total (over 2 acres)	46	26	54	55
2 acres and under, and landless	53	74	46	45
Total tenants	99	100	100	100

are unnamed, and should be named, in surveys, and that parish registers contain data which do not harmonise with either. Each source in turn throws doubt on another. Only the wills, once they have been carefully analysed, give a feeling both of reliability so far as they go, and also some kind of elementary image of the men who are only statistics in the surveys, rolls and registers. The wills do not, of course, set out to give the kind of total cross-section of a community which the surveys do, and they are therefore inadequate. However, the impressions gained from reading them are so strong that all the work done on obtaining an apparently 'complete' analysis from more adequate documents begins to seem merely a painful exercise in futility. Until one has more adequately translated the statistics into human terms, it seems that despite all the care one takes, the human beings have slipped between the meshes of the net, and that one has not yet begun to understand the real situation, which must have been so immediately apparent to the most illiterate peasant in every one of the alehouses of the villages concerned.

PART 2

The Schooling of the Peasantry

6

A general view of schools and schoolmasters

If we turn from the economic setting in which a village community lived, to attempt the much more difficult task of gaining some impression of the importance which religion and doctrinal thought had within such a community, we are at once faced with the question of the degree of education available to men and women below gentle status. It seems necessary to establish this before moving on to the fragmentary evidence which bears on belief at village level. If the man behind the plough could read, he was at once exposed to the propagandist religious literature which was pouring off the printing presses in the sixteenth century. He was no longer totally influenced by the opinions of his parish priest or minister, who, in turn, was no doubt influenced and controlled by the patron of his benefice. Instead, if a rudimentary education was available to the village, and if he had any leisure, he at once became free, or at least freer, of the whole world of religious dispute and conviction which made up so much of sixteenth- and seventeenth-century life and politics.

Here again, though, there is an economic link. The growth of a demand for education demands prosperity, which can enable families to spare children from the labour force. Great emphasis has been placed on the increasing prosperity of the farming classes during the sixteenth century, and the expression of this in a higher standard of living, shown in the proliferation of domestic offices in farmhouses. From Harrison's description of the novelty of pewter, feather beds, and chimneys in ordinary houses in the 1580s, to Hoskins's 'Great Rebuilding' and illustrations of the revolution in the size of houses of the yeomanry, it is the material effects of this new prosperity that have called for comment.[1] It is surely worth examining, though, the degree to which these economic changes freed sections of rural society to acquire new aptitudes, to become literate, and so to formulate attitudes

[1] William Harrison, 'An Historical Description of the Islande of Britayne' in Raphael Holinshed, *The Firste Volume of the Chronicles of England, Scotlande and Irelande* (1577). W. G. Hoskins, 'The Rebuilding of Rural England, 1570–1640', *Past and Present*, 4 (November 1953), reprinted in *Provincial England* (London 1965), pp. 131–48.

and opinions, and participate at the parish level in the reformation of the sixteenth century and the 'further reformation' of the seventeenth century.

Any lecturer to adult education classes in rural areas today has probably met the middle-aged members of farming families who were forced to leave school at fourteen after the end of the Second World War, not for any lack of ability, but because of the desperate shortage of farm labour. In the sixteenth and early seventeenth centuries, on the other hand, farm labourers were desperately seeking employment. Only yeomen farming sixty acres or more were in a position to employ servants or labourers regularly.[2] Since the thickly populated arable counties of eastern England probably still had numerically far more farmers of medium-sized holdings of thirty acres or less than yeomen holding substantial acreages, it seems likely that the children in these rural areas had little chance of much education, even if there were schools for them to go to.

The disadvantages of the ordinary village child, constantly reclaimed by mother or father to help with brewing, bird-scaring, hoeing, haying, and all the crises of the agricultural year, are vividly portrayed in a description of a Suffolk national school between 1860 and 1880. In the village of Blaxhall the farmers complained before a royal commission in 1880 that the loss of the school children's labour had affected their farming adversely, since they were unable to pay men's wages for the work the children were accustomed to do.[3] One boy, whose father was a miller with a smallholding in the fens near Ramsey, described his schooldays in the mid-1870s:

Attendance at the school warn't compulsory,[4] and all the summer months the older boys ... had to stop at home and go a-weeding or some such work in the fields ... I often wished my father were a bit more like other boys' fathers, as a good many o' my associates never looked inside the school. Arter I were about nine year old, I got real ashamed o' going to school when other folks went to work. One morning some men were working in a field as I passed on my way to school, and I 'eard one on 'em say 'Look at that bloody grut ol' bor still a-going to school. Oughta be getting 'is own living.'

After this, he hid in the ditches on his way to school to escape being noticed. He left at twelve.[5] It is admittedly dangerous to infer anything about seventeenth-century social conditions from those of the nineteenth century, but it is very difficult to believe that the village child of

[2] Thirsk, *Agrarian History*, IV, 652, 661.
[3] George Ewart Evans, *Ask the Fellows who cut the Hay* (London 1956), pp. 62, 172–6.
[4] For those children who lived more than two miles from the school.
[5] Sybil Marshall, *Fenland Chronicle* (Cambridge 1967), pp. 17, 21.

two centuries earlier can have been a great deal better off than his counterpart after the education act of 1870.

It is probable, therefore, that the children of labourers and farmers of holdings of only average size would have had little prospect of acquiring even a rudimentary education in the sixteenth and seventeenth centuries, even if provision existed for it. It thus suggests that any improvement in educational standards among classes below the gentry consisted in the emergence of a class of yeomen who were able to spare their children from the exigencies of the daily grind of keeping alive to acquire the inessential fripperies of education. Latimer's famous observation on the importance of the yeoman class in providing personnel for the Church was soundly based on the economic facts of life. In areas of arable farming like southern Cambridgeshire, where the size of farms was increasing during the period and the numbers of the yeomen growing, one would also expect a growing demand for education and an improvement in educational standards, although it might be confined to a small part of the population. Conversely, an area of small farmers like the fenland is likely to have had fewer literate-children. Literacy, or rather illiteracy, rates should, in fact, vary from area to area and to some extent follow differences in types of farming, and therefore in social structure. At the present moment, however, even this simple hypothesis remains unproven.

Much has recently been made of the 'educational revolution' of the late sixteenth and early seventeeth centuries.[6] The evidence for this is based, of course, on the intake of the universities and the functions and number of the grammar schools capable of producing such students, not on the extent to which the ordinary villager was taught to read and write, for the simple reason that the grammar schools and their products are easier to trace. There were two great periods of expansion in the universities, when the numbers of students rose steeply, one beginning in 1560 and reaching a peak in the mid-1580s, and the next beginning in 1604, after a lull, and reaching its peak in the mid-1630s.[7] During the latter, it has been very roughly estimated that two and a half per cent of the group of young men aged seventeen were going on to higher education.[8] The social composition of these university students has been exhaustively examined,[9] but more interest has been

---

[6] Lawrence Stone, 'The Educational Revolution in England 1560–1640', *Past and Present*, 28 (1964), pp. 41–80.
[7] *Ibid.* pp. 50–1 and Graph 1, facing p. 49.   [8] *Ibid.* pp. 57 and 68.
[9] By *ibid.* pp. 57–68, and by Joan Simon, 'The Social Origins of Cambridge Students, 1603–1640', *Past and Present*, 26 (1963), pp. 58–67. David Cressy corrects some of the figures cited by Mrs Simon in 'The Social Composition of Caius College, Cambridge 1580–1640', *Past and Present*, 47 (1970) pp. 113–15.

aroused in measuring the participation of the gentry and the professional middle classes than in measuring the participation of the sons of farmers and their servants, who as yeomen, husbandmen and labourers made up the bulk of the population. In a sense, an estimate of the proportion of the peasants' sons who went on to higher education is much less important than the much more difficult question of the extent of basic literacy amongst the mass of villagers. It is relevant, however, for the attainment of a university education can be used as one of the chief yardsticks of educational opportunity amongst the peasantry, and of the possibility of social advancement open to them.

Unfortunately, it is not possible to reach any conclusions about the numbers of university entrants originating from the families of yeomen, husbandmen, village craftsmen, or even smaller fry until the university matriculation registers and the college admission books begin to give the occupation of the entrant's father or, at the very least, to describe him as of an armigerous, gentle, clerical, or 'plebeian' family. Forty-seven per cent of matriculands at Oxford between 1575 and 1639 described their parentage as 'plebeian'. It is impossible to judge the proportion of these who came from a rural and agricultural background: 'plebeian' included sons of merchants, professional men, and artisans, as well as yeomen and labourers, and in fact covered every social group except sons of the new or old gentry, the nobility, or the clergy. In the same way, the admissions registers at Caius College, Cambridge,[10] which are the only printed Cambridge registers which give the parentage of incoming students in the sixteenth century, initially describe the fathers of a large proportion of the entry as 'mediocris fortunae'. The term apparently covered sons of the clergy and the professional and trading classes, as well as artisans and small farmers. The admission registers of St John's open in 1630.[11] In the peak decade of the 1630s when the Caius register becomes more precise in its terminology, twenty-five per cent of the intake were described as yeomen, farmers, husbandmen, plebeians, or 'mediocris fortunae'. At St John's, in the same decade, 117 men or 24 per cent came from the same background. In the 1690s after the end of the educational boom, the proportion of the intake from these social groups was reduced to fifteen per cent at St John's.[12] Men from rural backgrounds could make up as much as a quarter of the intake in some colleges during the educational

---

[10] *Admissions to Gonville and Caius, 1558–1678*, ed. J. and S. C. Venn (London 1887).
[11] *Admissions to the College of St. John . . .*, ed. J. E. B. Mayor and R. F. Scott (Cambridge 1882–1931).
[12] The whole of the foregoing passage is based on Stone, *art. cit.* pp. 64–6, with figures for the Caius intake corrected by Cressy, *art. cit.* p. 114.

boom of the 1630s.[13] Young men from rural, peasant, backgrounds certainly had the opportunity of a university education in the late sixteenth and early seventeenth centuries. Even if the quarter of the entrants at Caius and St John's who came from the peasantry represent a typical proportion in the university as a whole, we must remember that the section of society that they represented was, of course, much greater. Still, the opportunity existed, however rarely it was taken up.

There is a further general argument which suggests that some of the sons of the peasantry were able to benefit from a university education in the sixteenth and seventeenth centuries. It seems to be generally accepted, although exact proof is impossible, that the bulk of the parochial clergy, holding benefices with incomes which in many cases were totally incapable of supporting the incumbent in a way of life in any way superior to that of the bulk of his parishioners,[14] were men of humble origin.[15] At the same time, the evidence shows that the proportion of graduate clergy rose steeply. Only a fifth of the clergy instituted or beneficed in the diocese of Canterbury under Archbishop Bourghchier between 1454 and 1486 were graduates.[16] Between 1570 and 1580, 73 per cent of the men instituted to Ely livings were graduates, or had some university training.[17] Between 1660 and 1714, the proportion of university men instituted and beneficed in the diocese of Worcester was as high as 84 per cent. The largest group of Worcester clergy were of 'plebeian' origin.[18] If we make the

[13] For lack of more precise, and earlier, records, it is impossible to judge whether the farming classes were benefiting to a greater or lesser extent from the earlier educational boom of the 1580s, let alone trace the rise and fall of their prosperity measured in educational terms. Harrison's general remarks on the prosperity of yeomen in the 1580s suggests that they would then have been sending their sons to university as well as putting glass in their windows and adding brewhouses to their kitchens.

[14] P. Heath, *The English Parish Clergy on the eve of the Reformation* (London 1969), p. 173, shows that three-quarters of the parochial livings in England were probably worth less than £15.

[15] Christopher Hill, *Economic Problems of the Church* (Oxford 1956), pp. 208–9. Heath, *English Parish Clergy*, p. 137, supports this view, and cites the rare fifteenth-century example of John Pyndere, a bondman of Terrington in Norfolk, who was manumitted to take orders, and was parochial chaplain of Willingham in Cambridgeshire in 1462.

[16] This evidence, drawn from the register printed by the Canterbury and York Society, ed. F. R. H. Du Boulay, vol. 44 (Oxford 1957), p. xxix, is summarised with other evidence on the literacy of the clergy by Heath, *English Parish Clergy*, pp. 81ff.

[17] Felicity Heal, 'The Parish Clergy and the Reformation in the Diocese of Ely', *Proc. Cambs. Ant. Soc.* LXVI (1977), p. 159. Hill, *Economic Problems of the Church*, p. 207, gives figures showing a sharp rise in the number of graduate clergy between 1540 and 1640 in the diocese of Oxford.

[18] P. Morgan, 'The Subscription Books of the Diocese of Worcester and Class Structure under the Later Stuarts', unpublished Birmingham M.A. dissertation (1952), pp. 90–108, 111–39.

moderate assumption that the proportion of men of peasant origin entering the ministry remained the same during the sixteenth and seventeenth centuries (if this is wrong, it is more likely that the proportion rose than fell), then it is clear, since the proportion of the lesser clergy with degrees rose sharply, that a university education must have come more commonly within the reach of the farmer's son. General arguments suggest, then, that just as living standards improved amongst the yeomanry, so also did educational standards.

The hypothesis that different social structures produced different proportions of men free to take up educational advantages can, to some extent, be tested by examining the numbers of college entrants from the county of Cambridge and the Isle of Ely who were admitted to the colleges of Gonville and Caius and of St John's between 1558 and 1700. For if it is valid, the numbers of college entrants ought to be directly related to the number of families in an economic position to dispense with their sons' labour. Therefore, if there were numerically fewer yeomen in this situation in the Isle than in the county, the numbers of college entrants should reflect the situation.

The county and the Isle were strongly differentiated economically. The county was almost predominantly a barley-growing region. It remained arable, and almost unaffected by enclosure, throughout the period. In 1524–5, fifty-three per cent of those taxed in the great subsidy in southern Cambridgeshire were wage-labourers or servants earning 30s or less a year.[19] This is a much higher proportion than in those other countries, Leicestershire, Lincolnshire and Devon, studied in detail so far,[20] and is obviously related to the exclusively corn-growing nature of the Cambridgeshire economy, which demanded a very large labour force. All the available evidence goes to show, moreover, that during the sixteenth and seventeenth centuries a great deal of engrossing took place. Cambridgeshire society was further polarised socially. The number of yeomen increased, and so also did the numbers of the landless, which were already high. Only the villages on the northern edge of the county bounding the edge of the fen, like Willingham, developed differently. They resembled the villages of the Isle of Ely, which had a totally different economy, based on stock-raising. There, there were large numbers of farmers with relatively small holdings, and both fewer labourers and fewer men with larger farms.[21] A man calling

---

19 See above, p. 33.
20 Averages of 22 per cent in Leicestershire: W. G. Hoskins, *Essays in Leicestershire History* (Liverpool 1950), p. 129; 36 per cent in Devon: Finberg and Hoskins, *Devonshire Studies*, p. 419; 28–41 per cent in different areas of Lincolnshire: Thirsk, *English Peasant Farming*, p. 83.
21 Thirsk, *Fenland Farming*, pp. 39–41. Dr Thirsk's work is based on the Lincolnshire fenland, but the farms in the Isle of Ely seem to have been very similar.

himself a yeoman held a far smaller acreage, and left fewer goods at his death in the fen-edge villages of southern Cambridgeshire and the Isle than he did in the county.[22]

Between 1558 and 1700, a total of 236 men who were born in the Isle of Ely and southern Cambridgeshire came up to Gonville and Caius, and St Johns.[23]

	College		
	Gonville and Caius	St John's	Total
Entrants from county			
Gent.	36	11	47
Clergy	10	10	20
Other	21	7	28
Total	— 67	— 28	— 95
Entrants from Isle of Ely			
Gent.	10	6	16
Clergy	–	3	3
Other	5	8	13
Unspecified	3	5	8
Total	— 18	— 22	— 40
City	71	30	101
Total	156	80	236

Forty-three per cent of these were from the city of Cambridge alone, and can be discounted for these purposes. Seventy per cent of the remainder were from the county of Cambridge, and only thirty per cent from the Isle of Ely.[24] Allowing for the very different populations of the county and the Isle,[25] it seems that there were seven men coming up from the county to every four men from the Isle. The chances of a man from the county coming up were nearly twice as great. Dividing

[22] See above, pp. 144ff. The median yeoman farm in the 1660s was 92 acres, and the median wealth of yeomen dying in southern Cambridgeshire in that decade was £180. There were very few examples of yeomen from the edge of the fens coming into this category. My evidence suggests that a fenland yeoman with between 29 and 40 acres of arable and his fen-common, was, very roughly, in the same situation as his upland counterpart.

[23] Excluding the considerable numbers of boys from outside, who came to finish their grammar-school education at Ely or one of the schools in Cambridge itself. The registers of Christ's College and Peterhouse, which also provide information on schools do not usually give information on parentage. See below, p. 183, n. 44. Some of the 'gentlemen' were not, in fact gentlemen but yeomen. See below, p. 178, n. 26.

[24] Including the City of Ely.

[25] 5,091 occupied households in the Isle in 1674. *V.C.H. Cambridgeshire and the Isle of Ely*, IV (London 1953), p. 273. 6,952 occupied households in the county in 1664. My figures above, p. 16, n. 47, amended to include the hundreds of Staplehoe and Cheveley.

the entrants up socially is a risky business; those whose father's status was described as 'gentleman' by Venn include men whose fathers are known to have been yeoman farmers, and the clergy included sons of people like the master of Peterhouse at one end of the spectrum and those from the humblest livings at the other. However, if the pitifully small numbers of entrants of rural parentage who did not claim to be of gentle or clerical background are considered alone, it still seems that the chances of a county man from the peasantry coming up to college were nearly half as great again as those of his counterpart from the Isle. Such minute figures must of course, be treated with great caution. Twenty-eight men of peasant stock from the county, and thirteen from the Isle, acquiring an education up to university level, over a period of 140 years can hardly be claimed as a great educational boom.[26] Further-more, conclusions based on two registers could be totally misleading. If the Isle schools had special connections with a college, or colleges, whose registers are unprinted or do not give parentage, and if they in fact sent up far more entrants, this picture could be totally reversed. Insofar as it goes, however, the evidence suggests that the different social structures of the Isle and southern Cambridgeshire did have a consider-able effect, and that the areas with an enlarging class of substantial yeo-men were more able to benefit educationally. But the evidence also suggests that few Cambridgeshire yeomen were able to take the final step in social aggrandisement of sending their sons to college, even though the numbers might be greatly expanded if more registers were

[26] Half of these (15) came up to Gonville and Caius before 1590, and all but one, who was specifically said to be the son of a husbandman, were described as sons of men 'mediocris fortunae'. The term covers many different types of parentage (see above, p. 174 and Simon, 'Social Origins of Cambridge Students, 1603–40', p. 60). I have assumed that these men were of peasant stock, because they originated in vil-lages where there was no cottage industry, apart from the normal number of crafts-men supplying the community with essentials. The major flaw in my argument is that they could have been the sons of clerics. However, I think this figure of twenty-eight is a minimum rather than a maximum one for the peasantry, despite the difficulty over the Gonville and Cauis terminology, because I suspect that gentle status was claimed whenever this was possible. Venn mistranslated the term 'ingenuus' as 'gentleman' whereas in fact Dr Cressy has shown it meant 'yeoman' ('Social Compo-sition of Caius College, Cambridge 1580–1640', pp. 113–15). Henry Crispe, son of a yeoman of Willingham (see below, p. 180), who came up to Caius in 1627, is a case in point. I have not tried to draw any deductions on the period when farmers found it most possible to educate their sons to university level, because of these difficulties in terminology. On the face of it, it seems significant that half the men I have assumed to be sons of peasants came up before 1590, when the economic difficulties at the turn of the century began to loom, especially since only one of the registers supplies information for ths earlier period, and that is one from a college which later appeared to have a bias towards the gentry. I think it likely, however, that there were a good many Henry Crispes amongst those described as gentlemen's sons in the seventeenth century, and that therefore no conclusions can be drawn.

178

printed.[27] There are odd examples of men of peasant stock whose careers were so notable that they can be picked out without the aid of printed registers. John Richardson was born in Linton in about 1564, and went up to Clare. He became regius professor of divinity in 1607, and was one of the translators of the Authorized Version.[28] His father died in 1616, and 'John Richardson, Dr. of Divinity', was duly admitted to his lands as his son and heir. When his successor inherited in turn in 1626, the copyhold amounted to only about fifteen acres, so John Richardson seems to have been born of relatively very humble stock.[29] Yet it was not as humble as that of John Bunyan, who is the most outstanding seventeenth-century Puritan figure with a village background. He seems to have come from a declining yeoman family. His father held a cottage and nine acres, and eked out a living by tinkering. Yet, in his own words 'notwithstanding the meanness . . . of my Parents, it pleased God to put it into their Hearts to put me to School, to learn both to read and write'.[30]

The type of family which could normally afford to spare a son for college is exemplified by the histories of the Butler family of Orwell, in the uplands, and the Crispe family of Willingham in the fens. Both stood out as exceptional in their own villages.

Nicholas Johnson *alias* Butler of Orwell, who died in 1601, and who was described by his neighbours as a yeoman, was able to send his eldest son, Thomas, who was born in 1570, up to Gray's Inn. The inns of court are usually regarded as the most socially exclusive of the establishments for higher education. One of Thomas's younger brothers was literate and able to write a letter and address it to 'his loveing Brother Thomas Butler att his Chambers in Gray's Inn'. A second brother was able to write his name when he witnessed Thomas's will.[31]

Thomas put his legal education to good use. He acquired a lease of a large part of the Orwell demesne, and then brought a suit against some of his fellow tenants, when his actions eventually brought him into dislike.[32] He sent his eldest son, Neville, first to school at the Perse in

---

[27] The registers of Sidney Sussex contain details of parentage, for instance. Again, this judgement could be totally reversed, if many of the county schools happened to have affiliations with other colleges than Caius and St John's. Examination of entrants from other counties needs to be made, but can only be made by people aware of the social and economic structures concerned.

[28] J. and J. A. Venn, *Alumni Cantabrigienses* (Cambridge 1922–54), III, 452.

[29] C.R.O., Linton Court Minutes, R49/5/1, entries for 1616, 1625 and 1626.

[30] Roger Sharrock, *John Bunyan* (London 1968; first edn, 1954), pp. 9, 11–12. See also below, pp. 209–10.   [31] P.C.C., Wills, 18 Savile.

[32] All the details of the Butler family, except those on the size of their holdings, are taken from the depositions in this suit, P.R.O., E134, 3 Jas. I/East. 18 and a reconstruction of the family from the parish registers, *The Register of the Parish of Orwell, Cambs. 1560–1653*, ed. R. W. Whiston (Sedburgh 1912). See also Appendix 1.

Cambridge, and then to Christ's College in 1623, when he was fourteen. By the time Thomas died, in 1622, he was known as a 'gentleman'. He left his son all his books. His widow held ninety acres of copyhold arable in 1628 during the minority of her son, over and above an unknown amount of freehold and demesne leasehold.[33] Neville Butler sent his eldest son away to grammar school in Hertford, before he went up to Christ's in his turn in 1649. By the time his fourth son, John, was educable, there was a 'schola publica' in Orwell which prepared him for Christ's in 1661. John eventually became rector of Wallington. When Neville Butler died, after marrying an heiress, and buying the lands of the priory of Barnwell, one of the clauses in his will left £2 to his 'good friend' Mr John Noon of Clare Hall to preach at his funeral.[34] The Butlers had made the transition, both economically and in taste, from the yeomanry to the gentry.

George Crispe was the only man in Willingham, which lay on the edge of the fens, whose farm was comparable in size with those of yeomen in the upland part of southern Cambridgeshire. He held seventy-five acres of arable, both freehold and copyhold, in 1575, and stood head and shoulders above the other tenants. The most prosperous of them held under forty acres. George split his holding between his two sons, leaving the fifty-six acres of freehold to his son Henry and a full yardland of thirty-six acres of copyhold to William.[35] Even so, Henry Crispe still held the most considerable farm in Willingham in 1603. It was his son, another Henry Crispe, who went up to Gonville and Caius in 1627, who was described in the college register as the son of a 'gentleman'. For all that, when either his brother or his cousin, both of whom were unfortunately christened William, got into an altercation with a youth from a gentle family in the Isle of Ely in 1639, and told him that he was 'a better gentleman', the gentle family was so piqued by this language from what they described as 'an ordinary country fellowe' that they took the case to the court of Chivalry.[36] The Crispes had obviously not made the grade to gentility, in local eyes.

During the rest of the seventeenth century, the whole of the tenurial history of Willingham is one of the breakdown of holdings into smaller

[33] C.R.O., L1/1/130, pp. 73ff.   [34] P.C.C., Wills, 1675, fo. 42.
[35] See above, pp. 134, 150, 163.
[36] Case referred to by George Squibb, *The High Court of Chivalry* (Oxford 1959), pp. 175 and 209. I am indebted to my husband for this reference. I am also deeply obliged to Mr Francis Steer, Archivist to His Grace the Duke of Norfolk who made a special journey to Arundel and sent me a transcript of William Crispe's submission to the court (Arundel Castle MS, E.M.134), and notes on two other newly discovered documents in the suit (Arundel Castle MSS, E.M.3154 and 3155). It is most unfortunate that the documents cited by Mr Squibb, including the plaintiff's petition, cannot at present be found at the College of Arms.

and smaller units. It is no wonder that after 1627, despite the well-established school in Willingham,[37] no other Willingham boys, so far as is known, went up to college.

Illustrations of individual families who were able to afford university education do nothing, however, to illuminate the related, and in many ways much more important, question of the degree of literacy amongst the mass of villagers who could not hope to free their sons from farm labour for schooling which would lead to a university course. At the moment, the main statistical evidence bearing on literacy in the countryside is that a proportion ranging from seventeen to thirty-eight per cent of the signatories to the protestation oath of 1642 in each parish were able to sign their names.[38] In Essex, the ability to sign varied from twenty to seventy per cent over the county.[39]

This whole question of literacy is at present being examined by the Cambridge Group for the History of Population and Social Structure. When the work of the Group is completed, those interested in the quality of life lived in local communities will have as accurate a picture as it is possible to obtain of the extent of literacy at this level, measured solely in terms of the ability to sign one's name. The limitations of such a criterion are self-evident. It is impossible to gauge exactly the relationship between the ability to write one's own name and the ability to read, which is the real subject of inquiry for those who want to know how far the ordinary villager was open to external influences and pressures.[40] Furthermore, the two main classes of documents surviving from before 1700 which bear enough signatures to be analysed in this way are the depositions in ecclesiastical cases and the original wills. The former were signed by witnesses, who were necessarily chosen quite arbitrarily and came from every social group. The latter, which are more likely to be available for any particular community, have the considerable disadvantage that they were signed or marked by a man who was, more often than not, on his death-bed, judging by the rapidity with which the date of probate followed that of the will. He was probably therefore

---

[37] See below, pp. 192–5.

[38] Lawrence Stone, 'Literacy and Education in England 1640–1900', *Past and Present*, 42 (1969), pp. 100–1.

[39] Personal communication from Dr David Cressy.

[40] There seems to be a general impression that, although the relationship between the ability to sign and the ability to read is unknown, the two were related, and that reading ability very probably exceeded writing capacity. Discussed by Lawrence Stone, 'Literacy and Education', pp. 89, 98. V. E. Neuberg, 'Literacy in Eighteenth Century England: A Caveat', *Local Population Studies Magazine and Newsletter*, 2 (1969), p. 44, points out that eighteenth-century educationalists stressed that the teaching of reading was more important than that of writing, which did not necessarily follow it. At Orwell school, boys were taught to read and write, girls 'only' to read. See below, p. 203, n. 32.

much less able to make the effort to sign his name than usual,[41] and statistics drawn from the wills are suspect because of this. However, there is no better material available for the historian to work on.

Some insight both into the relationship between the abilities to write and to read and into the failing powers of testators is given in a dispute in 1578 concerning the will of Leonard Woolward of Balsham. He was a retired man who asked the young chirurgeon who was trying to give him some relief from pain in his last illness, to write his will for him.[42] He did this because he was living with his son and daughter-in-law, in the 'low chamber' off the hall, in his old age, and wanted his will made 'as pryvelye as mighte be', for he feared that if it were known to his son and his wife that he was going to leave some of his free land to someone other than them

he shoulde not be well tended & have that he woulde have, and if enye of his friends or acquintances . . . should write his sayd will, his sayd sonne yonge Lennard . . . woulde knowe of it, and soe laye on him that he shoulde not or coulde not make his wyll accordinge to his owne mynde.

He obviously felt that Balsham contained a number of 'friends and acquaintances' capable of writing his will, if he had not desired secrecy. His young doctor was in fact obliged to borrow 'pen, ynke and paper' from the house of John Allan of Balsham, who later witnessed the will, although he had not been present at its making. The implication is that as early as the 1570s there were in a village several members of the community who could write a document at need, even in a village like Balsham, where there were only isolated references to schoolmasters at work. Leonard Woolward himself had about twenty-four acres of free land, and so is likely to have been a fairly humble yeoman. The will was actually written on the day he died, although he could still sit up in bed. It was disputed by the family in the Consistory Court. In response to questioning, the young barber-surgeon replied:

That whether oulde Lenard Woolward in his lyef time coulde wrighte or noe this deponent knoweth not, for he saythe he never sawe him wryte, yet saythe that he hathe hard the sayd oulde Leonard saye that he cowlde wrighte, And further saythe that yf he the sayd oulde Leonard cowlde wrighte in his lyef tyme, yet that at the tyme of his will makeing, this deponent verelye belevethe that he cowlde not well write with ease or to his contentation, for that he was then verye oulde, & for that his sighte then fayled him muche, for this deponent saythe that ymediatelye after the wyll was wrytten he the sayd oulde Leonard toke the sayd will in his hand &

---

[41] See below, pp. 196–9.
[42] C.U.L., E.D.R., D2/11, fos. 259–61. I am deeply indebted to Mrs Dorothy Owen for drawing this particularly revealing case to my attention.

would have red it him selfe but sayd that his sighte was soe evell (excepte he had spectacles) that he coulde not reade it, & deliveringe it to this deponent desyred him to reade it, which he this deponent did accordinglye.

It is therefore perfectly evident that this old man was known to be able to read, and that the chirurgeon attending him was in no way surprised by this, although he was not entirely sure that he could write. Elsewhere in the chirurgeon's testimony, it appears that Leonard Woolward had an 'oulde parchment booke' in his house. On the very day of his death Leonard Woolward made an attempt to read the will written according to his directions, although he made no attempt to write. Reading was an easier skill.

In many ways it is premature to attempt to produce anything conclusive on literacy until the work of the Cambridge Group is complete. However, there are two ways in which it seems that this work can be supplemented. In the first place, bare statistics on literacy are in some ways uninformative unless they can be combined with information on the schools existing in the area from which they are taken. There is still a dearth of regional studies of schools,[43] particularly those which include full studies of elementary schools, since the latter involve working through all licences, visitations and subscriptions of schoolmasters in episcopal records.

In the second place, although the work of the Cambridge Group in examining literacy rates is irreplaceable, and cannot be done effectively on any small scale, there is still some advantage to be gained from examining literacy in a few communities which a local historian has already portrayed. There are obvious benefits in knowing something of the social structure of a community as well as the number of its inhabitants able to sign their names at a given date. I have therefore added an examination of literacy, based mainly on the testators' ability to sign their names to their wills, of three villages in Cambridgeshire between 1600 and 1700 to a survey of schools in the county.

CAMBRIDGESHIRE SCHOOLS AND SCHOOLMASTERS

The Ely diocesan records, for the period when references to schoolmasters abound, from 1574 to about 1628,[44] give a startlingly strong

---

[43] Like, for instance, Brian Simon's 'Leicestershire Schools, 1625–40', *British Journal of Educational Studies*, III (1954), 42–58; the survey of education in the diocese of Norwich in E. H. Carter, *The Norwich Subscription Books* (1937), pp. 81ff.; P. J. Wallis and W. E. Tate, 'A Register of Old Yorkshire Grammar Schools', *Researches and Studies*, XIII (University of Leeds 1956), 64–104, which confines itself to schools sending pupils to the universities.

[44] Elizabeth Key, 'Register of Schools and Schoolmasters in the Diocese of Ely, 1560–1700', *Proc. Camb. Ant. Soc.* (1980). I should like to thank Mrs Key very warmly for

impression that education was readily available in southern Cambridgeshire (see Map 11). There were twenty-three places where a school seems to have been kept more or less continuously during the sixty years.[45] Most of these were in the larger villages. The settlements on the fen-edge, which had had over a hundred households in 1563 (see Map 4) like Cottenham, Waterbeach, Bottisham and Fulbourn, had them. The larger villages in or near the Cam valley, like Great Shelford, Barrington, Sawston and Linton, which had accommodated over fifty households had them, and so also did the larger villages in the upper Rhee valley, like Melbourn and Bassingbourn. There is a remarkable degree of coincidence between the sites of these well-established schools and the sites of the present Cambridgeshire village colleges. At least eight of the present ten village colleges[46] lie where a school was well-established in the late sixteenth and early seventeenth centuries. The explanation lies either in the continued size of the village, which makes, and made, it a suitable settlement to provide enough work for a school, or in a combination of size and status. Market towns, like Linton, were obvious foci for schools, and were both easily accessible and much visited, so that they had a large catchment area. It is noticeable that the ancient market town of Bourn was the only settlement on the western clay plateau of Cambridgeshire to have a well-established school.

Apart from these twenty-three well-established schools, masters were continuously referred to in another nine villages either up to or after 1600. These villages also had scattered references in the later, or earlier, period, and they may well have had schools consistently for a much longer period. The records do not give the appearance of scrupulosity in licensing. A college entrant in 1589 who had been at school in Hauxton is a salutary reminder of the unreliability of the record. There is not

---

giving me unstinted access to this material, and information on it. Dr David Cressy, of Clare College, who has worked through all the visitation and licensing material of the diocese of Norwich, has very generously given me all the references he has found to teaching in the deanery of Fordham, which lies in the diocese of Norwich and the county of Cambridge. Map 11 is therefore based entirely on the work of Mrs Key and Dr Cressy.

[45] I have assumed continuity where there was a gap in the records for ten years or less. Records exist for the same man teaching for twelve years, like Mr John Jackson, vicar of Gamlingay, who was licensed from 1607 to 1619.

[46] Excluding Soham and Burwell village colleges, which lie in the deanery of Fordham in Norwich, for which there is little information. References to teaching were made for only four villages in the deanery in the entire seventeenth century. It may be significant that two of these were Soham and Burwell. Soham was endowed in the mid-seventeenth century. *V.C.H. Cambridgeshire and the Isle of Ely*, II (London 1948), 331–2.

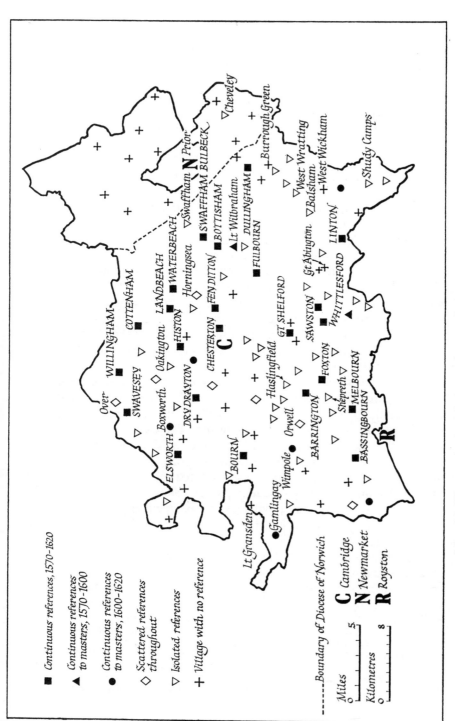

Map 11 The continuity of schools in Cambridgeshire, 1570–1620

a single mention of a master at Hauxton in either the sixteenth- or seventeenth-century documentary records.

Yet a third group of eight villages appeared in the records as having a schoolmaster both before and after 1600, and was referred to between four and six times altogether. In these villages, and those with even fewer references, it seems probable that individual masters rather than established schools were concerned. The high academic quality of many of these men[47] makes it seem very likely that they were the products of the bulge in university entrants in the period from the 1560s to the 1580s, and were reduced to searching for jobs wherever they could find them. The number of college entrants taught by men in villages which have no other record of a school gives the same impression that isolated individuals were often teachers in villages with no established school.[48] Detailed work on the careers of schoolmasters shows that many of them were very young men doing a short spell of teaching between graduation and getting a benefice elsewhere.[49] The spells for which they taught were therefore brief and there was little or no permanence. It is no wonder that endowment, even of a very humble kind, had the immediate effect of establishing a school, when there were so many graduates obviously seeking work which offered a steady income, however small.

Over is an example of one of these villages with a record of occasional teaching throughout the period 1574 to 1628. A master was licensed to teach young children there in 1583; in 1604 and 1607 Ezra Parkes was teaching there when the place was visited. The clerk who drew up the visitation book expected to find him there in 1610, but his name was crossed out, presumably because he had gone. By 1616, though, the vicar was schoolmaster there. These scattered references may well have indicated some continuity in teaching over a short period, and certainly did mean that the children in villages of this type had periods of several years when they could go to school at home, instead of walking to the nearest established school.

Finally, another forty-seven villages had up to three references to masters teaching in them between 1574 and 1628. Sometimes there was certainly a master in one of these villages for five or ten years; some-

---

[47] See below, p. 189.

[48] This confirms Professor Stone's impressions in 'Educational Revolution in England, 1560–1640', p. 46, that college entrants were often privately prepared in small hamlets. It is quite wrong to assume, as W. A. L. Vincent did in *The State and School Education, 1640–60, in England and Wales* (London 1950), that any village in which a college entrant was prepared automatically had a grammar school. His county lists are suspect for this reason.

[49] Elizabeth Key, 'Register of Schools and Schoolmasters in the Diocese of Ely, 1560–1700'. *Proc. Camb. Ant. Soc.* (1980).

186

times there was only a single reference. But in all, only twenty-two villages in the county had no schoolmaster licensed at any time between 1574 and 1628.[50] Most of them were very small.

The overall distribution of schools in the county shows that north of Cambridge the villages on the fen-edge both to the west and to the east were well provided with established schools, or schools where there was a fair degree of continuity. A child born here would rarely have to walk further than to the next village to acquire an education, if he could be spared from more pressing work. The river valleys and whole area south of Cambridge were also well provided for; again, a child would rarely have to walk further than the next village. The two exceptions to this abundant provision were the line of villages from Balsham out to Burrough Green, and the villages west of Cambridge on the clay plateau out to Bourn.[51] Most of these villages had schoolmasters licensed, or noted in visitations occasionally, but there was much less continuous schooling available here, and very often a child would be out of walking distance of a school.

This pattern of distribution fits very well with the economic differences between these areas of Cambridgeshire in the sixteenth and seventeenth centuries. The settlements on the fen-edge and in the valley area were expanding during the period, whereas those on the boulder clay to the west were shrinking. The villages on the chalk ridge were noticeably poorer than those in the rest of the county, judging from the much higher proportion of houses with only one hearth taxed there in the 1660s.[52]

It is important to know what type of education was available in these schools for the village child, but it is also difficult to establish this. The licences issued for schoolmasters between 1574 and 1604 sometimes simply gave permission to teach and instruct; but frequently the licence was issued for a specific function. These varied from 'to teach grammar', 'to teach the rudiments of gramar', 'to teach boys and adolescents to write, read and caste an accompte', 'to write and read the vulgar tongue' and 'to teach young children'. It looks, on the face of it, as though they were grammar and English schools, and that the latter were divided into the two types described by Professor Stone, petty schools teaching children to write and read, and those teaching English grammar, writing and arithmetic up to the age of sixteen.[53] Unfortunately, there is a great deal of inconsistency in the type of licence

[50] One of them was Little Gransden, see below, pp. 188–9.
[51] This scarcity of schools had a noticeable effect. There were fewer people on the clay plateau who could write their names (see below, p. 207, n. 7), Similar evidence does not exist for the chalk ridge.   [52] See above, pp. 22–3, 41–4.
[53] Stone, 'Educational Revolution in England, 1560–1640', pp. 42–4.

187

issued for the same village within relatively short passages of time. Licences not uncommonly specified the teaching of the 'vulgar tongue' or 'young children' at one visitation, and grammar at the next, or vice versa. Moreover, the college admissions registers gave evidence that boys were prepared in some villages in which, according to the episcopal records, there had never been a schoolmaster, or there was not a schoolmaster at the right time, or there was only a schoolmaster who taught the 'vulgar tongue'.[54] These suspicious contradictions make any attempt to establish a typology of local schools futile. For one thing, the definitions given in the episcopal records may not be reliable, for another, these small village schools probably changed in character remarkably quickly. Many existed over a brief period only, or for the working life of an individual teacher. Others, which apparently had no continuous history, may well have done so, and escaped episcopal notice. Castle Camps only had isolated references to a school. Despite this, Henry Reader, a husbandman, who deposed information against the 'ceremonious practices' of Nicholas Gray, minister of the parish, before Manchester's committee against scandalous ministers in 1643, partially begrudged them because his own refusal to comply forced him to move out of town 'beeing the means to deprive this deponent's children of the benefitt of the free school which there they enjoyed, to the great comfort of theire parents, being very ready and apt to learne'.[55] It is obvious that the records are only impressionistic, and the impression that they give is of flexibility and change.

The school held in Little Gransden should serve as a salutary reminder against too rigid definition. It escaped episcopal notice altogether, and Little Gransden was one of the few villages with no record of any teaching there. The existence of the school is known only because the tenants of Little Gransden fell out with the new lords of the manor in the early seventeenth century over the whereabouts of the demesne which they themselves had leased since the late fourteenth century. One of the witnesses in the consequent series of suits was an old gentleman settled in Lincolnshire, who deposed that he had known Little Gransden for sixty years 'for he was born in Great Gransden nearby and went to School in his youth in the chancel of Little Gransden'.[56] Another was Christopher Meade, gentleman, steward of the manor court, who likewise went to school in Little Gransden, and

---

[54] For a detailed list of schools which acted as 'grammar' or 'preparatory' schools in the county see my 'The Schooling of the Peasantry in Cambridgeshire, 1575–1700', *Land, Church and People*, ed. Joan Thirsk (Reading 1970), p. 127 n. 3.
[55] C.U.L., Palmer Papers, B/48, p. 16, being a transcript of B.M. Add. MS 5672.
[56] P.R.O., E134, 1649/East. I. He must have been to school in the late 1580s, according to his deposition.

therefore knew all the local gossip of the place.[57] He was responsible, in 1607, for searching the thirteenth-century episcopal surveys of Gransden and the medieval reeves' accounts, and tying these descriptions together with surviving earthworks to reconstruct the layout of the medieval demesne. This school at which Meade was trained, which did not even exist according to the diocesan records, evidently flourished in the 1570s and 1580s, and served as a preparatory school, at least, for the local gentry. It is impossible to believe either in the reliability of the records or in any interpretation of sixteenth-century local schooling which rests on a rigid typology of schools according to class. It is perfectly obvious that the children of Little Gransden who could be spared to go to school, including the children of the gentry, went along to the church chancel. How much they learnt there cannot be known. However, those who were later to go to university acquired an adequate foundation. And they all strengthened the common bonds of community which bound them, for, amongst other things, they talked about the rumour that houses had once stood in the Bury Close, and about the size of the yardland.

Although the schools may have changed rapidly in character between 1574 and 1604, the general quality of the masters teaching in them was extraordinarily high. Nearly two-thirds of the men licensed specifically to teach grammar are certainly known to have been graduates.[58] A number of the remainder may, of course, have graduated as well. Much more surprisingly, a third of the masters licensed merely 'to teach younge children to read write and caste accompte' were also graduates.[59] After 1604, however, when the licences stopped specifying the kind of teaching to be done, no generalisations can be made on the qualifications of teachers in different schools.

After 1628, until the Ely subscription books start in 1662, the only evidence available on schools is that provided by the college entrance books. Whereas a few villages had provided entrants in the earlier period (although nothing like as many as the grammar schools of Cambridge and Ely), no local school sent up an entrant in the boom years of the 1630s at all, while the schools of Cambridge and Bury St Edmunds became much more predominant. Local schools only really started sending up entrants again in any numbers in the 1660s. The period when college registers are helpful coincides with the period when the diocesan registers reopen.[60] Even after 1662, the references in the

[57] P.R.O., E134, 5 Jas. I/Hil. 26.
[59] Ten out of twenty-nine.   [58] Fifty-one out of eighty-one.
[60] Nine villages produced entrants for the colleges which have printed admissions books between 1660 and 1700. They were Orwell, 1661; West Wratting, 1666; Oakington (2 entrants), 1666; Bottisham, 1668; private school, Bourn, 1671;

records to schools are too scanty to give any real knowledge of the villages in the county which had schools functioning permanently. There is usually only one reference to a schoolmaster subscribing between 1662 and 1700; and the gap from the late 1620s is far too long to postulate continuity, although where there is a later reference to a school which had had a continuous record up to 1628, it is tempting to suspect it.

At least half the schools with continuous records between 1574 and 1628 reappeared at the end of the century. There was very little overlap between them and the places which sent up entrants to college. Again, it looks as if many of the latter were privately tutored by individual masters. However, Bottisham, which had had an early continuous record, and had been left a little bequest producing an income of a pound a year for teaching three poor children in 1639, managed to send a boy from the village up to college in 1668. Willingham, which was early endowed by public subscription, had masters who subscribed in 1666 and 1675, and an attorney from Cambridge sent his son there in the 1680s to be prepared for Eton. Endowments had an immediate effect. Dullingham had had a continuous record in the earlier period, but did not appear in the episcopal records of the 1660s. In 1678, Barradill Millicent left rents worth five pounds a year for teaching poor children in 'grammar and learning', and in 1679 a master subscribed, if only to teach writing and arithmetic. The most considerable endowment noted in the inquiry into charitable donations of the eighteenth century was at Haslingfield, where Simon Ertman left an income of twenty pounds a year in 1658. There had been scattered references to a master teaching there in the earlier part of the period, before 1628, but as a result of the Ertman endowment, masters from Haslingfield appeared five times in the episcopal records after 1662, more than from any other school.

The references in the subscription books are so thin that they can be used only as evidence of the existence of a school, not as evidence of its absence. It is not safe to suggest that no school existed where no schoolmaster subscribed. Therefore, although masters appeared in far fewer villages between 1662 and 1700 than between 1574 and 1628, it is impossible to say whether the ordinary village child had more or less chance of an education at the beginning or end of the seventeenth century. The only conclusion that can be drawn is that at the end of the century, as at the beginning, the areas best served by schoolmasters were the thickly settled edges of the fen north of Cambridge, and the

Shepreth 1671; private school, Swaffham Prior, 1678; Willingham, preparatory to Eton, 1685; Fordham, 1690.

valley of the Cam south of Cambridge. The western clay plateau and the poverty-stricken chalk uplands were still relatively unprovided for.

Even though schools seem so often to have been taught by young men before they obtained benefices elsewhere, it still seems true to say that, in the late sixteenth and early seventeenth centuries at least, the combination of the number of village schools in southern Cambridgeshire and the quality of the masters teaching in them should have given the Cambridgeshire peasantry ample, if erratic, opportunities for education. If their economic situation allowed them to benefit from their opportunities, then the literacy rates should have been fairly high.

7

The elementary ability to write: Willingham and Orwell

The communities I am concerned with were strongly contrasted socially. Willingham was a fen village, in which the economy was based largely on stock-raising rather than on the arable holdings. This economy produced a very different social structure from that of the uplands. In 1575, only one man held an arable acreage appropriate to a yeoman in the south of the county; the backbone of the community was formed by the holders of the twenty-eight half-yardlands. These men were only copyhold tenants of between thirteen and twenty-three acres of arable, but here, on the edge of the fen, they were men of substance, and in their wills they described themselves as yeomen. These wills give the impression of prosperity in the last quarter of the sixteenth century, at a time when the upland counterparts of such men were losing their holdings because they were unable to withstand the combined economic pressures of the price rise and frequent bad harvests. During the seventeenth century there was an influx of people into Willingham, and probably a rise in the resident population too, because the opportunities provided by the fen meant that it was possible to exist on a relatively small holding. The old half-yardland units, which had remained intact since the thirteenth century, broke down, and there was actually a diminution in the number of the landless and an increase in the number of tenants holding between two and fourteen acres, at a time when, in the uplands, the most noticeable movement was towards the polarisation of the size of holdings and an increase in the number of landless labourers.

Laurence Milford was the first schoolmaster known to have taught in Willingham. He was licensed to teach 'young children' in 1580.[1] He had obviously been living in Willingham before he was licensed there, for he acted as the regular scribe for the villagers' wills for the last thirty years of the century. He had no cottage when the place was surveyed in 1575, but must surely have been resident. In March 1578, John Loder of Willingham made a will which was written and witnessed by Laurence Milford, in which John left him the crops of one

[1] C.U.L., E.D.R., G/2/18.

'land' of meslin, one acre of wheat and 'my best hat'. In 1579, before he was officially licensed, Laurence Milford held a lease in Willingham.[2] When John Loder's brother, Robert, died in 1583, he left a pregnant wife, and specially provided in his will 'that if it be a man child that she go with all I will that she bring it up in learning til it comes to the age of sixteen years'.[3] He must have been thinking of Laurence Milford's school.

There was obviously some interest in education at Willingham, and in 1593 this bore remarkable fruit, for in that year the inhabitants endowed a school by public subscription.[4] The rector, Dr William Smyth, may well have been the initiator and driving force behind the foundation, for he seems to have been resident in Willingham for a considerable part of his incumbency from 1586 to 1601.[5] He had been a fellow of Kings before his appointment in 1586, and went on to be master of Clare in 1601. His name came high on the subscription list with a donation of one pound a year during his incumbency. Whether or not he was the initiator of the scheme, the really striking thing about it was the degree of support given by the villagers.[6] The 102 people who subscribed raised £102 7s 8d between them, and only five donations were of more than £2.[7] The core of the list was made up by the sixteen men who gave sums ranging from £1 up to and including £2, and the fourteen who gave £1 apiece. All the rest gave less than £1. Thirteen of the sixteen men who gave the largest sums were, or had been,[8] half-yardlanders. Another six of those who gave £1 were also half-yard-landers. Almost all the tenants of half-yardlands were represented

[2] P.R.O., E310/9/13. This reference is given in *Charity School to Village College*, produced by the Cottenham Village College Local History Group (1968), pp. 5–7, which discusses the early history of the Willingham school. The school has also been discussed by E. H. Hampson, *V.C.H. Cambs.*, II, 339.

[3] Robert Loder appears from his will to have held only a copyhold house and close, and one rood of free land. This is not the kind of holding one would suppose would keep a child at school until he reached the age of sixteen.

[4] C.R.O., P177/25/1, pp. 1–2. I am informed by Dr Roger Schofield that this subscription list is, so far as he knows, unique.

[5] Canon F. J. Bywaters, 'Historical notes', in *Willingham Parish Magazine*, January 1949.

[6] It is possible to identify a large number of the subscribers on the list of 1593 by using a combination of the surveys of 1575 and 1603, and abstracts of the court roll entries which give the descent of each holding between these two dates. Many of the tenants of 1593 can be identified with certainty by these means, and their wills give additional personal information.

[7] These were all made by people described as 'gentlemen' except for Anne Pearson, widow. I have been unable to identify any of them, except the lord of the manor of Burne. I have excluded his contribution, and the £1 a year given during the term of his incumbency by the rector.

[8] Two of them had, according to the rolls, surrendered their holdings in favour of their sons.

somewhere on the list, and almost all the larger sums given by villagers were given by them. This is the most concrete proof it is possible to have that the half-yardlanders of Willingham were indeed relatively prosperous. They could afford to give sums which amounted to more than two years' rent in most cases.[9] It is also proof they were sufficiently interested in education actually to dig into their pockets to give their children some chance of it. The half-yardlanders, although they were the most substantial villagers contributing, were not the only ones. Involvement in the plans for the school to the point of making a financial sacrifice on its behalf spread right down through Willingham society. There were examples of the younger sons of half-yardlanders, like Henry Bedall, who contributed 10s 2d, and held three and a half acres. There were also plenty of examples of cottagers like Matthew Ewsden, who had a lease to help provide a living for his five children,[10] and subscribed 4s, and of less fortunate landless cottagers like William Ridley, Simon Bissell and William Haynes who all contributed 8s or 10s.

It is impossible to gauge the motives of these men, but concern to provide some kind of education for their children was evidently uppermost. The school articles agreed by the inhabitants[11] laid down that only the children of men resident in Willingham should be taught in the school, and only if their families had made a contribution, with the notable exception that the children of the poor should be taught free. If a man either bought or rented a house or land in Willingham, his children were not to be eligible for instruction unless he made a contribution, if he was able to do so. Subscribers presumably made their gifts, therefore, specifically so that their children could go to school.

There is a certain amount of information which gives an indication of the number of these parents who desired education for their children, who were able to write their own names. Eighteen of the subscribers acted as witnesses to wills in the next decade or so.[12] Of these eighteen, only five, or just over a quarter, could sign their names. Naturally, however, the more prosperous men in Willingham acted as witnesses more often than their poorer neighbours. They are also easier to identify. Eight of the eighteen witnesses held a half-yardland, and they accounted for four of the five signatures.[13] One of them, William

---

[9] C.R.O., R59/14/8(b). The rents of half-yardlands varied between 14s 4d and 17s 10d, and were usually nearer the former.
[10] Will proved 1595. See above, pp. 141–2.   [11] C.R.O., P177/25/1, pp. 2–5.
[12] A mark or signature as a witness is a more reliable guide to the ability to sign than the mark or signature of a testator, which might so evidently be influenced by his illness or his physical weakness. See below, pp. 196–9.
[13] The fifth was a signature of a tenant of the sub-manor of Burne, who in fact held an acreage appropriate to a half-yardlander.

Ashman, may have even written a few wills on his own account. Half the half-yardlanders who witnessed wills, therefore, could sign their names. Not all the prosperous could sign their names, but on the other hand, all those who could do so were relatively prosperous. It is startlingly obvious that if only just over a quarter of the identifiable subscribers could sign, a very much lower proportion of the whole group of men who subscribed must have been able to do so, considering that the group contained a large number of unidentifiable, less substantial men. This lack of the elementary ability to sign amongst at least three-quarters, and probably more, of the subscribers to the school makes their desire that their children should acquire some elementary schooling even more poignant, considering the financial sacrifices that they were prepared to make to provide the opportunity.

Willingham school was upgraded in status when William Norton was licensed to teach grammar in 1596.[14] He remained there until 1607, and the seventeenth-century history of the school is as continuous as the records permit thereafter. It survived various vicissitudes in the eighteenth century, and functioned until its eventual closure by the Charity Commission in 1876.[15]

The vital question is how much difference the continuous existence of this subscription school, which had been set up by costly communal effort, made to the inhabitants. Unfortunately, this very question is almost impossible to answer. The education provided in the school was obviously an adequate one, or it could not have prepared Henry Crispe, son of a 'gentleman' of Willingham, for entry to Caius in 1627.[16] It is true that Richard Pearson, another son of a 'gentleman' of Willingham,[17] went to school in Huntingdon, rather than Willingham, for four years before going up to John's in 1658. Despite this, the place must have had some continuing merit at least as a preparatory school, or James Drake, attorney of Cambridge, would hardly have sent his son out from Cambridge itself to Willingham school before transferring him to Eton for the two years before his entry to Caius in 1685. The real interest lies less, however, in whether the school was fitted to prepare college entrants, than in how much it did to raise the standard of literacy of the more ordinary village families, who were not able to consider a university education for their sons.

There is, remarkably enough, some evidence which bears on this. In

---

[14] Laurence Milford remained in the village and continued to act as principal scribe for the villagers' wills until his death in 1604: Willingham Parish Register.

[15] *Charity School to Village College*, pp. 8–10, 50–1.   [16] See above, p. 180.

[17] I have been unable to find much material on the Pearson family. They were not considerable freeholders or copyholders in the 1575 or 1603 surveys; yet Anne Pearson, widow, gave £3 towards the school.

1677/8, an agreement on the management of the Willingham commons was signed or marked by ninety-five people.[18] No less than seventy of these wrote their names; seventy-four per cent of the commoners. This makes a really striking contrast with the situation at the end of the sixteenth century, when only a quarter, or twenty-five per cent, of the identifiable subscribers to the school could sign their names. Even if we take it for granted that every single non-commoning householder in Willingham was capable of writing his name,[19] nearly half of the heads of houses in Willingham must have still been able to do so.

A detailed examination of the scribes who actually wrote the wills which survive from Willingham shows that, although long series of them were written by the schoolmaster, Laurence Milford, a lessee of the sub-manor, or other local gentleman, or a tradesman, like Edward Negus, shopkeeper, who wrote most of them between 1661 and 1693, old Leonard Woolward of Balsham was right to feel he could have depended on 'friends and acquaintances' had he wanted them to write his will.[20] Four men from the Greaves family, who were half-yard-landers with twenty acres or so at the turn of the century, and therefore in this fenland village were substantial yeomen, wrote twenty-two wills between 1609 and 1647. Fifteen of them were by Thomas Greaves. Henry Halliwell, who was a representative of another family which held arable of between nine and twenty-two acres in 1603, wrote five wills between 1614 and 1619. John Pitts, who was described in his own will as a 'woolwinder' was responsible for three wills, and Henry Bissell, who was descended from the tenant of nine and a half acres in 1603, was responsible for two. Another six villagers wrote a single will apiece in the first part of the seventeenth century. There was a further series of six wills by Edward Allen, written between 1625 and 1630, and one series of fourteen by Robert Stocker made between 1631 and 1639. Neither family appears in the land survey of 1603, but both men wrote distinctly village hands. The school obviously produced a large number of fully literate villagers.

The other documentary material which shows the effect the school had is the ability of men, who were usually dying, to sign their wills, and this, as evidence, is fundamentally unsatisfactory. There are specific examples, apart from the detailed history of old Leonard Woolward,

---

[18] There were 107 houses with common rights in Willingham, but in 1603 several tenants had already acquired more than one.

[19] There were 150 houses, containing 159 taxable people, in Willingham, in 1666 (P.R.O., E179/244/22) and 150 houses, containing 152 taxable people, including the exempt, in Willingham in 1674 (P.R.O., E179/244/23). There were 153 tenants in the 1720s.

[20] See below, pp. 328–33, for a detailed study of the scribes writing wills in Willingham.

which show the obvious fact that a man's ability to sign his name deteriorated when he was on his death-bed.[21] Robert Caldecot, or Cawcot, of Willingham itself, was one such man.[22] He held between thirteen and fifteen acres of copyhold between 1575 and 1603, and subscribed 13s 4d to the school fund in 1593. In 1588, he witnessed a will, and was able to sign his name on it. In 1607, when he died, described as a 'yeoman', his staggering attempt at his initials was set down as a mark by the scribe, who wrote the will.

Orwell yields an even more striking example. Thomas Butler of Orwell had a first cousin, Nicholas Johnson.[23] Nicholas never left Orwell to acquire an education, as far as is known, but he was literate. He acted as rent collector for his cousin, and was able, in an Exchequer deposition, to identify the handwriting of Thomas Butler's brother, George. He was a churchwarden, and he acted as the scribe of some of the villagers' wills between 1614 and 1626. It was probably his nephew, another Nicholas Johnson, who frequently acted as a witness to wills with his second cousin, Neville Butler, Thomas's son. The contrast between the polished hand of one cousin, educated at the Perse and Christ's, and the rough village hand of the other, is a very illuminating one. Nevertheless, the younger Nicholas Johnson could write. When he died in 1648 he marked his will with an almost unrecognisable attempt at an 'N', though his cousin Neville witnessed it in his usual style.

Any estimate of ability to sign based on wills, therefore, presents absolute minimum figures of the proportion of the will-making population able to write their names; and it reflects the toughness of their constitutions, as well as their literary prowess. An analysis of signatures on the Willingham wills for the period 1600 to 1690 shows that fifteen per cent of the wills were signed.

It is a very great pity that hardly any will bear marks or signatures

[21] A further disadvantage is that very few people in any village communities discussed here made wills. In five villages, under two people per household assessed in the hearth tax made wills during the entire seventeenth century, including those proved in the Prerogative Court at Canterbury. If only the most prosperous, who were therefore more literate, tended to leave wills, the proportion of those unable to sign must in reality have been much higher.

[22] I am indebted to Miss Marie Rowlands for giving me a similar example which she found amongst the wills and inventories in the Lichfield Record Office. Samuel Freeman, an apothecary of Uttoxeter in Staffordshire, who must surely have been a fully literate man to practise his profession, marked his will, rather than signed it, in June 1696. On 5 July, a codicil was added, and whereas his mark on his main will approximated to rough letters, his mark on the codicil was a mere cross. On 15 July he was dead, and his inventory, as one would expect of a professional man, set a value on his books.

[23] See above, pp. 179–80.

Signatures of testators and witnesses, Willingham and Orwell

Robert Caldecot marks his own will in 1607

Robert Caldecot signs as witness to Anthony Haidon's will in 1588

Neville Butler and Nicholas Johnson sign as witnesses to
John Barton's will in 1637

Neville Butler, witness, and Nicholas Johnson mark Johnson's
own will in 1648

TABLE 15   *Testators signing and marking wills at Willingham*

	Yeomen and above		Husband-men		Labourers		Craftsmen		Women		No occupation given		Total	
	Sign	Mark	Sign	Mark	Sign	Mark	Sign	Mark	Sign	Mark	Sign	Mark	Sign	Mark
To 1600	0	1	0	0	0	0	0	0	0	0	0	1	0	2
1601– 1625	2	10	1	4	0	6	2	11	0	8	0	5	5	44
1626– 1650	4	4	2	19	0	10	2	9	0	7	0	4	8	53
1651– 1675	9	8	0	5	0	6	0	5	1	7	0	2	10	33
1676– 1700	6	16	0	5	0	3	2	5	0	7	0	3	8	39
Total to 1700	21	39	3	33	0	25	6	30	1	29	0	15	31	171

before 1600. As a result it is impossible to make any comparison of ability to sign before the endowment of the school and after it. However, one might expect some slight increase in the ability to sign amongst testators beginning in the 1620s and 1630s, if they had attended school in the 1590s. It does not seem to be there. The figures (shown in Table 15 above) give a slight impression of improvement in the second half of the seventeenth century, but this is too small to be statistically significant, and might be a mere chance.[24]

However disappointing the wills prove generally as a source of information on ability to sign, one inescapable conclusion emerges. At Willingham, yeomen were both better represented and far more able to sign their names than any other group. Over a third of the yeomen who made wills could do so. A sixth of the smaller group of will-making craftsmen could sign their names. A few husbandmen and one woman signed; no labourer could do so. Yeomen therefore stood out as a class persistently more able to afford an interest in education than any other, as commonsense suggests.[25]

It seems, therefore, that the school, even though it began with whole-hearted support and encouragement from the relatively rich and the relatively poor alike, and even though its rules laid down that the

[24] I should like to thank Dr R. S. Schofield for much general help and encouragement, as well as for detailed comment on these and similar figures.
[25] See above, pp. 171–3. Professor Stone shows that there was a very marked difference between the ability to sign of yeomen and husbandmen marrying by licence in the archdeaconry of Oxford and diocese of Gloucester in the seventeenth century. Between 71 and 72 per cent of yeomen, as against 43 to 52 per cent of husbandmen could sign: 'Literacy and Education in England, 1640–1900', p. 110.

children of the genuinely poor should be taught free, really benefited the sons of yeomen far more than any other class. The evidence of the commoners' signatures in 1677/8 supports this conclusion. The commoners were better-off than the community in general. They contained amongst their number a higher proportion of men with larger and more comfortable houses than their fellows. Only ten per cent of them had houses with a single hearth, against thirty-nine per cent of the villagers in general. Fifty-six per cent of those who could be identified in the hearth tax taken four years before, in 1673/4, had two hearths, against forty-one per cent of the villagers in general. Twenty-two per cent of them had three hearths, against only thirteen per cent of the whole village; and twelve per cent of them had houses containing four hearths or more, against only seven per cent of the whole village. These seem very arid and perhaps meaningless statements; but in fact, over the whole of Cambridgeshire, there was a strong correlation between the size of a man's house, judged on the number of hearths he was taxed on, and his wealth. The median wealth of men with one hearth was £24; that of a man with two hearths was £60; that of a man with three hearths was £141, and that of men with four hearths or more in their houses was £360. In any individual example, of course, the correlation might not prove correct; there are always exceptions. But in general the correlation was there.

The commoners who were unable to sign their names were either women or noticeably worse-off than their fellows. Just as women testators were noticeably illiterate as a group, so were women commoners. There were five of them, and only two could sign their names. Not a single identifiable one of the twenty-two men who were unable to sign their names lived in a house with three hearths or more. None of them, that is, was in the economic position of a yeoman, at least in the uplands. Literacy and prosperity were very strongly related. Henry Munsey, who lived in a house with only one hearth in 1674, and was able to sign his name as a commoner in 1677/8, was a highly exceptional man.

The community at Orwell was strongly contrasted with that of Willingham in many ways. A dependence on barley production and lack of common led it to near famine in 1612 and 1617, and the first thirty years of the seventeenth century saw a disappearance of many of the half-yardlands and yardlands, apparently under the same economic pressures as those at Chippenham,[26] although the evidence is not nearly so conclusive. The same years saw four or five prosperous yeomen families increasing their acreages, and the numbers of cottagers

---

[26] See above, pp. 66–70.

rising. Later in the century, the demesne farms were expanded, again at the expense of the farmers of traditionally sized holdings.

Orwell was, of course, much smaller than Willingham. In 1563 it was less than half the size, and in the 1660s it had fallen even further behind the expanding settlement in the fens as its own surplus population emigrated. The difference in the size of the two villages meant that Orwell had fewer yeoman families than Willingham, although they made up a slightly larger proportion of the village population.[27] Only the outstanding yeoman family in each village took what was perhaps the decisive step into the ranks of the gentry of sending a son up to university. The Butlers of Orwell seem to have started with more pretensions, and taken them further, than the Crispes of Willingham.[28] It is not surprising that no more than one family in each village considered university education as a possibility; the number of university entrants from rural backgrounds must have been directly related to the number of yeomen families in a position to make this sort of economic sacrifice. But if it is not too facile to suppose that the proportion of families who could free their sons to attend school should bear some relationship to the proportion of the people in the community who were later able to sign their wills at death, then the differing proportions of yeomen families in Willingham and Orwell should have made some difference to the basic literacy rates there. An examination of the Orwell wills, however, shows that the true position was not so simple.

The information given by the wills is frankly disappointing. It does nothing to prove this suggestion, and something to refute it. The number of wills surviving is really too small to show any changes over a period of time. The yeomen of Orwell shared the general inability to write the letters of the alphabet on their death-beds, and they did nothing to leaven the illiterate lump of their fellow villagers. Seventeen per cent of those who made wills at Orwell could sign, as against fifteen per cent at Willingham, but a much lower proportion of yeomen and a correspondingly higher proportion of husbandmen, signed at Orwell. Prosperity and elementary ability to write were therefore less clearly related at Orwell, where there was more economic polarisation of the community than at Willingham.[29]

[27] Orwell had four or five families with over 40 acres, insofar as one can judge on the basis of the copyholds alone. These accounted for 9 per cent to 12 per cent of tenants in 1602 and 1603, and the 1670s. Willingham had between five and eight families with over 25 acres, which I have suggested is roughly equivalent (see above, p. 177, n. 22). These accounted for 5 per cent or 6 per cent of the tenants in 1603 and in the 1720s. [28] See above, pp. 179–80.

[29] These figures are to some extent falsified by the fact that the most prosperous in the community tended to assume the aura of gentility, and get their wills proved in the Prerogative Court of Canterbury. The Butlers of Orwell did this, and so also did one

TABLE 16   *Status of testators signing and marking wills before 1700*

	Yeoman and above		Husband-men		Labourers		Craftsmen		Women		No occu-pation given		Total	
	Sign	Mark	Sign	Mark	Sign	Mark	Sign	Mark	Sign	Mark	Sign	Mark	Sign	Mark
Willing-ham	21	39	3	33	0	25	6	30	1	29	0	15	31	171
Orwell	3	13	3	15	0	5	2	6	2	10	1	6	11	55
Milton	6	9	1	9	0	6	0	4	1	4	2	6	10	38

TABLE 17   *Yeomen and other testators signing wills before 1700*

	Yeomen		Non-yeomen		All testators	
	Total no. of wills	% Signed	Total no. of wills	% Signed	Total no. of wills	% Signed
Willingham	60	35	142	7	202	15
Orwell	16	19	50	16	66	17
Milton	15	40	33	12	48	21
Total	91	33	225	10	316	16

If the proportion of those able to sign their names at death was approximately the same in Willingham and Orwell, it seems that the basic tenet that the number of smaller farmers in the fens should have led to a higher illiteracy rate is wrong, unless the wills which survive from Orwell are too small a selection to be representative.

Apart from the small numbers, part of the solution appears to lie in yet another major difference between the two villages: Willingham had a permanent school; Orwell did not. There were scattered referen-

or two Fairchilds, Godfreys, and other yeomen. It is fair to assume that a higher proportion of these men could sign their names than of those men whose wills were proved in the Consistory Court. The number of Orwell wills proved in the Consistory Court was so low that these Prerogative Court of Canterbury wills could make a considerable difference to the pattern. On the other hand wills of prosperous Willingham men, like Henry Crispe, also went to Canterbury. The proportion of wills in relation to the size of each community going to Canterbury was approximately the same over the seventeenth century, so it is unlikely that an analysis including all these Prerogative Court wills for both communities would be fundamentally different from one based on the Consistory Court wills alone. This conclusion is based on the *Prerogative Court of Canterbury Wills*, ed. J. C. C. Smith et al., IV–XII (London 1893–), covering wills proved in the Prerogative Court, 1584–1629, 1653–1660, 1671–1700; J. and G. Matthews, *Year Book of Probates from 1620–55*, I–VIII (London 1902–28), covering the years 1630–55; J. H. Morrison, *Prerogative Court of Canterbury: Wills, Sentences and Probate Acts, 1661–70* (London 1935). I have excluded the years 1653–60, when all wills were proved in the Prerogative Court in any case.

ces to a master teaching at Orwell from 1575 onwards, but they never amounted, in the episcopal records, to anything like Willingham's consistent record. Robert Clark was licensed to teach grammar there in 1587 after graduating from Queens' in 1583. There was a master there in 1590, and again in 1596. In 1609, William Barnard, the vicar, was teaching in Orwell. He may have done some sporadic teaching for some time, for he held the living until his death in 1644. He seems also to have acted as scribe for a number of the villagers' wills from 1615 to 1642.[30] However, no later visitation took notice of him as a teacher and, if he taught, it is obvious that his standard never came anywhere near that of the Willingham school. If it had done so, Thomas Butler would not have found it necessary to send his son Neville to the Perse in Cambridge before he went up to Christ's in 1624.[31] Nor would Neville Butler, in his turn, have sent his son away to school in Hertford before he went to college in 1649. Things must have changed considerably before 1661, for in that year Neville Butler's fourth son, John, went up to Christ's, after being prepared by 'Mr Griffen' at the 'schola publica' at Orwell. The school was still not permanently established,[32] but a Mr Wright was there in 1665 and John Lowe, 'schoolmaster', was buried in Orwell in 1689. It looks as if more schooling may have been available at Orwell in the second half of the seventeenth century.

There is another complicating factor in Orwell. The wills which survived are probably too small a group for statistical analysis and this may account for the disappointing results. These results are in any case in many ways at loggerheads with the general impression given by the wills that witnesses were highly literate. Such impressions, of course, are not capable of this type of analysis. There seem also to have been more scribes at work in Orwell. Many of the hands at work are unidentifiable, but many of those which are identifiable belong to the Johnson and Butler family. This leads to the suspicion that there may have been a tradition of literacy in some families which was not necessarily based on economic factors at all. On the Butler side of the family, of course, education was based on prosperity, from Thomas who went

---

[30] Nicholas Johnson appears to have written a parallel series of wills at approximately the same time. See below. pp. 324, 325.

[31] See above, p. 180.

[32] Until the incumbency of Dr Cobbatch, rector of Orwell, who died in 1748/9. The parish register records, 'Dr Cobbatch gave the school for ever.' His foundation appears to have spread literacy down the social scale. In 1775 the death of John Lawrence, 'labourer and Church Clerk', is likewise recorded in the register. Boys were taught to read and write and cast accounts, girls to read, as well as to sew, knit and spin. C. E. Parsons. 'Notes on Horseheath Schools and other Village Schools in Cambridgeshire', *Proc. Cambs. Ant. Soc.*, n.s., 16 (1920). p. 117.

up to Gray's Inn in 1589 onwards.[33] On the Johnson side of the family, however, it was not. Nicholas Johnson, the churchwarden who wrote a series of villagers' wills, had inherited about thirty-four acres in all. His brother Richard, who could sign his name on his death-bed, seems to have had a conventional fourteen-acre holding. The tradition continued, for Lawrence Johnson wrote a couple of wills at the end of the 1640s, and one of these was witnessed by Elizabeth Johnson, who was one of the rare women who could write her name clearly and well.[34]

Family tradition, cutting across economic divisions, may therefore be another reason for the apparently low numbers of yeomen, and the comparatively high proportion of husbandmen, who could sign their names at Orwell.[35]

The generally unsatisfactory and contradictory nature of the evidence at Orwell suggested the desirability of adding a third village study.[36] Milton, immediately north of Cambridge, had about 400 acres of fen common, which was obviously important in the economy, but it must have relied more heavily on its thousand acres of arable in the open fields than Willingham. The village was very small. It had only thirty-six households in 1563, and thirty-eight houses in 1664. The community based in this environment was a remarkably placid one, able to agree peaceably on the enclosure of its commons with its lord, and remarkably free from change. If the evidence of the surveys made of the place in 1599 and 1707 is to be trusted, the distribution of land changed very little during the seventeenth century. There were only four tenants with over fifty acres at both dates.

There was even less evidence for the existence of a school at Milton than at Orwell; only two references were found to a master teaching there in the entire seventeenth century. Even fewer usable wills survive for Milton than for Orwell, but, such as they are, they confirm the impression suggested by the Willingham evidence. Six of the fifteen yeomen who made wills at Milton signed their names; only four of the

---

[33] Joseph Foster, *Gray's Inn Admission Register, 1521–1889* (London 1889), p. 75. He had previously been at Staple Inn. The Butler wills themselves were proved in the Prerogative Court at Canterbury, and are therefore excluded from the Orwell analysis, which is based on the wills proved in the Consistory Court.

[34] For a detailed study of the scribes writing wills at Orwell, see below, pp. 323–8.

[35] Family literacy deserves separate study; the same thing was true of the Crispes at Willingham who likewise sprawled across class divisions.

[36] This should, of course, have been one of Chippenham where the disappearance of the husbandman was the most striking economic change in the period. Unfortunately I have not yet been able to work on the original wills from Chippenham which are much more numerous than the registered copies. They are at present being repaired and indexed. When this work is completed I hope to be able to make the comparison.

remaining thirty-three will-makers did so. Again literacy and prosperity were related, despite the absence of a school. At Milton, as at Willingham, the yeomen stood out as a group, which even at death retained the acquired skill of scrawling out letters far more markedly than any other section of the community.

8

The importance of reading in the village community

However helpful information on the proportion of villagers actually able to sign their names may be, statistics of this sort remain bleak and arid, unless some idea can be gained of the extent to which writing, and more particularly reading, entered into the ordinary life of the village community. Information of this kind can never be complete, and will never be capable of expression in statistical terms. It must necessarily be fragmentary and impressionistic. J. W. Adamson collected such information for the fifteenth and early sixteenth centuries, and showed, for instance, that 'Englische billes' were placed on the Norwich city gates in 1424. They were presumably intended to be read not only by the urban inhabitants but by country folk coming into market. By 1534, girls in Langham village on the borders of Essex and Suffolk could read Matins in English.[1] The number of devotional works, from Richard Whitford's *A Werke for Householders* printed in 1530, to Josias Nicholas's *Order of Household Instruction* which appeared in 1596, argues a market for such works,[2] although we do not know how far it was an urban market. We do know that in the 1530s and 1540s reformers had an active policy of reprinting and distributing Lollard books.[3]

The episcopate had an interest in disseminating orthodox theological literature in every parish, in the sixteenth century, quite apart from Cranmer's general argument, that the Scriptures ought to be read by all sorts and kinds of people and in the vulgar tongue.[4] One of Bishop Cox's special cares in his visitations[5] was to make sure that the church-

[1] J. W. Adamson, 'Extent of Literacy in England in the Fifteenth and Sixteenth Centuries', *The Library*, 4th ser., x (1930), 169–70.
[2] I am indebted to Professor Kenneth Charlton for these references and his opinion on this point.
[3] Margaret Aston, 'Lollardy and the Reformation: Survival or Revival?', *History*, LXIX (1964), 149–70, particularly pp. 156–61. Claire Cross has shown how active women were in collecting, distributing and learning by heart, Lollard books, even in the rural Chilterns. 'Great resources in scripture: women lollards 1380–1530', *Studies in Church History, Subsidia* I, *Medieval Women*, ed. D. Baker (1978), particularly pp. 368–73. [4] See below, p. 242.
[5] See for instance, his second visitation of 1564, E.D.R., B/2/4, fos. 91ff., and office court books of 1567, B/2/6, below, pp. 250 and 253.

wardens were actually in possession of the prescribed books, not only the Bible, but Erasmus's *Paraphrases*, the two volumes of the *Homilies*, the *Commonplaces* of Musculus, the Royal Injunctions, and various other works both theological and propagandist. When the books were not there, the wardens were required to get them, and were usually allowed only a fairly short space of time, of perhaps three weeks, to do so. This suggests that the book trade was functioning efficiently in the sixteenth century, so that even wardens of the remoter parishes could reasonably be expected to obtain a copy of Erasmus within three weeks. Other provisions made in the visitations suggest that just possibly more people were expected to be able to read in a parish than the minister. There was certainly little point in the emphais that the table of degrees of affinity and the Ten Commandments should be painted up on the walls, if no one could read them. Some smattering of letters, at least, was expected of the church clerk. In 1579, the parson of Dullingham, amongst other charges of nepotism, was said to have chosen his brother 'to be parish Clerke there, whoe is unlearned at all, and we think him not sufficient to serve that place'. The parishioners or wardens were directed to choose another clerk, 'for that the sayd Robert Tylbroke was altogither unlearned, and could not answere the vicar at prayres'.[6] The assumption is that a better-educated man would be obtainable. In Matthew Wren's visitation of 1639, the assumption was likewise that church clerks were literate, but also that literate men only formed a certain proportion of the community, as the entry for Caldecote shows. 'The clerk is illiterate,' it ran, 'and cannot be supplyed otherwise by reason of the scarcitie of people in the Towne, theire being but 16 families.'[7]

There is a further general argument, which must be treated with the greatest caution, which might imply that even when a schoolmaster was not licensed in the sixteenth century, some instruction leading to reading might go on. Cox also took great pains to see that his parish clergy actually performed their duty of catechising the 'pueri' or the 'parvuli' regularly, and also on the duty of their parents to send their children regularly to catechism. This was probably almost entirely learning by rote. But the combination of the extraordinarily high educa-

[6] E.D.R., D/2/10, fos. 151v–152.
[7] E.D.R., B/2/52, fo. 9. This evidence fits very well, incidentally, with the paucity of schooling in this clay area of Cambridgeshire. See above, p. 187. So does the evidence of the petition against Bishop Wren in 1640. This shows that, although in all the villages concerned, there were some men who could write their names, however crudely, in some settlements, like Willingham, there were far more inhabitants who were interested in the petition who could sign their names than in others like Toft and Eltisley, where the proportion of marks rose steeply.

tional quality of the parochial clergy,[8] this stress by the bishop on elementary religious instruction, and the provision of theological works in the churches and written precepts on their walls, might well have added up to some village children acquiring a smattering of letters, apart from the more orthodox schooling already discussed.

In Balsham, where no regular schooling was available, a small group was suspected of belonging to the Family of Love in 1574 but admitted merely to gathering together to study the Scriptures together in the evenings.[9] In 1578, a man was 'sellinge of lytle bookes in Balsham churcheyard'. A young barber-surgeon, who does not appear to have been very prosperous, since he was also a patcher of old clothes, and swore on oath that he would be 'worthe nothinge' if his debts were paid off, bought one.[10] There were, then, itinerant booksellers about, who appear to have caused no special remark. The way dissenting opinions could be spread about, if such book pedlars were at work, is obvious. When the Family of Love was examined thoroughly in 1580, six men from Balsham, including three of the suspects cleared in 1574, were imprisoned as obdurate members of the Family. The local leader of the sect, a glover from Wisbech, had over half-a-dozen books of Henry Niklaus's teachings concealed in his house, which were either read to, or available for reading by, other members of the sect. Obviously an urban craftsman was in quite a different position from a member of a rural community, and was much more likely to be able to read. Despite that, some Balsham men undoubtedly could read in the sixteenth century, and it seems likely that heretical opinion was spread amongst them by the printed word.

This is not the earliest reference in the diocese to the dissemination of dissent by the printed word. In 1553, when the Mass was reintroduced, a layman in Orwell spent an evening in the alehouse offering to show his friends a copy of a ballad against it called 'maistres mass'.[11] But the most conclusive and forceful argument for a widespread ability to read in the diocese, and the effect this could have on religious opinion, is the vivid account written by William Weston of the Puritan conferences in Wisbech in the late 1580s and early 1590s. The laity arrived at these with 'their horses and pack-animals burdened with a multitude of

---

[8] See above, pp. 175–6.
[9] It is interesting that one of the group, although he could presumably read, could only mark his name. Again, reading appears the easier skill. For the Family of Love in 1574, see John Strype, *The Life and Acts of Matthew Parker* (1711), pp. 472–3. For the obdurate members in 1580, see Gonville and Caius College MS 53/30, fos. 126v–129r and particularly fo. 73r, and below. pp. 255–6.
[10] He was the doctor who attended Leonard Woolward, see above, pp. 182–3.
[11] See below, p. 245.

Bibles' and diligently looked up, and argued over, each text cited by the preachers.[12] Here is rural literacy with a vengeance. Nearly a hundred years later, the Calvinist, Francis Holcroft, and the Quaker, Samuel Cater, met for a public debate in Thriplow. One of the questions at issue was whether grace was available to all, or only to the elect. Holcroft denied that the grace of God appeared to all, so Cater responded, 'I'll prove by the Scripture that it does, People look in your Bibles, and look into Titus 2.11 and you may read it as I say.' Holcroft read the text aloud, and altered it in the reading. He was at once challenged, and defended himself by replying, 'I read it as it is in the Greek; for it is not so in the Greek, as it is in our Book.' To which *an indifferent person,* standing by called unto him Francis, what do you bring your Bible hither for, if it be *wrong translated?* '[13] This was not only rural literacy, but critical literacy.

There are one or two fragments of information from wills which bear on reading in the period before the commonwealth, during which we know so little about schooling. John Tylbrooke, a thatcher, of Snailwell, in the archdeaconry of Sudbury, left his son John 'an english Bible to be given to him Immediately after my decease' in 1620.[14] Thomas Bowles, a fisherman of Willingham, left his 'eldest son William Bowles ... my bible, wishing him to use it to God's glory', in 1632. John Carter, a chandler, also of Willingham, interestingly left both his son William, and his daughter Sarah, Bibles in 1648. Women were not then excluded from reading the Scriptures themselves.

Herbert Palmer, the minister of Ashwell on the Cambridgeshire and Hertfordshire border, who set up a model Puritan household in the 1630s and provided a schoolmaster to teach those who repaired to him, regularly presented a Bible or 5s to any new communicant who could read. But by far the most revealing and vivid information on reading in the 1640s, or thereabouts, comes from Bunyan, who shows that whatever the situation had been before, there was a lively market for both popular and devotional works amongst villagers then. His limited education and poor background have been touched on earlier,[15] and yet he wrote:[16]

---

[12] See below, pp. 262–3.
[13] My italics. The quotations given here are taken from *A Relation of some of the most material Matters that passed in a Publick Dispute at Thriploe in Cambridgeshire ... 1676 between Francis Holcroft ... and Samuel Cater ....*
[14] Bury St Edmunds and West Suffolk R.O., Register Harold, fos. 568–9.
[15] See above, p. 179, and Roger Sharrock, *John Bunyan*, who discusses the books Bunyan's wife brought him.
[16] John Bunyan, *Sighs from Hell*, 2nd edn (1666?), pp. 147–8. The italics in the passage are his own.

Many a time the Preacher told me hell would be my portion . . . I remember he alledged many a Scripture, but those I valued not; the Scriptures, thought I, what are they? a dead letter, a little Ink and Paper, of three or four shillings price. Alas, what is the Scripture, give me a Ballard, a News-book, *George* on Horseback or *Bevis of Southampton*; give me some book that teaches curious Arts, that tells of old Fables; but for the Holy Scriptures I cared not. And as it was with me then, so it is with my brethren now.

Bunyan's first wife brought him in her dower two books, Arthur Dent's *The Plaine Mans Pathway to Heaven*, which ran to twenty-five editions between 1601 and 1640, and Lewis Bayly's *Practice of Piety*, which was likewise a devotional manual. So these books were certainly not all aimed at the urban market.

Unfortunately the probate inventories of Cambridgeshire only survive from the early 1660s, and they give hardly any information on the books to be found in the ordinary household. The Bible is occasionally mentioned in the houses of people who were not outstandingly prosperous. Richard Broomhead of Fenditton had a Bible, and his goods were worth £54 10s 10d when they were valued in 1669.[17] Robert Reynolds of Hauxton was only worth £18 7s 8d, or litle more than the norm for a labourer. He had a Bible, but he may of course have been a retired yeoman. The inventories of men from Chippenham show definitely that reading ability was certainly not confined to the prosperous. John Aves, who died in 1676, left goods worth only £9 6s 2d, and since he owed a baker of Fordham a bond for £4 10s 0d, his household possessions were put up to auction by the parish, which buried him and paid his arrears of rent. There is a pathetic note that his widow was the purchaser of the cradle in the sale. However, amongst the other bits and pieces were 'the bookes and debts' worth £1.[18] Richard Turner, a retired husbandman, who died in 1668, had no less than four Bibles, as well as some other small books valued at 30s in all. Ambrose Tolworthy, who died in 1652, had also retired, and owned very few household goods. Amongst them was an old Bible. Both of these men left a large proportion of their estate in bonds, and the inference is that they could read them. In some ways, the most interesting case was that of John Tolworthy, who was a barber, and may well have been itinerant, judging from the riding horse and its harness in the stable. His goods were only worth £12 19s 0d, but they included a Bible worth 5s. The entirely hypothetical picture of a travelling barber jogging round the

[17] The median wealth of the 18 labourers whose inventories occur amongst those presented in the Consistory Court of Ely for the 1660s was £15. That of the 24 husbandmen was £30. That of the 54 craftsmen was £40, and that of the 58 yeomen was £180. Analysis of all the inventories surviving for the decade gave a median of £40 for the area of southern Cambridgeshire.   [18] See below, p. 339.

edge of the fens with his Bible in his pocket is a fascinating one. It is noticeable that no books were listed in the very comfortable house of James Sleighton, which was later licensed as a Congregational meeting-place in the lifetime of his widow Ann.

But it is impossible to get an accurate impression of the number of households with Bibles from the inventories. The usual form of the inventories was to give a small notional value at the end for 'a bible and other lumber' or 'bible and other trashe', in the same way that small furniture in a room was often not described, but simply valued as 'other lumber'. It is quite evident that books were not worth listing, even if they were there, and that Bibles would not necessarily be entered separately. In 1666, Edward Hammond, a yeoman, of Willingham, left the scribe who wrote his will 'my book of martyrs'. It does not appear in his inventory. Nor do the three Bibles which Deborah Frohock, a Congregationalist widow of Willingham, left to her son Samuel in 1670, along with the provision that 'my executor see that my said son Samuel be virtuously educated and brought up in learning, and shall be put to the university as soon as he shall be of competent years'. The Frohocks, or Froggs, were newcomers to the village at the end of the sixteenth century, and were comfortable yeomen.[19] The only book apart from the Bible mentioned by name in these probate inventories of the 1660s is a copy of Gray's *Complete Horseman*, which was listed, along with a pair of pearl-coloured silk stockings, amongst the few possessions of a gentle-man who apparently died while on a visit to the county.

Reading obviously did not assume sufficient importance in the lives of most villagers for the books to be allocated special house-room. Of nearly 350 inventories which survive from between 1660 and 1670, only one single house apart from those of the clergy and gentry had a study in it. Thomas Laurence, a yeoman of Trumpington, whose goods were worth £138 when he died in 1669, had at least ten books in his study. The only other examples were that of Richard Wootton, a yeoman, of Ickleton, who had 'his books' and money, with a desk in his chamber, and perhaps best of all, Robert Tebbutt the younger, who was a bachelor, and died in Chippenham in 1682, worth over £400.[20] He had a little closet off the chamber over his parlour, which contained a silver tankard, two tumblers, two wine cups, seven silver spoons, and a parcel of books. It sounds as if Robert Tebbutt practised civilised living; how-ever widespread reading may have been, few of the Cambridgeshire yeomanry can have sipped wine as they read of an evening. The Teb-butts must have been at the point reached by the Butlers of Orwell by

---

[19] Dennis Jeeps checked these two inventories for me.
[20] See above, pp. 74–5.

the turn of the century; Thomas Butler with his legal training and his financial acumen, who left his books to his son Neville, may have thought of himself as a gentleman, but his neighbours probably thought of him as a successful son of old George Butler the bailiff; Neville Butler, on the other hand, disappeared both from the ranks of the yeomanry and Orwell society and reappeared as a member of the county committees and a gentleman.[21]

The inventories also give some indication of the importance of moneylending, and the way that even the humbler members of the community were owed cash, and held bonds for this. William Bourne of Cherry Hinton, who died in 1666, was a fell-monger. It was not surprising that he held £154 in bonds, since he must have travelled around the county collecting skins, and was an obvious person to give credit. But it seems that when men retired from active farming and took up residence with their sons or daughters, they often put their savings into bills and bonds. George Morling of Longstanton was described as a yeoman when he died in 1669, but he had no household goods apart from a few pairs of sheets. He had kept eleven hives of bees to care for in his retirement, but apart from these and his little flock of sheep, his property was in bills and bonds. Richard Caldecot was a husbandman, and was worth only £21 6s 8d. All this was in bills and bonds, except his own personal clothes, and a chest to put them in. Robert Cole of Duxford had a 'sole and only dwelling and lodging room' in 1662 and the furnishings were of the most meagre. 'One Hutch, one shouell and one Iron Rake, and an old bedsted' were priced at 3s 6d and his clothes and money in his purse at 5s. His whole estate was worth less, at £12 18s 6d, than that of the typical labourer. But in spite of his poverty, he held bonds worth 12s 10d. Thomas Doggett of Over, who was described as a 'labourer' by the appraisers who made up his inventory in 1666, held bonds worth over £76, although his personal goods were again of the poorest. He must have been putting his saved earnings out at interest for years. Most striking of all in some ways was Alice Scott, a spinster of Bottisham, who left only clothes and bonds worth £40 in 1669. These examples seem to represent standard practice. A series of thirty-one inventories which survive for Chippenham from 1576 to 1700 show that a third of the people who were well enough off to be appraised at death were involved in moneylending.[22] The three groups of people concerned were retired yeomen and husbandmen, prosperous craftsmen, and widows and spinsters. Although no inventories exist for the diocese of Ely

[21] See above, pp. 98, 108–11.
[22] Amongst the records of the Episcopal Commissary Court for Bury St Edmunds at Bury St Edmunds and West Suffolk R.O.

before 1660, the wills which survive give ample confirmatory evidence of the widespread use of credit, since they sometimes contain lists of debts both owing to, and owed by, the testator. In 1566, a yeoman of Orwell, Richard Kettle, drew up his will. He was owed £4 by a neighbour, over £6 by someone from the next village of Barrington, sums of between £1 and £8 by three men in Little Gransden, six miles away, and another £1 by a man in Royston, where Orwell people frequently marketed. John Hart, a husbandman of Milton, who died in 1588, was an extreme example of indebtedness. He owed money to fourteen men from seven villages including his own. All these villages lay within five or six miles, except Bourn, over ten miles away, where he owed the very large sum of £11.

It can be argued that people who entered into bonds were not necessarily able to read them,[23] provided they understood what they had signed or marked their names to. On the other hand, those who were owed sums on bond, who were most frequently yeomen, had a very powerful practical incentive to be able to read them. There must, indeed, have been a more powerful incentive for lenders of money to be able to cope with written figures than with letters. The written word cannot have been so inherently useful. If it was indeed normal for retired farmers and even widows and spinsters to hold their money in bonds, written notes of hand must have been extremely commonly exchanged amongst ordinary villagers, and it is no wonder that the ability to 'caste an accompte' was included as a basic skill with reading and writing in the curricula of many schools which set out to teach the humblest village child.[24] Simple accounting must have been a very necessary skill in the farming community if credit was so generously used.[25]

Even if the inventories give little direct information on the importance of reading in the community, a study of the growth of dissenting opinion in Cambridgeshire under the commonwealth gives a very strong impression of the vitality and fervour with which religious topics were canvassed in the villages in the 1650s and 1660s, and the extent to which the humblest, and even the women, joined in the debate. Many communities seem to have been hotbeds of religious dispute and

[23] For instance, John Aves of Chippenham, who may have been a scribe, died owning goods worth £9 6s 2d in 1676. A baker of Fordham, George Durrant, held a bond of his for £4 10s. George Durrant had been unable to sign his name when he appraised the goods of another Chippenham man in 1669. It is, of course, always possible that he was able to read, even if he could not write.

[24] See above, p. 187 and the curriculum of Orwell School, p. 203, n. 32.

[25] Miss Marie Rowlands, who has been working on tradesmen's probate inventories of Staffordshire in the late seventeenth century, has found the same or even greater use of credit amongst mercantile members of the community. It seems that credit extended throughout local society by this period and probably did so much earlier.

213

conviction. When the Baptist evangelist John Denne went on a preaching tour in the early 1650s, he was engaged in constant dispute with Ranters, and proto-Quakers like the 'maid' Isobel in the village of Kingston, who was convinced of the need to 'judge the Scriptures by the Spirit, not the Spirit by the Scriptures'.[26] She could presumably read them. The records of all the dissenting churches of Cambridgeshire give some intimations of the importance of the ability to read, and an impression that this was widespread. They are sprinkled with references which give at least indirect information on literacy. John Aynsloe, 'farmer', who lived in Over and was recognised as the teacher of the Quakers of Over, and indeed of Cambridgeshire – a sect which was described in such a derogatory way by the bishop in 1669 as 'all of very poor condition, scarce a yeoman amongst them' – could write a vivid letter. His accounts of the prosecution of the Quakers in 1660 and the conditions in Cambridge Castle at that time are horrifying documents.[27] It is perhaps not surprising that a recognised Quaker teacher, even if he was a local farmer, could write so fluently, and indeed there is some doubt about whether he did not originally come from a gentle family in Northumberland.[28] He was writing tracts for publication by 1664. It is perhaps more surprising that the otherwise unknown Baptist John Blowes of Bourn could in 1657 be disciplined into writing a letter of sorrow, apparently in his own hand, to the brethren he had duped on a visit to London by sneaking away leaving his bill unpaid.[29]

Much more general evidence is provided by the standard disciplinary practice amongst both Baptists and Quakers of writing letters of admonition to erring members who for some reason could not be visited. These were addressed to both men and women. The General Baptists of Fenstanton wrote a stinging letter to Jasper Dockwra of Bassingbourn in 1657,[30] after he had given persistent offence by going frequently to hear the minister of the Church of England. It is quite evident that this letter was intended to be read by Jasper Dockwra himself. The Baptists can scarcely have written it under the assumption that he would be obliged to take it to be read by the minister in question, or even by the parish clerk in Bassingbourn. The same argument applies even more strikingly to the letter of reproof addressed to Thomas Sterne of Haddenham in the Isle of Ely, after he had 'dishonoured' the

---

[26] *Records of the Churches of Christ gathered at Fenstanton, Warboys, and Hexham, 1644–1720*, ed. E. B. Underhill for the Hanserd Knollys Society (London 1854), p. 74 [henceforth, *Fenstanton Records*].
[27] Printed in J. Besse, *A Collection of the Sufferings of the People Called Quakers* (1753), 1, 89–91. See below, pp. 290–1 for an example of John Aynsloe's reports.
[28] M. Spufford, 'Dissenting Churches', pp. 224–37.
[29] *Fenstanton Records*, pp. 224–37.   [30] *Ibid.* pp. 213–23.

name of God by giving consent to the 'sprinkling' of his child. Thomas was invited to come to a general meeting at Fenstanton in 1658 to account for himself.[31] John Bunyan's Open Baptists also communicated with their congregations in the same way. In 1669 they addressed letters of encouragement to two men and to two women who were suffering in the persecution.[32]

There seems to have been a general assumption that members of the meetings could read, and could therefore commonly be addressed by letter. Indeed, much business between the elders of different congregations was conducted by correspondence, as the appeal addressed by the Baptists of Caxton to the various Baptist congregations in Cambridgeshire on behalf of John Wilson in 1654 bears witness.[33] John Wait, a yeoman of Toft, who was a local preacher affiliated to the Open Baptists of Bedford, sent them information by letter on the misdeeds of one of their members, who was begging from the brethren in St Neots in 1669[34] without the permission of his church.[35] Moreover, unless the ability to read was widespread it is impossible to comprehend why sectarian writers in the 1650s and 1660s fled to print to describe their disputes with each other. The number of tracts written by Baptists and Quakers to describe their quarrels, in Cambridgeshire alone, not to mention the dispute between the incumbent of Toft and Bunyan's Open Baptists, the writings of Henry Denne, Francis Holcroft and the Quaker Aynsloe, form in themselves a considerable bibliography. If their object was not to inform a wide local audience of theological wrangling and persecutions which affected them closely, it is almost impossible to imagine what it was, since only a proportion of these tracts had a straightforward theological argument, free from local implication.

Dissenting opinion continued to be spread under the commonwealth in Balsham by the printed word, as it had been in the sixteenth century. It was one of the villages in south-east Cambridgeshire with a small but

---

[31] *Ibid.* pp. 247–9.
[32] *The Church Book of Bunyan Meeting 1650–1821*, ed. G. B. Harrison (London 1928), pp. 39ff. [henceforth *Church Book of Bunyan Meeting*].
[33] *Fenstanton Records*, pp. 104–5.   [34] *Church Book of Bunyan Meeting*, p. 44.
[35] A certain amount of caution is necessary in interpreting this evidence, particularly in view of the statement of a miller's son from the fens in the nineteenth century that of the local preachers who served the local Wesleyan chapel, 'Some on 'em couldn't read at all, and had to learn by heart everything they were likely to want for the service, hymns and psalms and readings from the Bible and all the lot . . . Some on 'em could only put two or three words together at one time.' Sybil Marshall, *Fenland Chronicle*, p. 97. Still there is no doubt that the elders of the Baptist congregations in the seventeenth century wrote both the church books and letters of admonition, just as a yeoman of Croydon-cum-Clopton wrote, about 1690, the evilly spelt account of the life of the Congregationalist Francis Holcroft which opens the Great Gransden Church Book. See below, p. 226.

215

devoted group of Quakers. Their parish priest wrote an account of his spiritual struggles with them, before 1660, particularly with Robert Churchman and his wife, whom, he wrote with engaging honesty, he 'had a particular Eye upon . . . they being Persons of a very good Life and of a plentiful Estate, I was under a fear that their Departure from the Church might be a means to induce others to the same Practice'. He began his account by saying that the Quakers were 'very busie in enticing my People to a compliance with their Perswasions in Religion. This Design they did attempt to accomplish, by dispersing their Papers among them.' Quaker literature was, then, in general circulation, presumably not only among those of 'plentiful estate'. The parish priest began his wrestle with Robert Churchman, indeed, by desiring him 'that when any of their Books come to his Hand, he would do me the kindness to bring them to me, that we might read them over together, assuring him of no unwillingness in me to hearken to whatsoever should appear reasonable'.[36]

One direct and striking piece of evidence shows the way in which the written, as apart from the spoken, word could be responsible for the spread of dissident religious opinion, and could bring about conversion at the lowest social level. The General Baptist, Sister Sneesby of Over, was in 1654 in a state of great spiritual distress. She was tormented by the new Quaker teachings, and by the necessity to choose between them and her Baptist principles. In the end, she became a Quaker, and therefore formed one of that group which Bishop Laney had found of such humble origin. During her conversion to Quakerism, she was visited by Baptist messengers, who 'found [her] in a very sad and deplorable condition . . . We told her, that we heard that one of those commonly called Quakers was at her house and preached there; and we were afraid his preaching had brought her into that condition. She answered, that she could hear very little that he said [perhaps she was deaf]; but she said that she had read many of his books. Then we asked her whether the reading of them were not the cause of her trouble.' When she confessed that this might indeed be the root of her distress, she was advised 'to continue reading' the Scriptures.[37] In 1660, Widow Sneesby was amongst the Quakers imprisoned for not swearing the oath of allegiance. John Aynsloe sent a list of the prisoners to Quaker headquarters in London and annotated this with notes on their status.[38] He wrote of the small group of women of which she was one, 'they were

---

[36] Letter from John Taplow, Balsham, 1681/2, printed in William Turner, *A Complete History of the Most Remarkable Providences, . . .* (1697), pp. 128–9. Again, I owe this reference to Dennis Jeeps.
[37] *Fenstanton Records*, p. 120.
[38] 'Volumes of Sufferings', I (Friends' Meeting House, London), 110–12

most of them poor women and had nothing to live on but what they did labour for'. In his letter to London describing the prisoners he expanded this to explain that the women 'had little but as they did erne it by day labor'. This woman from Over, then, was in all probability either of a labouring family or reduced to day labour in her widowhood. Despite the poverty of her social background she had enough education to read Quaker literature, and the printed word conveyed a sufficiently powerful impression to her to bring about her conversion.[39] No more positive proof could exist of the importance of literacy in bringing about the spread of new religious opinion in the seventeenth century amongst people who were of far too humble status to be touched by any growth or decline of grammar school or university education. It will always be impossible to know, for lack of documentation, whether the ordinary villager was better educated in the sixteenth and seventeenth centuries than before the reformation. We can only state that the written word was a powerful and influential weapon at the parochial level in seventeenth-century Cambridgeshire, not whether it was more, or less, powerful than in the preceding period.

We can also show that yeomen, as a class, were more literate, and, indeed, the only class generally able to afford the luxury of developing skills which were not strictly necessary to the upkeep of their farms. The detailed village studies carried out in Cambridgeshire, however, do not offer any proof of the thesis that the uplands, with their more diversified social structure, produced communities of more literate people. The proportion of substantial yeomen in a community did not appear to bear any strong relationship to the basic literacy of that community, gauged by the ability to sign wills alone. If anything the reverse was true. The small number of college entrants from the Isle of Ely, compared with those from the southern Cambridgeshire uplands, did suggest, on the other hand, that yeomen from the uplands could afford to send their sons to university more often than those from the fens.[40] The more numerous, less prosperous yeomen in the Isle may

[39] It is difficult, but not impossible, to discover exactly what the Widow Sneesby was reading, apart from the Scriptures. John Aynsloe later lived in Over, of course, but there is no record of any work of his being printed until 1664. James Parnell was the Quaker apostle of Cambridgeshire, see below, pp. 228–9 and 281ff. He was active from the autumn of 1654 to the spring of 1655, and Sister Sneesby developed qualms of conscience in November 1654, at just the right date to be the result of his ministry. The only one of James Parnell's tracts which was printed before 1655 was *A Trial of Faith wherein is discovered the ground of the faith of the hypocrite which perisheth, and the faith of the saints which is founded upon the everlasting rock, etc.* (1654). Sister Sneesby was able to follow an intricate argument. The tract was later translated into both Dutch and French, so the Society of Friends must have thought it of considerable propagandist value.
[40] See above, p. 177.

have been less able to afford university education than their more sub-stantial brethren in the uplands, but larger numbers in communities in the Isle could perhaps afford elementary education. The history of the Willingham school shows that at the end of the sixteenth century there was in some places an interest in education which permeated whole villages, even though it did not enable the villagers to give their children any protracted schooling. The tremendous variations from parish to parish of numbers of people able to sign their names can perhaps be accounted for by the type of agricultural and economic background concerned.[41]

[41] See above, pp. 187, 207 n. 7.

PART 3

Parishioners and their Religion

Religion in two rural societies

THE HAY-HARVEST IN RUSSIA IN THE 1870s

The old man, holding himself erect, went in front, moving with long regular strides, his feet turned out, and swinging his scythe as precisely and evenly, and apparently as effortlessly, as a man swings his arms in walking. As if it were child's play, he laid the grass in a high, level ridge. It seemed as if the sharp blade swished of its own accord through the juicy grass . . .

The peasants began preparing for dinner. Some had a wash, the young lads bathed in the stream, others arranged places for their after-dinner rest, untied their bundles of bread and unstoppered their pitchers of rye-beer.

The old man crumbled some bread in a cup, pounded it with the handle of a spoon, poured water on it from a dipper, and having sprinkled it with salt, turned to the east to say his prayer . . . [When he had finished], the old chap got up again, said his prayer, and lay down under a bush, putting some grass under his head for a pillow.

Tolstoy, *Anna Karenin* (written 1874–6)
(Penguin Books, 1954), pp. 272–5.

If the Lark Rise people had been asked their religion, the answer of nine out of ten would have been 'Church of England' for practically all of them were christened, married, or buried as such, although in adult life, few went to church between the baptisms of their offspring... There were a few keener spirits. The family at the inn was Catholic and was up and off to early Mass in the next village before others had turned over in bed for an extra Sunday morning snooze. There were also three Methodist families which met in one of their cottages on Sunday evenings for prayer and praise... The Methodists were a class apart. Providing they did not attempt to convert others, religion in them was tolerated... Whenever she could obtain permission at home it was Laura's delight to attend [one of their services]... Permission was hard to get, for her father did not approve of the 'ranters'.

The Rector visited each cottage in turn, working his way conscientiously round the hamlet from door to door... The women received him with respectful tolerance. When the weather had been discused, the health of the inmates inquired about ... and the progress of the pig ... there came an awkward pause, during which both racked their brains to find something to talk about. There was nothing. The Rector never mentioned religion. That was looked upon in the parish as one of his chief virtues.

Flora Thompson (born 1876), *Lark Rise to Candleford*
(World's Classics, 1954), pp. 226, 223–4, 239–40.

9

Dissent before and after the commonwealth

The attempt to discover anything about the beliefs of the villager is even more difficult than the attempt to discover anything about his education. The first statistics dealing with religion are post-restoration, and come from the Compton Census of 1676, which was an attempt to discover how far, and where, dissent had spread under the commonwealth. Its figures have been much disputed,[1] but they form the most convenient starting point, with other post-restoration surveys like that of Bishop Laney of Ely, made in 1669, to gain some impression of what had happened amongst the peasantry under the commonwealth. It seems most feasible to start with these figures, and then work backwards in time to see what can be discovered of the Elizabethan genesis of dissent, if anything, before expanding on the growth of the various sects which flourished in Cambridgeshire, and discussing the social status of dissenters and their position in their communities. Finally, the most difficult task of all must be faced, that of trying to assess what importance individual religious convictions played in the lives of the common people.

In 1676, there were between four and five per cent of nonconformists in Cambridgeshire. The proportion was almost exactly typical of the country as a whole. An average figure is very deceptive, however, because nonconformity had obtained a really strong grasp in some areas and not in others. There were twenty-five villages in southern Cambridgeshire which, all the available records suggest, played a part as

---

[1] I have discussed them, and the other post-restoration sources in 'Dissenting Churches', pp. 67–94, particularly pp. 67–9, and in the 'Note on Compton Census', pp. 94–5. I have also discussed the post-restoration growth or decline of the various sects, and the antecedents of some of the present chapels claiming an early foundation. I have not repeated that discussion in this book. Wherever I refer to 1676, and give no reference, I am using the Compton Census, which is in the William Salt Library, Stafford. In the same way, if I refer to 1669, I am referring to the returns on nonconformist teachers, meeting-places, and the numbers and type of people attending them made by the bishop, Benjamin Laney, in that year. A reference to 1672 is to the licences issued for dissenting meeting-places and preachers after the declaration of indulgence of 1672. Both are printed in *Original Records of Early Nonconformity under Persecution and Indulgence*, transcr. and ed. G. Lyon Turner (London 1911), I, 34–42; II, 862–75 [henceforth Lyon Turner].

C Cambridge
N Newmarket
R Royston

Miles 0 — 5
Kilometres 0 — 8

▲ Baptist Churches in 1654
△ Baptist Conventicles in 1669
▲ Baptist Meeting Houses licensed in 1672
◇ Open Baptist Conventicles in 1669
◆ Open Baptist Conventicles licensed in 1672
◑ Quaker Meetings before 1669
. LINTON Place with 10 or more dissenters in Compton Census of 1676

Only one symbol is given where a sect had more than one meeting place or teacher in the same parish.

○ Quaker Meetings in 1669 (No Quaker licences were taken out in 1672)
◗ Meetings in Quaker Register for Cambridgeshire
□ Congregational Conventicles in 1669
■ Congregational Conventicles licensed in 1672
Ⅰ Presbyterian / Congregational licences in 1672
▼ Licences of unknown denomination in 1672, probably Presbyterian
‑‑‑ Boundary of Diocese of Norwich
⋯⋯ Congregational circuits of 1675

Map 12 Nonconformity in Cambridgeshire, 1654–76

centres of dissent. They all contained more than ten nonconformists, and they were grouped, in a noticeable pattern, on the fen-edge and in the fen, to the north-west and the north-east of Cambridge, and near and in the upper valley of the river Rhee, to the south-west of the county. The episcopal returns for the country as a whole showed that in 1669 the Presbyterians, with well over 40,000 adherents, were by far the strongest sect. The Baptists, with 7,000 or thereabouts, were equally noticeably the weakest. The Congregationalists competed with the Quakers for second place.[2]

This order was almost completely reversed in Cambridgeshire,[3] where the pitifully small group of thirty-odd Presbyterians put the county lowest amongst those which had Presbyterians at all.[4] The Congregationalists were, by Bishop Laney's reckoning, the strongest sect in the shire,[5] in 1669. There were just over 700 of them. Only London, Kent and Norfolk in eastern England, and Monmouthshire in the west, had more,[6] and apart from the last they all, of course, had much larger populations on which to draw.

The evidence for the early growth of the Congregational Church in Cambridgeshire is very scanty. The work of Francis Holcroft,[7] fellow of Clare, seems to have been fundamental. He accepted the living of Bassingbourn in 1655, and, according to tradition, founded a Congregational church there almost at once. Only the wording of the covenant which bound the members of the first church survives.[8] There is little evidence to show how extensive was the growth of the Bassingbourn church before the restoration, apart from the account of Richard Conder, junior, who became pastor of a branch of Holcroft's church at Croydon-cum-Clopton after his death in 1692. At about that time, when he was in his early forties, Richard Conder wrote a note on the work of 'God's servant' Francis Holcroft, at the beginning of his Church Book, which afterwards became the Church Book of Great Gransden.[9] In his account, he described how, after Holcroft had begun to preach at Bassingbourn:

[2] Lyon Turner, III, 119.
[3] Numbers of conventiclers tabulated by denomination in *ibid.* p. 110.
[4] *Ibid.* pp. 127–9.   [5] All these figures include the Isle.   [6] Lyon Turner, III, 130–2.
[7] For Holcroft, Bradshaw, and Holcroft's assistants Oddy and Lock, see Matthews, *Calamy Revised*, pp. 271–2, 69–70, 325–6, 371.
[8] Quoted by Robert Robinson, 'Historical Account', in his *Posthumous Works*, ed. B. Flower (Harlow 1812), pp. 257–9. For my general bibliography on Congregationalism in Cambridgeshire, see below, p. 287.
[9] H. G. Tibbutt, 'Pattern of Change', *Transactions of the Congregational Historical Society*, XX (1969), 170–3, and 'Memoir of the Late Rev. John Conder, D.D.', *Evangelical Magazine*, III (1795), 393–5. I am deeply indebted to Mr Tibbutt for his generosity in lending me his transcript of the beginning of the Great Gransden Church Book, before he printed it in 'Francis Holcroft', *Trans. Cong. Hist. Soc.*, XX, 295–301.

225

the lord oned him much in converchon of soolls and their began to be a talk of him, and my father being a ancient profeser then being feri son in this contri heard of his meting on one of the holi days as they calle them at Eastr or Whisantid. he maid his servant and chilldren to goo with him to the meeting thow it much displeased us and he preached then from them woords 'the ston that was regectid by yow builders is becom the head ston of the corner'.

and i being yong did not understand what he preached but thought he was a strang man to talk so much about stoons. and when wee cam away he followed us out and tallcked with my father about severall things, and my father being feri plain with him he askid him what he thought in him, and his ansour was that he toock him to bee on of the reformed prests of that day, and hee claped him on the shoollder and said 'thow dost not know my mind, but thow maist know it hearaftor'.

and soo hee partid with him and soon after the woorck of God went forward and soolls was convertid and the lord was much with him and soonn seet his hart to builld him an hows. and the lord's hand was seen in that day in calling seaverall of the yong schollers in the unifarciti which did preach about in the cuntri towns, as mister Oddi at Melldrid and mister Ecins at Chisell and mister Ponder at Whadon.

and God's servant, being ficxed for the rulls of God's hous, was soonne set apart pastor by mister Staloms and soom others which I hafe forgat, then being feri yong, but this I remember they cept the day and all the night after with great joy and singin. and I remember that my father and mother cam hom in the morning and as soonne as my mother had doon milleking shee cam in and toolld my father that shee must goo to Basingbon again, and they toock their hors and weent away.

their was shuch a mighti preasenc of God amongst them that they ware redi to forsack all to follow Crist.

Holcroft was obviously drawing large congregations to Bassingbourn before his ejection, although it sounds as if the formation of his church did not take place very long before 1662. Richard Conder added that his father 'stood out a priti whil' before he joined the covenant 'but the Lord brought him ... to see into it afterwards and in the time of builldin this church it was a tim of trobell, for now King Charls cam in and God's servant ... was turned out of the publick placises'.

After Holcroft refused to subscribe in 1662, he became a peripatetic minister in south Cambridgeshire, aided by a team of ex-fellows of Trinity, including Joseph Oddy. In Richard Conder's words, 'the woork of God went forward and their was daly adid to the church'. By 1663, he had meetings of several hundred people in southern Cambridgeshire and the neighbouring counties.[10] Most of his time between 1663 and 1672 was spent in prison, but according to tradition

[10] Lyon Turner, III, 294–6.

he was allowed out to preach. Conder testified that with Holcroft's imprisonment 'the churchis aflicton began upon her but the moar she was aflicted the moar she gru'. At the same time, Nathaniel Bradshaw, the non-subscribing rector of Willingham, continued to preach in his own house there as well as the neighbouring villages,[11] until he made the place too hot to hold him in about 1667. He then retreated to London for a space. Joseph Oddy took over his work and became the itinerant Congregationalist minister of north-west Cambridgeshire.

The Baptists, who were generally so weak, were extremely well established in Cambridgeshire in 1669. Their congregation in the county numbered over six hundred, and was probably more considerable than that of any other area except London and Buckinghamshire.[12] Kent and Sussex, in the south-east, also had a strong Baptist element. The only other counties where Baptists were found in considerable numbers were Wiltshire and Warwickshire.

The Baptist Church in Cambridgeshire owed its formation to Henry Denne,[13] the famous General Baptist preacher, whose publication *Christ, the Drag-net of all men*, set the note for his life. He was baptised in 1643 as a member of Lamb's church in Bell Alley, in London, and probably first evangelised in Cambridgeshire in 1644. He was also extremely active as a preacher and cornet in the army. He was presented to the living of Eltisley, in western Cambridgeshire, by Major-General John Disbrowe (Desborough) who was married to Cromwell's sister Jane, and became M.P. for Cambridgeshire in 1654, and a privy councillor Denne's main work in the county began in the 1650s with the gathering of the Fenstanton church. The first members of the

[11] Cottenham Old Meeting first Church Book (unprinted), p. 163.

[12] Lyon Turner, III, 133–6, discusses the Baptist figures. The order in which he lists the size of Baptist, or, indeed, any, congregations in the counties, depends on the theoretical size given to conventicles for which the bishops gave no number of attenders. Lyon Turner adopts the nominal figures of 90 and 50 for these meetings of unknown size, and gives two alternative tables for each sect, based on them. In these tables, Cambridgeshire, which certainly had 610 Baptists, plus three meetings of unknown size, comes out sixth and seventh respectively, well behind such counties as Kent, which had 236 Baptists, plus the members of 13 meetings of unknown size.
I feel myself that figures of 90 and 50 are much too large. The whole baptised membership of the church of Fenstanton and Caxton, which had been one of the strongest in the kingdom, was only 84 in 1676. This included many local meetings, which would have been listed separately by the bishops (*Fenstanton Records*, pp. 255–6). Quaker meetings were undoubtedly smaller than this, judging from the records of the prosecution of attenders under the second Conventicle Act in 1670. The largest Cambridgeshire meeting recorded was one of just over 20. If this figure of 20 is adopted for the Baptists, whose numbers were certainly diminishing under persecution, Cambridgeshire had more Baptists than anywhere except Buckinghamshire and London.

[13] For my general bibliography on the Baptists in Cambridgeshire, see below, p. 276 n. 21.

church all lived within easy physical reach of Eltisley, which was once described as 'an asylum for the most extravagant fanaticism . . . psalm singing was as heinous a sin at Eltisley as bending a knee to Baal, and it was then as much noted for the devout exercises practised there, as any other canting place within the kingdom'. Denne's son, John, became elder and recorder of the General Baptist Church which was established round the joint centres of Fenstanton in Huntingdonshire and Caxton in Cambridgeshire in the early 1650s. John Denne lived at Caxton Pastures, a farm in Caxton parish a mile or so from Eltisley, which therefore became one of the principal meeting-places of the church. The fullness and vivid reporting of the first Fenstanton Church Book, which covered the period up to 1659 and includes comment on the relations between the Baptists and other religious groups, makes it not only the most complete source for the history of the dissenting churches of Cambridgeshire but also the principal source for Baptist history under the protectorate. More important still, for those interested in doctrine at the village level, it is the only source yet known which gives an account, in reported speech, of the crises of conscience of the villager, caught up in the theological confusions of the 1650s. It is therefore more illuminating than any other material, and I have leant heavily upon it for the general impression of the religious atmosphere of the period which it gives. Even so, little is known of the origins of the other Baptist churches in Cambridgeshire, like those at Melbourn and Burwell, which were not affiliated to Caxton. These were conveniently listed by the Fenstanton Baptists in 1654, when they had occasion to send out a fund-raising letter, but little more is known of their early history.

There were probably over 600 Quakers in Cambridgeshire, but the county did not stand out as a predominant centre of Quakerism in the way that it did as a centre for Baptists. Yorkshire, in the north, and Wiltshire and Somerset in the south-west, all had over 1,000 Quakers. Almost all the eastern and south-eastern counties had over 600 apiece,[14] even though they were also mostly larger counties.

Organised Quakerism had first reached Cambridgeshire with the visit of Mary Fisher and Elizabeth Williams to the county town in 1653. In the following year, Richard Hubberthorne was jailed for visiting a woman imprisoned for 'testifying against a false prophet' in Cambridge. There they were joined by James Parnell, who was to be Cambridgeshire's principal Quaker apostle. He had heard, somewhere in the north, of two of his friends, who were presumably the two women

---

[14] Lyon Turner, III, 127–9. I have again used 20 as a theoretical number for meetings of unknown size.

visitors of 1653, being whipped for declaring the truth in Cambridge. He was moved to come to the town and there 'found those that were worthy that received me' before himself being jailed. Sometime after his release from prison in the autumn of 1654, Parnell returned to Cambridge, and spent six months evangelising and 'declaring the Truth in the Countries about', whence he found many 'that received the Truth gladly, but more Enemies'. By mid-1655 he was in Essex, where he was finally martyred, still only aged eighteen.[15]

It was no wonder that Parnell found some willing converts, for the records of the Baptist Church show that even before Elizabeth Williams and Mary Fisher reached Cambridge in 1653, spiritual seeking and unrest were extremely widespread at the lowest parochial level.[16] Converts were also made at a higher social level. In 1655, the year of Parnell's evangelism, James Docwra, a gentleman of Fulbourn, who was married to Ann, daughter of Sir William Waldegrave of Wormingford in Essex, settled a close of pasture and about sixty acres of arable in Fulbourn on his wife for 500 years. The income was to support various Quaker causes, including £3 a year towards the charges of 'Travelling Preachers and Horses at Cambridge'.[17] This argues a high degree of organisation by the end of Parnell's ministry. With both this, and popular support, it is not surprising that Quakerism flourished, and that despite the intense persecution suffered by Quakers, both under the commonwealth and later, a considerable hard core of adherents still remained in the late 1660s.

To the 'left' of the Quakers, a number of less reputable sects sprouted. The bishop of Ely appeared to be entirely unaware of the presence of Muggletonians in his diocese, but they flourished there. Ludovic Muggleton, who believed himself to be one of the 'two witnesses' of Revelations[18] with power to pronounce damnation or salvation to eternity, wrote in 1660 that his doctrine 'of the commission of the Spirit hath been very little received in the world; but the most that hath received it, is here in London, and in Cambridgeshire and in Kent'.[19] There were probably very few of them even so, but the

---

[15] For my general bibliography on Quakerism in Cambridgeshire, see below, p. 281 n. 41.   [16] See below, pp. 276–7, 283.
[17] W. Geoffrey Stevens, *Old-Time Links between Cambridgeshire and the Lake District*, vol. II, 'The Knights Hospitallers and the Docwra Family' (typescript 1966), pp. 27–31 (copy available in C.R.O.). Ann Docwra gave the 'Meeting House Yard' estate to the Friends in her will of 1700. The codicil of 1710 confirmed the annual payment of £3 for preachers, and added £20 towards a new burial ground. The present Meeting House was built in 1772.   [18] Rev. 11:3–6.
[19] *A Volume of Spiritual Epistles, being the Copies of Several Letters written by the last two Prophets, and Messengers of God, John Reeve and Ludowicke Muggleton* (1755), pp. 36*, 198–202, 307.

acrimonious correspondence between Muggleton and the new vicar of Orwell who had tried to get him arrested in 1666, is explained by Muggleton's comment in 1670.

There is one of our chief friends in Cambridgeshire dead, namely the widow Adams,[20] who lived at Orwell; but she was married about half a year to a friend of the faith, namely Thomas Warboyes, a very honest-hearted man ... but his daughter and son-in-law do live in Orwell still; but they being presented for not going to church, they do intend to remove from thence ... so that this house at Orwell, *hath been a place of entertainment like a stage town,* for many, twelve years to my knowledge; but now it will be broken up, and the Saints will be scattered, but not out of England.

The vicar, reasonably, objected to the position held by Orwell as a 'place of entertainment' for Muggletonians.

Despite their limitations, the arid figures and estimates given in the bishop's returns of 1669 partially reflect the successful evangelism of Henry Denne, James Parnell and Holcroft and his associates in the 1650s. The most central question to be asked is whether these great evangelist leaders of the separatist churches were responsible for the strength of nonconformist opinion in the villages – whether nonconformity was preached and spread from above, or whether the nonconformist apostles were giving form to opinions that already existed among the laity. Whether, in fact, dissent was disseminated mainly by educated men of particular quality, or at least particular zeal, or whether dissent already existed amongst the laity, and Parnell and Holcroft were only channelling and giving coherent shape to ideas that had already spread right down to the lowest social levels before the great days of the commonwealth evangelists. Was nonconformity a grass-roots phenomenon?

A tradition did exist, amongst the Congregationalists at least, that Holcroft was working on old-established foundations, when he gathered his church in the 1650s and 1660s. Calamy said that he 'fell in with the Old Brownists'.[21] Robert Browne, the arch-separatist, had spent nine years evangelising in Cambridgeshire and Norfolk after taking his degree in 1572–3,[22] and spending a little while in the model Puritan household of Richard Greenham, rector of Dry Drayton, before leaving for the continent in 1581. There are other hints of the same kind. An account has already been given of Richard Conder, junior, who wrote the Church Book of Great Gransden in the 1690s, and held meetings of the Croydon-cum-Clopton church in Cambridgeshire in the hall of

[20] See below, pp. 325–6, for her will.   [21] *Calamy Revised,* p. 272.
[22] Venn, *Alumni Cantabrigiensis,* I, 237.

his own farm at that time. He described his father, Richard Conder senior, as 'being a ancient professor'.[23]

The Conder family history shows us that Puritan ideas had been held amongst men of relatively humble stock long before the 1650s. Old Richard Conder, who forced his family, against its inclination, to go to Holcroft's early meetings, was said to be a dairy farmer. He was obviously a yeoman, but of relatively humble status for although he kept at least one living-in servant, his wife did the milking herself. Richard Conder was indeed an 'ancient professor' for in 1740 an old gentleman aged ninety or more told his great-grandson how he, when he was a boy

used . . . to accompany my father to Royston market which Mr Conder also frequented. The custom of the good men in those days was, when they had done their marketing, to meet together, and spend their penny together in a private room, when, without interruption, they might talk freely of the things of God; how they had heard on the Sabbath-day, and how they had gone on the week past etc. I was admitted to sit in a corner of the room. One day when I was there, the conversation turned upon this question, *by what means God first visited their souls and began a work of grace upon them.*[24] It was your great-grandfather's turn to speak and his account struck me so, I never forgot it. He told the company as follows: 'When I as a young man I was greatly addicted to football playing; and as the custom was in our parish and many others, the young men, as soon as church was over, took a foot-ball and went to play. Our minister often remonstrated against our breaking the sabbath which however had little effect, only my conscience checked me at times, and I would sometimes steal away and hide myself from my companions. But being dexterous at the game, they would find me out, and get me again among them. This would bring on me more guilt and horror of conscience. Thus I went on sinning and repenting a long time, but had no resolution to break off from the practice; til one sabbath morning, our good minister acquainted his hearers, that he was very sorry to tell them, that by order of the King and Council, he must read them the following paper, or turn out of his living. This was the *Book of Sports* forbidding the minister or church-wardens or any other to molest or discourage the youth in their manly sports and recreations on the Lord's Day etc. When our minister was reading it, I was seized with a chill and horror not to be described. Now, thought I, iniquity is established by a law, and sinners are hardened in their sinful ways! What sore judgments are to be expected upon so wicked and guilty a nation! What must I do? whither shall I fly? How shall I escape the wrath to come? And God set in so with it, that I thought it was high time to be in earnest about salvation: And from that time I never had the least inclination to take a football in hand, or to join my vain companions any more. So that I date my conversion from that time; and

[23] Quotation from H. G. Tibbutt, 'Francis Holcroft', p. 297.   [24] My italics.

231

adore the grace of God in making that to be an ordinance to my salvation, which the devil and wicked governors laid as a trap for my destruction.

Now this account of old Richard Conder's reaction to the proclamation of the *Book of Sports* takes us back to Charles I's proclamation of 1633. So sometime in the mid-seventeenth century a group of the farmers of western Cambridgeshire, who marketed in Royston,[25] met in one of the pubs there to 'talk freely of the things of God', and of their early lives. There certainly were 'ancient professors' about in the county, before Holcroft's work began in the 1650s. These may have been simply men of Puritan ideas who wished to see a further reformation, within the church of course; it was young Richard Conder's mother, who he wrote 'was on of the furst allmoast that was adid to lay the foundation, but my father stood out a priti whill and did not joyn with them upon the acount of the cofenant, for he was not clear in the cofenant nor the sealls of it . . . but the lord brought him'.[26] But even if these men began as Puritans within the church, they could, as in the case of the Conders, easily form the convinced members of a separatist church.

Fortunately we are not solely dependent on individual family histories to judge the extent or depth of the Puritan feelings in the county before the commonwealth. In 1640, a petition was made to parliament against the 'Tyrannicall courses and Administrations of Dr Wrenn, Bishop of Ely'.[27] The petition must date from 1640–1 when the Long Parliament was sitting. Wren, who was one of Laud's most trusted supporters, seems to have succeeded in making himself just as unpopular in his brief tenure of Ely, during the years 1638–40, as he had done in his previous tenure of Norwich.[28] The petition itself is in terrible condition, but three sections of it partially survive, covering eight hundreds of the county apart from Cambridge itself. These hundreds happen, perhaps by more than chance, to contain no less than twenty-two of the twenty-five villages which were focal points of dissent after the commonwealth. So if it is possible to identify the origins of the signatories to the petition, it should also be possible to tell whether Puritan feeling was indeed already established in Cambridgeshire before the work of the separatist evangelists. Incidentally, those who signed this document

[25] This, incidentally, tells us something of the reasons why market towns were so often dissenting centres. They were the natural meeting-places.
[26] For the Conder family history of dissenting opinions, stretching through four generations of Puritans and then Independent pastors from 1605 to 1781 see my 'Note on the Conder Family', *Trans. Cong. Hist. Soc.*, XXI (1972), 77–9.
[27] W. M. Palmer discussed this document, B. M., Egerton MS 1048, and printed the articles complained of against Bishop Wren in his *Episcopal Visitation Returns for Cambridgeshire* (Cambridge 1930), pp. 72–5.   [28] See below, pp. 265–8.

wanted no further reformation within the church; they asked specifically that Parliament should not only redress the wrongs done them by Bishop Wren but also 'be further pleased for the cleerer manifestation of God's glorie and the propagation of his holie word in the puritie thereof to abolish the government of bishops . . . and that a government according to the Holie Scripture maie be established in the Kingdome'. So there was no question in these men's minds that they wanted a total abolition of episcopal and traditional church government. One of the men who signed his name to it, very painfully, was a certain Richard Conder.

The petition is organised by hundreds. It is therefore not possible to tell from which village any particular signatory came, without further investigation.[29] A detailed comparison of the surviving legible names on the petition with the nearest subsidy which covers all the hundreds concerned, which was taken during 1641,[30] makes it possible to identify some of the communities from which the petitioners came. Lay subsidies became notoriously more unreliable as time went on in the sixteenth and seventeenth centuries. The values on which men were taxed became less and less related to their real incomes, and, more relevant for this purpose, they also included fewer and fewer names.[31] The subsidy of 1641 appears to contain between a third and a quarter of the names which appear in the hearth taxes later in the century.[32] So, not only do we have a petition ruined by wet, and wear and tear; we have, to compare with it, lists of names which are totally inadequate, of only the wealthiest third or quarter of the villagers in every settlement. The prospect is unpromising.

Given the unpropitious nature of the situation, the results one can obtain are truly astonishing. There are some five hundred recoverable names in the petition of 1640. Over 100 of these petitioners can be identified in the subsidy of 1641, as coming from a particular village. Some villages produced only one or two signatories from their wealthiest inhabitants who paid taxes; but nine villages stand out

---

[29] Palmer, *ibid.* p. 72, had a brief look at the petition, and identified one or two of the villages concerned by comparison with the subsidy rolls of 1640. He was wrong in assuming that the last section of the petition refers only to the three villages of Kingston, Eversden and Toft; it covers the whole of Longstowe Hundred.

[30] P.R.O., E179/83/411; E179/83/407; E179/83/408.

[31] Christopher Hill, *The Century of Revolution, 1603–1714* (London 1961), p. 52, and F. C. Dietz, *English Public Finance, 1558–1641* (New York 1932), pp. 382–93. Dietz does not, in fact, consider subsidies after 1621.

[32] For instance, Barrington had 25 people assessed in 1641; 81 householders were assessed in the 1664 hearth tax. Admittedly, there may have been a continuing population rise between 1641 and 1664; but all the available evidence at present shows that the population rise of the sixteenth century was checked, or at least considerably slowed down, in the early seventeenth century.

because they produced five or more signatories. Between them, these nine produced over half the identifiable signatories. All but two of these villages also later stood out as nonconformist centres in 1676.[33]

So, nonconformity demonstrably played a really strong part in the same villages in 1640 as it did in 1676. Of course, there were many fewer villages involved in 1640; and we can see which ones acted as nurseries for dissent. Those who were to form the Independent congregations were already dissenting in Willingham and Cottenham in 1640, but had not, interestingly, yet convinced any brethren in Oakington or Histon. Barrington, Meldreth and Melbourn were in fact Puritanical; but Orwell, Shepreth, Foxton and the rest of the subsidiary group of Congregationalist villages had yet to be touched. So, interestingly, had Bassingbourn, where Francis Holcroft held his living, and from which he formed his first church.[34] But the conclusion is inescapable. The Cambridgeshire laity, in some villages, were already convinced by 1640 that they wanted a total reform in church government; and their radical ideas were not planted in their heads by the dissenting evangelists Denne, Parnell and Holcroft, or even by the other clergy, who, with Holcroft, failed to subscribe in 1662.[35]

The depth of feeling involved, amongst yeomen, husbandmen and even labourers, can best be gauged by the complaints of some of the witnesses against 'scandalous ministers', deprived by the second earl of Manchester from 1643 onwards under parliamentary mandate.[36] John Cooke, a labourer, of Swaffham Prior, deposed against his vicar, Richard Peacock, that Mr Peacock had 'so behaved himself in church that this deponent and other persons hath tender consciences have been much grieved thereat ... (he) never preaches *but once a day*,[37] and never catechises the youth'. Thomas Norridge and Richard Parkin of Swaffham Prior, both yeomen, felt similarly about the daily preaching and

---

[33] Even the other two cases where there is apparently no connection between pre- and post-commonwealth dissent, are misleading. Willingham, which was undoubtedly one of the dissenting centres of the county, from other evidence, was omitted from the Compton Census and therefore does not appear on that map. Eltisley, which appears as a Puritan entry only in 1640, was the manor of the Desborough family and the parish which Henry Denne, the General Baptist missionary, used as a centre from which to found his church in the early 1650s. The General Baptists had succumbed to persecution by the time of the Compton Census, and Eltisley was no longer the base of a gathered church.

[34] See above, pp. 225–7. [35] See below, pp. 316–18.

[36] For the procedure involved see the 'Introduction' to *The Suffolk Committees for Scandalous Ministers, 1644–6*, ed. C. Holmes (Ipswich 1970), Suffolk Records Society, XIII (1920). I have taken these details from a transcript of B.M., Add. MS 15672 in the C.U.L., Palmer Papers B58, pp. 13–14, 10–11. I am very grateful to Mr Cedric Parry, of Keele, for drawing this source to my attention.

[37] My italics.

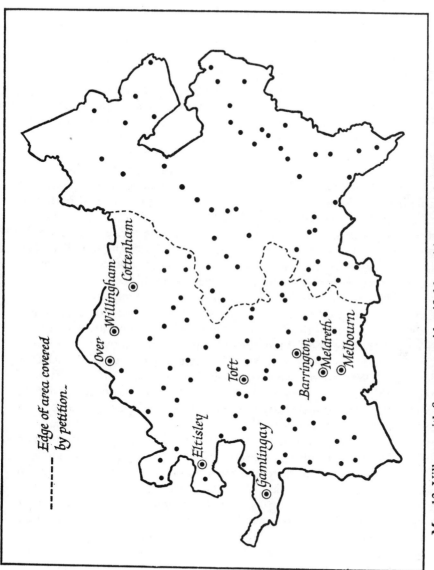

Map 13 Villages with five or more identifiable petitioners against Bishop Wren in 1640

Edge of area covered
by petition.

Over
Willingham
Cottenham
Eltisley
Toft
Gamlingay
Barrington
Meldreth
Melbourn

catechising. William Potter 'saith that on Feb. 25th last he brought his litle child to be baptised and desired Mr Peacock to do it without signing the sign of the cross but he refused . . . and deponent was constrained to get his childe christened by another minister at another church'. So William Potter was sufficiently determined to take his child elsewhere to avoid having his child signed with the cross.

Edward Sallesbury, a husbandman, giving evidence against Theodore Crossland, of Bottisham, complained not only about his 'superstitious works and popish innovations' but that for '4 or 5 years, and ever since he was vicar there, he never examined any, whether they were fit to receive the sacrament or noe; noe never prepared nor instructed them . . . neither did he ever preach to the edifying of them'. He had been absent for nearly five months and left an unfit curate in charge and 'one Lord's Day they had neither preaching nor praying in their church, *had not these deponents tooke care to provide one in his stead,*[38] 'tis probable they would have been destitute still'. The upshot of that particular case was that two of the deponents concerned, both husbandmen, received a warrant from Manchester to receive all rents and profits belonging to the vicarage, and see to the supply for the time being. So these men were to go out and find a minister whose doctrine and politics were acceptable to them, and they appeared capable of doing this.

The depositions made in 1643 against Nicholas Gray, D.D., of Castle Camps, in the south-east of the county by the Essex border, strongly suggest that some of the deponents belonged to a conventicle. Gray had been rector since 1630. Many of the witnesses had moved from Castle Camps, and now lived in Saffron Walden. Some, according to Henry Reader of Walden, a husbandman, had moved even further, 'divers of the inhabitants . . . were forced, the better to enjoy the peace of a good conscience and for their ease, to remove to several places, some beyond sea, and others to places in Essex'. An article of complaint made by several parishioners was that Dr Gray had rallied in a new communion table, set altarwise, with pictures set about it. Sarah Taylor, a widow, of Walden said she went to be churched about seven years since, but Dr Gray refused to do so unless she came up to the rails and so she was excommunicated. On being asked why she would not come up to the rails, she said 'That God's people did hold it unlawful to go up to the Rayles' and then Dr Gray said 'What do you talk of God's people? My conscience tells me that those you do account God's people are worse than swearers, drunkards, whoremongers and sabbath breakers.' The mention of 'God's people' makes the existence of a gathered church to which Widow Taylor belonged, very likely.

[38] My italics.

Other parishioners may not have belonged to a gathered church, but were thoroughly imbued with Puritan doctrine, emphasising the preaching of the word, and refusing to comply with Laudian 'innovations', even though they went through great distress at being deprived of the sacraments thereby. George Argent, a yeoman, said that Dr Gray refused to suffer a Mr Blackaby 'a godly minister' to preach a funeral sermon for one John Grigge, who had formerly received much comfort and counsel in the ways of heaven by the said Mr Blackaby, 'who being well known to this deponent and other neighbouring people, they went to another church to hear him'. The town had also provided a lecturer 'a very honest and able man' who had been turned out by Dr Gray. He had also often refused to let 'divers godly men' preach there. John Doughty, a husbandman,

saith that Dr Gray hath denied to him and many other of his parishioners the blessed Sacrament of our Lord's supper for not coming to the Rayles, which this deponent and others in their conscience could not yield unto, although in great humility this deponent and others hath entreated it at his hands, where their predecessors were wont to receive it. For this they were excommunicated for three years and much troubled by the Ecclesiastical Court where Dr Gray hath been judge himself, and have craved absolution divers times, but could not obtain it.

Despite the usual mixture of complaints against royalism and immorality as well as doctrine, there was enough protest of a purely doctrinal nature amongst the rural laity, to show that reformed convictions had made such an impact on them by the 1630s that many ordinary villagers were prepared to deprive themselves of attendance at the Sacrament, which meant a great deal to them, remove to other places if need be, and raise cash to pay for lecturers' stipends, rather than assent to practices they regarded as popish innovations. Labourers with 'tender consciences' were not rare in the diocese. The outburst against Wren in 1640 becomes much more comprehensible.[39] The tenets of the reformation, and the emphasis on preaching and the word, had become accepted at the lowest social levels. Many of the beliefs held by the villagers who laid information against their 'scandalous ministers' in the 1640s would have been acceptable to Bishop Cox of Ely, who was responsible for establishing the Elizabethan settlement in his see, and himself laid great emphasis on preaching and catechising. The willingness of his laity to sacrifice episcopacy, and their readiness to slip into separatism certainly would not have been acceptable. How long had this reception of reformed principles at the village level taken?

[39] All the complaints just discussed come from parishes in the diocese not covered by the petition, and all of them later provided members of nonconformist churches.

And if many of the laity of Ely were convinced that they wanted no more of their bishop by 1640, how long had this development of Puritanical feeling, which can be documented back to the 1630s, both in the complaints against scandalous ministers, and Richard Conder's dramatic conversion of 1633, been going on? It is demonstrably true, and no later myth, that Holcroft was building on old-established foundations in the 1650s, when he preached to 'ancient professors'. It is therefore necessary to examine, if possible, the truth of the tradition that he 'fell in with the Old Brownists'.

10

A general view of the laity in the diocese of Ely

LITURGICAL CHANGE IN THE REFORMATION

Recent years of liturgical change have brought home to both Anglicans and Catholics the degree of disturbance which is caused among the laity by the alteration of words, actions, and the position of church furniture, all of which have a symbolic part to play in the administration of sacraments. Very often this disturbance cannot adequately be expressed in any logical way; the reason is a very adequate one. If the function of a symbol is to 'represent the inexpressible in an unsurpassable way', then, as a Catholic has written, 'the Mass renders God present to us in an insurpassable way; in other words it is the symbol which communicates God to us'.[1] If the Mass, the Eucharist, or the Lord's Supper is that which in one fashion or another communicates the relationship of God to man, then interference even with the details of the forms of expression of this relationship is bound to cause concern amongst the faithful, which often they themselves cannot account for. A change in the position of the altar or holy table from the east end, where the celebrant stands in front of his people and mediates the Christian sacrifice, to the midst of the people in the nave, means much more than the mere rearrangement of a room. It symbolises a difference in the way the relationship between people and God is demonstrated. A change in accustomed language, even if it is archaic or foreign, is disturbing in the same way. Anglicans uneasy over the disappearance of the early celebration of Communion in favour of a parish communion, or over the loss of the order of service which has been familiar since 1662, or even the retranslation of the familiar but incomprehensible Lord's Prayer, and Catholics faced with translations of the Mass into the vernacular, or with a central altar, have all felt the same dis-ease, often without 'rational' justification. They are therefore more in a position to appreciate the impact that successive changes in the position of the altar, the translation of the familiar, if incomprehensible, Mass

[1] Donald Nicholl, 'The Return of Symbols', *The Life of the Spirit*, VIII (1953), 176. I am very grateful to Professor Nicholl for raising this issue with me, and discussing it.

into the vernacular of the Prayer Book of 1548, and the shift of doctrinal emphasis continued in its successor of 1552, must have had.

Even so, the impact must have been different, and greater, in a primitive rural society which was, from habit and by custom, a totally Christian one. The agrarian Orthodox communities of Greece, or the Catholic communities of south-west Ireland, which are completely and unselfconsciously involved in an almost casually unemotional way both with the ritual of the church's year, and with the seasonal demands of the land and the stock, one of which often mirrors the other, provide possible very rough images of the kind of community with which the reformers were concerned, and with those instinctive forms of expression with which they were tampering.

Homans in his work on the life of the English villager in the thirteenth century has described the function of religion as pre-eminently, and above all, one of ritual. 'It consisted of a series of actions to be performed in a particular way on particular occasions. Much importance was attached to the performance of the ceremonial in precisely the manner prescribed by tradition. The liturgy was treated as if it were an incantation of magic which would lose its virtue if it departed from the proper form in the slightest particular.'[2] If this description is even partially accurate, the magnitude of the disturbance in rural society caused by the reformation is thrown into sharper relief. The degree of disruption in the years between the 1530s and the 1660s probably lies behind the striking difference in the rôle religious affairs played in the part of an English rural community in the 1870s, in which religious affairs were a matter for embarrassment, and the completely instinctive practice in a Russian community at the same period.[3]

Although there were little signs of disturbance to start with in the diocese of Ely, the hundred years of liturgical change starting in the 1540s culminated in the explosion of the 1640s, and the growth of an uprooted, and sometimes lunatic, fringe of 'seekers' of one kind and another. Little articulate reaction to the first and most sweeping changes made in the 1540s and 1550s was recorded; but the depth of feeling aroused by the reversal of these changes in the 1630s, when the holy tables were, once more placed 'altarwise' and railed in in the east end by Wren, bears witness to the passionate depth of feeling which had been roused amongst the peasantry by the alterations in liturgy and sacraments. Labourers were worried by the sign of the cross in baptism, yeomen and husbandmen were ready to deprive themselves of the Sacrament of Communion, which they still valued, because they would not

---

[2] G. C. Homans, *English Villagers of the Thirteenth Century* (New York 1960), p. 391.
[3] Shown in the two passages quoted at the beginning of Part 3.

come up to new altar-rails which, indifferent in themselves, had become symbols of this change in the fundamental relationship expressed in the Communion and therefore turned into a cause of profound disturbance.[4] Church clerks were willing to defy episcopal authority and carry the 'new' altar back to its position in the nave as a communion table.[5] All demonstrated how deeply the beliefs of the laity had been affected. In some cases, they were so deeply affected that no sect could hold the allegiance of the most vulnerable.[6]

Bishop Goodrich ruled from 1534 to 1554. He was a man of genuine Protestant convictions, despite his nominal reconversion under Mary at the end of his life. He supported Bishop Ridley in the debate over the doctrine of the Eucharist set forth in the Prayer Book of 1548,[7] and appointed Protestant chaplains within his own household. He was probably responsible for appointing Cox, who was later to prove both one of the outstanding reformers and the most outstanding bishop of Ely of the century, to the archdeaconry of Ely. He also promoted the known Protestant, Launcelot Ridley, Bishop Nicholas Ridley's first cousin, to the living of Willingham.

Since it fell to him to enforce the Henrican reformation, he was, perhaps, responsible for the most disturbing set of episodes in the spiritual lives of the laity, for the initial changes in liturgy and church order, altering traditional habits of worship established over centuries, were bound to be the most dislocating.

Bishop Goodrich's first major task was the proclamation of the royal headship of the church in a letter written in 1535, which was to be read from every pulpit in the diocese. The episcopal seal which witnessed the authenticity of the letter was to be shown to the congregations.[8] It is interesting that the bishop's seal was thought to be obviously recognisable. The importance that the Pope's headship of the church held in the thoughts of the laity cannot be gauged. The authority of the bishop known to them was evidently thought to be an adequate counter-weight. Robert Parkyn, the 'conservative late-medieval Catholic' who retained his benefice near Doncaster from the 1540s to his death in 1569, and wrote a *Narrative of the Reformation*, was certainly much less concerned by the abolition of papal authority than by changes in ritual.[9] It

---

[4] See above, pp. 236–7.   [5] See below, p. 268.   [6] See below, pp. 349–50.
[7] A. G. Dickens, *The English Reformation* (London 1964), p. 218.
[8] Felicity Heal, 'The Bishops of Ely and their Diocese during the Reformation Period: Ca. 1515–1600', unpublished Cambridge Ph.D. thesis (1972), p. 68. Many of my statements on the diocese in the sixteenth century are drawn from this thesis. I am extremely grateful to Dr Heal for allowing me to use her work, and quote her, in this generous way [hereafter Heal, thesis].
[9] A. G. Dickens and Dorothy Carr, eds., *The Reformation in England to the Accession of Elizabeth I* (London 1967), pp. 140–2.

is safe to assume that the next changes, which made a direct impact within the familiar parish churches of the laity in which they met regularly, which acted as a centre for community business as well as worship, and for which they were partly physically and financially responsible, meant more.

In 1541, the proclamation that every church should have a copy of the Bible of 'The Greatest Volume' was sent to every parish in Ely, and a copy read from the pulpit, and fixed to every church door.[10] Some of the churches in the diocese already had an English Bible by 1539, in response to Cromwell's injunctions of 1538.[11] Half the cost of this was borne by the parishioners themselves. In return, Coverdale's version of the Scriptures came for the first time within the reach of every literate parishioner. He, or even she, could also read Cranmer's preface,[12] which stated that 'to the reading of the Scripture, none can be enemy . . . It is convenient and good the Scripture . . . be read of all sorts and kinds of people, and in the vulgar tongue.'[13]

In the same year, 1541, Goodrich mounted an attack on image-worship, in response to a royal request to Cranmer. All clergy were required to make a search for any bones or images to which the people still made secret offerings, and to discover if any monument was venerated. The bishop was to be notified at once if superstitious practices were discovered. If the search was fruitless, the priest was to obtain the certificate of three 'trustworthy' parishioners that no memory of image-worship was kept alive in the community.[14] The certificates and court records do not survive; it would be interesting to know how superstitious practices were safely concealed at, for instance, Horseheath, where the veneration of a cross with figures on it earned Cox's severe censure in 1579,[15] or at Brinkley, where Goodrich himself later discovered traditional forms of worship continuing.

The introduction of Communion in both kinds in 1547, followed by the first English prayers within the Mass, in the spring of 1548, and its replacement by the Eucharist of the first English Prayer Book, which became the only legal form of worship on Whitsunday 1549,[16] seems to have passed without remark in the Ely records, although this must have been by far the most startling event to take place so far within the parish churches. Even the most illiterate, and least intelligent in every village must have become aware of the magnitude of the changes that were

10 Heal, thesis, pp. 81–2.
11 E.D.R., B/2/2. Dickens and Carr, *The Reformation in England*, p. 82.
12 To every edition after the first. *Idem*, pp. 112–13.
13 Dickens, *The English Reformation*, pp. 133–7, for the Great Bible and its effects.
14 Heal, thesis, pp. 80–1.
15 E.D.R., D/2/10, fo. 228.   16 Dickens, *The English Reformation*, p. 219.

taking place. It is only possible to deduce from the sole recorded reaction to the reintroduction of the Mass in 1553 that splits in village
opinions did indeed develop just here.

The next sweeping innovation, the rearrangement of church interiors,
the destruction of the altar, and its replacement by a 'decent table suitable for the administration of the sacrament of the bread and wine',
which followed the introduction of the vernacular, and demanded the
active and physical participation of both clergy and laity, did not pass
without comment. At the very end of 1550, Matthew Parker and
Edward Leedes, the diocesan chancellor, began a tour of the various
deaneries of the diocese to address meetings of the clergy on the change.
Robert Parkyn's most violent criticisms were reserved for the change in
position of the table, which he described in detail, and the words of
administration of the Communion used in the Prayer Book of 1552.
'Oh, how abominable heresy and unseemly order was this,' he wrote.[17]
Perhaps the tour made by Parker and Leedes was necessary. Again,
there is no evidence of the immediate impact in the diocese of Ely,
although   there is evidence that the reintroduction of the Mass only
three years later, in November 1553, and its reabolition only six years
after that, in 1559, bred both direct opposition and an insecure and
cynical attitude on the part of churchwardens. Cox found in his primary
visitation in 1561, that the area in the church chancels where the altar
had stood had not been decently paved and whitened in several places.
This was perhaps not entirely surprising since the altar had by now been
removed twice and replaced once, within ten years. There can by now
have been no generally accepted position for the altar, no certainty
about what it represented, and no feeling that its present position was
permanent, and so that the expense of paving was worth it. It is no wonder, therefore, that the churchwardens of Great St Mary's did not sell
their vestments and plate until between 1567 and 1568.[18] The wardens
of Holy Trinity, Cambridge, did not sell their 'alter stone' until 1573.
Churchwardens cannot have been the only members of the laity who
either expected, or feared, further reversals and innovations. Bewilder-
ment must have been common, and many people profoundly shaken by
so much interference with traditional forms of expression, which were
suddenly no longer traditional.

Few heretics were persecuted in the diocese under either Goodrich or
his Marian successor Thirlby. Goodrich appears in any case to have

---

[17] He passed the first Prayer Book with comparatively little comment. Dickens and
Carr, *The Reformation in England*, pp. 141–2.

[18] Churchwardens' Accounts of St Mary the Great, Cambridge, ed. Foster, *Proc.
Camb. Ant. Soc.* (1905), p. 164. Accounts of Holy Trinity deposited in the C.R.O.
personally searched by Mr Farrar for me.

tried to avoid persecution and to have treated offenders very leniently.[19] But those men who were charged with doctrinal error show clearly the different straws blowing in the changing winds of the 1540s and 1550s.

Three priests in the diocese were charged with doctrinal offences in the late 1530s. Two of them offended by holding reformed views which were at least ten years ahead of their time. Both made an attempt to administer Communion in both kinds to their congregations in 1537. In the case of the vicar of Caxton, it was a very crude attempt. He gave his parishioners ale to drink after administering the bread on Easter Sunday.[20]

In 1554, twenty per cent of the priests in the diocese were deprived, mainly for marriage. Only four of them were well-known Protestants. One of them, John Hullier, was martyred.[21] The laity also were affected. As early as 1540, before any of the liturgical changes in the village churches which might have been expected to start debate and argument, two laymen from Sawston were accused of heresy. William Potton admitted to having said that the picture of Christ in the roodloft was in fact a picture of the devil. He thus became the first known forebear of Dowsing in Ely. William Thornton successfully denied the rather curious charge brought against him, which was presumably a reaction against Mariolatry, of saying Christ had no mother for 'he saide that the holy goste was bothe his father and moother'.[22] The cases are particularly interesting, since the Huddlestons of Sawston Hall were resident lords of almost all the manors in the village, and were also one of the few families in the county to remain obstinate papists throughout the period. Their influence does not seem to have cowed their tenants.

The charge brought against Humphrey Turner of Girton, also in 1540, who denied the utility of infant baptism, was more serious, and he was pronounced a heretic. Even so, only public penance and abjuration of his beliefs was required of him.[23]

The spread of reformed opinions amongst the laity is witnessed to by the reaction to the Marian reintroduction of the Mass at Orwell, in 1553. Thomas Dobson, the vicar, was a married priest, and the wardens and questmen reported that he

contynnyn with his wife did take upon hym to saye masse and before he came to the alter, he used himself unreverently saying we must go to this gere with laughter and in toying so moch that the peple was so offended at his so prophaynly usying of that holy mystery that some of them coulde not abide but departed oute of the church, other some taryed was so slandered

[19] Heal, thesis, p. 76.   [20] *Ibid.* p. 74.   [21] *Ibid.* p. 96.
[22] *Ibid.* p. 76.   [23] *Ibid.*

that they were dryven into a great hevyness and fere that some were thereby confirmed in their lewdness. Also that he did not take holy water and holy breade for the space of xx weekes after we had masse in our churche by meanes where off we cannot think but that divers others did with lesse reverence and with wors will receive the same. Also we do present that Thomas Cundall as it is reported and certified by an honest and credible persone that beyng in an ale hous and talking of the Sacrament office did saye it is no better than this: and with those words he made a fyllip with his fingers and the said Thomas Cundale at a tyme of the elevacon dothe leane himself backward uppon the foremost stahll in the church without any reverence in externall gesture to the great offence of thos that be in the bodye of the churche. Also he promised that he would let one see a ballatt that is yntitled maistres masse.[24]

The parishioners of Orwell were therefore clearly split into two groups in 1553. There were those who were so offended by the behaviour of their priest in celebrating what they still thought of as a holy mystery that they either left the church or were driven into 'great hevyness' by his actions if they remained.[25] There were also those who had learnt to snap their fingers at the Mass. Thomas Cundale was not the only parishioner to behave in this way, for he obviously found a ready audience for his talk of the Sacrament in the alehouse he frequented, as well as a reader for the derogatory printed ballad he had. This audience was presumably drawn from those who were 'confirmed in their lewdness' by the priest's behaviour at the reintroduction of the Mass.[26]

The descent of reformed opinions at Orwell cannot be traced, since the records do not permit this.[27] In the 1670s, Orwell had both absolutely and proportionately more dissenters,[28] who were both Congregationalist and Muggletonian, than any other village in the county. It may be pure coincidence that it is one of the two villages where reactions amongst the laity against the Marian counter-reformation are recorded. Certainly, and surprisingly, considering the even spread of nonconformist opinion throughout the community at Orwell in the 1670s,[29] there were no identifiable signatories to the petition against Wren from the most prosperous section of the community taxed in 1641.[30]

The other village was Willingham, where Launcelot Ridley was the incumbent.[31] The spread of reformed opinions amongst his parishioners

[24] 'Churchwardens' Bills or Returns for the Deanery of Barton', *Proc. Cambs. and Hunts. Arch. Soc.*, v (1930–7), 263.
[25] The wardens and questmen obviously felt this way themselves, or such a full report of Thomas Dobson's behaviour would not have been made.
[26] Thomas Dobson later became the incumbent of Bassingbourn. See below, pp. 248–9.
[27] See below, pp. 253, 255, 265.
[28] Fifty-eight nonconformists. See below, p. 300.
[29] See below, pp. 301–2.   [30] See above. pp. 233–4.   [31] See above, p. 241.

there is witnessed by testators from Willingham, who showed in their wills that by the 1540s they believed that they depended for salvation on Christ's merits alone.[32] Ridley developed an ingenious device for escaping the effects of his deprivation, which was nominally for marriage, at the beginning of Mary's reign. He leased the parsonage before his deprivation, to his relation, Henry Ridley. According to the new rector, Thomas Parkinson, who was unable to gain possession, and eventually brought a Chancery suit against him. Launcelot Ridley had been resident in the parsonage most of the time since the lease had been made.

To whom [Parkinson explained] not only the said woman to whom he was unlawfully mariid divers and sondrey tymes Resortyd to the said parsonadge but also the said Henry Ridley his said supposid leese and divers marrid preistes of erronious opinions and corrupt Judgements wher they usse divers secreth commnicacons to the offence of the conformable parishioners ther and the evell example of all other evill doers and the incorigment of such as be of there pernicious secte.[33]

Independent confirmation that some of the laity of Willingham were convinced Protestants comes from the story of Henry Orinel of Willingham, who, in about 1555, travelled to Colchester.[34] In his words, 'The cause of my repayre there at that tyme was: that I was desirous to provide that my conscience should not be entangled with the Popish pitch.' He was not alone, or unknown in Colchester, which was

at that tyme frequented, because it aforded many godly and zealous Martyrs, whiche continually with their bloud watered those seedes which by the preaching of the worde had been sowne most plentifully in the hartes of Christians in the dayes of good King Edward. This town for the earnest profession of the Gospell became like unto a Citie upon a hill and as a candle upon a candlesticke gave great light to all those who for the comfort of their conscience came to confere there from divers places of the Realme, and repairying to common Innes had by night their Christian exercises, which in other places could not be gotten.[35]

---

[32] See below, pp. 334–7.   [33] P.R.O., C1/1373.
[34] The story is given in Strype, *Annals of the Reformation*, II, 596–7, who took it *verbatim* from William Wilkinson's preface 'A very brief and true description of the first springing up of the Heresie termed, The Familie of Love, which containeth the places where, and the parties by whom the said Heresie was broached' to his *A Confutation of Certain Articles Delivered Unto the Familye of Love* (1579) reprinted as no. 279 in *The English Experience*, by the Da Capo Press (Amsterdam 1970). According to Wilkinson, Orinel was living in 1579, and it sounds as if they had talked together. Strype gives Orinel's name as Crinel; Wilkinson has it in both forms. There are no Crinels in the Willingham parish register, but there are numerous Orinels.
[35] For a cooler appraisal of the Colchester Protestant congregation, see Dickens, *The English Reformation*, p. 275.

So Orinel, at an inn,

met with divers of mye acquaintance, as also with strangers, who came thether to conferre concerning the safetie of their conscience, where William Raven of St. Ives who came thither at that time with me and was my bed-fellow, having likewise fled beying in danger for Religion.

The scene in the inn at Colchester is painted with extraordinary vivid-ness. It was full of earnest seekers after salvation. Despite the reputation of the town for martyrdoms, a Dutch heretic, Christopher Vitells, who was a disciple of the founder of the Family of Love, Henry Niklaus, was there preaching Familist doctrines openly. His chief opponent in the debate which developed on the divinity of Christ was a 'servant to Mr Laurence of Barnehall in Essex'. When the serving men failed to refute, or reinterpret, a Pauline text, it was to the horror of 'two women Gospellers' who were present, as well as Orinel, the Willingham hus-bandman, and his friend from St Ives. Orinel was so disturbed that, as he said, 'I was fully mynded to go to Oxford to aske connsaile of Bishop Ridley and M. Latimer concernyng that matter, had I not met with some man, to satisfie my conscience in the meane season.'

Here indeed is theological debate amongst the common laity; ser-vants, husbandmen and the women who were to predominate in so many dissenting congregations in the seventeenth century, were all present at this heated overnight argument in the 1550s. One of the most striking things about the scene is that it is recorded by accident. We would have no knowledge of it at all, if the eager young student Henry Wilkinson, who was anxious to define and refute the doctrines of the Family of Love for his bishop, had not sought out Orinel twenty years later, simply because he was known to have heard an evangelist of the Family speak. The details of the setting, and the protagonists involved, held neither interest nor surprise for Wilkinson. He only put them down to give the context in which Vitells, the heretical joiner, preached. We are left in complete ignorance of the frequency of such travelling and argument. The very fact that Wilkinson records it all with so little sur-prise, and in so matter-of-fact a way, suggests that it was to him commonplace.

The astonishing picture of a husbandman of Willingham, who farmed a half-yardland in 1575,[36] travelling to Colchester to refresh himself with spiritual exercises, meeting several friends there, unable to resolve doubts about the doctrine of the divinity of Christ, and seriously con-sidering travelling on to Oxford to get help from Ridley and Latimer, gives a brief and illuminating picture of the way the rural laity were

[36] See above, Table 8, p. 135.

247

involved in the doctrinal developments of the reformation and counter-reformation. It is given substance by the simple fact that over half the 135 Marian martyrs whose status is given by Foxe, were rural labourers.[37] The next largest group were women. It is therefore impossible that Orinel was an isolated figure, and unlikely that he was the only husbandman in Willingham to be spiritually committed to reformed precepts in this way.

Even though Ely provided few martyrs under Mary[38] other information bears indirect witness to the depth of the reception of Protestant feeling in the diocese. The dedicatory clauses of the wills of the peasantry in Willingham show a strong emphasis on justification through Christ's merits alone, from the 1540s, despite a minor fashionable swing back to traditional formulae in a few cases under Mary.[39] Perhaps the scarcity of Catholics in the diocese, even in the great anti-Catholic scare of the 1580s, is the most telling evidence of all.[40] But consideration of the bizarre changes in Bassingbourn brings home more than anything else the profound alteration in the generally accepted attitudes of the laity in the first half of the sixteenth century.

In 1511 a play on 'the holy martyr St George' was performed in Bassingbourn on St Margaret's Day. Bassingbourn was a large and prosperous village, but all the same, twenty-eight townships round about contributed sums, which went towards the purchase of a 'play book', garments, minstrels and 'waits' from Cambridge for three days, and bread, ale and victuals for the players. Among the townships contributing to an occasion that was obviously a very grand one, judging only by the amount of roast mutton consumed, were those later dissenting centres, well known to Holcroft in the seventeenth century, and the despair of the episcopal officials, Litlington, Orwell, Meldreth, Shepreth, Fowlmere and Foxton. An image of St George was purchased at considerable expense out of the proceeds. When the church goods of Bassingbourn were listed in detail in 1498, they were extraordinarily rich, and included four chalices, four crosses with hangings, a pyx of silver with a crucifix, four altar cloths and frontals for the high altar,

---

[37] Dickens, *The English Reformation*, pp. 266–7.
[38] One clerical martyr from the county, and two laymen who belonged to a Protestant group which was headed by the village constable, from Wells, in the Isle. J. Strype, *Ecclesiastical Memorials*, III (2) (Oxford 1822), 554–6, who gives the fullest list according to Professor Dickens (*The English Reformation*, p. 266), only lists the places from which martyrs come, and their numbers, not their names. The two laymen from the Isle were burnt in 1555, and the county martyr in 1556, according to this list. I suspect, if I am right about the depth of the reception of reformed feeling by this date, that the lenient administration of the diocese was responsible for the comparative lack of persecution in Ely.
[39] See below, p. 334.   [40] See below, p. 255, n. 70.

and six or seven altar cloths and frontals each for the Altar of Our Lady and St John's altar, cloths for veiling the images of Mary and John, the high crucifix and the 'other images' and 'four suits of vestments for priest, deacon and subdeacon, coloured purple, blue and red, and one for the salutation of our Lady', as well as nine other assorted sets of vestments for Sundays, ferial days and Lent. There were also at least five mass books, two of which were printed, and a new and old antiphonary, a legendary and four processionaries, an epistle book, two manuals, an old psalter, a Bible and another book.[41]

Under fifty years later, in 1557, Thomas Dobson, the once-married vicar of Orwell, who had offended some of his parishioners there so deeply over the reintroduction of the Mass and said 'we must go to this gere with laughter', was presented as a suitable incumbent to this parish. He had obviously found it wiser to conform.[42] There is no record of unrest in the parish over the attitudes of their new priest, although it had once enjoyed revelry so much, and had found no offence in images or vestments. In the late sixteenth and early seventeenth centuries whatever nascent Puritanism there was at Bassingbourn and to the region immediately around it was fed by Master William Bradshaw. He had first been admitted to Emmanuel College, Cambridge, in 1589, before becoming a fellow of Sidney Sussex College. He 'gave a weekly lecture at Abington about eight miles from Cambridge, at the instance of Master Pigot, a religious gentleman . . . and also . . . a weekly lecture with some other ministers, at Bassingbourn, not far thence distant . . . and then to Steeple Morden by master Martin who held the appropriation and entertained him as a Lecturer, in regard of the infirmitie of the partie that was possessed of the Vicarage'.[43] In the 1650s, the first covenanted Independent church in the county was gathered there.[44]

THE SEARCH FOR PURITANISM AND EARLY SEPARATISM

The obvious way to see whether the theory of the seventeenth-century nonconformist that the roots of their beliefs ran back to forebears in the sixteenth century and particularly to Robert Browne's activities, is to see whether these supposed forebears and their opinions left any trace in the regular diocesan visitations conducted in the sixteenth century, by the bishop of Ely, and in the cases he conducted by virtue of his office in his consistory court against parishioners in spiritual and moral error.

[41] Bassingbourn Churchwardens Accounts, C.R.O., P11/5/1.
[42] See above, pp 244–5.
[43] Samuel Clarke, *A Generall Martyrologie*, p. 102.
[44] See above, pp. 225–6.

The dating of the growth of the Puritanism which was so predominant in the diocese in the next century is so difficult, and indeed, so impossible that suspicion must rest, despite the lack of definite evidence, on the whole period from the 1540s onwards.

The lack of interest shown by the episcopal courts in the beliefs, as opposed to the morals, of the laity, can be demonstrated from the records of Cox's episcopate. Ely was fortunate in having a man of the calibre of Bishop Cox at its head during the Elizabethan settlement. As well as becoming a leading exponent of the *Via Media* himself by the 1570s, anathematising papist and Puritan alike, he was resident in his diocese. He rarely left his local manors after 1566, except on formal business as a prince of the church. He was no longer temperamentally 'progressive' on his appointment and by 1571 had lost all sympathy with 'radical protestantism'.[45] At least five of his visitations were conducted partly by Cox in person. The visitation records of a bishop as zealous as Cox for sound reform and conformity should therefore mirror any turbulence caused by Robert Browne's teachings, and reflect the growth of any strong heretical feeling amongst the laity. But, as Dr Heal has written, 'The clergy occupied such an important part in the records of Cox's episcopate that it is difficult to avoid the feeling that the laity were somewhat neglected, and that there was a tendency to underestimate the degree of independent thought of which they were capable, and the importance of increased literacy, and of the dissemination of the Bible.' The only visitation articles which survive from Cox's episcopate show that this was indeed so.[46] Elementary religious instruction, punctual attendance at church every Sunday, and morality, were to be the objects of inquiry amongst the laity, with the single exception of 'whether there be any persons that . . . presume to exercise any kind of ministry in the church of God without imposition of hands, and ordinary authority'.

Cox's visitations and office books[47] show the normal exercise of an Elizabethan bishop's administrative powers, together with a certain reforming zeal of his own. Above all, he laid emphasis on an active, preaching ministry. He showed particular concern over absenteeism and pluralities amongst his clergy, although there were not often cases

[45] Patrick Collinson, *The Elizabethan Puritan Movement* (London 1967), pp. 61 and 117.

[46] W. H. Frere, ed., *Visitation Articles and Injunctions*, III (1559–75) (London 1910), 296–302. See particularly articles 4, 5, 18, 20, 30, 33. Dated by Frere to 1571, but by Felicity Heal to 1567 or 1570.

[47] The following conclusions are based on examination of Cox's visitations of 1564 (C.U.L., E.D.R., B/2/4) and 1579 (E.D.R., D/2/10, fos. 150ff.) and office court books for 1567–8 (E.D.R., 8/2/6), 1568–70 (E.D.R., D/2/8), and 1576–9 (E.D.R., D/2/10).

as shocking as that of the vicar of Longstanton. In 1564, this vicar had been absent from his cure for twenty years, being a canon of St Paul's. Not surprisingly, the church was ruined, the register not kept, and the children not taught the catechism.[48]

Many of the livings in the diocese were extremely poor. No less than sixty-two per cent of them were impropriated, that is, had the major part of their profits in the form of the 'great tithes' mulcted from them for the benefit of a lay rector. This was a full twenty per cent higher than the national average in 1603. The situation came about as the result of a combination of both ex-monastic impropriations, and impropriations for the benefit of colleges within the university. Bishop Cox was perfectly justified when he complained in 1563, 'my diocesse is very miserable, for almost all is improperede'.[49] As a result, any reforming bishop was bound to be waging a ceaseless battle with non-residence and pluralism amongst his clergy, for these were the two inevitable consequences of parochial poverty. The likelihood of clerical absenteeism has always to be remembered in Ely, and set against the natural advantage the see drew from its proximity to the university, an unusually well-qualified clergy.[50]

Cox and his administrators took great pains to see that sermons were preached at least quarterly,[51] the Queen's Injunctions read, and that each parish church had all the volumes of theological and propagandist literature prescribed by law.[52] Churchwardens were constantly in trouble for lacking one or another of these volumes, and having to obtain them. Cox also showed great concern for the teaching of the young. In his visitation of 1564 there were constant presentments like those of the curate of Castle Camps who did not teach the *pueri* their catechism, or the rector of Little Gransden who *non docet Parvulos*. In the parishes of West Wratting and Grantchester it was, unusually, said to be the fault of the parents 'and Maisters' that the children were not sent to catechism.[53] The charge made in 1579 against the vicar of Swaffham Bulbeck was unusually precise. He 'dothe not instruct the youth and servants of bothe sexes in the catechism, he takethe not the names of the youthe that cannot say the catechism. He admittethe some to

[48] E.D.R., B/2/4 fo. 176.
[49] Heal, thesis, p. 111. A third of the parishes in the whole diocese were held by non-residents in 1561, when the situation was, admittedly, particularly bad. Of the 152 benefices in the diocese 98 had been held by the monasteries and colleges between them before the reformation.
[50] See above, pp. 175–6.
[51] I have not attempted to chronicle the gradual improvement in educational standards and preaching amongst Cox's clergy; the subject has been extensively dealt with by Dr Heal in her thesis.
[52] See above, pp. 206–7. [53] E.D.R., B/2/4, fos. 119, 154, and D/2/10, fo. 167.

the Communion, that be above xx yeres oulde which cannot say the Catechism.'[54] The wardens of Bulbeck appear to have been unusually vigilant. In 1569, they had brought a charge against Lucy Neales that 'she did receive the Communion and could not saye the lords prayre nor the articles of here beleffe'. She had, as a result, both to confess her fault publicly after the reading of the Gospel on the following Sunday, and learn the Lord's Prayer and the Creed and say them to the vicar within three weeks.[55] Such meticulous care and oversight did not penetrate always, and probably did not do so often, to the communicating laity; but it is perhaps remarkable that it ever did.

Neglect of church buildings and inadequate church furniture gave cause for concern also, and formed one of the most bulky items in the office books. Reading the presentations for repairs and neglect gives a disturbing, and perhaps erroneous, impression of the degree of decay of church buildings by the 1560s. *Ruinosa* was an adjective which was probably lightly used, and it would probably be unwise to stress the amount of dilapidation too far, although the uncertainties of the last twenty years may well have led both parishioners, and a new class of lay rectors, to neglect their responsibilities towards a building the uses of which had now become ambiguous and debatable. Certainly the account of the state of Shepreth church in 1579 is too precise and vivid to allow of any doubt of the state of repair there. It also gives a clear indication of the way the function of a church was now thought of by the parishioners, not as the place where the Sacrament was re-presented, but as the place where the word of God was read. 'The chancel', they deposed 'is not repaired ... that lyeth more lyker a swines style than a place to hear gods worde red in, and fyled with birds and owles to the great annoyance of the parishioners there in could frost rayne and snowey weather'.[56] The bishop's officials were involved in constant battles with rectors, like Edward Bland of Toft, who was excommunicated twice in 1569 for failure to repair the chancel which was 'redy to fall downe'.[57] Occasionally they met an unforeseen and ironical check, as they did at Waterbeach in 1579, when, the wardens presented, if the church 'be not repaired in a very short time, it will be utterlye spoiled and fall downe. And we have often times complayned of that but no remedye is had therefor, my L(ord) of Elye is proprietarie thereof.'[58]

After the amount of liturgical change and expense involved since

[54] E.D.R., D/2/10, fo. 50.   [55] E.D.R., D/2/8, fo. 55v.
[56] E.D.R., D/2/10, fo. 165.
[57] E.D.R., D/2/8, fos. 21v and 29v, 49, 40v, 44, 59 and 60v.
[58] E.D.R., D/2/10, fo. 181v.

the 1540s it was not surprising that some wardens found themselves without the proper vestments and plate. Things were curiously confused at Barton in 1569,[59] when the wardens were presented not only for lacking a 'lynnen Clothe, and a coveringe of buckram for the communion table', but also for having 'a chalys insted of a cuppe'. Some of the poorer parishes like East Hatley and Tadlow had no communion table at all in 1564.[60] Hatley, which only had nine households in 1563, still did not have a 'fair table' for the Communion in 1579, nor a silk or buckram cover for it, nor the Homilies, the Paraphrases, Musculus, the Injunctions or any register, even though 'one person doth write the names orderly'.[61] Nor did they have a surplice. But the wardens of bigger parishes like Impington were also presented for lacking a communion table in 1564 and Boxworth for only having an 'insufficient' one in 1570. The wardens of St Vigor's parish in Fulbourn still lacked a communion cup in the same year. The new wardens of Bourn at the end of 1570 were in an unusual amount of trouble 'for they have not in their parish church a perfecte Byble, a decent coveringe and a fayre lynnen cloth for the Communion table, a perfecte Communion Boke, A Chest sufficient for the poor mans stockes, And that the church ys unrepayred'.[62] It was well into the 1580s before parish churches were re-equipped with 'decent' and adequate furnishings for their functioning under the ecclesiastical settlement of 1559.

Most emphasis was then laid by Cox on the residence of the clergy, preaching at least quarterly, the acquisition of the prescribed books by every church, and the regular catechising of the laity. But apart from noticing absenteeism from church, Dr Heal says, there is no evidence in Bishop Cox's 'letters or his records that the independent rôle of the laity, or their support for puritanism, were important matters for him'. It was the morals, not the opinions, of the laity which took up a great deal of the attention of Cox and his officials. 'Scandalous living', not heresy, was the prime concern of the ecclesiastical officials. There were odd presentations for non-reception of Communion, as well as absenteeism, but the vast bulk of the office cases dealt with were made up of one sort of licentious living or another. Adultery, fornication, pre-marital pregnancy, the old case of bigamy, failure to marry after betrothal, or, once married, to co-habit with one's spouse, together with a bit of scolding, backbiting, and brawling between neighbours made up the vast mass of the consistory court's business.

---

[59] E.D.R., D/2/8, fo. 22v.   [60] E.D.R., B/2/4, fo. 163.
[61] B.M., Harleian MS 594, fos. 196r–200v (Episcopal returns for 1563), and E.D.R., D/2/10, fo. 194.   [62] E.D.R., B/2/4, fo. 178; D/2/8, fos. 116v, 88 and 117v.

A nice example of the type of business that mainly occupied the court was produced by a group of cases from Graveley in 1570. The rector was presented because there 'was no sermon this whole year, neyther that he readeth the Queenes Maiesties Injunctions'. The farmer of the rectory was charged because 'the chancel both in stone worcke and timber worcke ys utterly decayed'. The wardens lacked 'the principal Articles of Religion' and Thomas Wasse was suspected of adultery with Richard Hobson's wife, who was also charged, and possibly with Richard Farmer's wife as well. He failed to clear himself, and was enjoined to 'stand iij severall Sundays or holye dayes in the church porch of graveley from the second peal to morning prayre untill the readinge of the second lesson, be clothed in a white shete downe to the ground, a white wand in his hand and ij papers with great letters of abhomynable Adultrye, thone uppon his backe and thother uppon his brest'.[63] Thomas Wasse, and William Shankes of Landbeach, who 'by common report and fame hath forsaken his wife and followed a mayde his harlotte by the space of a yere . . . and hathe kept and maintained the same harlott at Cambridge wynde mill' represent the largest group of sinners to appear in the consistory court in Cox's time. To the twentieth-century reader treatment meted out to these people seems unlikely to stimulate genuine penitence, or indeed any reaction but resentment. It certainly caused considerable resentment at the time. John Taylor of Longstanton appeared in court in 1579 charged with 'indecent and unseemly speeches towards the parson there (Mr Howgrave) sayeinge that he wolde see him (meaninge . . . Mr Howgrave) hanged before that he wolde doe enye penance'.[64] In 1608, William Day of Westley Waterless appeared for 'rayleinge uppon Nicholus Carpenter Apparitor of this Courte and calleing him knave and sayeing that he had a knaves office'.[65]

There were a few cases in which the human dilemma concerned was recognised, like that of Luke Barefoot of Eltisley who, when in 1570 he was presented as having been 'absent from the Communion the day yt was appointed to be celebrated' answered 'his wyf recevyed the holy Communion ye same day, and that he had ij or iij small children at whome, which he was constreyned to tend and kept the same daye. And that he himself the next tyme that the holy Communion was celebrated, did recyve.' William Kirke of Stow-cum-Quy was in a similar dilemma, and was also presented for absence from church in 1570. He confessed the truth of the charge, but claimed he was driven by necessity, since his wife was 'lyinge in chilld bed, and also his

[63] E.D.R., D/2/8, fo. 115r and v, 131; D/2/10, fo. 25.
[64] E.D.R., D/2/10, fo. 242.   [65] E.D.R., B/2/28, fo. 12v.

children wanted succor, for the which he was then compelled to travell in fetchinge meal from the myll and suche other lyke'.[66] Both cases were dismissed. The dilemma of both men is given point by the case of the woman from Duxford, who in 1579 brought her child to church and 'disturbs the minister very much in service time', and when told to amend her fault 'useth lewd speech'.[67] She asked public pardon ultimately. The dilemma is not unfamiliar to modern parents, but no satisfactory compromise between obligatory attendance at church under penalty of fines for failure, and the problem of what to do with young children, seems to have been worked out in the sixteenth century.

An unusual degree of tolerance was exercised also towards Helen Ormes of Sawston, who in 1579 was presented 'for not receiving Communion for four or five years and remaining stubborn'. She was also dismissed, when she was deposed to be 'besydes hir wyttes'.[68] But moral lapses met with short shrift and sharp penance.

The emphasis in the ecclesiastical court on morality was further stressed at the end of 1570 by presentments of churchwardens 'because they have not certified quarterly the names of all swereres, blasphemers, drunkards and adulterers'.[69] Only 37 out of 346 cases in a register of excommunications made in the diocese between 1571 and 1584 were based on doctrine, or failure to communicate, or to attend church.[70] The minds and opinions of the laity, the common people of God, did not seem to Cox and his ecclesiastical officials to have merited any attention. The sole exception was the extent of surviving Catholicism.

The point is made with considerable force when the growth of the sect of the Family of Love in the diocese is considered. Henry Orinel of Willingham was not secure from further pressure by the Familist evangelist Christopher Vitells, when he returned home in 1555. Vitells passed through Willingham when he was 'wandryñg uppe and downe the Country (to visit his Disciples)' and sent for Orinel 'to come and speak with hym at an Alehouse, but I sent hym word that I would not come at hym'.[71] Willingham lay on the old main road, which is now a

---

[66] E.D.R., D/2/8, fos. 124v and 81.
[67] E.D.R., D/2/10, fo. 211.   [68] E.D.R., D/2/10, fo. 153v.
[69] Abington-cum-Shingay and Melbourn. E.D.R., D/2/8, fos. 128 and 129.
[70] E.D.R., B/2/9. Noticed and briefly commented on by Collinson, *The Elizabethan Puritan Movement*, p. 40. Sixteen of these were papists excommunicated in the great scare of 1581/2, or soon after. The number of proven Catholics was very low, and remained so in the diocese (there were only ten in the part of the county of Cambridge covered by the diocese of Ely in 1676 and ten more in the parish of Cheveley in the county of Cambridge, but the diocese of Norwich). This scarcity of Catholics of determined opinions in the 1580s is in itself indirect witness to the strength of reformed opinion amongst the laity.
[71] W. Wilkinson, *A Confutation of Certain Articles*, p. vi. See above, p. 246, n. 34.

driftway, from Cambridge to Ely. Vitells was obviously more successful in his preaching in some quarters than he was with Orinel, for in 1561 two Surrey men 'told how one of their congregation of the Family had sent for a wife from the Isle'. The adherents of the sect must therefore have been known to be established there by then.[72] In 1579, Cox encouraged William Wilkinson to expose the beliefs of the Family, and his book was dedicated to Cox 'because that within this Isle of Ely and otherwise within your Lordshypes Dioces, divers doe suspect that ... dayly those swarmes increase which in the end ... will wonderfully disquiet and molest the Church of God'. At the end of 1580, nearly seventy supposed adherents of the Family were examined by a Commission which included Richard Greenham, and fifteen men and women were imprisoned as members.[73] Cox had personally visited at least some of the deaneries in his regular visitation the year before,[74] but there is no trace of a single one of these people in the returns for any of the parishes concerned – even Balsham which produced six, and Shudy Camps which produced five, obdurate members of the Family of Love for Cox and his commission to imprison in the following year. This neglect is even more curious in the case of Balsham where Andrew Perne, rector of Balsham and dean of Ely, as well as five times vice-chancellor of the university, master of Peterhouse, and master-trimmer of sails to whatever ecclesiastical wind blew, had carried out his own investigation into a small group of six suspects in 1574.[75] Three of Perne's suspects, cleared in 1574, appeared again as obdurate in 1580. Their existence must have been well known; but the visitation of 1579 showed no care to investigate their opinions. Other matters preoccupied the churchwardens more. At Cottenham,[76] for instance, four couples had begotten children before wedlock, the schoolmaster had no licence, and Thomas Hawkins would not pay 16d for church repairs and maintain his part of the churchyard wall. Perhaps worst of all was the case of William Starling who 'misbehaved himself in church by sleeping ... and being rebuked by one of the questmen, he did give him froward answers'. But no one thought to mention that John Essex had odd opinions, although Cox imprisoned him at the end of 1580 as a member of the Family.

Despite persecution, the Family survived; the wills of four of fifteen

---

[72] Dr Heal has expanded the work she did on the Family of Love in her thesis in 'The Family of Love and The Diocese of Ely', *Studies in Church History*, 9 (Cambridge 1972), pp. 213–22.
[73] Gonville and Caius College, MS 53/30, fos. 126v–129r, and particularly fos. 72v–73r.   [74] E.D.R., D/2/10, fos. 150ff.
[75] Strype, *The Life and Acts of M. Parker* (1711), pp. 472–3. See above, p. 208, for the literacy of the Family.   [76] E.D.R., D/2/10, fos. 176–7.

of the named adherents from the county who were imprisoned in 1580 can be traced.[77] They show various interesting features, common to later dissenting groups. All four died between 1601 and 1623, at least twenty, and up to forty, years after their discovery. They were all therefore young men when they were converted. Even these four wills show that the Familists intermarried across the county, as well as within their own villages, and managed to maintain contact with each other across considerable distances.[78] Dissent and separatism was in the sixteenth century, as it was later, a family phenomenon.

Nothing can illustrate the limitations of sixteenth-century visitation returns and court books more clearly as guides to the genesis of dissent than the complete failure of the Ely records to document the growth of the Family. Concentration on morality, rather than belief, was general in the later sixteenth century, however. As Dr Marchant has pointed out, much of the 'reinvigoration of church discipline' of the period was directed against what was strongly felt to be 'the permissive society of the 1550s'.[79] The point could not be better reinforced than by the figures he prints covering the type of presentment made in office cases in deaneries as far apart as Yorkshire, Cheshire, Suffolk and Somerset from the 1590s to the 1630s.[80] Everywhere cases of sexual immorality formed the largest group of cases presented, and usually the outstanding group, with the single exception of the deanery of Sudbury in the 1630s, where non-attendance at Communion loomed even larger. Furthermore, there were always more presentations for recusancy than for nonconformity. The latter were a negligible group. In his *Puritans and Church Courts in the Diocese of York*, Dr Marchant shows how, during the period when Puritanism was established in the diocese – for which, after all, the high commission records do survive and enable a very complete picture to be gained – practically no attention was paid to it. Archbishops Grindal and Sandys were actively concerned with the establishment of a preaching ministry. Piers, who from 1589 to 1594 made an 'increased effort to enforce conformity', in his visitation of 1594, discovered no more than two Puritans in his entire diocese. When men like Christopher Shute, who was presented for nonconformity after eighteen years in his living, were themselves members of the high commission, at a time when the Archbishops' attention was almost entirely directed to establishing an active preaching ministry, it is no wonder that 'the establishment of Puritanism cannot be adequately

---

[77] John Tayler of Balsham, Consistory Court of Ely, Wills, Liber Morley, fo. 86; Henry Mersley or Mershe of Balsham, Liber X, fo. 306; Thomas Hockley of Horningsea, Liber W, fo. 132; John Essex of Cottenham, Liber Z°fo. 256.
[78] See below, p. 264.   [79] Marchant, *The Church Under the Law*, pp. 240–1.
[80] *Ibid.* p. 219.

illustrated from court records for the very reason that relatively little action was taken against nonconformity in the diocese in Elizabethan times'.[81] Archbishop Matthews, who ruled over the see from 1606 to 1628, excelled in toleration, and in his time the founder of the Grindletonians, Roger Brearley, preached unsilenced for fifteen years in the district of Craven and held conventicles there. None of the laymen who attended these conventicles was prosecuted in the attack made on the Puritans in 1627, although their names were given. This was one of the areas in which Quakerism later flourished. If this was the general approach to lay nonconformity before the Laudians, and it appears that it was, it is impossible to wonder why the sixteenth-century roots of seventeenth-century dissent amongst the laity cannot be documented. The ecclesiastical courts were generally not interested, and so the records do not exist.

A partial exception can be made for the archdeaconry courts of Essex and Colchester, where the godly were regularly presented from the 1580s for travelling on Sundays to hear an acceptable sermon, if they happened to have a non-preaching incumbent. Sometimes the place of origin of the absentees was recorded; sometimes they were even licensed to attend church elsewhere; and sometimes there were even descriptions of a conventicle in the Act Books.[82] At Ramsey, in 1581, a dozen villagers gathered in a clearing, which was regularly used as a preaching place, 'to eat roast beef and goose while listening to one William Collett, who expounded St John's Gospel from a ladder'.[83]

Ely does not provide any examples which are as happily vivid as this. Nowhere do the records speak of the exposition of St John's Gospel from a ladder. There were certainly parishes which had a suspiciously high number of absentees, who were absent not merely because they were scandalous livers, or feared to be taken up for debt, or because they had to get the crops in whether it was in the time of divine service on a sabbath or not, but for some other, unstated reason. Only the parishioners of East Hatley in 1580, 'doe goe to other churches to sermons' according to their wardens.[84] Quite often, parishes

---

[81] R. A. Marchant, *The Puritans in the Church Courts in the Diocese of York, 1560–1642* (London 1960), pp. 16–25, 29–43, particularly pp. 40–1.

[82] The movement has been analysed by Professor Collinson, both in 'The Godly: Aspects of Popular Protestantism in Elizabethan England', *Papers Presented to the Past and Present Conference on Popular Religion* (1960), particularly pp. 11–16, and *Elizabethan Puritan Movement*, pp. 372–82.

[83] Collinson, 'The Godly', p. 16. It is possible that the courts of Essex reflected more of the Puritan activities of the county because of the avowed anti-Puritanism of Aylmer, bishop of London from 1576. Collinson, *Elizabethan Puritan Movement*, pp. 201–2.   [84] E.D.R., D/2/10, fo. 194.

which had a noticeable number of absentees, or wardens who failed to make returns of absenteeism, were later dissenting centres. At the end of 1570, the wardens of Litlington, Orwell and Steeple Morden were all presented, not for failing to report scandalous livers, but for 'not takeing the forfeiture of xijd of negligent comers to the church'.[85] All of them admitted the charges. The most general charge was made by the new wardens in 1579 at Sawston. They reported, suspiciously,

We doubte not but that manie have deserved by reason of wilfullness and otherwise to have paid the forfeture ... howbe we cannot learne that it hathe been taken with us of longe time, ffor if it had been trewlye taken ... either the poore mens boxe shoulde have ben better stowed with money, or ells our churche manye times better filled with people.[86]

This charge was too general and was allowed to lapse, but Bottisham, Chesterton, Meldreth and Thriplow,[87] all of which had active dissenting histories later, provided lists of four or more absentees without reason in the late 1560s or 1570s. The Swaffhams were also noticeably turbulent parishes. Such evidence is of the slimmest and most insubstantial kind, and will not serve to illustrate the origins of dissent in Ely amongst the laity. There is no evidence which will serve in the absence of information from the diocesan records, except that of the growth of the Family of Love, and a couple of fragments which came from the long vacancy of the see after Cox's death in 1581 until the appointment of Martin Heton to the see in 1599.

Despite Cox's conservatism, and antipathy to radical Puritanism, the need to promote an active Protestant preaching ministry still weighed so heavily with him that he was responsible for appointing to livings several men who were later to refuse to conform to Whitgift's Eleven Articles of 1583. It was typical of him that he used Richard Greenham so many times, to confer with recusants in doubt,[88] as well as to confute the members of the Family in 1579,[89] despite Greenham's lengthy 'answere to the Bishop of Ely' in 1573,[90] in which he refused to wear the surplice or use 'the communion book'. Such men were too valuable to him to lose. It was typical of Cox, and his desire for an educated clergy and instructed laity, that he supported Grindal in 1576

---

[85] E.D.R., D/2/8, fos. 128*v*, 121*v*, 128.   [86] E.D.R., D/2/10, fo. 153*v*.
[87] E.D.R., D/2/8, fos. 1*v*–2*r*; D/2/10, fos. 18*v*, 210, 245*r* and *v*.
[88] As, for instance, with Mistress Mary Johnson of Tadlow, who was directed to confer with him 'in certaine points to be perswayded to receyve' in 1580. E.D.R., D/2/10, fos. 195*v*–196*r*.
[89] See above, p. 256. Greenham drew up his own set of articles to be presented to the Familists, as well as those presented by the general commission.
[90] *A parte of a register* .... (Edinburgh or Middleburg (?) 1593), pp. 86–93.

when he refused to suppress the spiritual exercises and prophesyings taking place in the counties.[91] Cox wrote to Burghley

I trust ... her Maiestye seking especiallye the glorye of god, and the quiet and nedeful edyfyinge of her Peple, may be moved to have Further Consideracion of this matter. And when the greate ignorance, Idlenesse and lewdnesse of the greate number of Poore and Blinde Prestes in the Clergye shalbe depelye weyed ... it wilbe thowght most necessarye to Call them and drive them to some travayle, and exercise of gods holy word, whereby theye maye be the better able to discharge ther Bounden duty towards thee Flocke.[92]

This attitude of Cox's is probably responsible for the poor response Robert Browne met with round Cambridge amongst the Puritans in the early 1570s, because they felt that the authority of the bishops was 'tolerable' even if it was not scriptural; on the grounds that the bishops did preach the word of God.[93] The particular bishop they had in mind must necessarily have been Cox.

In 1582, soon after Cox's death, and the beginning of the vacancy, came the meeting of 'three-score ministers appointed out of Essex, Cambridgeshire and Norfolk' at Cockfield, near Bury, which shortly led to a general conference in Cambridge, and ultimately to the establishment of the Presbyterian *classis* at Dedham on the borders of Essex and Suffolk in the same year.[94] The minutes of the *classis* are far from illuminating on the degree to which the Cambridgeshire clergy were involved. Richard Greenham was the sole parochial priest listed as a member of the *classis*; the rest, like Chaderton, Harrison and Perkins, were notable scholars, publicists, and were all fellows of colleges.[95] Chaderton was frequently applied to by assemblies which were formed from elected members of small *classes*, debating matters of moment. The 'brethren at Cambridge' were likewise consulted.[96] There was one Cambridgeshire organisation of ministers, however, as various entries show. Bancroft wrote, 'within a while after, viz 1587 (as I suppose) there was in like sort an assemblie or Synode helde of the Cambridgeshire brotherhood, accompanied peradventure with some of other

[91] Collinson, *Elizabethan Puritan Movement*, pp. 191–6.
[92] B.M., Lansdowne 2529. Dr Heal says that Cox assured Burghley that there had been no Puritan exercises in the diocese, but as I read the letter, he only expresses his disapproval of unauthorised exercises.
[93] B. R. White, *The English Separatist Tradition* (London 1971), p. 46.
[94] Collinson, *Elizabethan Puritan Movement*, pp. 218–32, for the formation and scope of the *classis*.
[95] *The Presbyterian Movement in the Reign of Queen Elizabeth as illustrated by the Minute Book of the Dedham Classis 1582–1589*, ed. R. G. Usher, Camden Soc., 3rd ser. VIII (1905), pp. xxix, and xxxv–xlviii. [Hereafter cited as *Dedham Minutes.*]
[96] *Ibid.* pp. 13, 50–1.

shires', and 'In the yeare 1589 there was another Synode or generall meeting helde in Saint John's College in Cambridge.'[97] The latter meeting was purely academic and theological, and at it, according to Bancroft, the Presbyterian *Book of Discipline* was amended. It is more interesting that in 1587 or 1588 there was a synod held at Stourbridge Fair, which sounds as if it was a regular meeting-place.[98] It may only have been so because such a large gathering gave an ideal opportunity for concealment. Perhaps the laity were not involved in any way. Yet the occasion was used as one for public preaching. Puritans regularly discoursed there to both locals and travellers from all over the country.[99] The fair provided a very large audience, for according to its charter of 1589 it 'far surpassed the greatest and most celebrated fairs of England . . . purchasers coming from all parts of the realm'. It specialised in wool and hops, as well as sheep and cattle, and also provided a magnificent and curiously non-Puritanical rowdy background for preaching. It has been described as 'having developed to a fantastic degree the gay, licentious side of fairs', with 'its inns and theatres, its fortune tellers, its harlots and "Lord of the Taps" '.[100]

Stourbridge Fair continued to draw the attentions of preachers both orthodox and unorthodox. It acted as a magnet for evangelists, both because of the numbers present and its unholy character. In 1678, Ludovic Muggleton, 'the last true Witness and Prophet unto the Man Christ Jesus, glorified', wrote to his kinsman Roger Muggleton, 'I had great hopes to have seen you at Cambridge. I went about the fair at Sturbridge to find you out, and so did several others of our friends, persons of quality, from London, and out of the country, *knowing that I would be there.*'[101] The fair was obviously a recognised meeting-place.

If there was an organised meeting of the 'Cambridgeshire brotherhood' of Puritan clergy in the late 1580s, as Bancroft's comment suggests, it would be very strange indeed if at least those eleven Puritan ministers who had refused to subscribe to Whitgift's articles in 1583 were not involved. They included Edward and Thomas Braine, the incumbents of Grantchester and Comberton, and the incumbents of

[97] *Ibid.* pp. 11, 19.   [98] *Ibid.* pp. 17 and 20.
[99] Alan Everitt, *Change in the Provinces: The Seventeenth Century* (Leicester 1969), p. 42, taken from Collinson's 'The Puritan Classical Movement in the Reign of Elizabeth I', London Ph.D. thesis (1957), p. 772n. The reference does not appear in Professor Collinson's book. I am very grateful to Professor Everitt for supplying me with it.
[100] The whole description of the fair, and the quotations come from Everitt, 'Trading at Fairs', Thirsk, *Agrarian History*, IV, 535–6.
[101] My italics. *A Volume of Spiritual Epistles, being the Copies of Several Letters written by the last two Prophets and Messengers of God, John Reeve and Ludowicke Muggleton* (1755), p. 473. See above, pp. 229–30, and below, p. 295.

Leverington, Tydd St Giles and Wisbech in the Isle. When they appealed against suspension in 1584[102] they agreed to the use of the Book of Common Prayer, but listed practices which were repugnant to them, including 'the execution of Church government by one man'. The main ground of their appeal, which was supported by a letter from most of the chief gentlemen of the county, was

> the miserable plight of the poore people, hungring after the foode of the word, who being bereft of us, are allmost without all hope of having learned and godlie ministers to reside and continue among them ... before we came to them thei had none that did carefullie teach them and whollie reside with them: and manie of our livings are meanlie sufficient, and most so verie poore that some of us have spent of our owne and partlie have bene mainteined by our good friends.

The ministers of Norfolk in a similar position claimed that if they were deprived, Brownism would spread amongst their people.[103] It is perhaps significant that, despite Browne's early wanderings in the shire, and Holcroft's claim to have met with 'old Brownists', the Cambridgeshire ministers threatened in 1584 claimed that their deprivation would lead to the spread of the beliefs of the Family of Love. Their parishes, they said, were at present clear of Familism, but places near were 'infected with the Familie of Love'. They may of course have used the spread of Familism as a threat simply because the scare of five years ago would be readily recalled.

Only one of the ministers concerned ultimately lost his living. The rest continued to be presented at visitations during the vacancy, and were occasionally suspended, but then outwardly conformed to regain their livings. It is more than likely, therefore, that some, at least, of these men put into practice amongst their laity the kind of practice that was used at Dedham. The Dedham minutes give a rare illustration of the part played by the parishioners of the *classis*. In 1588, 'a publike fast was agreed upon to be very necessary and first to confer with the Auncients of our parishes about it, and they to intimate it to the rest'.[104] The Jesuit priest, Father William Weston, observed very large assemblies of Puritans from his prison in Wisbech Castle in the Isle of Ely from the beginning of his imprisonment there in 1588. His account is justly famous, but rarely quoted in full.

> From the very beginning a great number of Puritans gathered here. Some came from the outlying parts of the town, some from the villages round

---

[102] New style. Letter printed in *The Seconde Parte of a Register...*, ed. A. Peel (London 1920), pp. 227–30.
[103] Collinson, 'The Godly', p. 15.   [104] *Dedham Minutes*, p. 68.

about, eager and vast crowds of them flocking to perform their practices – sermons, communions and fasts. (The keeper of the prison, and his whole family, were Puritans, and the justices were sympathetic to them.) This was their ceremonial. In the first few hours there were three or four sermons, one after the other, and the remainder of their devotions. They then went to communion, which they would receive from their minister, not on their knees or standing up, but walking about, so that it could be called in a true sense a Passover. They also held a kind of tribunal, where the elders took cognizance of the misdoings of their brethren and castigated them at discretion. Each of them had his own Bible, and sedulously turned the pages and looked up the texts cited by the preachers, discussing the passages among themselves to see whether they had quoted them to the point, and accurately, and in harmony with their tenets. Also they would start arguing among themselves about the meaning of passages from the Scriptures – men, women, boys, girls, rustics, labourers and idiots – and more often than not, it was said, it ended in violence and fisticuffs.

All this the Catholic prisoners, looking through the windows of their cells, were able to watch; for it did not take place in one of their temples or houses, but on a large level stretch of ground within the precincts of the prison. Here over a thousand of them sometimes assembled, their horses and pack animals burdened with a multitude of Bibles. It was a wretched and truly pitiful sight, but in some ways it was comic and laughable for the onlookers. When the gathering broke up after a long fast and an entire day spent in performances of this kind, they went off to a vast and elaborately set-out feast. And the affair concluded.

Later their first fervour slackened. Their chief supporters were removed from the scene, and they began to dwindle away and look for other places which they considered more suitable for the celebration of their sacrilegious gatherings.[105]

There is then, proof, for the first time in the late 1580s and 1590s that large numbers of the laity in the diocese, 'men, women, boys, girls, rustics, labourers and idiots' had been influenced by Puritan teachings, and were actively involved in doctrinal disputes. The picture of their horses and pack-animals loaded with Bibles, and all the members of the congregation assiduously looking for the texts cited by the preachers, and arguing over the meaning, shows better than any other source the way the common people had been affected by the reformation and the growth of literacy. Erasmus's 'wish that all good wives read the Gospel and Paul's Epistles ... that out of these the husbandman sang while ploughing, the weaver at his loom',[106] had indeed come true. Here were the people of the diocese 'arguing amongst themselves about

---

[105] William Weston, *The Autobiography of an Elizabethan*, trans. and ed. P. Caraman (London 1955), pp. 164–5.
[106] J. Huizinga, *Erasmus of Rotterdam*, Engl. trans. (London 1924), p. 110.

the meaning of passages from the Scriptures'.[107] Such people were willing to travel very long distances to attend meetings. When he died in 1601, Thomas Hockley of Clayhithe in Horningsey, one of the Familists imprisoned in 1580, left a bequest of £10 to 'his loving friend' William Bridge of Shudy Camps,[108] over fifteen miles away at the other side of the county, who had also been imprisoned in 1580. Hockley also had a close friend in St Ives, over twelve miles away in the other direction, on the Ouse. The Familists obviously travelled as far, in their efforts to maintain contact, as the seventeenth-century dissenters.[109] If separatists behaved in this way, devout Puritans would too, and some of them must have come from the county, and not only from the Isle. Some travelled even further. The name of John Klerck, a cobbler, of Newton, south of Cambridge, appeared in the marriage register of the English residents in Amsterdam in 1604. He was accompanied by a woodworker and a girl from Cambridge itself, and three girls from Wisbech.[110] A few went to New England.[111]

Just as Orinel's evidence on the state of affairs in Willingham in the 1550s stands alone, so does Weston's on the mass meetings of Puritan laity in the 1580s and 1590s. He implies these meetings in Wisbech faded out, after about six years of his imprisonment.[112] He also implies

[107] See above, p. 209, for a more detailed discussion of such a debate in the 1670s, involving argument over the merits of translation.

[108] Cambridge University Archives, Consistory Court Wills, Liber W, fo. 132.

[109] See below, pp. 345ff.

[110] T. G. Crippen, ed., 'The Brownists in Amsterdam', *Trans. Cong. Hist. Soc.*, II (1905), 160–72. Not all the exiles who appear in this register of marriages in Amsterdam between 1598 and 1617 were in fact Brownists, but there seems to have been no reason for Robert Browne's depression to be found in Cambridgeshire and the Isle of Ely; on the face of these figures alone, Cambridgeshire, Norfolk and Suffolk produced 6 or 7 *émigrés* apiece.

[111] I have not found any very satisfactory evidence on the degree of emigration to New England. *The Topographical Dictionary of 2885 English Emigrants to New England, 1620–1650*, by Charles Edward Banks, ed. Elijah Ellsworth Brownell (Philadelphia 1937), pp. 12–13 lists twenty-nine emigrants from Cambridgeshire. Three of them were from the Isle, and twelve from the town of Cambridge itself. Unfortunately it is impossible to discover from the text the date on which any particular individual sailed, and therefore, to see whether, for instance, most of the fourteen who went from the county went during Bishop Matthew Wren's tenure of Ely from 1638 to 1640. Three members of the Desborough family, which was to sponsor Denne's work in Eltisley after 1650, went from Eltisley to Connecticut before 1650 and two humbler members of the laity of Eltisley also went to Connecticut or Massachussetts, Woodditton, which was a Baptist meeting-place by 1654 (see below, p. 279) lost two emigrants, and isolated individuals went from Borough Green, Comberton, Elsworth and Cottenham. It is obvious that this record is very incomplete, for those who left Castle Camps (see above, p. 236) are not included. But it is also clear that the exodus from Cambridgeshire was not on the scale of that from Norfolk, Suffolk and Essex, which produced 168, 298 and 266 emigrants apiece (Banks and Brownell, map).

[112] Weston, *Autobiography of an Elizabethan*, p. 165.

that the 'sacrilegious gatherings' continued elsewhere, in places 'more suitable'. But again, as it was impossible to trace the descent of Protestant conviction in Willingham and Orwell from the 1550s, so also is it impossible to trace the linear descent of the opinions of these Puritans of the 1590s, to their spiritual offspring of the 1630s.

An excursion into early seventeenth-century visitation records only proves a negative point further. The notable Arminian, Lancelot Andrewes, who was bishop from 1609 to 1618, was known as a persecutor of Puritans when he was translated to Winchester.[113] His private chapel at Ely was known as a place both of devotion and ceremonial worship. The man who preached that, when in the presence of God, 'our "holiness" should have a kind of beauty with it', and that God, who gave the body, should be worshipped with the body also, and 'he will not have us worship him like elephants, as if we have no joints in our knees', was not likely to countenance 'seditious conventicles'. Nor would he, who preached against 'worship with our hearts, and not our hats, as some fondly imagine',[114] have agreed with the protest of James Percival, who refused in 1639 to do more 'bodily Reverence to the name of Jhesus than to ye name of "Father" '.[115] But his visitations of Ely in 1610–11, 1617, and a metropolitical visitation of 1615–16,[116] all prove as uninformative as those of Cox in the 1560s and 1570s. None of the villages which were to emerge as dissenting centres stood out in any way.

The reasons why episcopal visitations so signally failed to record the growth of Puritanism, or even of separatism, become apparent when Bishop Matthew Wren's first visitation of 1639[117] is examined. It should have been revealing, because Matthew Wren was Laud's most trusted trouble-shooter; he had been posted to one of the most difficult dioceses in the country, Norwich, to deal with the Puritans there, even against the express wishes of Elizabeth of Bohemia, who wished to put in her own nominee. In Norwich he was outstandingly successful by Laud's standards. The degree of this success may be gauged by the boatloads of Puritan emigrants he was responsible for launching, and the Puritan lecturers he was responsible for exiling, and by the fact that he attracted the attention of no less a person than Prynne, who under a pseudonym wrote a pamphlet, *News from Ipswich*, which ran to three editions.

[113] P. A. Welsby, *Lancelot Andrewes 1555–1626* (London 1964; first pub. 1958), pp. 113–17.
[114] *Ibid.* pp. 126–30 for these quotations from Andrewes's *Sermons* and the description of his chapel at Ely.   [115] See below, p. 270.
[116] Visitations of 1610–11 (E.D.R., B/2/31, fos. 56–106), 1613–16 (E.D.R., B/2/33) and one described as of 1617 (E.D.R., B/2/37) in which most of the actual proceedings date from 1619.   [117] E.D.R., B/2/52.

Professor Trevor-Roper gives Wren a most striking testimony: 'If ever Laud's methods could have eliminated Puritanism in England, Wren would have eliminated it. He was the archbishop's most efficient disciple, a man of strong intellect, and fearless determination. No single bishop of Laud's creation was so hateful to the Puritans.' He survived howls for revenge, maintained the dignity of a prince of the church in the Tower through the civil war and the interregnum, refused to buy his liberty by recognising the protectorate, negotiated with the exiled court for the restoration of the church, and on its restoration, returned triumphantly to his diocese to defy the intervention of Charles II. Professor Trevor-Roper also describes Wren not merely as a 'bigot' but as a governor, who knew his business and did it with determination.[118]

When Wren was moved to Ely, in 1638, he was presumably moved because it was a diocese of greater standing and revenue. Ely was rich, although it was small, and had been surpassed in the *valor* of 1535 only by Winchester, Canterbury and Durham. Under Elizabeth, the bishop of Ely ranked seventh in precedence. His personal reputation makes it likely that Wren was also moved because trouble was known to be brewing there. His visitation of 1639 ought therefore to reflect any trouble which did exist, particularly since he already knew his diocese. He had been not only a scholar and then a fellow of Pembroke, but also vicar of Teversham in 1615.[119] It is possible in this particular instance to examine the sympathies of many of the active laity in the parishes, upon whose attitude Wren depended, because lists survive of the names of the churchwardens and questmen in each parish who were responsible for the presentments upon which the visitation rested.[120] The names of the parochial laity responsible for the returns on which Wren acted, can therefore be compared with the names of the laity petitioning against the 'government of bishops' a year later.[121]

If the episcopal visitation is a revealing document for our purposes,

[118] H. R. Trevor-Roper, *Archbishop Laud 1573–1645* (London 1962; first pub. 1940), pp. 313–14, 426–7. See also pp. 172, 204–6, 247, 359, 404. R. W. Ketton-Cremer, *Norfolk in the Civil War* (London 1969), ch. 4.
[119] *D.N.B.*, xxi (1937–8), p. 1009.
[120] E.D.R., B/2/50, fos. 1–22. This document is in fact a list of the names of the wardens and the questmen for the diocese in 1637 and 1638, produced for the metropolitical visitation of 1638, but B/2/51, a similar list for the episcopal visitation of 1638–9, seems to contain only the names of the 'new' wardens and questmen of 1638 in B/2/50, together with some additional 'assistants', who were often the wardens or questmen of 1637. I have therefore taken B/2/50 as a basis for analysis, to cover both the lay officials of 1637 and 1638. I have already written up my findings, which were mainly based on the visitation of 1639 and its attendant documents, in 'The Quest for the Heretical Laity in the Visitation Records of Ely in the late Sixteenth and early Seventeenth Centuries', *Studies in Church History*, 9 (Cambridge 1972), pp. 223–30.   21 See above, pp. 232–4.

the visitation made by Matthew Wren in 1639 should show unmistakably the presence of strong Puritan feeling, at least in those nine villages which a year later came out so strongly in favour of the abolition of the episcopate. At his visitation he asked specifically whether there were any 'abiding in the Parish' who do 'at any time preach or maintain any heresie contrary to the faith of Christ'; whether there were any who affirmed that the form of consecration of bishops, priests and deacons, or the government of the church, was unlawful or anti-Christian; or whether any had been to unlawful assemblies, conventicles or meetings.[122] Wren, unlike Cox, was well aware that the opinions of the laity were of importance. His visitation returns should surely pinpoint just those parishes where, a year or so later, so many signatories were found to petition for 'government according to the Holie Scripture'. But they do not do so; or at least only do so for one of the nine parishes concerned.

The returns made to Wren's visitation of 1639 show clearly his aims and objects in the diocese. He objected to the habit, which was clearly universal, of Communion being received in the body of the parish churches, and he wished the communion tables to be moved to the east end of the chancel, steps or 'ascents' to be made up to them, and for them to be railed. He also wished the reading desks to be moved from their, again apparently universal, position in the nave, to face eastwards, away from the congregation. Almost all the churchwardens in the county were directed to 'turn the reading deske'. Further, he wished every pew to be uniform in height, apparently so that the congregation, when kneeling, could still see eastwards. He thus must have made an enemy of almost all the squires or persons of pretension in the county, by directing that their pews, which in size accorded with what they felt to be their rank, be cut down. Sir Thomas Cage of Longstowe, for instance, had a pew five foot high which was to be made uniform with the others in the church. Wren was also anxious to see that due reverence was observed in the liturgy; that the laity should bow at the name of Jesus, kneel at appropriate points, and not leave unceremoniously before the blessing. The wearing of hats in church was the kind of behaviour calculated to rouse him. He did not like the use of the church as a community centre either; announcements of the next manorial court leet to be held, or of lost property found, made in church, bothered him. So did the keeping of fire buckets and ladders there. He also showed a justifiable concern for neglected fabric.

With such a bishop, and with a considerable group of potential

[122] Chapter I of 'Articles to be Inquired of Within the Diocese of Ely', *Documents relating to Cambridgeshire Villages*, ed. W. M. Palmer (Cambridge 1926), p. 444.

Protestant parishioners amongst the laity of Ely, one would expect Wren's visitation of 1639 to indicate clearly those parishes which the petition of 1640 has identified for us. The easiest way of testing the degree to which the visitation is a clear guide is to look at what it has to say about just those nine parishes with a strong Puritan bent.

There was no doubt about the strength of feeling against these 'innovations' at Toft. The curate there was presented for administering the last Easter Communion in the body of the church. The parish clerk, William Aungier, was presented as being responsible for moving the communion table back from its 'new' position behind the rails, so that Communion could be administered in the position that the laity had presumably come to accept, since Bishop Cox had finally persuaded them into it at the Elizabethan settlement. A whole group of parishioners connived at this, and were presented also. John Bunyan spoke at meetings in a barn belonging to one of the Aungier family in the 1650s.[123] But none of the other eight parishes appeared in this way. At Melbourn, where an early Baptist church in Cambridgeshire was founded under the commonwealth, all that appeared in the visitation was that John Scruby refused to kneel at the altar-rails to receive Communion, and Timothy Atkin irreverently called a court leet after service. The visitation is scarcely an accurate guide to the underlying ferment in Melbourn, where in 1640, eleven named ringleaders, one of whom had been a churchwarden in the previous year, of a mob of a hundred or so, first beat up, and then ran out of town, the sheriff's collectors of ship money.[124] Later in the year, five men signed the petition for the total reform of church government.

A careful examination of the visitation entries shows that a detail in the return for a parish will often confirm previous suspicions, raised by other firm evidence, but that visitation entries taken alone are in no way reliable or clear guides to the state of feeling and doctrine, as opposed to morals, in a parish.

The reason why the visitation records are such unreliable guides to doctrinal deviations in a parish becomes plain when the opinions of the churchwardens, who were responsible for drawing up the *comperta*, on which the episcopal officials proceedings were based,[125] are examined.

---

[123] See below, p. 273.
[124] A. Kingston, *East Anglia and the Great Civil War* (London 1897), p. 21. Another account is given in W. M. Palmer and G. Porter Chapple, *A Nonconformist Bi-Centenary Memorial* (London 1895), pp. 7–10.
[125] Dorothy M. Owen, 'Episcopal Visitation Books', *History*, XLIX (1964), 186. I would like to acknowledge my indebtedness to Mrs Owen, the Ely Diocesan Archivist, for much general help and time spent assisting me, although the opinions expressed here in no way necessarily coincide with hers.

In two of the deaneries concerned, Barton and Chesterton, men who were wardens or questmen in 1637 or 1638 seem to have made up something like a tenth of the adult male population.[126] The nine villages with numerous petitioners for a reform in church government had fifty-eight men who held office as churchwardens or questmen in 1637 or 1638. No less than twenty-two of these, well over a third, signed the petition demanding 'government according to the Holie Scripture'. Those of the parochial laity who wanted a further reformation in the church, or even a complete break with tradition, therefore had a deliberate policy, or were naturally drawn, to take up office in their parishes. The figures are adequate proof that this is so. It is therefore no longer surprising that the visitations, based on returns made by men who were often of Puritan disposition, did not uncover the Puritanism which men like Matthew Wren were so eager to destroy. If Nicholas Grey at Bassingbourn, where Holcroft 'gathered' his first church, and Benjamin Metcalfe, the farmer whose son later founded the Baptist church at Melbourn, and Richard Staploe at Eltisley, which was the base from which the General Baptist Church in Cambridgeshire was evangelised, were questmen or churchwardens in 1637 and 1638, it is not surprising that their parishes did not appear as centres of potential Puritan revolt in Wren's visitation of 1639. It was hardly in their interests to call their bishop's attention to their own activities, which they sincerely considered to be godly.[127]

It is not possible to make any generalisation on the accuracy with which episcopal visitations elsewhere reflect doctrinal change amongst the laity. We can only say that in the 1630s, in the diocese of Ely, Puritans who wanted further reform, within or even outside the established church, deliberately filled a high proportion of lay parochial offices, and that the visitations drawn up on the presentations they made are

---

[126] This is a very rough estimate, based on a comparison between lay office-holders, and numbers of householders in the same areas in the hearth tax. It cannot be pushed far, both because it ignores any growth of population there may have been between the 1630s and 1660s, and because some householders in the 1660s were women, who were naturally ineligible for lay office. Moreover, the number of office-holders for any parish was relatively static, while some Cambridgeshire villages were over four times the size of others.

[127] I have not examined the method of election of churchwardens in the parishes concerned. This would have to be done separately for each parish, since so wide a variety of customs seems to have governed the election; see W. E. Tate, *The Parish Chest: A Study of the Records of Parochial Administration in England* (Cambridge 1946), pp. 84–5. It would be particularly relevant to know whether any attempt was made to replace the 'town meeting' or 'vestry' which commonly chose the parish wardens at Easter, by 'select' vestries only containing conformable men, in the puritanically inclined parishes of Cambridgeshire in the late sixteenth and early seventeenth centuries (Tate, pp. 13–20). If such an attempt was made, it seems from the opinions of the wardens who served under Wren that it failed.

unrevealing for that reason. We can probably extrapolate backwards in time, at least in this diocese, and say that Elizabethan and Jacobean Puritans may well have been active in the same way. Visitation records are no guide to the opinions or doctrines of the laity in the late sixteenth and early seventeenth century; possibly because the laity had such a formative hand in their composition, as well as because in the sixteenth century at least, the very subject of parochial doctrine below the level of the gentry appeared to lack importance to the episcopate.

There is one further point to be made. Bishop Wren was primarily a trouble-shooter, dealing particularly with Puritans. In the visitation of 1639, there is just one list for a county parish, and two for city parishes, of people who refuse to bow at the name of Jesus, or do other similar reverence at appropriate times. Four men were presented at Great Eversden,[128] headed by John Wilson, who 'doth not kneele and doe due reverence in the Church . . . nor bow att the name of Jesus, nor stand up at Gloria'.[129] At St Clement's in Cambridge, three men were presented for not bowing at the name of Jesus, and the splendid defence of one of them, James Percival, is recorded in the visitation. He says 'that he doeth noe other bodily Reverence to the name of Jhesus than to the name of "Father", and that God requires noe more'. There were other sporadic recordings of people here and there in the county for similar offences. But interestingly enough, not more than nineteen people altogether were presented in Cambridgeshire for irreverence.[130] Twenty-one recusants were named. It is a very bizarre reversal of what we know to have been the true situation, from the complaints made against scandalous ministers in the 1640s, which went back to the 1630s. We know without a doubt that, by this time, Richard Conder was giving thanks for the 'work of grace in his soul' that had been brought about by the reading of the *Book of Sports* in 1633. We are indeed, in reading this visitation, looking through a glass darkly. The fears of the 1580s had left a lasting impact, and lists of the recusants in the county, one of the least papistically inclined in the country, were presented, as was required by law. The living, and relatively new, menace to the episcopal authorities was not yet expressible within the form of this visitation. No

---

128 There were not enough identifiable petitioners for Eversden to make it an outstanding Puritan parish in 1640, although many of the barely legible signatories and markers at the bottom of the petition bore surnames common in that area. The men who made them may not have been wealthy enough to be assessed in the subsidy, and therefore to be identified by me.

129 E.D.R., B/2/52, fo. 15v.

130 Admittedly the wardens of Trinity parish in Cambridge itself had obviously given up, and recorded merely 'some comes late to Church and some bows not att the name of Jesus and some goes out of the Church before the blessing be pronounced'.

reader, however attentive, could possibly suppose from this document that in the following year well over five hundred signatures, from only half the county would be raised against the whole existing system of church government, from the common people alone.

11

Fragmentation and the growth of sects

THE FAILURE OF THE PARISH CHURCH

The ecclesiastical history of the twenty-five years from 1640 onwards was marked by two drastic changes of personnel among the parochial clergy, as first the Laudian and royalist sympathisers lost their livings, to be followed in their turn by those unable to conform to the settlement of 1660. It has been estimated that some thirty per cent of English livings were under sequestration at some time between 1643 and 1660 and that twenty per cent of the restoration clergy were ejected over the country as a whole.[1] The reformation itself had probably obtruded itself far less on the ordinary parishioner than did this 'further reformation' so much desired by the Puritans.

Cambridgeshire was as much, or more, affected by the deprivations as the rest of the country. The county contained 121 parishes.[2] Forty-five of these lost their incumbent in the purges of the 1640s and 1650s.[3]

[1] A. G. Matthews's figures, discussed by A. Whiteman, 'The Restoration of the Church of England', in *From Uniformity to Unity 1662–1962*, ed. G. F. Nuttall and O. Chadwick (London 1962), pp. 34–5. Figures of ejections for 1660–2 calculated from pp. 35, 155 n. 1, and 169 n. 2.

[2] Including those of the deanery of Fordham in the diocese of Norwich, which lay within the county, but excluding the urban parishes of Cambridge, Royston and Newmarket. The livings of Croydon-cum-Clopton, which were consolidated under James I (Lysons, *Magna Britannia*, II, 172) have been counted as one, as have the livings of Great and Little Childerley, which together had only three inhabitants taxed in 1524, and Hauxton-cum-Newton, which were taken together in the visitation of 1539. The double parishes of Cambridgeshire present another problem from the depopulated ones. I have counted Histon St Andrew and St Etheldreda, where the church of St Etheldreda was pulled down *c.* 1600, as one, and Burwell St Mary and St Andrew, where St Andrew was probably pulled down in the seventeenth century as one (Lysons, pp. 214 and 98). Swaffham Prior, where the benefices of St Mary and St Cyriac were united in the 1660s, I have also counted as one. Fulbourn St Vigor and All Saints, and Duxford St John and St Peter which still had separate livings in the eighteenth century (Lysons, pp. 196 and 182) I have counted as two each, together with Longstanton St Michael's and All Saints. I have not allowed for pluralities.

[3] All information on the sequestred royalist clergy in the following chapter is taken from A. G. Matthews, *Walker Revised, being a Revision of J. Walker's Sufferings of the Clergy during the Grand Rebellion, 1642–60* (Oxford 1948). [Henceforth, *Walker Revised.*]

Another fourteen incumbents were ejected between 1660 and 1662.[4]

Even though almost exactly half the Cambridgeshire parishes were entirely undisturbed by sequestrations or ejections, and did not even have contentious clergy who were, later in their careers, deprived elsewhere, it is probably impossible to overestimate the magnitude of these changes to the laity. In half the parishes of the diocese, the incumbent continued to officiate as before, but changed his Prayer Book for a Directory. On the other hand, over a third of the parish congregations saw their parson or vicar removed in the first stages of reform; and about a tenth saw their minister dispossessed in the early 1660s. A hard core of seven parishes in the thick of the struggle experienced both.[5]

The state of the parish of Toft, where an active and acute struggle over the position of the communion table, involving a considerable body of the parishioners, had been going on in 1639[6] shows the way that doctrinal dispute could eventually lead to a complete breakdown in the functioning of the church: it stopped fulfilling its rôle both as a sacramental and as a preaching body. In 1644, the absentee rector was ejected by the second earl of Manchester. Amongst the other charges brought against him by the parochial witnesses were both that his curates observed ceremonies, and that perhaps understandably, in view of the reception these 'ceremonies' had met with from the Puritans in the parish, he had failed to provide for the cure at all since June 1643. John Ellis was apparently put in as rector in 1650, after, presumably, no provision had been made for the cure for six years.[7] At some point before 1659, relations between him and his parishioners became so strained that they beat him up. Bunyan regularly held a meeting in the parish, and attenders apparently made a habit of heckling neighbouring clergy after sermon-time. Toft had not suffered worse than usually in being left without a minister for so long. The next parish of Caldecote was likewise left without a pastor between the sequestration of its incumbent in 1644 and the presentation of Thomas Smith, the Cambridge University Librarian, to the living under the great seal in 1650.[8] Smith carried on a vigorous running battle with Bunyan's converts in Toft, and in 1659 wrote, 'The

[4] A figure of 11%. Clergy from: Abington Pigotts, Bassingbourn, Cheveley, Cottenham, Fowlmere, Hardwick, East Hatley, Swaffham Bulbeck, Swaffham Prior and Willingham, together, according to Calamy, with those from Croydon-cum-Clopton, Dullingham, Litlington and Meldreth. A. G. Matthews has been unable to find supporting evidence for the latter. All information on nonsubscribers from *Calamy Revised*.

[5] Cheveley, Cottenham, Fowlmere, Hardwick, East Hatley, Swaffham Bulbeck, Swaffham Prior.   [6] See above, p. 268.

[7] See Henry Downhall in *Walker Revised*, p. 79.   [8] *Ibid.* p. 86.

Lord's supper, which the primitive and best Christians received every day ... the people of your Town have not desired, as I hear, these fourteen years.'[9] This means that the Sacraments had not been administered at Toft ever since, presumably, the rector had stopped providing for the cure in 1643.

In 1653, in Worcestershire, Richard Baxter set up a voluntary association, to try to prevent exactly the collapse of the church as a functioning body so clearly illustrated at Toft. After the purges of the 1640s, came the Presbyterian attempt to establish the classical system of church government over the whole country. This was probably never adopted in Cambridgeshire,[10] even after the parliamentary ordinance on church government in 1648, unless the tiny group of Presbyterians at the end of the 1660s in the town of Cambridge itself was a surviving remnant.[11] Even where Presbyterian government had been both organised and fully adopted, as in London and Lancashire, it had decayed after the army's triumph in 1648. Classical discipline could only be enforced at the parochial level with the aid of civil power, and this, after 1648, was not forthcoming. The decline of discipline and the unfilled elderships meant that the Lord's Supper was infrequently administered, since there were strong Presbyterian objections to admitting parishioners to the Sacrament without previous examination by the elders. The parishioners in many places objected to this practice, often for reasons which appear congenial, as did those of St Bartholomew Exchange, in London, who desired their minister 'to deliver the Sackariment to all his parish to beget love one with another'.[12]

Baxter's aim was to establish a church discipline that would be acceptable to the parishioners generally, and yet be sufficiently rigorous to prevent 'the more religious people from separation, to which the unreformedness of the Church, through want of discipline, inclined them'.[13] The members of Baxter's association were, he said, 'a company of honest, godly, serious, humble ministers in the county where I lived, who were not one of them (that associated) Presbyterian or Independent, and not past four or five of them Episcopal; but disengaged, faithful men'.[14] These ministers had to work on, according

[9] All information from Thomas Smith, *A Letter in Defence of the Ministry and against Lay Preachers* (1659) printed with his *The Quaker Disarm'd*. See also below, pp. 285–6.
[10] W. A. Shaw, *A History of the English Church During the Civil War and Under the Commonwealth 1640–60* (London 1900), II, 373–440, prints the available evidence, with a county summary on pp. 29–33.
[11] See above, p. 225.   [12] Shaw, *ibid.* p. 149.   [13] Quoted by *ibid.* p. 154.
[14] The single Presbyterian minister of Worcestershire was not associated, and only one of the five or six of the Independents of the county were. Most of those who

to Baxter 'an honest, humble tractable people at home, engaged in no party, Prelatical, Presbyterian or Independent; but loving Godliness and peace and hating schism as that which they perceived to tend to be the ruine of religion'.[15] It is very probable that Baxter describes here the mental state of the vast majority of English parishioners, described by the extremists on either hand as apathetic.

Cambridge did, like many other counties, follow the lead of the voluntary association set up by Baxter in Worcestershire in 1653, even though the Cambridge Voluntary Association had few active members. Those meeting in 1657 and 1658[16] were concerned to remedy those evils first amended by Baxter. The association observed that, as at Toft, the Sacrament of the Lord's Supper 'hath in some places been foreborne for a long time', and resolved that intending communicants should be examined by the minister, judging that 'as the case now standeth, wee esteem it the best course for the Minister to judge who is ignorant and scandalous, except it bee in such congregations where the Minister hath, or can [have,] some convenient assistance'.[17] It sounds as if attempts to set up eldership in Cambridgeshire had met with no more popularity than elsewhere.

Some of the ministers who were later to refuse to subscribe were amongst the most vigorous supporters of the Cambridge Association, including Abraham Wright, Jonathan Jephcot, the Presbyterian, and Nye and Bradshaw, the Congregationalists,[18] although the rest were, presumably like all Baxter's members, 'disengaged faithfull men' who saw the need to establish some kind of norm in parochial life.

Even if the Cambridgeshire clergy had formed an active voluntary association as soon as Baxter had shown the way, they would already have been too late.[19] The field was 'white already to harvest'. Those who signed the petition against Wren in 1640 were ripe for action, and ready to be led. Yet in a very real sense, the Baptist, Quaker and Congregationalist evangelists were reaping where they had not sown. The vacuum of the next thirteen years was filled by the growth of the separatist sects. The scribe of the Bedford Church, which was later

---

did not associate were the 'weaker sort of Ministers whose sufficiency or conversation was questioned by others. As also some few of better parts of the Episcopal way.' Quoted by *ibid.* p. 164.   [15] *Ibid.* p. 154.

[16] There were never more than twenty-five sympathisers at any *classis* meeting, although the contemporary list of Cambridgeshire incumbents included in the *classis* minutes gave 108 names. 'Minutes of the Cambridge Classis', printed as pp. 189–204 of *Minutes of the Bury Presbyterian Classis, 1647–57*, Chetham Society Publications, ns, xxxvi (1896).

[17] *Ibid.* p. 194.

[18] Although Holcroft did not attend meetings.   [19] See below, pp. 276–8, 281–3.

to become John Bunyan's Open Baptist Church, began his book with a little historical account, expressing the 'seeking' attitudes of those who were to become members, on the formation of the church in 1650:

In this town of Bedford, and the places adjacent, there hath of a long time bene persons Godly who in former times even while they remained without all forme and order as to visible church communion ... were very zealous according to their light, not onely to edify themselves but also to propagate the Gospell ... Men that in those times were enabled of God to adventure farre in showing their detestation of the Bishops, and their superstitions. But as the saide these persons with many more, neither were, nor yet desired to be imbodied into fellowship according to the order of the Gospel: onely that they had in some measure separated themselves from prelaticall superstition; and had agreed to search after the non-conformity men such as in those days did beare the name of Puritanes.[20]

These 'seekers' who had already expressed their opinion on government by prelates in 1640 seem first to have been organised 'into fellowship according to the order of the Gospel' in Cambridgeshire in the General Baptist Church led by Henry Denne.

GENERAL BAPTISTS

The records of the Baptist church of Fenstanton are not only the most complete source for the history of dissenting churches of Cambridgeshire but are also the principal source for Baptist history under the protectorate.[21] The first members of the church were baptised in 1644 and 1645, beginning with Rebecca Denne. The eleven Baptists gathered in these years all came from Caxton and Fenstanton, with Rebecca Denne herself from Eltisley where her husband's living was. The first members were therefore within easy physical reach of Henry Denne's living. Eltisley was described by the Tory, Noble, as 'an asylum for the most extravagant fanaticism ... psalm singing was as heinous a sin at Eltisley as bending the knee to Baal, and it was then as much

---

[20] *Church Book of Bunyan Meeting*, fo. 1.
[21] The career of Henry Denne is described in most works on the General Baptists. It is given in the introduction to the *Fenstanton Records*, pp. v–xxiii. Adam Taylor, in his *History of the English General Baptists* (London 1818), I, described both Denne's career and the history of the Fenstanton church, pp. 99–100, 101–7, 137–57, 218–24. W. T. Whitley listed Denne's printed works in *A Baptist Bibliography*, I (London 1916). B. Nutter, *The Story of the Cambridge Baptists* (Cambridge 1912), mainly concentrated on the central figures in the Baptist Church rather than its local developments. See also J. H. Wood, *Condensed History of the General Baptists of the New Connection* (London 1847), pp. 119–28.

noted for the devout exercises practised there, as any other canting place in the kingdom'.[22] The main period of Baptist evangelism was however from 1651 to 1653. In this period, there were over 130 baptisms, nearly ninety of them in 1652. From 1664–5 there were between eight and twelve converts a year, and at that point the list of baptisms breaks off until a few were added right at the end of the century. The first volume of the Church Book of Fenstanton itself, as opposed to the baptismal list, was not filled until the beginning of 1659, when the records were still being kept, for the last entry records that the new book is to be begun, and the old one read over and approved at the following general meeting. So perhaps the Caxton baptisms really did come to an end in 1656, while the other records continued. At the sister church of Warboys in Huntingdonshire which was also founded by Henry Denne, the majority of members were recruited at roughly the same time as at Fenstanton and Caxton, but the baptisms trickled on in small numbers until 1658, with one in 1662 and four in 1664, before they stopped for over twelve years.

The main period of formal Baptist recruitment, then, was in the early 1650s.[23] The account of Henry Denne's evangelising activity, and the picture of the gradual development of church organisation which is given by the *Fenstanton Records*, confirm the crucial importance of this time. In 1653, Henry Denne proposed that the general meeting at Fenstanton was much at fault in not obeying the command 'go, preach the Gospel to every creature', considering that there were 'many towns hereabout that have no teachers'.[24] As a result he was sent on a preaching tour early in 1654, which circled round to the west and south of Cambridge through from Kingston, Toft and Harston[25] and Shelford and so into Essex. The evangelists returned by Royston and Melbourn, where they met with the 'brethren' in both places. It is noticeable that, on the whole, the messengers tended to stay with those who were already at least semi-converted, like Paul Wayts and his wife in Toft who 'seemed to continue zealous and to be affected with their sense of the want of things of God'.[26] At Harston, the 'brethren' met together with the evangelists. Only at Shelford is it

---

[22] Quoted by E. B. Underhill in his introduction to the *Fenstanton Records*, p. x.
[23] The records of the Bedford Open Baptist Church show a slightly different pattern of development. [24] *Fenstanton Records*, pp. 71–2.
[25] I have identified 'Hawson' as Harston, instead of the more likely-sounding 'Hauxton', because a Baptist conventicle met, and was licensed in 1672 at 'Harstoln' (Lyon Turner, II, 872) where there were twenty dissenters of otherwise unknown denomination in 1676.
[26] *Fenstanton Records*, p. 75. Probably an ancestor of the Open Baptist John Wait of Toft who held a meeting in Toft in 1669 and was excommunicated by Holcroft's Independent Church in 1671.

recorded that 'the people seemed very well affected to that which was spoken, although it had not been heard in the like manner before'. The assumption is that elsewhere the Baptists' message had been heard.[27] Yet even in Shelford, the messengers used as a base a house where the wife had recently been baptised.

The whole account of the tour gives the impression that the evangelists were more concerned with maintaining contact with those who had lapsed or strayed from orthodoxy than preaching in new areas for the Baptists. The impression that the principal difficulty lay in providing any kind of regular support for a village congregation, rather than in attempting conversions in the first place, is confirmed by such appeals as that from brother Cranfield of Over who in 1655 'did earnestly desire on the behalf of many people in that town, that our brother Denne should come over thither to preach publicly'.[28] There had been a steady stream of converts from Over ever since the *Fenstanton Records* opened. It seems likely that, when Henry Denne suggested his evangelising tour, he had in mind that few villages had a resident or easily reachable teacher rather than that few villages had ever heard the Baptist message. This had very likely been spread in the 1640s.

The growth of the church organisation in the early 1650s also gives the impression that the principal work of forming the churches had been completed, and they were now feeling their way towards a regular administration. By the end of 1652, Henry Denne was suggesting that births and marriages amongst the congregation should be recorded 'for the preventing of danger and trouble that otherwise may come upon us'.[29] Two years later, the maintenance of regular contact between the independent Baptist congregations was felt to be a necessity, and quarterly meetings of the elders of all the country churches were started in Cambridge, 'for the better attaining to and retaining of, unity and order in the churches'.[30] These meetings of elders were regularly kept up and were concerned with both administrative and theological affairs. In 1655, for instance, they decided that no one should travel from place to place without the consent of his congregation, that is, his formal dismission; that every member of the church should 'sit down' with a particular congregation and be responsible to it, and that each congregation should keep a register of the names of the members.[31] An effort was being made to give some formal order and stability to the congregations.

The main congregations had been formed well before their elders

[27] *Ibid.* p. 77.   [28] *Ibid.* p.14.   [29] *Ibid.* p. 18.   [30] *Ibid.* pp. 126–7.
[31] The Fenstanton list of baptisms was probably drawn up in response to this order.

instituted regular meetings in 1654. Happily there was some correspondence in 1654, in an effort to raise funds for a member whose barns and crops had been destroyed by fire, and John Denne in Caxton made a note of the congregations to which he sent his appeal. This list of the congregations therefore should include all those early Baptist meetings in the vicinity which were established before the voluntary association began its work of trying to prevent schism in the church, and also those which were established before the onset of persecution. Apart from the congregations in the Isle and in Huntingdonshire it included three main groups of meetings outside Cambridge itself. One copy of the letter went to Woodditton and the places adjoining. Woodditton lies on the Suffolk border in the diocese of Norwich, and the places adjoining must have included the church of Dullingham, whose elder John Ray was a sufficiently influential Baptist to be sent on special missions by the association of elders.[32] A second copy of John Denne's letter went to the churches at the unidentifiable 'Salsham' and 'Wigan' and at Burwell, also in the diocese of Norwich. A third copy went to Balsham, which lay like Woodditton up on the chalk hills near the Suffolk border, and to Wilbraham. The last letter went to Harston, which, though an outlying part of the Caxton congregation, obviously had to be communicated with by letter, and to Melbourn and to Royston. Meetings in all these places had existed by the time Henry Denne made his tour in 1653.

In Melbourn, the redoubtable Benjamin Metcalfe had already had dissenting ideas in 1640 when he was responsible for turning away King Charles's collectors of ship money in true Hampden fashion.[33] His son, Benjamin the younger, who was born about 1626, became a corporal in Cromwell's Ironsides. After his discharge, he returned to Melbourn, probably about 1651, married, and formed the Baptist church there which Bishop Laney was to note with such disgust in 1669 as a meeting of about twenty 'Farmers, Labourers and most women'. The meeting survived and a Richard Metcalfe was deacon

[32] *Ibid.* pp. 141, 144–6 and 238–9. James Parnell in *The Watcher* (1655), p. 222 says that Ray comes from 'Wickombruch', Suffolk.

[33] W. M. Palmer assembles some details of the Metcalfe family's career in *A Non-conformist Bi-Centenary Memorial* (London 1895), pp. 7–14. I am very much obliged to the kindness of Mr Kenneth Parsons, of the Cambridge University Library, for supplying me both with a copy of his bibliography on the Cambridgeshire Baptists, and also, by personal communication, for giving me the date of death of Benjamin Metcalfe, senior, the organiser of the ship-money riot, and the approximate date of birth and details of the career of his son, Benjamin Metcalfe junior, the founder of the Anabaptist group in Melbourn. He has also given me details of the first Melbourn Church Book, which unfortunately only contains sketchy minutes for 1704 to 1740, but does cover Richard Metcalfe's family and deaconate.

of the church between 1705 and 1707. He was probably a great-grandson of old Benjamin Metcalfe who led his community into revolt in 1640. Dissent as a phenomenon transmitted through the family deserves more attention.[34] The history of the Conder family, which likewise produced four successive generations first of Puritans, and then of Independent, not Baptist, pastors between 1605 and 1781, provides an exact parallel, in a different sect.[35]

Most of the pastoral work of the Baptists recorded in the *Fenstanton Records* was concerned, however not with missions but with converts lost to other sects. A dispirited minority had been so disturbed that they could ultimately give their allegiance to no sect at all.[36] The major controversies of the period were so frequently disputed that they were eventually listed by Henry Denne, together with the appropriate scriptural authorities on which both sides of the arguments were based, for the guidance of his congregation. Denne's intent was that every member of his congregation should be acquainted with the scriptural arguments against the General Baptist position, and be able to answer them. He defined the main controversies as, firstly, 'whether Christ died for all men, or only for some'; secondly, whether baptism was relevant to infants or only to believers; thirdly, whether God was the author of sins and therefore the origin of evil; fourthly whether the 'ordinances'[37] of God, as 'prayer, exhortation, baptism, breaking of bread, etc.', were superseded; and lastly, whether it was possible for believers to fall away.[38]

Of these, the controversy over whether the Sacraments were super-seded gave most trouble to the Baptists. The most persistent friction in the early 1650s was with the Quakers, whose conviction of the spirit indwelling within them led to their claim that the Scriptures could be tested by the spirit within, rather than the other way round. The logical extension of this argument led to the claim that scriptural authority for a practice was not necessary, provided the light of Christ within sanctioned it.[39] The Ranters formed the lunatic fringe to the 'left' of the Quakers, and claimed that not only were they possessed by the Spirit, but that all their actions were thereby justified.[40]

[34] See above, pp. 256–7, for intermarriage in the Family of Love.
[35] See above, 232 n. 26; and below, pp. 295–6 for the Congregationalist Crabb family, and p. 508, for the Peacheys, who illustrated sectarian division within the family. [36] See below, pp. 349–50.
[37] Sacraments. See G. F. Nuttall, *The Holy Spirit in Puritan Faith and Experience* (Oxford 1946), ch. 6, 'The Spirit and the Ordinances', pp. 90–101.
[38] *Fenstanton Records*, pp. 83–4.
[39] Nuttall, *The Holy Spirit in Puritan Faith*, pp. 155–6.
[40] The Quaker rebuttal to this was not to deny that the Ranters possessed the Spirit, but an appeal to judgement based on 'by their fruits ye shall know them'. James

QUAKERS

Organised Quakerism came to Cambridgeshire in 1653.[41] In that year Mary Fisher and Elizabeth Williams visited Cambridge and 'discoursed about the things of God with some young Scollars'. The following year, Anne Blacklin was sent to prison for 'testifying against a false prophet in Cambridge'. Meanwhile, James Parnell, who was to be the principal Quaker apostle of Cambridgeshire, heard somewhere in the north of two of his friends, presumably the two women visitors of 1653, being whipped for declaring the truth. He was imprisoned for 'setting up a paper in the Market . . . which is a Libell against the ministers and Magistrates of the said Town',[42] early in July 1654. Richard Hubberthorne made a brief visit to Cambridge probably during the same period, and held meetings unmolested, but was arrested after his return

Parnell wrote, 'We are accused to be at one with the Ranters . . . we abhor their Principles in our Hearts, and deny any Liberty to the Flesh, or any light or loose or vicious Conversation, which they live in.' p. 111.

[41] Information on the persecution of individual Quakers is taken from the MSS 'Volume of Sufferings' preserved in the Friends' Meeting House, London, I, pp. 101–35, covering Cambridgeshire and the Isle of Ely. The original book of sufferings of the Cambridgeshire meetings, from which the transcripts preserved in Friends' House were presumably made, did not survive. The first sufferings book in the Cambridgeshire Record Office covering Cambridgeshire as well as Huntingdonshire only begins in 1756. Most of the information from the 'Volume of Sufferings' is printed in J. Besse, *Collections of the Sufferings of the People called Quakers* (1753), pp. 84–99, but he sometimes leaves out entries, or vital information, like the name of the village from which the particular sufferer comes. The humbler the Quaker, the more risk of omission. The rest of the history of early Quaker evangelism in the shire can be pieced together from G. F. Nuttall (ed.), *Early Quaker Letters from the Swarthmore MSS to 1660* (London 1952) [henceforth cited as *Early Quaker Letters*], particularly numbers 57, 76, 83 (Richard Hubberthorne from prison in Cambridge), 84 (Margaret Killam to George Fox), 367 (George Whitehead at Cottenham and Ely), 440, 476 and 486. James Parnell, referred to in letter 83, gives his own account of his Cambridgeshire ministry in the 'Fruits of a Fast' printed in *A Collection of the Several Writings Given Forth from the Spirit of the Lord, through that Meek, Patient and Suffering Servant of God, James Parnell* (1657) [henceforth cited as *A Collection*]. His disputes with the Cambridgeshire Baptists are described by him in detail in *The Watcher: or . . . A Discovery of the ground and end of all forms, Professions, 'Sects' and opinions* (1655), printed in *A Collection*, pp. 180–229. The Baptists' own account of Parnell's visit to Littleport and his disputes with them is printed in *Fenstanton Records*, pp. 144–7. The two accounts, taken together, make entertaining reading. The pamphlets published in the dispute by Parnell, John Wigan, Alderman Blackley, Henry Denne, the Quaker John Crook, and others are listed in Whitley, *A Baptist Bibliography*, I, under 'Cambridge', 'Henry Denne', and 'J[ohn] C[rook]'. The minutes of the Quarterly Meeting of Friends in Cambridgeshire and the Isle of Ely survive from 1673, C.R.O. R59/24/1/5. The register of Quaker births, marriages and deaths is in the P.R.O., R.G./6/1219.

[42] In the words of the Mayor, William Pickering. *The Immediate Call to the Ministry of the Gospel witnessed by the Spirit, With a true Declaration of the persecution and Suffering of Richard Hubberthorne, James Parnell, Ann Blayling . . .* (1654), p. 8. Other relevant passages giving dating are on pp. 2 and 4.

281

at the end of July 1654 and joined Anne Blacklin who had already, according to him, been imprisoned for over three months, and Parnell, who had been imprisoned for nearly three months. In September 1654, they were visited by Margaret Killam, who reported her visit to George Fox. A little while after his release, Parnell returned to Cambridge. There he spent six months 'declaring the Truth in the Countries about and many I found that received the Truth gladly, but more Enemies'. By the middle of 1655 he was in Essex, where he was finally martyred, still only aged eighteen.[43]

Official Quakerism is supposed to have reached Cambridge in 1653, then, and the main evangelising effort was undoubtedly made by James Parnell in the first half of 1655. Despite this official chronology, Quakerism, or Quaker ways of thinking, seem to have reached the villages even before the visit of Elizabeth Williams and Mary Fisher to the county town in 1653. When the Baptist records open in 1651–2, they show the elders in correspondence with two families at Yelling, just over the Huntingdonshire border. They write, 'we do much rejoice to hear of the great manifestations of God (if it be as ye say) has been pleased to give unto you ... but, beloved, we wonder much that you are in doubt how you should try the spirits ... know ye not ... that you ought to try the spirits by the scriptures? ... and in no wise receive any inward manifestations contrary to the written word'.[44] When the response came back, it showed that the writers had fallen into the crude error which so easily developed out of Quaker thinking, of seeing the Scriptures as a possibly conflicting alternative to the inner light of Christ, rather than as an extension of it. 'Now we would know whether the scriptures give life, or Christ?'[45] The whole of the Baptists' pastoral work of 1652 and early 1653 before the Quaker missionaries even arrived, shows them struggling with villagers who claimed a special revelation, and freedom from 'ordinances', whether or not this led them into the Ranter error of justifying sin. The Widow Pepper of Over, which was to be a Quaker centre, in early 1653, told the messengers who asked her to come to meetings, 'I cannot walk in these low dispensations; for God hath manifested himself to my soul, that I am his, and he is my God, and that he hath done by his spirit.'[46] In June

---

[43] There is a discrepancy in the evidence here. Stephen Crisp in his testimony to James Parnell (printed at the beginning of *A Collection*, unpaginated) says Parnell came to Essex at the beginning of 1655 and was arrested in the middle of the same year, implying that he was evangelising there for the whole of the first part of the year. In fact, Parnell's account of his dispute with the Cambridge Baptists in March, April and May 1655 makes it clear that these three months formed part of his six-month period in Cambridgeshire. He cannot have moved permanently to Essex until after March, although he may, of course, have made a short visit earlier.

[44] *Fenstanton Records*, pp. 3–4.   [45] *Ibid.* p. 10.   [46] *Ibid.* p. 41.

1653, when she was again requested to walk in the ordinances of God, she replied, 'I find no comfort in them, and to walk in them I should but show myself a hypocrite. I have received greater manifestations; for God dwelleth in me, and I in him. And now I see that to love, to clothe the naked, and to feed the hungry is enough.'[47] The Ranter extremes were reached by people like the Ofleys of Fenstanton itself, who not only denied ordinances, but claimed that they personally were grown to perfection, unlike the apostles, that all things, including themselves, were God, Who was the author of all actions, and that therefore sin no longer existed.[48] The Baptist records give the impression that spiritual seeking and unrest was extremely widespread at the very lowest parochial level, amongst women and girls and labourers in the villages, and that the Quaker position was reached, or nearly reached, before the arrival of the Quakers, The account of Henry Denne's evangelist tour in the autumn of 1653, at least nine months before Parnell's ministry began, confirms this, for his chief disputes were with Ranters, and with Quakers like the 'maid' Isobel at Kingston who 'tried the Scriptures by the Spirit and not the Spirit by the Scriptures'.[49]

With this background, it was no wonder that the official Quaker effort, as Parnell himself said, bore fruit, and that on his first coming to Cambridge, he 'found those that were worthy that received me'.

The first persecutions of villagers, as opposed to Quaker missionaries, for going to meetings and public testifying are recorded in 1655 and 1656. They show that Quakerism had taken root in both the south and the north-west of the county. Men from Royston and Meldreth were imprisoned in Cambridge Castle in 1655 for meeting on the first day, evidence that Royston meeting was under way. In the same year, Anne Norris of Swavesey was 'moved by the Lord to beare her testimony against the preist of Over in the Steeplehouse' and went to prison for six months as a result. Her husband, who was nearly eighty, was fined in the same year for riding on the sabbath, because he had been caught on his way to a meeting two miles away from Swavesey. For refusing to pay, he also was imprisoned, and so they were both kept from their six children who were still 'not able to guide themselves'. A week after his release from prison, Boniface Norris died. So began the long series of painful family disruptions, and the imprisonments which sometimes led to martyrdom, which the village Quakers were to suffer over the next twenty years.

The Norrises were not the only Quakers in Swavesey. In 1656, two Swavesey men were fined for 'entertaining the people called Quakers'.

[47] *Ibid.* pp. 46–7.   [48] *Ibid.* p. 8.   [49] *Ibid.* p. 74.

The Register Book of the Cambridgeshire Friends which records the marriages back to 1657 is preceded by a list of the nine Cambridgeshire meetings. Five of these, Swavesey, Over, Willingham, Oakington and Cottenham, lay close together in this area, north of Cambridge on the fen edge. When Quakerism died in Balsham and Linton, its other main strongholds in the south of the county, it remained strong here. The persecutions, particularly after the conventicle act of 1670, show that meetings were then held, or at least broken up, most frequently in Swavesey and Over, although Oakington meetings were not unknown. They were all attended by people from the whole group of villages, and also by others from Cottenham and Willingham. George Whitehead was in Cottenham in 1656.[50] He, Richard Hubberthorne, and Alexander Parker visited the county periodically and advised in local problems, but after Parnell's six months in the county, Quakerism was sufficiently firmly established to supply its own leaders. By the onset of full-scale persecution in 1660, John Aynsloe, a farmer living in Over, was established as the Quaker spokesman.

Many of the Quaker converts were inevitably gained from the Baptists, as they were elsewhere. These converts often went through great distress. The effects of this in the mind of one woman in Over, who was later said to make her living by day labour[51] were recorded by the Fenstanton messengers when they visited her in January 1655, probably just at the time of James Parnell's crusade.[52] 'Sister Sneesby' was found 'in a very sad and deplorable condition. She wept as soon as she saw us, and desired us to pray for her; for she was much troubled in her mind.' When John Denne was desired to preach publicly at Over by the Baptists there in mid-1655, possibly to counteract the effects of the Quakers' work there,[53] he found Sister Sneesby finally 'turned aside from the truth, denying the holy scriptures, the ordinances of God and the church of God'.[54]

While this struggle for souls was going on at a village level, to the distress of the Sister Sneesbys, it was no wonder that public relations between the Quakers and the Baptists were very bad. James Parnell opened the real hostilities in March 1655 by sending a series of queries to the Fenstanton Baptists challenging them to justify their position. By choosing to attack the Denne church, he presumably took the most active Baptist centre within reach. When his queries remained unanswered, he took himself to Fenstanton in person, 'freely declaring the truth of God'. His meeting, as he obviously intended, turned into a public debate with the Baptists, who were led by a certain Richard

[50] *Early Quaker Letters*, no. 367.   [51] See above, pp. 216–17.
[52] *Fenstanton Records*, p. 120.   [53] *Ibid.* p. 147.   [54] *Ibid.* pp. 148–9.

Elligood. The serious argument on the necessity of baptism, and on whether the spirit should be tried by the letter of the Scriptures or not, degenerated into a verbal free-for-all. The debate, and the series of letters between the Fenstanton elders and Parnell which followed the meeting, were full of personalities, on the level of Parnell's 'the Lyar is of the Devil and therefore is Elligood'.[55]

The tone of the public debate held in Cambridge the following month between Parnell and the Baptist Doughty, before 'a multitude of Rude People and Brutish Scholars'[56] was no better. The height of ill-feeling between Baptists and Quakers was reached in May 1655 when the Baptist John Ray was sent by the association of elders to try and correct the errors of the Littleport meeting. There, no less than twelve of the twenty-one members had turned Quaker, including the elder, Samuel Cater.[57]

The relationship between the sects continued to be extremely bad. John Bunyan, the Open Baptist, gave credence to the tales circulating about the Quakers after two of them had been brought to trial at assizes in July 1659 on a charge of witchcraft, and himself issued a paper on the subject. This called for a Quaker rebuttal, which it promptly got: 'Thou has shamed thy self in believing such lyes . . . to render the innocent odious.'[58]

The only signs of tolerance were shown by Henry Denne, who took up his pen a month or so after the witchcraft episode to refute, on the Quakers' behalf, the charge made against them that refusal to swear the oath of abjuration was itself tantamount to an admission of popery.

Yea, the Argument, were there any force in it would prove the poor Quakers to be very Mahumetans, and Atheists; which I hope no man is yet so mad as to conceive of them. For were there an Oath exacted of them, to swear that Mahomets Religion is false . . . or to swear there is a God, which none but Atheists (if they) would scruple at, yet Quakers would refuse both the one and the other, standing to their principles.[59]

Denne's pamphlet makes most impressive reading, for the accuracy with which he meets Thomas Smith's attack on the validity of ministry outside the Church of England by a counter-attack on the break in

---

[55] Parnell, *The Watcher*, p. 185.   [56] *Ibid.* p. 202.
[57] *Fenstanton Records*, pp. 144–7.
[58] Alderman James Blackley *et al.*, *A Lying Wonder Discovered and the Strange and Terrible Newes from Cambridge proved false, with an answer to John Bunion's Paper touching the said imagined witchcraft* etc. (1659).
[59] Henry Denne, *The Quaker No Papist, in Answer to the Quaker Disarm'd, or, a brief Reply and Censure of Mr. Thomas Smith's frivolous Relation of a Dispute held betwixt himself and certain Quakers at Cambridge* (1659).

Anglican episcopal ordination under Elizabeth, but most of all for the charity and large-mindedness with which he defended not only the Quakers, but the papists themselves, as well as those unwilling to swear, as a matter of belief, that purgatory and transubstantiation did not exist.

Is not the Imputation (that Papists believe that faith is not to be kept with heretics, and are therefore themselves totally untrustworthy) proved manifestly to be false, by continuall experience of Protestants treating, commercing, and dealing with Papists as confidently and constantly as with those of their own profession? ... May not a man be a good Subject, because he thinks that Christ is in the Sacrament, and that Good Works merit salvation?

Possibly Denne's understanding of the Quaker position was gained at a meeting between Quakers and Baptists in May 1659, when Alexander Parker wrote to George Fox that he had been to Eltisley: 'The man's name that did desire the meeting was one Desborough, *an ancient professor*, he is uncle to Major General Desborough.'[60] There 'a Baptist teacher'[61] spoke who is likely to have been Henry Denne or his son. A laconic entry in the Quaker 'Volumes of Sufferings' shows that if there was a genuine improvement in relations between the Baptists and Quakers as a result of this initiative, it had evaporated fifteen years later. In 1674–5, when John Elger of Papworth was fined two steers for going to a meeting at the house of Elias Woodward in Eltisley, the information had come from 'James Desborough of Eltisely Informer'.

By 1657 and 1658, then, when the Cambridge Voluntary Association was active,[62] the harvest, already ripe in 1640, had been reaped. The gathered churches of the General Baptists and the Quakers had been formed by the mid-1650s and it is possible that at roughly the same date, the members of the Calvinist Congregationalist church at Bassingbourn had already covenanted to give themselves up 'to the Lord, and to one another'.

CONGREGATIONALISTS

While the Quakers and the Baptists were struggling with each other, the Congregationalists, who were to be the strongest dissenting group in the county, were gaining ground. Their combination of Calvinism in

[60] My italics. It sounds as if the uncle of the patron of the Eltisley living, and so of Henry Denne, was one of those 'non-conformity men such as in those dayes did beare the name of Puritanes', like old Richard Conder. See above, p. 227–8 and 264 n. 110. Quotation from p. 276.
[61] *Early Quaker Letters*, no. 476.   [62] See above, p. 275.

the Presbyterian mould, combined with their own ideas on church government, must have appealed to Cambridgeshire farmers. Unfortunately materials bearing on the growth of the Congregational Church are very thin indeed, apart from Richard Conder's life of Holcroft. There is no rich source like the *Fenstanton Records* or even the Quaker 'Volumes of Sufferings' to illuminate its progress. This can only be pieced together from a very few scraps of information.[63]

In 1654, Margaret Killam reported that while she was in Cambridge she went to a church 'where most of those meets which are comers from the other priests, and have one, as they say, that speaks freely without hire'. Perhaps Francis Holcroft, fellow of Clare, was there.[64] He was by this date already preaching as a supply at Litlington, in south-west Cambridgeshire. He had been drawn to offer his services there, so the story goes, by seeing the horse which was brought to collect the regular preacher, also a fellow of Clare, go away riderless from the college gate, Sunday after Sunday.[65] In 1655, he accepted

---

[63] The main material on the growth of the Congregationalists in the county is contained in the following bibliography.

Robert Robinson, 'Historical Account' in his *Posthumous Works*, ed. B. Flower (Harlow 1812), pp. 257–9. Most of Robinson's material is drawn from the near-contemporary account of Francis Holcroft's work preserved at the beginning of the Great Gransden Church Book (see above, p. 225), which appears to be the only seventeenth-century documentary evidence on the spread of Congregationalism in Cambridgeshire, apart from the list of members of the church made in 1675 (Bodleian MS, Rawl. D1480). The wording of the covenant taken at Bassingbourn was recorded in the Gransden Church Book, when the members of the Croydon church renewed their covenant in the 1690s. An article entitled 'Statistical Survey of Dissent' in the *Congregational Magazine or London Christian Instructor*, II (1819), 437, also records the Bassingbourn tradition, as, in a modified form, does the first surviving Church Book of Cottenham Old Meeting (in the keeping of the secretary and deacons, to whose kindness I am much indebted). The latter only begins in 1780, and includes two passages of meditation on the earlier history of the church inserted amongst the minutes of meetings in 1823 and 1829 (pp. 107–8 and 163). The writer of the second seems to have had an earlier Church Book in front of him. W. T. Whitley, 'Willingham Church', *Congregational Historical Society Transactions*, XII (1933–6), 120–30, prints 'An Authentick Account of the Church of Christ at Willingham from the year 1662 to 1781', probably written in 1811. The first Church Book of Willingham Old Meeting, which opens when the Willingham church split from that of Cottenham in 1726, contains a contemporary account of the foundation of the church there. It quotes a letter gathering information, possibly from Robinson, and contains the account of Bradshaw given by Calamy on pp. 40–1. The only other possible reference to early Congregationalism in the county is the reference made by the Quaker Margaret Killam in 1654 (*Early Quaker Letters*, no. 83). Dr Nuttall suggests that this separatist congregation might well have paved the way for the work of Holcroft and Oddy after 1662. A. G. Matthews, 'The Seventeenth Century', in *Congregationalism through the Centuries* (Cambridge 1937), pp. 45–7, was baffled because he had not been able to find any trace of a Congregational church nearer to Cambridge than Wisbech at this time.

[64] Biography in *Calamy Revised*, pp. 271–2.

[65] Robert Robinson, 'Historical Account', in his *Posthumous Works*, p. 257.

the living of Bassingbourn, next door to Litlington. Since in 1650, the previous minister had been described as 'a very honest man', but one who had 'grown old and worne, and hath not a good delivery, and the parish is very great',[66] Bassingbourn must have had a considerable period of neglect. Holcroft almost at once founded a Congregational church there,[67] which was said to be attended by 'a great many people of other parishes, as well as of his own, besides several of both town and gown from Cambridge'. The covenant which bound the members together survives. It ran:

We do in the presence of the Lord Jesus, the earthly crowned King of Sion, and in the presence of his holy angels and people, and all beside here present, thoroughly give up ourselves to the Lord, and to one another, by the will of God; solemnly promising and engaging in the aforesaid presence, to walk with the Lord and with one another to the observance of all Gospel ordinances, and the discharge of all relative duties in this church of God, and elsewhere and the Lord shall enlighten and enable us.[68]

Apart from the actual wording of the covenant at Bassingbourn there is no evidence of the scope of Holcroft's work at this time. Possibly he evangelised the parishes round about, and laid the foundations on which he built Congregationalism in the county between 1662 and 1669, in this period in the late 1650s. However this may be, Congregationalism in Bassingbourn itself did not survive. The bishop wrote in 1669 that there was no conventicle of dissenters there, though 'some few go to other places'. It was Holcroft's ejection in 1662 which 'appears to have converted him from being the minister of a small parish, to be an apostle chosen and called, to bear the Gospel testimony from village to village'. It is impossible for lack of material to tell what progress he had already made, when, in 1660 the king came into his own again, and the relative freedom of the last twenty years came to an end. But there is one indirect argument which does suggest that the spread of Congregationalist doctrine did take place late, and certainly not before 1662. There is a conspicuous lack of any account of controversy with the Calvinist Congregationalists in either the General Baptist or the Quaker records. Neither sect was slow to resort to print to set their discords before the general public. The Quakers did eventually fall foul of the Congregationalists, over predestination to damnation. A public debate was held, and the record printed;[69] but this did

[66] Parliamentary Survey of 1650, abstracted in C.U.L., Palmer Collection, B3/3.
[67] See Robert Robinson, 'Historical Account', pp. 258–9 and the *Congregational Magazine or London Christian Instructor*, 'Statistical Survey of Dissent', p. 437.
[68] Quoted by Robinson, *ibid.*
[69] *A Relation of some of the most material Matters that passed in a Publick Dispute at Thriploe in Cambridge-shire the 15th day of the 2d Month 1676 between Francis*

not happen until as late as 1676. It is impossible to believe that Denne, who wrote *Christ the Drag-net of all men*, would not have taken issue with Holcroft, who stated, 'There is none shall be saved but such as are elected', if Holcroft had been preaching widely before Denne's death in the early 1660s.[70] There is also a very noticeable lack of Calvinist terminology in the dedicatory clauses of Cambridgeshire wills. References to election were very rare indeed.[71]

THE RESTORATION AND PERSECUTION

The restoration brought to an end the period, which had lasted from at least 1649, during which dissent had been able to spread in relative freedom. The notable exception to this freedom had been that of the Quakers, whose opinions were persecuted from the formation of the sect. The Cambridgeshire Quakers had already suffered fines and imprisonments for several years when, in 1660, they and other non-conformists were hit by the first of the waves of persecution which were to continue until brought to an end in 1687 by the declaration of indulgence. For this reason, the Quakers' fortunes were a little different through the 1660s and 1670s from those of the other, orthodox, sects. The sect had had no room for the half-hearted since its inception, since it was under constant pressure. There was no reason why the number of Quakers should fall as persecution began, and creep up again as persecution eased off, since persecution was already the constant state of affairs for them. Over the next twenty years, therefore, the 'Volumes of Sufferings' record Quaker names which recurred as often as not, again and again, as their possessors were gradually stripped of their goods over a decade or so and reduced to the state of John Smith of Over, who, by the end of 1670, had several charges of attending meetings against him, and eventually had two cows taken from him 'being all he then had'.[72]

The first period of persecution lasted from 1660, through the passing of the act of uniformity and the first conventicle act proscribing meetings, until the fall of Clarendon in 1667 and the adjournment of parliament from 1667 to 1669, brought some relief. The Quakers were probably the worst sufferers. Even before the restoration, they had been obvious scapegoats for communal feelings of superstition and xenophobia, as the credence given to charges of witchcraft brought against them

Holdcraft, and Joseph Odde . . . on the one Party, and Samuel Cater with some others on the Friends of Truth called Quakers. The quotation from Holcroft is on p. 7 of this pamphlet. [70] See below, p. 293.
[71] See below, pp. 343–4. [72] 'Volumes of Sufferings', I, 121.

in 1659 showed. These charges were linked with an unpleasant little tale of the defilement of an altar in Norwich, in a way well calculated to rouse feelings of disgust and hostility in the reader.[73] Their unprotected situation also laid them open to the accusation of secret alliance with the papists.[74] This accusation, as Henry Denne pointed out in their defence, had previously been levelled at the Presbyterians by the Episcopalians in a political smear-campaign, and, then, by the Presbyterians and Episcopalians together, at the Anabaptists.

But the suspicion not so well fastening upon them, 'tis at length derived upon the Quakers; and there it may probably rest and thrive, inasmuch as the Quakers are a people, as to matter of conversation, most estranged from the fashions of the world, and as to matter of interest, I think so unprovided of all humane help, that they are as little able to vindicate themselves as the Papists, and consequently must be content to be both abused alike.[75]

The unpopularity of the Quakers brought mob violence down on them in Cambridge by April 1660, when the meeting in Jesus Lane was broken up, the house wrecked, two women stabbed in the street and blood drawn from another couple of dozen attenders. The Quakers wrote a letter of complaint to the King, quoting the declaration of Breda against him and adding bitterly, 'now heere all may see what muddy waters this fountain of Cambridge streams forth'.[76] But by the beginning of the following year, their refusal to swear the oath of allegiance got them into worse trouble, and Cambridge gaol was filled with Quaker prisoners.[77] They were kept under evil conditions, which were described by John Aynsloe, their spokesman:

some of us are kept in and not suffered to go out at all to ease themselves but might doe it where they lye, and others of us shut up in dungeons and

---

[73] Anon., *Strange and Terrible Newes from Cambridge, being a true Relation of the Quakers bewitching Mary Philips*, etc. (1659). Replied to by Alderman James Blackley et al., *A Lying Wonder Discovered and the Strange and Terrible Newes from Cambridge proved false, with an answer to John Bunion's Paper touching the said imagined witchcraft*, etc. (1659).

[74] By no less a person in Cambridge than the University Librarian. Thomas Smith, *The Quaker Disarm'd, or the True Relation of a Late Publick Dispute Held at Cambridge by Three Eminent Quakers against One Scholar* (etc.) (1659).

[75] Henry Denne, *The Quaker No Papist, in Answer to the Quaker Disarm'd, or, a brief reply and Censure of Mr. Thomas Smith's frivolous Relation of a Dispute held betwixt himself and certain Quakers at Cambridge* (1659). Both the public controversy over Quaker witchcraft and that over Quaker popery blew up in August 1659, after the witchcraft trial at Assizes on 28 July 1659, so it seems likely that there was a general mood of popular feeling against them then.

[76] 'Volume of Sufferings', I, 167.

[77] Sir Thomas Sclater, one of the Cambridgeshire J.P.s made brief notes in his diary on this. They are printed as 'Commitments at Cambridge, 1660–1', *Journal of Friends' History Society*, xx (1923), 32.

holes where they keepe their fellons and witches and Murderers and soe thronged that they have but roome to stirr one by another and the places doe smell soe nastily that it were enough to poyson any creature but the Lord is our preserver . . .

Worse still, these prisoners were of all ages, all conditions and both sexes, and their imprisonment had bitter consequences for their families. The worst-hit village was Swavesey, from which twenty-three people were taken, including men whose families were wholly dependent on their trade and who were now reduced to destitution. All adults were removed from some houses, leaving in one case two small children 'left as in the streets without habitation'.[78]

Other records show the effect on the rest of the denominations of this governmental action. In 1660, the Bedford Open Baptist Meeting, which was later to evangelise Gamlingay and parts of western Cambridgeshire, was turned out of St John's Bedford, where it had been meeting. By 1661, the minutes noted 'some of our brethren and sisters have neglected to come to our Church meetings'.[79] There was a temporary recovery in 1664, but from then until 1668 the record lapsed entirely. When it resumed, the first business was the admonition of 'many of the friends having in these troubleous times withdrawn themselves from close walking with the Church'.[80] There was therefore a falling-away from 1661 until a revival began in 1668, after the pressure had eased off a little.[81]

The fate of the Caxton and Fenstanton Baptists is obscure. Their Church Book, kept so meticulously by John Denne, was filled at the end of 1658,[82] and the new one, which was supposed to be started at the following meeting, did not survive. One or two fragments, presumably from it, covering parts of 1677 and possibly 1676, with a single entry for 1687, were found amongst the papers of the sister church of Warboys, which was united with the Fenstanton church in the early eighteenth century.[83] With these fragments were the two registers of the Fenstanton congregation, one the list of members presumably drawn up in 1650 on the instance of the elders, and the other on 29 August 1676. The two lists show that a great change had taken place in the church in the interval. The first list is significantly headed 'a register for the congregation belonging to Caxton, County Cambridge,

---

[78] 'Volume of Sufferings', I, 109.
[79] *Church Book of Bunyan Meeting*, fo. 25.   [80] *Ibid*. fo. 27.
[81] The history of the Gamlingay Baptists, who in 1670 were united to those of Bedford, suggests a rather different pattern. There was a large group of adherents in Gamlingay in 1669, and it looks as if they had suffered less in the preceeding few years than their Bedford brethren (see below, p. 313).
[82] *Fenstanton Records*, p. 250.   [83] *Ibid*. pp. xxiii–xxiv.

and Fenystanton, County Huntingdon'.[84] It shows that the church in Caxton was the strongest after Fenstanton itself in the early period, with fifteen baptised members. Eltisley, the real base of the church, was fourth strongest, with ten members. Altogether, the church members were drawn from thirty villages, thirteen of them in Cambridgeshire.[85] By 1676, the catchment area had become very much smaller. The congregation was drawn from only seventeen places, and only five of these were in Cambridgeshire. Moreover, not a single member in 1676 lived in either Caxton or in Eltisley. John Denne, who had lived at Caxton Pastures throughout the 1650s, had moved to St Ives, where he was licensed to preach in 1672. It seems that some disaster had hit the Cambridgeshire part of the Fenstanton church.

By happy chance, the Quaker records give some clue to what this disaster had been. Some Baptists, like the Quakers, had conscientious scruples to swearing the oath of allegiance.[86] In his letter reporting the Quaker trial at the assizes in 1660,[87] John Aynsloe recorded 'Severall of Bunion's People and alsoe Baptists' were tried along with the Quakers. Among them was

one John Denne, a teacher amongst them, to whom the Judge was very harsh, more than to any other of the prisoners, ... and did much upbraid him for getting up into the pullpitt for he and some others had crepen into a Steeplehouse to shelter themselves from the King's late proclamation against meetings in private. And it became a greater Snare to him for he was taken in the Pulpitt not haveing orders as the Judg said.

John Aynsloe's report makes it seem likely that the flourishing Baptist meeting, based on Caxton where John Denne lived, had attempted to take refuge in the parish church of Eltisley a mile or so away across the fields, where his father Henry still probably held the living.[88] John Aynsloe did not report the outcome of the trial in full, but the collapse of the Cambridgeshire section of the Fenstanton church seems very likely to be related to the penalties it now suffered.[89] It is sad that this was the result of all the devoted work of the elders in the 1650s, about which more is known than in any other commonwealth church. The Baptists collapsed only in this west Cambridgeshire area; the Huntingdonshire section flourished and the later evidence shows that the Baptists in south and east Cambridgeshire at Melbourn and the Wilbrahams showed more pertinacity than their brethren round Caxton. Whatever happened to the latter, John Denne did not lose the regard

---

[84] *Ibid.* p. 251.   [85] Excluding the Isle of Ely.
[86] *Fenstanton Records*, pp. xxi–xxv.   [87] 'Volumes of Sufferings', I, 113–14.
[88] Henry Denne is supposed to have died in 1661. *Fenstanton Records*, p. xxii.
[89] John Denne himself swore the oath and put in bond for his good behaviour on this occasion, according to Aynsloe.

of his Baptist colleagues, for in 1672 it was he who took out the licences of all the Baptist meetings of Cambridgeshire and Huntingdonshire.[90]

The Congregationalists were not affected as early as the Quakers and Baptists by persecution because they had no qualms about taking the oath of allegiance. Indeed, such evidence as there is shows that the powerful Congregational Church of Cambridgeshire was formed in the 1660s, and probably the early part of the decade, when the Baptists were under heavy pressure and losing members. Some clue is given by the tradition that Nathaniel Bradshaw who was ejected from Willingham rectory in 1662, continued to 'Preach in his own and other Families' for some years before the 'Providence of God gave him the Liberty of a Pulpit in a small Village, which he us'd with so much Prudence and Moderation, that he was conniv'd at for about Five Years.'[91] Bradshaw was the only ejected minister, apart from Holcroft and his team, who left a really lasting mark in the form of an active dissenting congregation at Willingham.[92]

This same period while Bradshaw was being 'conniv'd at' saw Holcroft at his great work. One modern writer has suggested that 'There cannot have been any other county in England at this period (1660–90) when Congregationalism within so short and so extraordinarily difficult a time took such lasting root.'[93] Holcroft's Congregational Church was fully formed by 1669 when the bishop noted the conventicles belonging to it.[94] Commonsense suggests that the most active period of formation would have been immediately after Holcroft's ejection before the passing of the first conventicle act and the five mile acts made things more difficult. An informer's report,[95] which can probably be dated to 1663, and which states that Holcroft had meetings of three hundred and more at Barley in Hertfordshire, and of many hundreds in Cambridge itself, and that his assistants Oddy and Lock held large conventicles at Meldreth and had a circuit in Cambridgeshire, Bedfordshire and Hertfordshire, seems to prove that this was so.

In 1798, the Rev. Thomas Hopkins began the *History of Lynton Congregational Church* of which he was pastor. He reported that a church member who was then upwards of ninety-four years of age remembered hearing her mother say 'she used to go to hear preaching in the neighbouring woods in the night for Fear of their enemies'. Other elderly people had the same tradition handed down from parents

---

[90] Lyon Turner, III, 299–300.   [91] *Calamy Revised*, pp. 69–70.
[92] Even that was nursed by Oddy, one of Holcroft's helpers during the difficult period until Bradshaw returned after the act of toleration. See above, p. 234; and below, pp. 316–18, for the influence of the non-subscribers.
[93] A. G. Matthews in *Congregationalism through the Centuries* (1937), p. 54.
[94] Lyon Turner, I, 36–41.   [95] Discussed in Lyon Turner, III, 294–5.

and some pinned it down to the Horseheath and Hare Woods about four miles from Linton. This tradition, if it had any substance, probably referred to a time not only before the act of toleration, but before the declaration of indulgence. If so, the picture of preaching in the woods at night, for fear of enemies, gives some idea of the way in which Holcroft's work was carried on after the conventicle act.

Hopkins also described the chapel which the Congregationalists of Linton built only ten years after toleration, in 1698.[96] The description gives a vivid impression of the simplicity of reformed worship, and the predominance in it of the preaching of the word from the dominating pulpit. It also illustrates the family pride in dissent, and the way non-conformity was handed down within the family, as it had been in the Conder family of Croydon and the Metcalfe family of Melbourn. It also shows that Congregationalism had acquired great social respectability by the end of the eighteenth century at Linton, where the squire had his own pew, despite the fact that the meeting-house stood next to a tan yard, since the ground had originally been given by a tanner, 'which rendered it most unpleasant'.

The pastor of Linton in the late eighteenth century wrote of his chapel,

In appearance it was rather rough, the shape was like unto a barn divided into three bays, to be converted into a barn again if persecution revived . . . the doors opened outside, the windows were all provided with shutters to prevent their being broken into by persecuting men, the shutters being drawn up with pulleys. As you enter, opposite the doors, stands the pulpit, with a large Cumbrous sounding board over it. In front of the pulpit is a long table pew across the building capable of holding thirty persons or more, with a large brass chandelier hanging over it. There is a square pew for the Squire, lined with green baize surrounded with silk curtains, with a devotional table in the centre; other large square pews lined with green baize capable of seating fourteen or fifteen persons, other pews in variety, some long, some square, some three-cornered, it appeared that each one built his pew as he pleased. On either side of the pulpit galleries were erected in 1704, and in front of the pulpit was a circular gallery where the singers like the sons of Asaph had their place. On the walls were many monumental tablets in memory of worthy men, the Malns, Jacksons, Fords and Taylors, whose voices once filled the house with praise.[97]

[96] Copy of first trust deed in 'Notes on Linton Congregational Church', C.U.L., W. M. Palmer Collection, B4/1.
[97] Taken from the typescript précis of the *History of Linton Congregational Church 1798–1894*, by the Reverend Thomas Hopkins *et al.*, in the C.U.L., W. M. Palmer Collection, B3/8. This building was pulled down in 1818, according to Hopkins, and the materials were used in the present meeting-house which stands at right-angles to the original building in Horn Lane, Linton.

A dissenting ancestry was a matter for pride.[98]

The history of conflict between the General Baptists and the Quakers, which was often deliberately provoked by one sect once the other was established in a village, illustrates a very important point. Once dissent or separatism in any form existed, it was likely to be spread by argument and debate, and further fragmentation was likely to follow. It is only necessary to look at the map showing the distribution of dissent between 1654 and 1676 (Map 12, above) in the county to see that this was so. Perhaps the most outstanding example of fragmentation was Over, where there was a small group of Baptists in the 1650s and a Baptist meeting-house was licensed in 1672. Over was the home of John Aynsloe and there was also a strong Quaker meeting there in the 1660s. However little they approved of each other, both parties must have been united in their detestation of the 'Prophet Ludowicke Muggleton' who evidently visited the place several times with 'several other friends who had the assurance of salvation abiding in them'. This is apparent from one of Muggleton's typical formal letters of blessing, written as late as 1681, to a woman of Over, in which he wrote, 'I do pronounce and declare you, Sarah West, one of the blessed of the Lord, both in soul and body, to all eternity.' In the letter he rebuked her for not asking his blessing on one of his previous frequent visits to Over: 'I speak this not to daunt you for your neglect, but do say unto you, as Christ said unto Martha, who was troubled with many incumbrances about victuals to entertain Christ and his disciples; for indeed your husband and yourself did entertain us with several feasts, as princes, which will not be forgotten as long as any of us do live.'[99] Neither Baptists nor Quakers exhibited spiritual pride on this scale. The incumbents of Over, presented by Trinity College,[100] may possibly have tolerated the work of Holcroft and his assistants, which led to the recording there of yet another conventicle, of Congregationalists, in 1669. But the presence of the Quaker Aynsloe, the Baptists, and the visits of Muggleton were certainly not matters for self-congratulation.

Oakington and Willingham both had Quakers and Congregationalists. In the early 1670s the staunch Congregationalist Crabb family of Little Wilbraham was joined, and challenged, by the equally staunch Quaker family of John Prime. The Crabb family was another in which

[98] The post-restoration growth or decline of the various sects and the antecedents of some of the present chapels have been discussed by me in 'Dissenting Churches', pp. 67–95. I have not repeated the discussion here.

[99] Ludovic Muggleton, *A Volume of Spiritual Epistles ... etc.* (reprinted by subscription, 1820), pp. 497–8.

[100] Which had over twice as many fellows ejected in 1660 as any other Cambridge college, *Calamy Revised*.

dissenting opinions could be traced through several generations. In 1716, Sarah Crabb, aged twenty, the daughter of Widow Crabb of Little Wilbraham, was baptised as a Congregationalist in Cambridge along with her eighteen-year old sister, 'after her experience of the work of God laid upon her soul in the law of the church'. These were presumably the great-grandchildren of Moses Crabb, a water-miller, who held a small conventicle in his house in 1669. In 1679, four Crabbs, and a Crabb son-in-law were presented by the wardens at the visitation for joining conventicles. The validity of Sarah Crabb's marriage was also doubted by her co-villagers. The Sarah Crabb baptised in 1716 was presumably her grandchild, and one of the fourth generation to experience spiritual convictions deep enough to lead her to separate herself from her natural village community.[101]

The villages lying on the chalk ridge which carried the Icknield Way across south-eastern Cambridgeshire were almost untouched by organised dissent. The exception was Balsham, which had a history of separatism reaching back to the Family of Love in the 1580s. A group of Baptists existed in Balsham in 1654, but by 1669 there were tiny conventicles of both Baptists and Quakers there.

Even where the early dissenting history of a village was entirely that of the growth of one sect, as soon as Congregationalism started to expand rapidly in the 1660s the inherent vulnerability to fragmentation of any sect was shown.[102] Melbourn had had an Anabaptist tradition since the Metcalfe family established it, at least by the end of 1653 and probably before. However, in a visitation of 1679 twelve of the seventy families in Melbourn were said to be 'Wolcroft's disciples'. In 1690, the lord of one of the manors of Melbourn gave £15 a year to establish a school for forty children 'of the poorer sort' from Melbourn and Meldreth 'being Protestants and the children of Protestants of the Church of England as it was then by law established, and no other'.[103] Again the depth of the doctrinal and divisive rift within the village community itself is brought home. This was new. However, Congregationalism gained so strong a footing in Melbourn that, at some point in the next thirty years, the old Bassingbourn and Meldreth church moved its meeting-place there. Between 1716 and 1717 the charming house of brick which is still used by the Congregationalists today was built in Melbourn. Appropriately enough, a Bassingbourn man, John

---

[101] M. Spufford, 'Dissenting Churches', pp. 82–3.
[102] Meldreth, which itself was sending a couple of Quakers to meeting in Royston in 1655, was a Congregationalist stronghold by 1663.
[103] *Report of the Commissioners Inquiry Concerning Charities*, XXIX (1937–8). 76–7. I am grateful to Miss Angela Black, of the Cambridge Record Office, for drawing this to my attention.

Jermans, a tailor, was one of the first feoffees of the new meeting-house. The Melbourn meeting, with four hundred hearers, was one of the best-attended in the county.

Just as Congregationalism moved into Melbourn to challenge the Baptists, it moved into Linton to challenge the Quakers. There is no surviving evidence that there was any early Congregationalism at Linton, apart from the tradition of the church there that during persecution the oldest members had been to hear preaching in the woods a few miles away. Apart from this the early dissenting history of the place was all Quaker. The Linton meeting was the only really sizeable and strong one, apart from those round Swavesey and Over. It had its own meeting-house by the early eighteenth century. However, only ten years after toleration, in 1698, the Linton Congregationalists were planning to build their own chapel. Doctrinal convictions not only divided villages, but families within them. The uncommonly named Peacheys of Soham not only provided elders of the Quaker church, but also a member of Holcroft's church, listed in 1675, who was later admitted to the Rothwell Congregational Church.

Dissent then bred dissent. Once it had taken root, fragmentation followed. The environment which tended to encourage dissent to take root in the first place has yet to be considered. It is particularly important to consider this, since some parts of the county, notably a large number of villages on the clay to the west, another coherent group in the valleys of the Granta and Cam downstream from Linton to the Shelfords, and a little group of four sparsely settled parishes round Carlton on the top of the chalk ridge to the south-east of the county, were almost entirely conformist. This demarcation between dissenting and conformist areas still needs investigation.

12

The possible determinants of dissent

It has become fashionable to attempt to account for the distribution of religious phenomena by explaining them in terms of the social and geographical backgrounds in which they flourish or wither away. There is no doubt much merit in this approach. It can also lead to over-simplification of an extraordinarily naive kind. The Indian geographer Kuriyan, for instance, has accounted for the readiness with which Christ's disciples followed him by pointing out that 'the fishermen of Galilee were nomadic by virtue of their occupation. Fishing was a haphazard business, and hence their readiness to uproot themselves and chance the integrity of a wandering teacher.' On the other hand, 'The men of Nazareth were patient cultivators . . . like all cultivators they were rooted to the soil, and could rarely move away from their homes as the land has to be constantly tended. The horizon of their minds was limited to the walls which shut in their corner of the earth, and by nature, they were against novelty and change.' Few converts were there-fore made in Nazareth.[1]

Much more subtle arguments have recently been advanced by Pro-fessor Everitt for the distribution of nonconformity in country parishes in England in more recent times. Basically, he suggests that dissent could flourish in large parishes, mainly in fen and forest regions where manorial control was weak, in boundary areas, or in decayed market towns, where control was likewise weak.[2]

The description of the growth of dissent in Cambridgeshire has already shown that 'a countryside of patient cultivators . . . rooted to the soil' was not by any means necessarily one in which the horizon of the people's minds 'was limited to the walls which shut in their corner of the earth'. The peasants of Cambridgeshire were certainly not by nature against novelty and change. However, it is still necessary to discuss whether dissent was more likely to flourish in one or other of

[1] Quoted without comment by J. D. Gay, *The Geography of Religion in England* (London 1971), p. 17.
[2] Alan Everitt, 'Nonconformity in Country Parishes', in *Land, Church and People*, ed. Joan Thirsk, *Ag. Hist. Rev.* 18 (1970), pp. 178–99, especially pp. 188–97.

the two very dissimilar types of community I have discussed, the polarised corn-growing villages of the 'uplands' or the stock-rearing, more egalitarian, communities of the fens.

It would also be interesting to know whether dissent gained an equally strong hold throughout the whole of village communities, or whether, for instance, yeomen, whose superior economic status led to a higher degree of literacy,[3] were even more likely to adopt dissenting opinions.

By confining myself to the village members of dissenting groups, I am only examining dissent amongst 'the lower classes', by some definitions. But I have demonstrated the very great economic divisions within rural communities. I am myself extremely chary of using the word 'class' of the many, and important, different strata within village communities, even by the end of the seventeenth century. Phrases like the 'agricultural petite bourgeoisie' leave me very cold indeed. Certainly there were clear and well-marked economic differences between yeomen, husbandmen, labourers and craftsmen, as the very different value of their goods at the time of their deaths shows.[4] As we have seen, these economic differences were becoming increasingly emphasised in upland Cambridgeshire by the polarisation of agricultural society in the seventeenth century, as corn-growing became more and more an occupation for the farmer with over forty-five acres. Economic differences in themselves, however strong, do not necessarily make for social cleavage, however. Fathers in this county tried to provide all their younger sons with either an acre or so of land, or a cash sum with which to set up a cottage, even if the eldest was to inherit the main holding. This constant paternal effort to provide all the members of a family with at least a toehold on the land meant that the immediate members of a family could, and did, sprawl right across the economic divisions within a village, and comprehend, at one extreme yeomen who were turning into gentry, and at the other landless labourers with only a cottage to their name.[5]

Dissent, as we have already seen, was frequently a family phenomenon. The natural corollary to the spread of the family across economic divisions suggests that dissent also spread right through a community. As well as examining the type of economy in which dissent flourished best, and the degree to which it spread throughout these

[3] See above, pp. 199, 204–5.
[4] The median wealth of the eighteen labourers whose inventories occur amongst those preserved in the Consistory Court of Ely records from the 1660s was £15. That of the twenty-four husbandmen was £30; that of the fifty-five craftsmen was £40, and that of the fifty-eight yeomen was £180.
[5] See for instance above, pp. 85–6 and 106–7, 111–12.

societies, or was confined to certain social groups within them, it is necessary to consider the other possible influences at work.

If a village had only one lord, who was resident, his influence might obviously have a considerable effect. A village with a non-resident lord would be in a very different position. So also would the community which was more normally found in Cambridgeshire, a multi-manorial settlement which frequently had a multiplicity of lords many, or all, of whom were non-resident. The influence of the clergy is another obvious factor which should, in theory, have influenced the peasantry. The shepherd should lead his sheep. The presence or absence of a school made for greater or less literacy, and so laid the villagers open to new opinions transmitted by the printed word. We have seen how this could bring about conversions.[6]

THE SOCIAL SPREAD OF DISSENT IN CORN-GROWING AND FENLAND COMMUNITIES – ORWELL AND WILLINGHAM

Orwell and Willingham were economically contrasted almost as completely as it was possible for any two villages to be, as my detailed studies of them above have shown. Orwell, which had fifty-eight nonconformists in the Compton Census, had more than any other parish in the county, even though it was only an average-sized village on the edge of the clay uplands, with fifty-odd houses in the 1670s. Most of these dissenters were Congregationalists, although there were also Muggletonians there.[7] Orwell was one of the main centres where Francis Holcroft's team of helpers worked. It was noticed by the bishop in 1669, and a licence was issued for a meeting-place there in 1672.[8] In 1675 a list was made of the members of Holcroft's church in Cambridgeshire which survives, in a very corrupt form, in the Bodleian Library.[9] One of the sections of this list contains church members drawn from Orwell and three neighbouring villages. This joint congregation, which had 124 members, was the strongest in the county.

By comparing the Congregational list with the hearth tax taken a year earlier, it is possible to identify most members of the church from Orwell who were also heads of households. The uses of the hearth tax are not exhausted there, fortunately. There is no doubt that entries in the tax lists form a general, if not a precise guide, to the economic position of those taxed. In the seventeenth century, retired or declined yeoman farmers could be found, like their counterparts today, hanging

[6] See above, pp. 215–17.　　　[7] See above, pp. 229–30.
[8] Lyon Turner, I, 36; II, 863.　　　[9] Bodleian MS, Rawl. D1480, fos. 123–6.

on in houses they could not afford to keep up; but as an overall guide, the tax is adequate.[10]

Nearly a quarter of the householders of Orwell who were taxed on their hearths in 1674 were identifiable as nonconformists.[11] This is an astonishingly large proportion, for heads of households alone are being considered here. The amount of trouble caused by the dissenters of Orwell is indicated by a couple of entries in the churchwardens' accounts. Between Michaelmas 1668 and Michaelmas 1669, and again in the following year, no less than seven applications were made for a 'warrant for the phanaticks'. The parish register, too, gives ample evidence of the amount of nonconformity there, for the deaths of dissenters were sometimes recorded even though they were not buried in the churchyard. It was not always possible to carry the corpses elsewhere and the disgusted scribe recorded several times in the later seventeenth century that someone had been 'buried with the burial of an asse' in a close or orchard.

Who then are these Orwell dissenters? A comparison of the size of their houses recorded in the hearth tax with those of the remainder of the community shows that they were distributed throughout every layer of village society from the top to the bottom, and that there were, if anything, slightly more poor men among them than among their conforming fellows.[12] John Howard, senior, who paid tax on five hearths and is therefore likely to have been a considerable yeoman, was a dissenter. So was John Adams, who had a more modest house with only two hearths. This had been one of the meeting-places of the conventicle in 1669. John Adams was one of the few remaining small yeomen of Orwell who held only about twenty acres of arable in the 1670s; most of them had been squeezed out in the engrossing process which had been going on throughout the century. When he died, as an old man, in 1691, he left £91, a barely adequate estate by yeomen standards. Three of the twelve

---

[10] The median wealth of those who died in southern Cambridgeshire in the decade 1661–70 and can be identified in a hearth tax return as occupants of houses with one hearth was £24; that of a man occupying a house with two hearths was £60; that of a man with three hearths was £141, and that of a man with four or more hearths was £360. Compare with the figures in n. 4, p. 299; above. M. Spufford, 'Significance of Hearth Tax', pp. 53–64.

[11] Twelve out of fifty-two householders. I have throughout, in identifying nonconformists, used a combination of the 1674 hearth tax, P.R.O., E179/244/23, with Lyon Turner, the Congregational church list of 1675, and, where there were Quakers, the 'Volume of Sufferings', I, 101–34 in the Friends' Meeting House, London and the Quaker Register for Cambridgeshire, P.R.O., R.G./6/1219. I have also used as supplementary evidence two episcopal visitations, of 1679 and 1682, which contain many names of parishioners presented for attending conventicles, without, of course, their adherence. E.D.R., B 2/6, fos. 13–28v and 39–53v.

[12] See Table 18.

301

dissenting householders of Orwell who appeared in both the 1674 hearth tax returns and in the rental of the 1670s were holders of half-yardlands like John Adams, but another three were certainly cottagers with a very small acreage. Half of the dissenters in the hearth tax returns paid on only one hearth. There is no doubt that Congregational opinions had gained as much hold on the poor, by village standards, as on the rich. Richard Barnard, who had a cottage with one hearth in 1674, was constantly in trouble with the ecclesiastical authorities for not going to the parish church. He must have been a devoted adherent, for his orchard was commonly used for Congregationalists' burials. When he died in 1693, he was described by his neighbours as a husbandman, and was by then an impoverished one, for his goods were valued at £15. Edward Caldecot, who likewise paid tax on one hearth in 1674, was also paying a cottager's rent of 3s 4d in the 1660s, and was really poor, for he was possessed of goods worth only £5 when he died in 1690. Nonconformist opinions, and prosperity, bore no relationship at all to each other in Orwell.

Willingham, on the edge of the fens, was three times the size of Orwell. Its minister, Nathaniel Bradshaw, was a non-subscriber, whose proud boast it was that he had left 'four score and ten praying families' there at his deprivation.[13] By 1669, there was a flourishing Congregational conventicle there. It had about a hundred hearers, taught by Francis Holcroft and Joseph Oddy. Many of the members came from other places, and they were, in Bishop Laney's words 'all very meane, Excepte some few yeomen'. A licence was obtained for Willingham in 1672, and it remained a Congregational centre. A few Quakers appeared there in the 1670s also. The Congregational church list of 1675 again lumps together Willingham members with those from two neighbouring villages, but once again some of the householders can be identified by comparing the list with the hearth tax return of the year before. An agreement on the use of the Willingham fens was marked or signed by all of the commoners in 1677–8 and another comparison can be made with this.[14] It is unfortunate, for these purposes, that the membership of the church was, as usual, predominantly female. Only twenty-two of the seventy Congregationalists in the Willingham section of the church list were men. All the remainder were, as usual, women and it is almost impossible to trace a woman's status unless her husband is named. However, of the twenty-two men in Francis Holcroft's church who came from Willingham, Oakington and Over, fourteen appeared in the hearth tax return for Willingham, or in the commoners' agreement, or in a list of presentments of Willingham people for failure to

13 *Calamy Revised*, p. 69. See above, p. 293.   14 C.R.O., R59/14/5/9 (f).

attend church made in 1673.[15] So about two-thirds of the male membership of the church came from Willingham, and it is possible to examine their backgrounds and see if the bishop's judgement that they were 'all very meane' was a partial statement or not.

Willingham, like the other fen-edge villages, was pastoral. The social and economic structure of the villages was entirely different from that of the upland villages like Orwell. Whereas, on the uplands, the tenants of half-yardlands had been losing their holdings since the end of the sixteenth century because small-scale corn-growers were unable to withstand the continued pressures of the price rise and bad harvests, here, on the edge of the fens, such men were men of substance, because of their common rights and the cattle that went with their holdings. These villages were not economically polarised in the way that arable, upland, villages were. They had a lower proportion of the houses of landless or near-landless men, with only one hearth, and a much higher proportion of the houses of the moderately prosperous with two or three hearths. Commoners were more prosperous than their fellows, and were more likely to have larger houses. Every single one of the nine male Congregationalists named in Francis Holcroft's church list of 1675, who was identifiable in the tax list of 1674, lived in a house with two or three hearths. The Willingham Congregationalists were not, therefore, like their fellow members at Orwell, distributed throughout the village community. They were neither drawn from the poorer thirty-nine per cent of the villagers who lived in houses with only one hearth, nor from the most prosperous seven per cent of the householders who had bigger houses with four or more hearths. They came from the relatively comfortable and substantial middle section of this village community. All but one of them were also literate, in the sense that they could write their names, which usually seems to indicate the ability to read. Francis Duckins is a good example. He was one of the foremost of the church members, because his house was one of the meeting-places of the conventicle in 1669, and was the one chosen to be licensed as a meeting-place in 1672. It was taxed on three hearths in 1674. The bishop or his officials, were plainly out of touch with the nuances of village society when they described these people as 'all very meane'. They were nothing of the kind: they were the small yeomen-graziers who formed the backbone of Willingham society.

The same judgement applies to the Quakers of Willingham, about

---

[15] Dennis Jeeps kindly drew my attention to this list in a book of miscellaneous court records (E.D.R., D2/54, fos. 39v–40v). This list adds thirteen more male non-churchgoers, who do not appear either in Congregational or Quaker records, but who do appear in the hearth tax, to the nine identifiable male Congregationalists and four identifiable Quakers who also appear in the hearth tax.

whom the bishop wrote in even more depreciating terms than the Congregationalists. Four Quakers of Willingham can be identified in the 1674 hearth tax returns. Three of them had houses with two or three hearths and one had an outstandingly large house with five hearths. The two Quakers who appear among the commoners could both sign their names. All but two, or possibly three, of the additional thirteen non-churchgoers of 1673, whose denominations are unknown, also lived in houses with two or three hearths. This meant that the overwhelming majority of nonconformists in Willingham were comparatively prosperous. When the bishop wrote of the local dissenters in the terms he did, he was either making a deliberate attempt to minimise their importance within their own communities, or he was genuinely ignorant of the difference between a day-labourer and a fenland yeoman.

A close look at the dissenting members of two village communities at the same date therefore gives a very different impression of their status. In one, nonconformist opinions had spread throughout the villagers, from the prosperous to the poor. In the other these opinions were almost entirely confined to the comfortable middle stratum of smaller yeomen. The most likely reason for this surprising result is that it ties in, in some way, with the very different social situation in the upland and the pastoral villages. I still cannot understand why Congregational opinions should make no appeal to the poor of Willingham, while they did to the poor of Orwell, when the kinship network spread as widely across social stratifications in one village as in the other.

I have not here been dealing with a group of statistical significance; a dozen Congregationalist and Muggletonian householders in Orwell and another couple of dozen Congregationalist and Quaker householders in Willingham do not make a sample.[16] A brief look at the distribution of Congregational and Quaker views at Cottenham, which is both close to Willingham and comparable with it economically, shows that a rather larger number of dissenters there seemed to be well-off than in the community at large, but the phenomenon was not so clearly marked as at Willingham. It was not found at all among the Quakers in Swavesey, which was then a small port and market town on the edge of the fens. Swavesey was the nursery of Quakerism in this part of the county, and the early Quakers, involved in the mass arrests of 1661, were as usual, predominantly female; but they were also predominantly poor. Four of the nine men involved were labourers, whilst three others were craftsmen.

---

[16] Unlike the work of Cole and Vann on the early Quakers which dealt with significant numbers. See Alan Cole, 'The Social Origins of the Early Friends', *Journal of the Friends' Historical Society*, XLVIII (1957), 99–118 and R. T. Vann, 'Quakerism and the Social Structure in the Interregnum', *Past and Present*, 43 (1969), pp. 71–91.

TABLE 18 *Economic status of dissenters in 1674*

	Orwell						Willingham					
	Identifiable dissenters		Others		All villagers		Identifiable male dissenters		Others		All villagers	
	no.	%	no.	%	no.	%	no.	%	no.	%	no.	%
Large houses – four hearths and over	3	25	8	20	11	21	1	4	9	7	10	7
Modest houses – two and three hearths	3	25	19	47	22	42	22	88	60	48	82	54
Small houses, cottages – one hearth	6	50	13	33	19	37	2	8	56	45	58	39
Totals	12	100	40	100	52	100	25	100	125	100	150	100

By 1674, the Quakers of Swavesey were better-off, but two of the half-dozen who appear in the 1674 hearth tax returns were still occupants of houses with only one hearth. This certainly does not tie in with the picture of Willingham dissenters as a prosperous group, nor, incidentally, does it tie in with Vann's suggestion that first-generation Quakers were more prosperous than converts after the restoration.[17] It looks as if the situation in Willingham may have been atypical.

The obvious next step to be taken to obtain a complete picture of the spread of dissent within rural society is to analyse the whole of the Congregational church list for Cambridgeshire, together with the Quaker records and the pitifully small list of the General Baptists at this date who had managed to survive persecution, in conjunction with the whole of the 1674 hearth tax returns for the county. But unless this is done on a basis of the very different farming regions within the county, or any other county treated in this way, one will lose sight of the economic realities in the search for what Vann has splendidly called 'the protection of the law of large numbers'.[18] It is extremely dangerous to stick an arbitrary label on the tenant, farmer, owner or occupier of twenty acres and call him a 'yeoman', when in an upland area producing sheep and corn he is likely to have been a husbandman struggling along under severe pressures, and in the fens or the forests, a comfortable farmer enjoying reasonable spending power. If it is worth looking at the distribution of dissent amongst the peasantry at all, the structure of the communities concerned must first be fairly well known.

This interim examination shows, first, that nonconformist opinions could and did obtain as strong a hold on an upland village growing corn as in a fenland village growing stock. The totally different economic backgrounds of the two communities made no difference to their common position as seed-beds of dissent. Secondly, dissenting opinions were not confined to the 'wealthy' by village standards, but could also be held by the very poor, even though they made more appeal to the 'wealthy' than the 'poor' in Willingham.

THE INFLUENCE OF LORDSHIP

The only thing Orwell and Willingham had in common was the absence of a resident lord. The effect of lordship, and its absence, on a community's beliefs must therefore be considered. The opinions of the lord certainly were recognised, at the time, as a factor to be reckoned with. John Bunyan, who knew his Cambridgeshire as well as his Bedfordshire, warned against landlords, in the 1660s:

[17] Vann, *art. cit.*, p. 78.   [18] *Ibid.* p. 91.

Oh what red lines will those be against all these rich ungodly Landlords, that so keep under their poor Tenants, that they dare not go out to hear the word for fear their Rent should be raised, or they turned out of their houses.

Interestingly though, ungodly landlords were generally classed by Bunyan along with other heads of smaller communities, those of individual households rather than villages. He railed equally against

mad brain'd blasphemous Husbands that are against the godly and chaste conversation of their Wives; also you that hold your Servants so hard to it, that you will not spare them time to hear the word, unless it be where, and when, your lusts will let you. If you love your own souls, your Tenants souls, your Wives souls, your Servants souls, your Childrens souls ... if you would not bear the ruin of others for ever . . .[19]

He ended up with a plea for relaxation of patriarchal authority, when this was set against attendance at meetings, in general. Not only landlords, but husbands and masters were potential villains of the piece to Bunyan.

Certainly landlords could, and did, interfere with the spread of separatist opinions. When Henry Denne went on his evangelising tour in 1653,[20] the minister and the 'chiefest men of the town', created trouble for the Baptists despite the popular desire to hear them,[21] in 'Hawson' and Shelford. The kind of dislike felt for Baptists in some quarters principally amongst the landed classes, was shown very clearly in Shelford, where a potential convert confessed under pressure that he 'hired a farm of Mr Bendich, and if he should know he was baptised he would turn him out'. 'I told him', replied Henry Denne, 'that the earth was the Lord's and the fullness thereof, and wished him to trust God and he would be a better landlord than Mr Bendich.' Like the rich young man asked to give away all that he had, the convert replied he 'would consider of it'. One cannot help but sympathise with his predicament. Henry Denne had after all a living at Eltisley.

There are other examples of interference by landlords. In 1669, Bishop Laney reported of the small settlement of Shingay-cum-Wendy that there was no conventicle there, 'though some be affected to it. Yet Sir Thomas Wendys care restrains them.' In 1676, there was no nonconformist in the place, although there was one papist.

Impressionistic evidence, however, is not enough. The tabulation of those villages which appeared as very markedly dissenting[22] in 1676,

---

[19] John Bunyan, *Sighs from Hell*, 2nd edn (1666?), pp. 101–2.
[20] See above, pp. 277–8.   [21] *Fenstanton Records*, pp. 81–2.
[22] Over twenty and between ten and nineteen dissenters respectively in the Compton Census.

TABLE 19 *Villages with large numbers of dissenters in 1676*

Village	Dissenters		1640 petition	Population		Manorial status		School	Clergy
	no.	%		Size	Density				
Orwell	58	24	No	Av.	Av.	Single	Non-R.	Scattered refs.	Seq.
Thriplow	48	30	No	Av.	Av.	Split	–	Isolated refs.	–
Gamlingay	44	6	Yes	Large	Av.	Split	–	Continuous after 1600	Resigned to avoid seq.
Over	42	8	Yes	Very large	Dense	Split	–	Scattered refs.	–
Barrington	40	22	Yes	Large	Dense	Nearly single	Non-R.	Continuous	Seq.
Shepreth	39	22	No	Av.	Dense	Split	–	Isolated refs.	–
Oakington	37	21	No	Av.	Av.	Split	–	Isolated refs.	Seq.
Burwell	33	6	Outside area	Very large	Av.	Split	–	Outside area	Seq. *classis*
Bassingbourn + Kneesworth	30	6	No	Very large	Av.	Split	–	Continuous	– *Classis* (= non-sub.)
Linton	28	6	Outside area	Very large	Dense	Single	R.	Continuous	Seq. *classis*
Melbourn	26	10	Yes	Large	Av.	Split	–	Continuous	Seq. *classis*
Litlington	24	18	No	Av.	Av.	Split	–	Isolated refs.	*Classis* (= non-sub.)
Soham	21	4	Outside area	Very large	Av.	Split	–	Outside area	Seq. *classis*
Harston	20	11	No	Av.	Dense	Split	–	Refs.	–

Village	Dissenters		1640 petition	Population		Manorial status		School	Clergy
	no.	%		Size	Density				
Willingham	at least 20	?	Yes	Very large	Av.	Nearly single	Non-R.	Continuous	*Classis* (= non-sub.)
Toft	16	19	Yes	Av.	Av.	Single	Non-R.	Isolated refs.	Seq.
Chesterton	15	–	Outside area	Very large	Dense	Single	Not known	Continuous	Seq.
Swavesey	15	–	No	Very large	Dense	Nearly single	R.	Continuous	–
Cottenham	14	–	Yes	Very large	Av.	Split	–	Continuous	Seq. *classis* (= non-sub.)
Great Wilbraham	13	–	Outside area	Av.	Av.	Single	Non-R.	Isolated refs.	Seq.
Histon	12	–	No	Large	Dense	Single	R.	Continuous	Seq. *classis*
Meldreth	12	16	Yes	Av.	Av.	Split	–	Isolated refs.	Seq.
Shudy Camps	11	–	Outside area	Av.	Av.	Split	–	Isolated refs.	–
Stow-cum-Quy	11	14	Outside area	Av.	Dense	Single	R.	Isolated refs.	– *Classis*
Fowlmere	11	–	No	Av.	Av.	Split, becoming single	R.	Isolated refs.	Seq. *classis* (= non-sub.)
Kingston	11	12	No	Small	Sparse	Single	R.	No refs.	Seq.
Foxton	10	–	No	Av.	Av.	Split	–	Continuous	–
Fulbourn	10	9	Outside area	Large	Av.	Split, becoming single	Non-R.	Continuous	– *Classis*

TABLE 20 *Villages without dissenters in 1676*

Village	Population		Manorial status	School	Clergy
	Size	Density			
Abingdon-iuxta-Shingay	Very small	Sparse	R.	No refs.	– (Non-sub.)
Little Abingdon	Small	Av.	Non-R.	No refs.	–
Babraham	Small	Sparse	R.	Isolated refs.	–
Boxworth	Small	Sparse	Non-R.	Continuous after 1600	–
Brinkley	Av.	Av.	R.	Isolated refs.	–
Carlton-cum-Willingham	Av.	Av.	Split	Isolated refs.	–
Comberton	Av.	Av.	Split	Scattered refs.	– *Classis*
Croxton	Small	Sparse	R.	Scattered refs.	–
Elsworth	Large	Av.	Non-R. to 1656, then R.	Continuous	– *Classis*
Great Eversden } Little Eversden	Av.	Av.	Single	Isolated refs.	Seq.
Fen Drayton	Av.	Av.	R.	Isolated refs.	Seq.
Little Gransden	Av.	Av.	Non-R.	No refs.	Seq.
Grantchester	Av.	Av.	Non-R.	Isolated refs.	Seq.
Graveley	Small	Av.	Non-R.	No refs.	–
East Hatley	Very small	Sparse	R.	No refs.	Seq. (non-sub.)

Village	Population		Manorial status	School	Clergy
	Size	Density			
Hildersham	Small	Av.	Single	R.	Isolated refs.	–
Impington	Av.	Av.	Split	–	No refs.	–
Knapwell	Av.	Av.	Single	Non-R.	No refs.	Seq.
Lolworth	Small	Av.	Single	Non-R.	Isolated refs.	–
Pampisford	Av.	Av.	Split, then single	Not known	Isolated refs.	–
Sawston	Large	Dense	Single	R.	Continuous	–
Great Shelford	Large	Dense	Split	–	Continuous	–
Little Shelford	Av.	Av.	Single	Not known	No refs.	–
Shingay-cum-Wendy	Both very small	Sparse	Single	R.	No refs.	–
Stapleford	Small	Av.	Split	–	No refs.	–
Teversham	Small	Av.	Split	–	No refs.	Seq. *classis*
Westley Waterless	Very small	Av.	Single	Non-R.	Isolated refs.	–
Weston Colville	Av.	Av.	Single	R.	Isolated refs.	–
Whittlesford	Large	Dense	Single	Non-R.	Continuous	–
Wimpole	Small	Sparse	Single	R.	Continuous after 1600	Seq.

Dissenters (Table 19)

Notably dissenting villages have been taken to be those with ten dissenters or more in the Compton Census. They have been arranged according to the number of dissenters. There are twenty-eight villages on this table, but only twenty-five have been used in the text, since Burwell and Soham were in the diocese of Norwich and so outside the area covered by the 1640 petition and the school material, and Willingham, although known to have at least twenty dissenters in 1675, was not included in the Compton Census. The percentages here have been calculated from the figures given in the Compton Census itself of conformists and nonconformists, with all their limitations.

1640 petition (Table 19)

'Yes' or 'No' to whether or not the village produced over five identifiable petitioners.

Population

The criteria of size are:

Very large = in twelve largest villages in the county: over 110 taxed in the hearth tax
Large = in largest quarter of villages: 70–110 taxed (excluding largest twelve)
Average = in middle half of villages: 30–70 taxed
Small = in smallest quarter of villages: 20–30 taxed (excluding smallest twelve)
Very small = in twelve smallest villages: under 20 taxed

The criteria of density are:

Dense = over 35 taxed persons per 1000 acres
Average = 14–35 taxed persons per 1000 acres
Sparse = under 14 taxed persons per 1000 acres

Manorial status

Single = only one manorial lord
to single has been added R. = manorial lord Resident
or non-R. = manorial lord non-Resident or institutional
Nearly single = primarily in the hands of one manorial lord, but with an unimportant smaller manor also
Split = village divided amongst two, or more, main manors

School

The criteria relate to the material in Part Two above, pp. 183–7

Continuous = references suggest the continuous existence of a school throughout the period 1570–1620
Continuous after 1600 = modification of 'continuous' category
Scattered refs. = scattered references throughout period, but not enough to suggest that there was a continuous school, although there
may well have been, but that there was certainly schooling frequently available
Isolated refs. = isolated references which suggest that schooling was sometimes available in the village
No. refs. = no references, which suggest that schooling was never or only very occasionally available in the village

Clergy

Seq. = sequestered
Classis = member of the Cambridgeshire *classis*
Non-sub. = non-subscriber

together with those which appeared as totally conformist in the same year is revealing, when the various possible determinants – lordship, the record of the incumbents, the evidence for a school and the size of the place – are added.[23] There is one initial difficulty. If a community is described as dissenting because it has a 'large' number of nonconformists in absolute terms, these nonconformists may have formed a fairly small percentage of the community as a whole, if it was a large one. Gamlingay, for instance, had forty-four dissenters, who made life impossible for the incumbent, ran the school, and obviously formed a focal point amongst the population. Yet they only made up six per cent of it. In a small village, like Caldecote, two dissenters in 1676 might make up over five per cent of the total returned in the census, although they obviously would have had to go elsewhere for meetings, and were probably both isolated from their churches and ostracised within their communities. Villages have been classified as 'very dissenting' or 'dissenting', on outright numbers, therefore, but percentages have been added as a corrective.[24]

At first sight, there appears to be a strong correlation between the degree of manorial subdivision in a parish, and the extent to which dissent was found there. The converse was also true; there was a co-incidence between parishes containing single manors, and conformity. Almost exactly half of the twenty-five parishes which stood out in the Compton Census as centres of dissent were held by more than one lord and frequently by many. Not one of the fifteen villages which were markedly dissenting, with a group of over twenty nonconformists in 1676, had a resident single lord,[25] until Sir Thomas Sclater built a fine house near the market town of Linton which he bought in 1675, and started a vigorous and totally ineffective persecution in his capacity as a justice of the peace. Most of these dissenting centres were subdivided anyway. They were also markedly large settlements; manorial subdivision and the consequent lack of control which favoured the growth of dissent, may well in itself have been merely a by-product of settlement size.

No less than four-fifths of the completely conformist villages of southern Cambridgeshire in 1676 were also contained within single manors; although only one-third of their lords appear to have been

---

[23] See Tables 19 and 20 throughout this discussion.

[24] Percentages of dissenters against the total numbers returned for the parish in the Compton Census by the incumbent, although the Census is unreliable as a guide to population. See my 'Note on Compton Census', pp. 94–5.

[25] The correlation between manorial subdivision, non-residence and dissent still existed if the proportion of dissenters in a community, not the absolute number, was considered.

resident. Again, manorial subdivision or the lack of it was related to the size of the settlement; an abnormally large number of the entirely conformist villages were small in size.[26] Professor Everitt's thesis must be admitted: dissent was related to lack of manorial control. But it can be refined upon. Wherever a settlement was large, whatever its economy, whether it lay in the fens or forests, or even in open-field arable country, manorial subdivision was to be expected and dissent might therefore flourish. A small settlement was better controlled, and therefore the inhabitants had less chance to pursue their beliefs.

Even so, determinism must be avoided. It is vital to remember that although a conformist resident lord of a manor may have been able to quash his tenants' dissenting opinions, this did not mean that they did not exist, or that the peasantry never had any leanings that way. They obviously did, in both Shelford and Shingay, for instance. Lordship could act as a check; it did not prevent initial seekings after independent religious initiative.

Moreover, as in any matter capable of statistical proof, any particular case may well prove to be an exception. Individual examples of the influence exercised by landlords are not entirely satisfactory. Even when the parish and the manor coincided in the seventeenth century, it is often impossible to discover whether the squire was resident, and if he was, what attitude he took towards dissenters. Even when both these facts are known, the lord's influence was not always conclusive, as Sir Thomas Sclater discovered at Linton. The example of families which had, or should have had, a controlling influence in two or more parishes, which yet developed very different religious complexions, casts more doubt on the theory that the landlord's influence was the decisive one. The Paris family of Linton, who were notable recusants, nationally known, had owned Linton itself since the fifteenth century, and hardly seem to have promoted any really extensive growth of Catholicism, or prevented the spread of dissent there. They also owned Little Abingdon and Hildersham, in entirety. Both parishes lay near Linton, and both remained conformist, according to the Compton Census. The Huddlestons were also recusants, although they were only of local, not national, notability. They lived at Sawston, which they owned in entirety by the late sixteenth century. It remained conformist. So did Whittlesford, which the family acquired in 1556.[27] There was a large number of freeholders then, and the place appeared abnormally prosperous from the hearth tax returns, so the lord's influence should not have weighed

[26] 14 out of 30 (47%) against 30 out of 122 (25%) with below 30 taxable houses in the 1664 hearth tax.
[27] T. F. Teversham, *History of Sawston* (Sawston, 1942–7), I, 69–72.

unduly heavily and dissent might well have developed, given inclination. It did not, although the village lay immediately to the east of a large group of parishes evangelised by Holcroft. Yet the third Huddleston estate, which covered nearly all the parish of Great Wilbraham, supported a very lively and flourishing group of Anabaptists, who can scarcely have met with approval from their lords, any more than they did from their bishop. Histon, where the recusant families of Coles and later, Harries, were resident, supported a dissenting conventicle in 1669. The Cutts family, which acquired Swavesey under Elizabeth, lived there, and also died there, judging from their fine marble monuments in Swavesey church.[28] They owned all but a very small part of the parish. Yet Swavesey was perhaps the most active Quaker centre, and notable as the place from which Anne Norris went, 'moved by the Lord to bear testimony against the priest of Over in the Steeplehouse',[29] in 1655. The Cutts appear to have had no influence against them, if, indeed, they tried to exercise it. Yet their manor at Lolworth, which covered the whole of the tiny parish, and at Boxworth, which they likewise owned in entirety, remained entirely conformist.

There was, then, a connection between weak lordship and flourishing dissent; but it was not deterministic. It seems very likely that the places where dissent flourished, the larger villages with denser populations, were also more manorially subdivided. There was less subdivision in the shrinking villages of the clay plateau, the small but densely settled villages of the river valleys, and the sparsely peopled conformist group on the eastern chalk.

THE INFLUENCE OF THE CLERGY

There is also a strong connection between another of the possible determinants of dissent, the influence of the clergy, and the places in which dissent flourished in the 1670s. It is an unexpected one, however. Usually the attitude of the incumbent, and therefore of the patron who stood behind him, is considered as a possible influence which was probably reflected strongly in the attitudes of a community. A comparison of the clergy deprived in the 1640s for Laudian practices, royalist views, or moral lapses, in the Cambridgeshire parishes which either had large numbers of dissenters or remained impeccably conformist, shows that there was indeed a connection. It was a surprising one. Far from Laudian incumbents influencing their flocks, some flocks had decided views on the fate of their shepherds. Cambridgeshire parishioners were not docile; and, as we have seen, their Puritan opinions were already formed in

[28] Lysons, *Magna Britannia*, II, 264.   [29] See above, p. 283.

many places before the civil war. Fourteen clergy were deprived, on the complaints of their parishioners, in the twenty-five parishes which were later dissenting.[30] This amounted to over half of the incumbents. Only seven, or under a quarter of the clergy were sequestered in the thirty parishes which were later to be completely conformist. The abnormality of both the high rate of sequestration in dissenting parishes and the low rate in conformist parishes, is seen clearly when it is compared with the thirty-seven per cent of the clergy who were sequestered in the county as a whole.[31] The well-known sufferings of Dr Manby of Cottenham[32] illustrate very well the fate of one of these Laudian incumbents presented to a Puritan parish. The rectory of Cottenham was worth £500 a year, and was one of the most valuable in the county. The bishop was the patron, and it was perhaps natural that Manby should be presented in 1635: he married the bishop's daughter. Their tenure of the rectory was uncomfortable to say the least of it. Manby's wife and five small children were turned out with brutality by his own parishioners acting as sequestrators after his imprisonment.

Meate was att the fire, roasting for dinner, they seized that, and gobled it upp and left none for the owner, but putt us into the streete, the heavens to be our covering and ground our lodging, for they took not care, to provide an habitation for us, and every one was afraid to give us shelter.

wrote his youngest daughter later.[33] When the family was eventually restored to the living in 1660, the animosity against it was so great that, the same child wrote, the

very children were soe full of hatred, takeing it from their parents, that if I and my sister had stragled (*sic*) out on a holliday, to see them play, the would leave off, and not company with us, and myself being very young att schoole with a master in Cottenham, where boyes and girles were brought together, att play time in the yard some boyes pretended to espy a wonder ... and I running among the rest to see, a boy, sone to an adversary, took up a forke, and thrust the tines into my head, a little above my forehead, the scarse I have yett to be seene, my father durst noe more lett me goe amongst them.

In Cambridgeshire, in the 1640s, a Laudian incumbent appears to have been helpless if his parish had already decidedly Puritanical or separatist views. These shepherds did not lead their sheep; they were frequently bitten by them.

The degree of lasting influence which the non-subscribers of 1662 did

---

[30] See above, pp. 234–8, for examples of these complaints.
[31] See above, pp. 272–3.   [21] *Walker revised*, pp. 83–4.
[33] Frances King. She was an unweaned babe in arms when Manby was sequestered in 1643; a copy of her letter adding to Walker's original account of her father's sufferings, written in 1704, is in the C.U.L., W. M. Palmer Collection.

or did not have in their parishes can to some extent be gauged by the episcopal inquiries of the late 1660s and 1670s. Fourteen ministers, or eleven per cent of the clergy, were non-subscribers.[34] Henry Denne would undoubtedly have been added to their number, had he not died, probably early in 1662. Holcroft and Denne, Nathaniel Bradshaw of Willingham who stayed and worked in the county after his ejection, and his brother-in-law John Nye in the next village of Cottenham,[35] undoubtedly left their mark, even though it was made by fostering, not initiating, dissenting opinions already present in 1640. The work of the Presbyterian, Jonathan Jephcot, who ministered in Swaffham Prior right through from the 1630s to 1662 was the direct ancestor of that of Mr Thomas Cawdwell, who despite his poverty, need of books and large family, was doggedly holding a meeting there in 1690.[36] David Foot, ejected from Swaffham Bulbeck in 1662,[37] had been preceded by no less than three other ministers holding the cure from 1645 to 1651, who were all non-subscribers elsewhere in 1662. But, again, the Swaff-hams had an uneasy sixteenth-century ecclesiastical history, and the opinions of their ministers under the commonwealth may well have been determined by those of their parishioners rather than the other way round. The complaints against Peacock, of Swaffham Prior,[38] suggest that this is the true explanation, even though there is no proof of dissent there in 1640, since the parishes lay outside the area of the petition against Wren.

The examples of other non-subscribers show clearly how the influence of the minister could fail to determine the attitudes of his people. The point is readily illustrated by two reports on Abraham Wright of Cheveley made under the commonwealth. Abraham Wright was ejected in 1660, and his parish was chiefly remarkable for having no less than ten papists in 1676. There were then only two nonconformists there. In 1650, the Cheveley bill reported that Wright 'is a man altogether unfit for the place, a proud, contentious and covetous person, little religion or anything that is good in him, they generally desire a better and heartily pray for the same'. On the other hand, only a little later, 'Mr Abraham Wright is by divers certification represented to us as an able, honest man.'[39] Mr Isaac King at Abington Pigotts, was 'an able paynfull man', and had been there since 1645,[40] but he and Richard Kennett at East Hatley,[41] who both went in 1662, left parishes

---

[34] See above, p. 273 n. 4.   [35] *Calamy Revised*, pp. 69–70 (Bradshaw) and 369 (Nye).
[36] *Ibid.* p. 298, and A. Gordon, *Freedom after Ejection* (1917), pp. 12–13.
[37] *Calamy Revised*, p. 204.   [38] See above, pp. 234, 236.
[39] C.U.L., W. M. Palmer Collection, Notes of Parliamentary and Parochial Surveys under the Commonwealth, B3/3, and *Calamy Revised*, p. 548.
[40] *Calamy Revised*, p. 309.   [41] *Ibid.* p. 305.

which were only later remarkable for their conformity. Kennett had been preceded by another non-subscriber, and before that by a Laudian who also seems to have been an undesirable,[42] but, in this apparently ideal environment, dissent did not flourish.

The non-subscribers of 1660–2 thus tended either to leave parishes which had already had a dissenting history, and continued to have a dissenting faction, or to have had no effect at all in their ministry.

THE INFLUENCE OF SCHOOLING

Literacy could bring about conversion through the printed word; the presence of a school could therefore have been an encouragement to dissent. Again, there is an apparent correlation between the availability of schooling, and dissent. Only eight of the thirty entirely conformist villages had continuous, semi-continuous, or even scattered references to teachers at work in the 1676 Census. Twenty-two, or over two thirds, had isolated references or no references at all. As against this, twelve, or less than half, of the twenty-five dissenting villages had few, or no, references to teachers. The rest were comparatively well provided with educational facilities. Yet again, the correlation is misleading. The villages with good schooling records were large or prosperous ones,[43] which also had large numbers of nonconformists. Good opportunities for schooling, like manorial subdivision, were normally a by-product of the size of the settlement. Moreover, if only the places with a high proportion[44] of dissenters are considered, only two of them had continuous references to schools. Therefore no discernible connection between dissent and the availability of schooling exists.

We are therefore forced to the tautological conclusion that large settlements tended to contain larger number of dissenters than small ones. They also tended to be more manorially subdivided, and have more opportunities for education available. The absence of nonconformity in the less thickly settled areas of the county seems to be more related to the presence of fewer potential converts than to any other more subtle reason. Greater manorial control and less schooling in smaller settlements may have had something to do with it, particularly in the river valley area below Linton, but both of these were in a sense themselves a by-product of size. The only startling fact to emerge is the way the clergy not only failed to change the pattern of anti-episcopal feeling which had emerged in Cambridgeshire by at least the 1630s, but were actually the victims of their parishioners.

[42] *Ibid.* p. 386, and *Walker Revised*, p. 80. [43] See above, p. 184 and Map 11.
[44] Eleven villages with ten per cent or more of dissenters.

13

The reality of religion for the villager

Much has been said of the areas in which dissent gained a footing amongst the laity, its strength, and the time when it may have gained this strength. Little has been said, so far, of the much more important matter of its quality. It is just here of course that the attempt, which is perhaps ludicrous enough anyway, to gauge the opinions and devotional life of the ordinary villager is most likely to break down, for the ordinary villager is not an articulate man. It is just here, also, that the attempt is most important, for if we have no idea of the importance that these people's beliefs had to them, the numerical counting of heads is a sterile exercise at best. But there is a certain amount of evidence which does bear on the faith of the laity. It has one very important limitation. Very little can ever be said of the way that the beliefs of the orthodox amongst the laity affected them. Orthodoxy, like happiness, has no history. We can scarcely say anything of the overwhelming mass of parishioners who went on going to their parish churches, whatever the changes in liturgy and belief imposed on them. Amongst them were presumably some who went, not solely because worship was required of them by ecclesiastical law, but because they had a meaningful faith. But this faith has no history. Perhaps we can catch an echo of its existence from time to time. In 1639, the churchwardens of Horseheath in Cambridgeshire complained that both the rector and the curate had been negligent in wearing their surplices at baptisms. They apparently wanted a conforming minister. It is just possibly not pure coincidence that it was in Horseheath also, in 1579, in one of Bishop Cox's visitations that there was said to be a 'stone cross in the church yard there, with ymages uppon it, which . . . the Towne there, when they come by it, to the church there, do make great reverence'.[1] Horseheath was very obviously traditional in its habits of worship, even though attempts were made to break the habit. In 1580, a satisfactory report was given to Bishop Cox that 'the cross and ymages are deformed quite'.

The evidence that does exist on the depth to which the ordinary villager could be stirred and the sacrifices that he, or she, was prepared

[1] See above, p. 242.

319

to make for his beliefs under the commonwealth comes from dissenting sources. So far, the only genuine voice of a parishioner breaking through in the episcopal visitations of the bishop himself has been that of the man from St Clement's who justified his not bowing at the name of Jesus in 1639 by saying that he did no other bodily reverence to the name of Jesus than to the name of 'Father' and that God required no more.[2] Here, suddenly, is the authentic note. But such notes are very rare, amongst diocesan records at least, and mainly come from dissenting sources. There is at least enough evidence to show that when a recent writer has said 'the true spirit of popular involvement with the Church . . . has very little to do with credal commitment, nor did it ever have',[3] he was mistaken, at least about the seventeenth century. If we generally lack articulate statements from the ordinary villager, the deficiency is to some extent supplied by the books of the dissenting churches which open in the seventeenth century, and are often very full and explicit. Furthermore there is one source, and one only, which can be used to show the way in which, at the parish level, the reformation gradually obtained a hold on the mind and devotions of the laity.

WILLS AND THEIR WRITERS – ORWELL, DRY DRAYTON AND WILLINGHAM

Once in his life, and once only, the ordinary villager, yeoman, husbandman, labourer or craftsman, might make at the beginning of his will, a statement which bore on his religious beliefs.[4] The first bequest in a will was of the soul. This may appear strange to modern eyes, but the reasoning behind it is made plain in the will of a maltster of Orwell in Cambridgeshire, Thomas Brocke, in 1597, whose will began, 'First as thing most precyous,[5] I Commend my soule to God the father my Creator.' A testator with Catholic beliefs may well leave his soul to 'Almighty God, the Blessed Virgin Mary, and the whole company of Heaven', or some equivalent phrase, and a testator of Puritan or Calvinistic beliefs may well leave his soul to 'Almighty God and his only Son our Lord Jesus Christ, by whose precious death and passion I hope only

[2] See above, p. 270.
[3] A. W. Smith, 'Popular Religion', *Past and Present*, 40 (1968), p. 186.
[4] The major part of this section, first appeared as a paper in *Local Population Studies*, 7 (1971), pp. 28–43 which provoked an interesting comparable study of Matlock wills in the following number, 8 (1972), pp. 55–7. This on the whole reinforced the conclusions I have drawn here, although both it, and the correspondence on my article (*idem*, pp. 64–7), suggested that will formularies must have been in circulation. Dr Capp has produced evidence of one such formula, which first appeared in an almanac of 1657 (*Local Population Studies*, 14, p. 49). This appears to be the earliest cheaply available in mass circulation, although lawyers' formularies like *Simboleography*, first published in 1590, existed. (Eric Poole, *Local Population Studies*, 17, pp. 42–3 and Spufford, *idem*, 19, pp. 35–6.)
[5] This phrase is not common form. I have come across it nowhere else.

to be saved', or some other similar phrase. Any will which mentions the Virgin, the saints, or the angels may be suspected of Catholic tendencies. Any which stresses salvation through Christ's death and passion alone, or the company of the elect, may be thought of as Protestant. In between, lie a vast number of indeterminate neutral wills, which simply leave the soul to 'Almighty God, my Creator', or in which the stress on salvation through Christ appears so minimal, that they cannot be classified. The spectrum of these clauses is very wide; but because of their existence, historians seeking to penetrate the iron curtain which hides the religious opinion of the really humble laity, below the social level of parish priest or minister, in the upheavals of reformation or counter-reformation, sometimes analyse them in an attempt to establish what was going on at the parochial level.[6] These statements are almost too brief to be treated as evidence by those accustomed to dealing with the verbose and well-documented gentry; but they give enough to piece together a patchwork picture.

Unfortunately there is one major technical difficulty, which has not been given attention, in doing this. For most purposes, the content of the will itself is all that matters; the identity of the scribe who wrote it is irrelevant. For this particular purpose, the identity of the scribe might be all-important. A very high proportion of villagers' wills were made in the testator's last illness, on his death-bed, when he was 'sicke in bodye and Fearing the hasty calling of death'.[7] It is almost common form to get, at the beginning of a will, a statement that the testator is 'sick in body but thanks be to God of good sound understanding and memory' and extremely rare to get the opposite statement, which headed the will of William Griggs, a yeoman of Orwell in 1649, that he made his will

beinge in good healthe and body [but] Considering the frailty of this life, although there is nothinge more certaine than death, yett there is nothing more uncertaine than the tyme of the coming thereof ... now intending the disposition of my landes ... in this tyme of my good health and memory for the better quieting and satisffying my mynd and conscience whensoever it shall please God to visit me with sickness.

[6] Professor Dickens has used these differences effectively in Nottinghamshire and Yorkshire wills to illustrate the progress of the reformation amongst the laity. A. G. Dickens, *Lollards and Protestants in the Diocese of York, 1509–1538* (London 1959), particularly pp. 171–2 and 215–17. Dr David Palliser has used wills to illustrate the progress of the reformation in York, and has raised the problem I here discuss, that of the influence of the scribe. D. M. Palliser, *The Reformation in York 1534–1553*, Borthwick Papers 40 (London 1971), pp. 18–21 and 32. Both Professor Dickens and Dr Palliser take cross-sections of wills proved in years of significant religious change. For the reasons which have led me to adopt a different, and less obviously revealing method, see below, p. 335 n. 35.

[7] A comparison of the date the will was written, and the, usually close, date of probate, shows this.

A man lying on his death-bed must have been much in the hands of the scribe writing his will. He must have been asked specific questions about his temporal bequests, but unless he had strong religious convictions, the clause bequeathing the soul may well have reflected the opinion of the scribe or the formulary book the latter was using, rather than those of the testator.

I have therefore considered the whole question of the identity of the scribes who wrote villagers' wills in relation to the historical points to which the identity of the scribe may well have been crucial, the content of the clause bequeathing the soul.

The case of old Leonard Woolward of Balsham may be recalled here,[8] because from it, it was evident that the circle of people who could be asked to write a will was wide. Quite obviously Leonard Woolward had a number of 'friends and acquaintances' whom he could have asked to write his will, and he thought first of them, not instinctively of the minister, curate or parish clerk. The implication is that as early as the 1570s, there were in a village several members of the community who could write a document at need, even in a village like Balsham, where there were only isolated references to schoolmasters at work.[9] Since Woolward desired secrecy, his choice fell on the doctor, who came from another village altogether.

There is a modern case, which shows how traditional methods of making a will persisted, although in this case, the instinctive first choice of the testator was a gentleman. Leonard Woolf[10] writes of a time in about 1918, when the farm carter of Rodmell in Sussex

came to me and asked me to make his will for him. He had several sons and one daughter and he wanted me to write out on a sheet of paper a statement, which he would sign in the presence of his children and of me, saying that he left everything to his daughter. I told him that this would not be a legal will and that he ought to go to a solicitor and sign a proper legal will. He refused to do this and said that if I would do what he asked, his sons would carry it out after his death. So I did what he asked. I wrote out the statement and took it round to his cottage one Sunday morning. He, his sons, and his daughter were all there in their best clothes. I read aloud the document and he signed it and they all thanked me and we shook hands. When he died, everything went to the daughter without difficulty.

It is obvious therefore that in the search to identify scribes, not only the incumbent or his curate, who may seem the obvious choice, but the

---

[8] See above, pp. 182–3.   [9] See above, Map 11.
[10] Leonard Woolf, *Beginning Again* (London 1964). Mrs Elizabeth Key noticed this case.

322

local gentry and the whole circle of literate villagers who were the friends and acquaintances of the testator, must be considered.

There is an obvious, major difficulty in identifying the hand of the scribe who wrote a particular will, for the local historian who is not a highly trained palaeographer. Any reasonably formalised hand of the late sixteenth and seventeenth centuries, once the writer was educated beyond a certain point, has so many features in common with any other that the non-specialist may well pause. There is one redeeming feature. A local historian working on a particular community, and on all the surviving wills for that community, is limiting himself so strictly by date and by place that only a small number of scribes are likely to be at work at any one time.

The smaller the community for a pilot study in some ways the better. Orwell, with its fifty-odd houses in the 1670s and its lively history of dissent among the laity[11] is therefore an ideal village for experimentation. Between 1543 and 1700, ninety-nine wills of which the originals survive were proved in the Consistory Court although until the 1580s, the 'originals' were mostly office copies,[12] and therefore useless for these purposes.

It is possible to make at least a reasonable guess at the identity of the scribes who were responsible for a surprisingly large number of these wills. Sometimes the scribe was the only witness of one or more wills who could actually sign his name; sometimes his hand was the only one even approximately of the same type in a run of wills, and he was also a witness to all of them. In order to tell whether or not the clause bequeathing a soul to Almighty God was dictated by the testator's opinions, or by the scribe's, at least two wills in the same hand are necessary, and obviously, a much longer run is desirable.

The Orwell wills include half a dozen written by identifiable scribes, but they all appear to have written only one will apiece. They are therefore useless for comparative purposes. Often the scribe's name is unfamiliar to the historian of the parish, and he may therefore have been an outsider, and possibly a notary or ecclesiastical official. There were four pairs of wills by the same scribe, one series of three, by George Holder, a villager, who held at least an acre of freehold in the defective survey of Orwell made in 1607, and two very interesting series of four. One of these was by John Martin, about whom nothing is known, and the other by Neville Butler. He had been educated at the

---

[11] See above, pp. 300–2.

[12] The initial custom seems to have been to return the true original, signed or marked by the testator, to the executors, and retain an office copy for the court. At some point in the latter sixteenth century, this custom changed, and the original document was retained for registration, and an office copy, presumably, given to the executors.

Perse and Christ's, and was the grandson of a yeoman. He ended up buying the lands of the dissolved priory of Barnwell, becoming a gentleman, and disappearing from the Orwell scene. There were also, most usefully for comparative purposes, two longer series, overlapping in date. One group of six wills was written by Nicholas Johnson between 1614 and 1626. He was one of Neville Butler's father's first cousins, was frequently a churchwarden, and was tenant of fourteen acres of copyhold land.[13] William Barnard, M.A., rector of Orwell from 1609 to 1644, who held a licence to teach there, wrote twelve surviving wills during his incumbency, between 1615 and 1642.

Nicholas Johnson, who was described as the 'well beloved in Christ' of Catherine Rutt of Orwell when she made him the supervisor of her will in 1614, probably had his own religious convictions. Not only Catherine Rutt's testimony, but his career as a churchwarden bears this out. In all six of the wills he wrote, the clause concerning the soul is so nearly identical, that if there were any doubt that the scribe's hand had been identified correctly, it would be disposed of. Every one read, 'I commend my soul into the hands of almighty God that gave it me ... when it shall please God to take me out of this present world.' Whatever the opinions of the testator, they did not influence Nicholas Johnson, who started off each will in his accustomed fashion, which unfortunately did not reveal much of his doctrinal position.

Each of the four men who wrote a pair of wills apiece in the seventeenth century, as well as George Holder, who wrote three at the beginning of the century, also used his own common form. Lawrence Johnson, one of the numerous literate Johnson clan, wrote an entirely neutral phrase in his horrible hand at the end of the 1640s, 'I bequeath my soul to Almighty God.' George Holder wrote with slightly more Protestant emphasis in each of his three wills, 'I commend my soul to God the Father my Creator, and his son, Jesus Christ my Redeemer.' John Wicks took up a slightly stronger position again in 1640, and wrote, 'I bequeath my soul to God my Maker expecting [or believing] to be saved by and through the merits of Christ Jesus my Saviour and Redeemer.' Matthew East, at about the same date, wrote more strongly still. Both his wills contain the phrase, 'I commend my soul into the hands of Almighty God who gave it to me assuredly trusting through the death and passion of his son Jesus Christ to be saved.' Ambrose Benning, who appears as 'Mr Benning' in a rental of the 1670s, and was probably a freeholder and a gentleman, again adopted his own formula. Again, if there was any doubt of the correct identification of

---

[13] See above, pp. 108–11, for the whole Butler family, and pp. 179–80 and 197 for the education of Neville Butler and Nicholas Johnson.

a hand which only occurs twice, six years apart, it would be resolved by the identical wording: 'I commend my soule into the hands of god my maker, redeemer and preserver, in an assured hope of a joyful resurrection through the meritts of Jesus Christ my saviour.'

It appears quite clearly that each of these half-dozen men adopted his own formula, and that the religious conviction of the scribe, not the testator, is apparent in the will.

This provisional conclusion can be taken further, by looking at the series of twelve wills written by the rector, William Barnard, between 1615 and 1642. William Barnard's phraseology was not much more striking than that of his churchwarden, Nicholas Johnson. Eight of his twelve wills bequeath the soul of the testator to 'the hands of God Almighty my Creator, [Saviour] and Redeemer . . . whenever it shall please the Lord to take me to his mercy'. They were all written before 1636. In 1637, he added a new phrase which appeared in three of the remaining wills and strengthened his formula by the expectation of a 'joyful resurrection to life eternall'. But in the will of Richard Flatt, made in 1636, a strongly individual piece of phraseology was inserted within William Barnard's formula. Richard Flatt commended his soul

Into the hands of God Almighty, my maker, my Saviour and Redeemer, *trusting to be saved by the only sufficient merits of Jesus Christ my Saviour . . . when it shall please the lord in mercy to take me out of this world, being fully assured that this my mortal body shall one day put on immortality, and being raised again by the virtue of Christ's resurrection, I shall live forever with him.*

Here is a piece of Pauline theological thinking, which is so far outside the scribe's usual formula that it seems for the first time that a testator feels sufficiently strongly for his opinions to come through clearly into his will. In any long series of wills for any one village, there are a large number of individual formulas which occur, and some deviants which fit into no pattern. It looks from the example of Richard Flatt, as if these deviants can be taken to reflect the genuine convictions of the testator; the rest reflect the opinions of the scribe, who may, of course, have been a villager also.

This suggestion is strengthened by examination of the four wills John Martin appears to have written. Two of the testators, Mary Barton and Elizabeth Adams, were members of strongly nonconformist families.[14] Their wills were witnessed by Simon Grey, who was also a nonconformist,[15] as well as by John Martin. The other two wills were written

[14] Lyon Turner, I, 36. Elizabeth Adams was one of the most prominent Muggletonians in Cambridgeshire (see above, p. 230).   [15] E.D.R., B/2/6, fos. 51–52v.

for men who do not appear on the dissenting church lists, or as absentees from church in the episcopal records. Simon Grey witnessed one of the latter, as well as those of the dissenters; but it had a purely neutral clause commending the soul of the testator into the hands of Almighty God, its maker, despite being drawn up and witnessed by dissenters. The last of the four was also neutral. The wills of Mary Barton and Elizabeth Adams were, however, highly individual. Mary Barton bequeathed her soul into the hands of Almighty God her maker, 'hoping through the meritorious death and passion of Jesus Christ my only saviour and redeemer to receive free pardon and forgiveness of all my sins'. She also spoke of the temporal estate that 'God in his infinite mercy has lent me in this world'. So did Elizabeth Adams, the notorious harbourer of Muggletonians, though she felt that her temporal estate had pleased 'God far above my deserts to bestow upon me'. The clause in which Elizabeth Adams bequeathed her soul had the same sense as Mary Barton's but it was not phrased in the scribe's identical wording. She ended her will with an injunction to her son and principal heir that related worldly prosperity to prudence, which I have not seen duplicated anywhere else: 'As Soloman said to his son "My son fear thou the Lord and the king, and beware that you live not above your living especially in the beginning for fear that will bring you to wanton necessity, both in the midst and the ending."' It was not apparent from her will that she was a very important Muggletonian, but it was apparent that she was a woman of strong opinions.

This scribe then wrote dissenters' wills which expressed the testators' strong sense of justification by faith, but did not dictate the form when a more neutral phrase was required. Neville Butler likewise wrote two wills which were neutral and simply bequeathed the soul to God that gave it[16] but two in identical wording when more appeared to be called for. Richard Johnson and Robert Bird both left their souls

With a right good will ... to god that gave it whensoever it shall please him to take it out of this transitory life hoping by his infinite mercy and the only merryt of my saviour Jesus Christ that it shall again put on this my corruptible body of flesh and that they [*sic*] shallbe made partakers of everlasting life.[17]

[16] Wills of Richard Kettle and Robert Adam.
[17] This example is a confusing one, because the phraseology Neville Butler uses and his emphasis on the resurrection of the body echoes almost exactly that of his grandfather Nicholas in 1601 (P.C.C., 74, Woodhall) and his great uncle Henry in 1594 (P.C.C., 32, Dixy) although his own father, Thomas, wrote a neutral clause bequeathing his soul in 1622 (P.C.C., 18, Saville) and his own will 'all written with my own hand' only expressed his belief in justification by faith, not in the resurrection of the body (P.C.C., 1675, fo. 42). We may here be getting an example of the

One further interesting point emerges from the Orwell wills. The vicar, when he was present as a witness, and not as a scribe, was not necessarily deferred to over the form of the clause bequeathing the soul. Roger Davis, clerk, wrote his own will in 1580,[18] and appears to have been a Protestant, for he bequeathed his soul to 'Jesus Christ in faith in whom I hope undoubtedly to be saved.' He witnessed a will couched in similar terms for John Adam, yeoman, in 1569, but the two others he witnessed for John Johnson, husbandman, in 1568, and Edmund Barnard, another husbandman, in 1595, both had neutral clauses bequeathing the soul. John Money, the vicar in 1595, witnessed Katherine Ingry's will in that year, and she also simply bequeathed her soul to Almighty God. Nicholas Butler, who had the same faith in the resurrection of his temporal body that was later expressed by his grandson Neville, as a scribe, both witnessed Katherine Ingry's will along with the vicar, and had his own will witnessed by the vicar; but his faith in the resurrection of his earthly body seems to have been entirely his own, and was not dictated by John Money.

The saddest example of the lack of influence of an incumbent is provided by Richard Greenham of Dry Drayton. Greenham was incumbent of Dry Drayton from 1570 to 1591, and his was the first model Puritan parish in the country. He

spared no pains amongst his people, whereby he might advance the good of their souls: His constant course was to preach twice on the Lords day, and before the evening sermon to Catechize the young people of the Parish. His manner also went to preach on Mundayes, Tuesdayes and Wednesdayes and on Thursdayes to catechize the youth and again on Fridayes to preach to his people . . . besides his publick preaching and catechizing, his manner was to walk out into the fields and to conferr with his Neighbours as they were at plow.

He won a widespread reputation as a comforter of people of distressed and tormented conscience, and so can have been by no means an unsympathetic personality, although it may have been a little irritating to have the ploughing interrupted by spiritual advice. He was practical, despite this, and his people's succour in times of bad harvest.[19] Moreover, he should have had more impact because the preceding rector had committed adultery with a parishioner in 1568 and, failing to perform penance, remained excommunicated and publicly denounced from April to June 1569.[20] A greater contrast between this man and his

scribe's own religious beliefs, rather than the testator's, but it is interesting that he only applies it when it is called for, and does not automatically write a phrase expressing his own opinions.   [18] It ends 'per me Rogerum Davys'.
[19] See above, pp. 51–2.   [20] E.D.R., D/2/8, fos. 9v, 11, 20, 27.

successor, who spent his uneasy nights in prayer and rose at dawn to preach, could surely not have been found. Yet Greenham left Dry Drayton after twenty years, partly because of 'the intractablenesse, and unteachablenesse of that people amongst whom he had taken such exceeding great paines'.[21] Unfortunately, this impression was not merely Greenham's subjective judgement on his labours, made in a fit of depression. Judging from the wills, the souls of the people of Dry Drayton were tough and strong ground. Fifty-four originals survive which were written between Elizabeth's accession and 1630. Two-thirds of these were either entirely neutral, or incorporated a lukewarm Protestant phrase mentioning 'Jesus Christ my saviour and redeemer' that certainly carried no conviction. Only eight were written during Greenham's incumbency, and four of these were completely neutral. He wrote two others himself, and his own phraseology commended the testator's soul to

my alone and Omnisufficient saviour Jesus Christ who as he hath all only redeemed me so I do fully believe that I shalbe saved oonly by the fruit and merit of his passion and sufferyinge for my synnes, confessynge that for my synnes I am unworthye of the least mercies of god, yet for his sake, that I shall by faithe possesse and enioye the Kyngdome of heaven prepared for all the Children of God whereof I am one.

Only four wills in the forty years after Greenham's incumbency stand out because they contain dedicatory clauses revealing doctrine or teaching, and two of these are irrelevant because they were written by public notaries. Not until 1611 did a widow begin her will by leaving her soul to 'Almighty God my Father trusting through the precious death and passion of Jesus Christ to have free forgiveness and pardon of all my sins and to be saved.' Another widow wrote similarly in 1619. There is less feeling of convinced Protestantism in the wills of Dry Drayton than any other parish I have examined. The influence of the rector or vicar certainly did not dictate the attitudes of his parishioners.

The same features found amongst the Orwell wills are also found amongst the much more numerous surviving wills from Willingham. There are nearly 250 wills written between the 1570s and 1700 by an identifiable scribe, although fifteen of these are the only ones by that particular scribe, and are therefore useless for comparative purposes. Amongst the scribes, there are a considerable number of series by the same man. Laurence Milford himself wrote fifty wills between 1570 and 1602, beginning before he was first licensed as a schoolmaster to 'teach young children' in 1580,[22] and continuing after William Norton, the

---

[21] Samuel Clarke, *A Generall Martyrologie*, pp. 83–7.
[22] See above, pp. 192ff., for the work of the Willingham school.

curate, was licensed to teach grammar in 1596. After experimenting with various formulae in the 1570s and 1580s, hoping to 'obtain everlasting joys and felicitie' for the soul, he went through a neutral phase before settling down in 1590 to the constant usage of one of his early experimental formulae, 'I bequeath my soul into the hands of God the father, and to Jesus Christ my saviour, by whose merits I hope to enjoy his everlasting rest.' William Norton wrote only four wills, and bequeathed the soul in an unusual Trinitarian form to 'God Almighty, Father, Son, and Holy Ghost.' This was obviously entirely his own.

Laurence Milford was succeeded as the principal Willingham scribe, not by Norton's successor as schoolmaster, John Nixon, who taught and was curate in Willingham from 1608, but by John Hammond, a local gentleman who was lessee of the sub-manor of Burne in Willingham. He, with a relation of his, Edward, wrote over thirty wills between 1609 and 1639. He also acted as a scribe when a petition against the charges of fen-drainage was drawn up.[23] His phraseology was again almost identical throughout the wills that he wrote. He had been very heavily influenced by Milford. He strengthened the Protestant element and added 'by whose only merits and mercies' to Milford's formula. Otherwise he duplicated it. There were only three wills in the Hammond series which varied from the standard opening in any way, and none of them, with the possible exception of his own, was of importance. John Gill, a labourer, who died in 1623 hoped to enjoy everlasting rest 'after this transitory life ended'. Philip Fromant, a husbandman, trusted to obtain 'remission of all my sins'. When John Hammond himself wrote his will in 1637, it became evident that a genuine faith lay behind his standard Protestant formula, for he left his soul to

Almighty God my creator, and to Jesus Christ my redeemer, by whose only mercies and merits (*Sealed unto me by their blessed Spirit*) I trust to obtain forgiveness of all my sins and to enjoy their everlasting rest.

The laity of Willingham are known from other sources to have been particularly zealous Protestants. They probably had secret conventicle meetings in Mary's time, and were anti-episcopal in the late 1630s. From these beginnings, a strong and lasting Congregational Church developed under the commonwealth. Quakerism was present there too.[24] Laurence Milford, either in his work as teacher or as scribe, unfortunately seems to have made such an impact on the people of Willingham, that their individual convictions, which were undoubtedly

---

[23] B.M., Add. MS 33466, fo. 190. I am indebted to Mr Dennis Jeeps for lending me his photostat of this.
[24] See above, pp. 302–4, and my 'The Dissenting Churches', pp. 70, 76–7.

strong in very many cases, are masked in their wills by his phraseology. The early wills of the seventeenth century do provide ample evidence that old Leonard Woolward of Balsham was right to feel he could depend on 'friends and acquaintances' to write his will, if not to keep it secret, for enough villagers acted as scribes in Willingham to prove the point.[25] In all, fifty wills were written by yeomen from the Greaves family, by Henry Halliwell and Henry Bissell, Edward Allen and Robert Stocker who each wrote several. A further half-dozen wills were written by other villagers who only wrote one apiece. All these wills began either with a neutral clause, or with Laurence Milford's standard clause, or with Hammond's variant on it. Only John Pitts, 'woolwinder', stood out in any way. He wrote three wills between 1617 and 1626, all using the Milford phraseology, but his own will, made in 1631, was couched in stronger terms. His soul was left to the 'hands of Almighty God my Creator hoping for remission of my sins by the death and passion of Jesus Christ my redeemer'. Unfortunately John Pitts's own will was an isolated one, written by Thomas Ambler, so it is impossible to tell whether John Pitts made a fuller and more revealing assertion of his faith on his own death-bed, or whether Thomas Ambler was asserting his own beliefs.

The strength of Protestant feeling in Willingham, combined with Laurence Milford's influence, makes the wills of the villagers so consistently Protestant, that, as in any orthodox group, it is impossible to tell how far individual feeling is involved, even when minor variants in the phraseology do occur, since the sense is so uniform. Occasionally individual testators do stand out, just as Richard Flatt did in Orwell. Robert Shilborn wrote the will of Thomas Lambert, who was a husbandman, in 1625, and that of Thomas Bowles, who was a fisherman, in 1632. There was no doubt at all of the strength of the convictions of Thomas Lambert. Shilborn wrote for him,

I bequeath my soul to God that gave it trusting in the only merits of Jesus Christ my saviour and redeemer for the forgiveness of my sins, and that death shall be an entrance for me into a better life.

The will ended with the desire that

The Lord out of his never decaying or failing mercy be a husband to my wife and a father to all my children.

Thomas Bowles's will contained the tell-tale bequest, 'To my eldest son William Bowles . . . my bible wishing him to use it to God's glory.'[26]

Although the influence of Laurence Milford at last declined, the

---

[25] See above, pp. 182 and 196.   [26] See below, p. 336.

Willingham scribes continued each to write their own standard formula. There was one important change. From the 1650s, the testator's customary bequest of his body to the churchyard for burial, which followed that of the soul, was replaced by a phrase leaving the burial of the body to the discretion of the executor or to 'Christian' burial. This may well reflect the growth of the nonconformist element in Willingham. But Congregationalist or Quaker wills cannot be picked out as such from the phraseology. They can sometimes be identified by virtue of local knowledge. Two Henry Orions wrote thirteen wills between 1634 and 1648, and 1659 and 1667. They were probably father and son, and of humble stock. There had been no Orions in Willingham in 1603, but the family held twelve acres of arable there in the 1720s. Both men wrote a roughly standardised form of will, bequeathing the soul to 'God that gave it to me, and to Jesus Christ my redeemer by whose mercies and merits I hope to have forgiveness of all my sins and to have a Joyful Resurrection at the Last Day.' The emphasis on the resurrection was typical of them; the formula was their own, but some of the testators obviously had religious convictions, which were hidden behind the devout but customary formula of the scribes. John Carter, a chandler, whose will was made in 1648, left both his son and his daughter Bibles. Mary Marshall, the widow whose will Henry Orion wrote in 1669, left Francis Duckins a bequest of £2. She did not appear to be related to him, and he was a leading Congregationalist in whose house the conventicle met in 1669.[27] This is not proof that the Orions were writing for Congregationalists, particularly since the very last will in the series, in 1667, expressed the, by now, unusual desire to be buried in the churchyard; but there is a suspicion. It is partially confirmed because the Henry Orion alive in the 1720s had his house licensed as an independent meeting-place.[28]

The same suspicion applies to Edward Negus even more strongly. He wrote forty-three wills in an educated hand between 1661 and 1693, mostly with a brief clause bequeathing the soul into the hands of God and the body to the ground in Christian burial. Until 1670 he usually wrote, when he came to the disposal of the testator's goods, 'touching such worldly estate as God in his Mercy far above my estates has been pleased to bestow upon me'; after 1670 he dropped this additional clause also. But there was no doubt that he was writing the wills of convinced Protestants. In 1669, the will of Edward Hammond, 'yeoman', who was one of the sons of John Hammond who had acted as a scribe

---

[27] Lyon Turner, I, 38.
[28] This information also comes from Mr Dennis Jeeps who likewise kindly provided me with additional information on Negus.

earlier in the century, contained the clause, 'I give unto Edward Negus my book of martyrs.' Deborah Frohock, a Congregationalist widow, left her son Samuel three Bibles in 1672. Four of the fourteen men who were known to be Congregationalists in Willingham in 1675[29] had their wills written by Negus. A suspiciously large number of the witnesses to wills written by him also appeared with absence from church in an ecclesiastical court of 1673. But despite this, individual conviction did not come through Edward Negus's accustomed phraseology, except in the case of two men, William Bowles, a yeoman, in 1673, and John Allen, a maltster, in 1686, both of whom trusted in a joyful resurrection at the last day. Neither was known from other sources to belong to a particular sect. Negus himself held the lease of a shop in 1665, and does not appear to have been involved in agriculture at all.

Robert Osborne wrote eleven wills between 1665 and 1693 in a village hand, and wrote a much more vivid clause, but one which was still in a common form peculiar to himself, bequeathing the soul 'Unto the hands of God that gave it to me trusting through the merits of Jesus Christ my redeemer, to have a joyful resurrection at the Last Day.' One of the eleven wills was written for one of the Willingham Quakers, and a second was witnessed by another Quaker.

The clauses in wills bequeathing the soul of the testator to God are therefore mainly couched in whatever phrase the particular scribe was accustomed to us and, taken alone, tell little or nothing, of the testator's opinions. But just as the strength of Richard Flatt of Orwell's convictions in 1636 broke through his rector's common formula, so also did a handful of the Willingham wills reflect, in the strength of their language, what must have been the strength of the dying man's faith. John Osborne, who only wrote one will in 1668, must have been closely related to Robert, because their hands were so alike. Even though the will cannot be compared with any others written by John, it is impossible to believe that anything but the feelings of Thomas Staploe, the testator, lie behind the last and only statement of faith which he ever made.

I . . . calling to remembrance the uncertain state of this Transitory life that all flesh must yield unto death when it shall please God to call . . . first being penitent and sorry from the bottom of my heart for sins past most humbly desiring forgiveness for the same, I give and commit my soul unto Almighty God my Saviour and Redeemer in whom and by the merits of Jesus Christ, I trust assuredly to be saved, and to have full remission and forgiveness of all my sins and that my soul with my body at the General Day of resurrection shall rise again with joy receive that which Christ hath prepared for his *elect and chosen.*

[29] See above, pp. 302–3.

It seems from this analysis that for any village there will often be two or three scribes writing wills at any one time, and a large number over a period of a hundred years. They will range from the lord or lessee of the manor, to the vicar, curate, church clerk or churchwarden, to the schoolmaster, a shopkeeper, or any one of the literate yeomen or even husbandmen in a village who could be called in to perform this last neighbourly office for a dying man. If the village lay near a county town, it was possible for a public notary to be called in, although I have less evidence for this practice.[30] Most of these scribes evolved their own slightly different formulae for bequeathing the soul, which can be traced through most, or all, of the wills they were responsible for. If the scribe was an identifiable villager, as he often was, one is still getting irreplaceable information on the doctrinal convictions of the peasantry, of course, since the scribe came himself of humble stock, like the Greaves, or John Pitts or Edward Negus of Willingham, or Nicholas Johnson or George Holder of Orwell. Even when the rector, like William Barnard of Orwell, or the schoolmaster, like Laurence Milford of Willingham, is the scribe, one is still getting information on whatever doctrine is generally accepted at village level. It is a great mistake to assume the docility of the normal parishioner. If the rector of Cottenham, which was a radically nonconformist village in the seventeenth century, felt unable to let his children out to play after one of them had been attacked and scarred for life with a fork in the schoolyard by a 'sone to an adversary',[31] it is scarcely likely that such an 'adversary' would call on the rector to make his will, while the choice of potential scribes was, as I have shown, wide. It is therefore safe to assume that, however near death the testator was, he still exercised a choice over his scribe, as Leonard Woolward did. He probably did not influence the form of the preamble the scribe normally used, unless he had abnormally strong convictions, but he is highly unlikely to have chosen a man whose general opinions were strongly opposed to his own.

Wills can, therefore, be used as Professor Dickens used them, to show a swing away from the cult of the Virgin and the Saints in the 1540s and continued into the 1550s, but he was entirely right when he added, 'The results should not be presented in any spirit of statistical pedantry.' The evidence is not statistical. It is wrong for the historian to assume that if he takes a cross-section of 440 wills proved over a

---

[30] Samuel Newton, a public notary, wrote and signed as such, the will of Edward Daintry the elder (husbandman) of Milton in 1664. Likewise John Brayshaw, a public notary, wrote the will of John Foot, a husbandman of Milton in 1628.
[31] See above, p. 316.

particular period, he is getting 440 different testators' religious opinions reflected, unless of course the wills also come from 440 different places. Even then the scribe might have a determining influence. One is still getting evidence on the attitudes of the peasantry to whatever ecclesiastical settlement was in fashion, but it would take a much more stringent analysis to show how much evidence one is getting, and to eliminate more than one of a series of wills written by the same scribe. On the other hand when a testator had strong religious convictions of his or her own, these may come through, expressed in a variant of the formula usually used by the scribe concerned. If any local historian wishes to study the religious opinions of the peasantry, he should look for these strongly worded individualistic clauses which occur in any run of wills for a parish, which alone record the authentic voice of the dying man.

THE OPINIONS OF THE TESTATORS – WILLINGHAM, ORWELL, CHIPPENHAM, SNAILWELL AND MILTON

The series of wills which survive for Willingham show very clearly the limited way in which the dedicatory clauses in last wills and testaments reveal the opinions of the testators. An analysis of the wills from the 1540s on gives an overall impression of deep Protestant feeling. Thomas Payge, who in 1545 left his soul to Almighty God, 'trusting through the merits and death of his only son Jesus Christ I have forgiveness for all my sinnes' was typical. The sole Catholic will dated a few months after Edward VI's accession to the throne, which mentioned the company of heaven, was an isolated example of individual obstinacy. However, fashion was generally followed, and one scribe at least[32] reverted to a more Catholic terminology under Mary. Half the Marian wills mentioned the holy angels in heaven, the Blessed Virgin Mary, the fellowship of the saints, or the holy company of heaven. The wills did not reveal the existence of a Protestant conventicle in Willingham under Mary,[33] although again obstinate individuals like Isabelle Ragge, who left her soul to Almighty God, 'trusting surely through the merits and death of his only son Jesus Christ that I shall have forgiveness of my sins and that after this present life I shall have life everlasting', sometime at the end of Mary's reign in 1558, stood out against the prevailing trend. So did a handful of Catholic testators, who, as late as 1567, were still bequeathing their souls to Almighty God and all the holy company of heaven, even in Willingham, which was certainly a village where

[32] These early wills are office copies only, so the identity of the writer cannot be traced.
[33] See above, p. 248.

reformed principles were early received and became part of the life of the laity themselves. Parishioners were not all docile sheep, and these stubborn people of conviction were always to be found in every parish.

Just as the wills do not reveal the existence of a Protestant conventicle under Mary, the dedicatory clauses much later, during and after the commonwealth, do not reveal the existence of widespread dissent either. One cannot find dissenters by looking at the terminology of their wills, although the absence of a clause bequeathing the body to burial in the churchyard is suspicious. The wills do not, therefore, mirror the 'ecclesiastical history' of the community from which they come in any reliable way.

Nor is there even any negative connection between a common-form dedicatory clause, and a genuine absence of conviction on the part of the testator.[34] A dedicatory clause with no special features whatsoever does not show that the testator lacked positive beliefs. It only tells us that, if they existed, we shall never know what they were. Despite all their limitations, though, wills are the only source which, in parish after parish[35] illustrate the slow swing amongst the rural laity from Catholic views, from the hope of the dying man or woman to join the holy company of saints, to a reception of reformed opinions, and the ultimate hope in justification by Christ 'by whose bloodshedding only I trust to be saved'. The change was profound and must have represented a profound change in the feelings and attitudes of the parishioners. It is therefore well worth documenting the chronology, which varies from parish to parish. Moreover, there are enough individuals and idiosyncratic dedicatory clauses scattered amongst the wills to show that not only was there a general reception of Protestant belief amongst scribes but that also it obtained a deep spiritual hold on many individuals.

Even after the formula used by Laurence Milford had been so generally adopted in Willingham as to mask individual piety almost entirely[36], some wills still contained their own theological emphasis. A husbandman who died in 1570 left his soul to 'Almighty God my Creator and Maker and to Jesus Christ my own Saviour and Redeemer, and with all holy spirits to rest with Abraham, Isaac and Jacob.' In

[34] See above, pp. 331–2, Edward Hammond and Deborah Frohock.
[35] I have chosen to work through the wills for a handful of parishes, rather than use the more obviously revealing method of taking a cross-section of wills proved in any year, or years, of significant religious change. This is because each parish has its own scribes, its own sets of common forms, and even, I feel, its own variety of thought. It is only by working through the whole run of surviving wills for a parish that, with all its limitations of spread over a hundred years or so, the method of expression peculiar to that community can be identified; so also then can those individuals whose beliefs were too strong to be expressed adequately within the common framework.   [36] See above, pp. 329–30.

1571, Robert Adams, husbandman, betrayed the existence of Calvinistic feeling in Willingham when he trusted 'through His merits to be saved in heaven *amongst his elect*'.

In the period from 1570 to 1639 when the influence of Milford and Hammond as scribes was so strong, there were still testators, like Christian Ewsden, in 1615, whose wills used individual terminology. Christian Ewsden was the widow of a cottager who had provided for her lovingly on his death over twenty years before.[37] John Williams wrote her will for her, and in it she rendered her 'soul unto Almighty God my creator, through the mediation of Christ Jesus my sole redeemer and only saviour'. Williams also wrote the will of another poor woman, Alice Fromant, 'almswoman' who left her soul 'into the hands of Almighty God my creator hoping to be saved by the death and passion of Jesus Christ my redeemer'. The phraseology would not appear distinctive if it did not come as such a refreshing change in the middle of a run of over ninety wills using almost identical wording. As it is, it shows the importance which the religious beliefs of two very poor elderly women had in their lives.

In 1632, Thomas Bowles, a fisherman, bequeathed 'my soul into the hands of Almighty God my maker, trusting in the only and all sufficient merits of my saviour Jesus Christ for the forgiveness of my sins and salvation'. The phraseology again stood out; the way it accurately reflected personal conviction was further emphasised by another bequest in the will, 'I give to my eldest son William Bowles also my bible wishing him to use it to God's glory.' Perhaps he did; it may have been the selfsame William Bowles 'yeoman' whose will stood out amongst the neutrally phrased wills written by Edward Negus, because when it was written in 1673, the testator trusted 'in the righteousness of Jesus Christ that I have a joyful resurrection at the last day'.

John Crouch, a yeoman who died in 1667 and had been a petitioner against Bishop Wren in 1640, was perhaps naturally more prolix.

Principally I commit and commend my soul into the hands of God my loving father in Jesus Christ verily believing through the only death and merits of my alone lord Jesus Christ to have full and free pardon of all my sins, and to be made partaker of life everlasting.

Examples like this can be multiplied; but all they do is provide more minute dots in a Seurat-like picture, which shows that, however great the limitations of wills to provide a religious framework of the doctrinal history of a parish may be, they still prove conclusively that personal faith in the mediation of Christ and redemption through Him had per-

[37] See above, p. 141.

colated right down through Willingham society and obtained a hold on the many very disparate people within it, from almswomen to yeomen. The wills of the other villages which I have examined in detail confirm this picture, although the timing of the change was often quite different.

Orwell had a married priest who was not disposed to reintroduce the Mass in 1553. From their reactions to his behaviour, it also seems to have been split already between those parishioners incensed by their priest's behaviour, and those inclined to make an alehouse mockery of the Mass and circulate ballads called 'maistres masse'.[38] Yet both the only surviving original wills from Orwell from the 1540s are Catholic in form, and so is one of 1558. The straightforward Protestant wills do not start until 1569. Judging from this alone, the Willingham wills with their Protestant emphasis in the 1540s, reinforced the general history of a village in which a husbandman could seriously think of going off to Oxford in Mary's time, to get his theological doubts sorted out by Bishop Ridley himself.[39] But there was no doubt of the strength of Protestant feeling in Orwell later.

Chippenham, and its little neighbour Snailwell, may have lain in the deanery of Sudbury, which Marchant described as 'very much under Puritan influence'[40] but the wills which survive for these villages[41] show no trace of the trend which was so apparent in Willingham, the typical acceptance of justification by faith by the 1540s. In 1543, William Masse, of Badlingham hamlet in Chippenham, left his soul to 'Almighty God, our ladye St Mary and to all saints' and further willed 'that a priest sing in Chippenham church and pray for my soule at the feast of the nativity of our lord next coming v days'. He was not alone. William Chapman of Chippenham left his soul to 'Almighty God, our ladye St Mary and to all the company in heaven' in the following year. Trimming the sails to the winds of ecclesiastical fashion came hard in Chippenham, and the strain can be felt in the dedicatory clauses. In 1552, under Edward VI, the will of Robert Clement of Chippenham started off with a magnificent all-inclusive clause:

I bequeath my soule to almyghtie god to rayne withall saintes in hys kyngdome through the merytes of Jesus Christ the sonne of the blessed vyrgyne Marye and oure only saveour.

---

[38] See above, p. 245. [39] See above, pp. 246–8.

[40] Marchant, *The Church under the Law*, p. 209.

[41] I have used registered copies only for these villages. Fifty-three survive for Chippenham, and twenty-three for Snailwell between 1502 and 1700, in the Bury St Edmunds and West Suffolk Records Office. The originals were unavailable when this text was written.

It is impossible to fault the perfect unity of what, unhappily, became thought of as opposing theological beliefs here. One would like to know whether Robert Clement, or the vicar, Robert Webster, who was one of his witnesses, was responsible for the composition of the clause.

If it was the vicar, his next effort slipped a bit, because he also witnessed the will of William Clarke, which bequeathèd his soul to Almighty God, simply, but was headed, gratingly, in the 'first yeare of the raigne of oure soveraigne Ladye Marye . . . defender of the faythe and upon yearthe of the churche of England and Ireland the supreme head'. Political acumen seems to have failed him a little. Even in 1559, towards the end of Elizabeth's first year on the throne, Thomas Porye of Badlingham still left his soul to Almighty God 'desiring him of his mercy that I may rest with all the holy company of heaven'. He was witnessed by some of the most substantial inhabitants of Chippenham, including Edmund Francis,[42] engrosser and rising yeoman.

Elizabeth had been on the throne five years when the first Chippenham will with a slightly Protestant emphasis was written. The pen of Robert Webster, clerk, who witnessed, may have been responsible, and if it was, it seems to have creaked and jerked again; there is a certain lack of wholeheartedness and fullness in Thomas Kynwardine's bequest of his soul to 'Almighty God which is the saviour of the world.' It was 1566 before William Haylock left his soul 'to Almighty God to Jesus Christ my maker and redeemer trustinge to his passion to be partaker of his resurrection' in the first fully Protestant phraseology. After this, all the Chippenham wills were either Protestant or neutral. Between 1592 and 1617, Nicholas Allen, the vicar of Chippenham wrote, or witnessed and probably wrote, half a dozen wills.[43] It is evident that Nicholas Allen was a teaching minister, from the will of the husbandman John Lyvechild, written in 1599, which leaves 'Mr Allen for his paynes taken with me, a combe of rye'. It is also evident that he was a Protestant, for all six wills have devout Protestant dedicatory clauses. But interestingly, none of the six duplicates the phraseology of another. They all differ, from John Mayor's dedication of his soul 'into the hands of almighty god hoping to be saved by the precious bloodshedding of our saviour Jesus Christ' to Garrard Grime's 'into the hands of Almighty God hopeing to be saved by the death of our lord Jesus which he suffered for all mankind'. Possibly Nicholas Allen's teaching went more than skin-deep, and we have here the individual reflections of it

---

[42] See above, p. 84.
[43] See will of John Tebald, of Chippenham, written 5 April 1605, which closes 'per me Nicholas Allen vicarium de Chippenham, huius testamenti scriptore'.

338

in the words of his dying parishioners. At the least, he bothered to think afresh every time himself.

Most of the yeomen who were outstandingly noticeable as economically successful in Chippenham in the seventeenth century were also responsible for strongly worded and individual dedicatory clauses in their wills. John Kent, in 1625, left his soul 'into the hands of Almightie god my Creator and Jesus Christ my saviour and Redeemer hopeing to be saved by his death and bloodsheddinge'. Thomas Dillamore,[44] who was still agile enough to sign every page of his will, hoped 'through the merrittes of Jesus Christ my saviour to be made partaker of life everlasting'. John Hodgkin[45] almost, but not quite, repeated his hope. The aged James Cooke, yeoman, of Badlingham,[46] who kept all his money in bonds, was much fuller than usual. The body of his will begins:

First and above all things I commit and commend my soule into the hands of Almighty God my creator assuredly in and through the meritts, mercies mediacion and intercession of Jesus Christ my ever blessed Saviour and Redeemer to have full and free remission of all my sins and to be made partaker of everlasting happiness in his heavenly kingdom.

In 1682, Robert Tebbutt, the younger,[47] left his 'soul to God my Creator trusting for salvation through the lone meritts of his blessed son Christ Jesus my Saviour'. Otherwise from 1661 to 1665 the half-dozen surviving wills seem to have been written by John Aves, who wrote a standard phrase bequeathing the souls of his testators 'into the hands of almighty god my creator, trusting through the merits of Jesus Christ my saviour to be made partaker of everlasting life'. Judging from his fate, employment as a village scribe was by no means a lucrative by-employment.[48]

Chippenham was, then, strongly Protestant, but the reception of Protestant ideas came later there. Although the wills bear witness to individual testators' feelings, as elsewhere, they do not provide evidence of much of the religious history of the place. There is nothing to show, in the wills, that a section of Francis Holcroft's church list of 1675 was headed 'Chippenham, Snail' etc.' or that Ann Sleighton's house was licensed as a meeting-place in 1672. Nor is there any reason, except for the sword and bandolier in his inventory, to suspect from his will that the first Robert Tebbutt's convictions were strong enough to take him into the civil war, for his will was written in John Aves's own common-form. Nor is there any reason either to deduce that the strength of conviction of Richard Parr, vicar of Chippenham from 1658 to 1664, who

[44] See above, pp. 76, 81–2, 86–7.
[45] See above, pp. 85–6.
[46] See above, p. 80.
[47] See above, pp. 74–5.
[48] See above, p. 210.

started life as a husbandman's son from Lancashire before going up to St John's, and who witnessed the same will, would make him a suitable chaplain for the household of Henry Cromwell at Spinney Abbey after 1664.[49] Nor indeed could the strongly Cromwellian affiliation of the landowners of Chippenham[50] be deduced from their tenants' religious opinions, which read strongly, but no more strongly than any other Cambridgeshire parish at this date. Nor could the presence of Samuel Fairclough, a considerable scholar, lecturer in Hebrew and Logic in the University of Cambridge, who was ejected from his living in 1660, be deduced in Chippenham, where he was licensed to preach as a Congregationalist in 1672.[51]

Snailwell, from its wills, seems to have reached a Protestant attitude before Chippenham. Strangely enough, the first two Protestant wills which survive for Snailwell are Marian. They differed in terminology, and were witnessed by different men, so seem to reflect independent but coinciding opinions. There was no doubt about either, but Dorothy Smythe, whose will was made at the beginning of 1558 (n.s.) was particularly clear. She left her soul 'into the merciful hands of god trusting to be saved by the meryts of Christes deth and bloodshedding'. Robert Eyton's will two years later made one of the very rare allusions to the Trinity. He commended his 'soul unto the holie trinitie, trusting to be saved by the onely merites and death of our saviour Christe'.[52] After this, the Snailwell wills were consistently Protestant, when they were not neutral, differing only in their degree of fervour. Martin Warren, a very considerable yeoman[53] whose will was made in 1600, was a Calvinist. He bequeathed his soul 'into the hands of Almighty God hoping by the death and passion of Jesus Christ to come to *the place prepared for his elect*'. In 1606, Thomas Gilbert who was also one of the prosperous yeomen of Snailwell, commended 'my soul unto God the almighty, not doubting but that my salvacion is all readie purchased by the death and passion of Jesus Christ'. This, and the will of John Howlett, another yeoman made in 1610, which left his soul to Almighty God 'my Creator, and to Jesus Christ my redeemer, and to the holy ghost my comforter, hopeing to be saved by faith only in Jesus Christ and by no other meanes or merits', both bear the marks of individual belief.

The parish of Milton lay near Cambridge, and coincided with the single manor, which was held by one of the few recusant families in Cambridgeshire. The Cookes, lords of Milton, were persistently in trouble under Bishop Cox[54] and their successors the Harrises fared no

---

[49] *Calamy Revised*, p. 381.   [50] See above, p. 74, n. 35.   [51] *Calamy Revised*, p. 188.
[52] He was witnessed by the vicar of Exning, so this may be a scribal idiosyncrasy.
[53] See above, pp. 80–1.   [54] See, for instance, E.D.R., D/2/10, fo. 180v (1579.

better under Bishop Wren. Wren's visitation of 1639 can probably be trusted to reflect the numbers of recusants accurately[55] and in that year there were six recusants in Milton, all belonging to the Harris family, together with two of their maidservants. The influence of the lords of the manor does not seem to have had any effect on the parishioners, although it is possible that the very late inclusion of some Catholic clauses in wills of the last decade of the sixteenth century have something to do with their presence. The rectory was not theirs, but King's, however. Despite both recusant lords and the influence of King's, the place had one infrequent Congregationalist conventicle of 'a great many', most admittedly from other parishes, meeting there in 1669. Some of the conventiclers were 'of Ability, mostly the contrary', Bishop Laney typically wrote. But Congregationalism gained no lasting hold in Milton; there were no licences granted there from 1672, only one resolute papist, and no nonconformists, according to the Compton Census in 1676.

Only four original wills survive from Milton, drawn up before Mary's reign, and the three from the 1530s and 1540s are all neutral. Not surprisingly, the will of Alice Feston, made in the fourth year of Mary's reign, was straightforwardly Catholic; but Harry Hart, like Robert Clement of Chippenham,[56] attempted a compromise solution in the following year, although the balance was not perfect as it was in Robert Clement's will. He left his soul to God Almighty, the Blessed Virgin Mary and to all the holy company of heaven, trusting 'bye the meryts off chrystes passion and shedynge of hys preciouse blode to have remyssyon off mye synnes and lyfe everlastinge'. Thomas Eversden's will, in the first year of Elizabeth's reign, repeated a similar formula, including the reference to the Blessed Virgin. Perhaps the influence of William Gotobed, the curate, who witnessed both, was at work. If so, he remained consistent both in his adherence to an unfashionable stress on justification through Christ, under Mary, and admission to the equally unfashionable company of heaven, under Elizabeth. Eleven years after she had come to the throne, Gotobed witnessed the will of Geoffrey Holmes, 'the unprofitable servant of God', who did

wythe a free heart Render and geve agayne in to the handes of the Lord my God my spyrite wych he of hys fatherlye goodnes gave unto me bye this means makying me a lyving creature. Doubting nothing but that this mye lord god for hys mercye sake thorows the precyous blood shedyng of hys dearlye beloved sonne chryste Jesus mye onelye savyour and Redeemer that he wyll Receve mye soule unto his glorye and place me in the companye of the heavenly angels and the blessed sayntes.

[55] E.D.R., B/2/52, fo. 35.   [56] See above, p. 337.

Geoffrey Holmes seems to have had strong convictions of his own any-way. Not only did his will continue to consign his body to the earth until the general resurrection, 'when we shall all appear before the iudgment seat of Christ Jesus and I shall receive it again by the mighty power of Christ', but he also made the only reference I have seen in a will to marriage as a sacrament, 'as touching my wife, with whom I coupled myself in fear of God and living with her in the blessed estate of wedlock through whom by the blessing of God I have had my daughters'.

The reference to the holy angels and the blessed saints which appeared in Geoffrey Holmes's will was dropped in John Foote's will in 1572, which Gotobed witnessed also. And yet as late as 1592, Ursula Barnard bequeathed

> my soul into the hands of the lord my God nothing doubting but that this my lord God for his mercy's sake set forth in the precious blood of his blessed son Christ Jesus our alone saviour and redeemer will receive my soul into his glory and place it in the company of his heavenly angels and blessed saints.

She commended her body to the earth

> faithfully believing that according th'articles of our belief at the great day of the general resurrection I shall receive it again not mortal, corruptible, Weak and Vile as now it is but a body immortal, incorruptible, strong and in all points perfect.

Another will of about the same date is in very similar phraseology. Yet the laity of Milton, and their curates and scribes, gradually abandoned the balance between Catholic and Protestant clauses, and settled down into a general acceptance of Protestantism, which just occasionally went deeper.

Eighty-one wills survive for Milton before 1700, thirty-two of which are neutral. Another thirty-five, from 1567 onwards, express a general hope in justification by faith, like John Richards, husbandman, who died in 1568 and left his soul into the hands of Jesus Christ 'by whom I hope ever to live'. A considerable number of these put the hope more strongly, like John Graves, a yeoman, who over a hundred years later, in 1674, resigned his soul to 'God that gave it, hoping for mercy and acceptance through the alone merits and satisfaction of my crucified Saviour'.

Half a dozen wills were so individual that the convictions of the testators shine through the crabbed hands of the scribes. Edward Leach, a labourer, made his will well before his death in 1644,

Forasmuch as death is certain but the day and hour uncertain, and because there should be no controversy after my death for my goods and possessions, and for the maintenance of love and peace in the world.

He gave and committed his soul

into the hands of god my creator Redeemer, and sanctifier, fully trusting and assuredly believing to be saved only by the death and resurrection of Jesus Christ, the son of god, and by no other means.

Although the histories of small communities reflect national events local affairs have their own momentum also. It is both significant and pleasant that a labourer of Milton should have been thinking of the maintenance of love and peace in the world, and among his family and friends, when his small goods were divided up, at the same time as the civil war lurched on its unwieldy way and affected the maintenance of the commons of Milton itself. The convictions of the labourers were also those of the yeomen. Ellis Richards, in 1676, bequeathed his soul

into the hands of almighty god my creator, assuredly hoping by and through the merits and mediation of my blessed Saviour Jesus Christ to obtain and full Remission and pardon of all my Sins and to be made partaker of everlasting Joy and felicity when this mortal life shall have an end.

But amongst all the testators of Milton, Robert Trigge, a yeoman whose will was made in 1681, was the only Calvinist. He committed his soul

into the hands of almighty god, my Creator and Redeemer in whom, and by the merits and righteousness of the lord Jesus Christ I trust ... assuredly to be saved and to have full remission and forgiveness of all my sins, and that my soul with my body at the general resurrection of the just shall rise again with joy and possess and inherit the kingdom of heaven prepared for *the elect and chosen of God* [my italics].

Close study of the wills of orthodox villagers bears out the general impression given by the *Fenstanton Records*, of a society in which even the humblest members, the very poor, and the women, and those living in physical isolation, thought deeply on religious matters and were often profoundly influenced by them. This comes through despite all the difficulties caused by scribes repeating common-form clauses. So does the type of conviction held generally in Cambridgeshire by its villagers after Elizabeth's accession. It was generally reformed, generally Protestant, it laid great emphasis on salvation through Christ's death and passion alone, but it was not Calvinistic. Very, very few wills mention election; Martin Warren of Snailwell, Robert Adams and Thomas Staploe of

Willingham, and Robert Trigge of Milton, were very isolated individuals.[57]

The wills, with all their limitations, do therefore permit a glimpse into the importance religion had, even amongst orthodox villagers. No doubt many of them felt as neutrally as the phraseology of their wills would suggest. Others, who belonged to no sect so far as can be discovered, were men and women of conviction, who probably felt as strongly as those dissenters to whom we must turn for practical illustrations of real strength of feeling.

— DISSENTERS —

MEMBERSHIP OF THE GATHERED CHURCHES

Where direct verbal evidence is missing, other evidence, less direct but no less telling, must be admitted. The distances the members of a gathered church were prepared to walk to a meeting, and the fines the members were prepared to pay for going there are pieces of evidence of this kind. If a relatively poor man was prepared to give time, energy, and above all money to the service of his particular brand of faith, his convictions must have been both deep and genuine.

For their adherents, the nonconformist churches which formed under the commonwealth were very different bodies from the 'natural' parish communities which they replaced. The parish community was that of the village, bound together in its working life by the communal discipline of the open fields and the manor court, turned to prayer. Every villager, whatever his spiritual state, and however advanced or non-existent his spiritual life, was automatically a member of the all-inclusive church to which he was bound to go on Sundays. Membership of a nonconformist group was by conscious choice and election, and therefore involved the believer in the entirely different group of like-thinking people. These 'gathered' churches cut across the boundaries of parish and village. They enforcedly drew in their members from a wide area, since most villages only provided a couple of active dissenters. The physical problems of getting to meetings and communications were therefore absolutely fundamental to the villagers who formed the congregations of the dissenting churches.[58]

---

[57] If predestination to salvation became a commonly held tenet among Cambridgeshire villagers, it must have done so after the commonwealth, when Holcroft was spreading the principles of his Calvinist Congregationalist Church. See above, p. 288. Thomas Staploe appears on p. 332, Robert Adams on p. 336, Martin Warren on p. 340 and Robert Trigge on p. 343.

[58] Although it is well to remember that large distances were commonly covered, chiefly to get to market, and that George Mitchell of Eltisley in Cambridgeshire earned the wrath of his brethren by not turning up to meetings half a mile away 'seeing he could go ordinarily three or four, and sometimes seven or eight miles to

The reality of religion for the villager

The records of the General Baptist Church of Fenstanton, which lies just over the Cambridgeshire border in Huntingdonshire, illustrate very clearly the difficulties of maintaining communication between the members of the congregation. John Denne, son of Henry Denne who founded the church[59] and held the Cambridgeshire living of Eltisley, was elder and recorder of the Fenstanton church and lived a mile or so from Eltisley in Caxton parish, at the farm called Caxton Pastures.[60] The church of Fenstanton met as commonly in this Cambridgeshire farmhouse as it did in Fenstanton. From time to time, it held general meetings in other Cambridgeshire villages as well: Eltisley, Papworth Everard and Bourn were among them. The members baptised between 1644 and 1666 came from no less than thirty villages and towns in Cambridgeshire, Huntingdonshire and Bedfordshire.[61] The practical problem that this scattered membership presented is most vividly brought home by a letter written from Fenstanton in answer to an inquiry made in 1653 by some Lincolnshire brethren about the grounds on which the Cambridgeshire and Huntingdonshire Baptists broke bread 'in remembrance' at supper and at feasts at Fenstanton.[62] In his reply, John Denne cited his scriptural reasons for the practice, and then added 'and for a feast of love in the church of God, if the Scripture had not spoken at all of it ... yet we find it very necessary, the brethren coming from far, that the congregation should be refreshed before it be dismissed'.[63] When James Parnell, the Quaker, argued with one of the Baptist elders in Fenstanton in 1655, he scoffed at his adversary and recorded 'at last he shuffled away, under Pretence that he had far to go'. The reason given may have been an excuse in the circumstances, but for all that is likely to have been true.[64]

The way the organisation and disciplinary procedures of the dissenting churches developed in the early stages is often a reflection of this simple problem of communications and distance. In 1654 the church of Fenstanton decided that every member should be present at the assembly of the congregation on the first day of the week unless he or she was prevented by sickness.[65] This ruling presented obvious difficulties. The records of the church show that when enough converts existed in any sufficiently remote village, they held their own meetings for worship there, although for disciplinary purposes they attended the general meeting wherever it was held. Four people from Harston were baptised before 1646, for instance. When Henry Denne made an

the riotous assemblies of wicked persons ... and that upon the first day of the week'. *Fenstanton Records*, p. 162.
[59] See above, pp. 227–8.   [60] *Fenstanton Records*, pp. xxii–xxiii and 100.
[61] *Ibid.* Church Register, pp. 251–4.   [62] *Ibid.* p. 61.   [63] *Ibid.* p. 70.
[64] James Parnell, *The Watcher*, p. 186.   [65] *Fenstanton Records*, p. 126.

evangelising tour in 1653 he stayed at 'brother Raymond's house' in Harston and 'the brethren that night met together with us; we prayed with them and stayed with them'.[66] Later that year, Denne made two converts in Great Shelford but he took them to Harston for baptism. Obviously the little group there was faithful, and met regularly. For all that it remained entirely subject to Fenstanton, and when there was disciplinary trouble there with an ex-elder who beat his wife 'and that in the open street',[67] it was necessary for the general assembly at Caxton to rule when he was reconciled to his church after repentence that 'a time should be appointed when the brethren there might assemble ... it being concluded that what should be done at that time should be in as full force as if it had been done at the general meeting of the congregation'.[68]

The Baptists of Harston were fortunate to be numerous enough to hold meetings together. Others were not so lucky. By far the largest part of the Fenstanton Church Book is made up of the reports of messengers sent by the congregation to visit and admonish the backsliders, the lazy, and those who found themselves confused, in the theological melting-pot of the 1650s, on matters of doctrine. Many of these people must have been in the situation of Jasper Dockwra of Bassingbourn, who 'confessed that he being alone a long time was much discouraged and at length did go to the Church of England'.[69] It is impossible, from historical evidence, to estimate the stresses on these early converts, and the degree to which they were, by their conversion, cut off from their 'natural' communities. The question is absolutely fundamental, since it seems likely that the village community was split from top to bottom in the seventeenth century on ideological grounds for the first time in its existence. It is difficult to imagine the depth of feeling and tension aris-

[66] *Ibid*. p. 75.   [67] *Ibid*. p. 211.
[68] *Ibid*. p. 240. There seems however to have been no organised method of dismission at this early stage. It is true that in 1653, the elders told William Marriat of Eynsbury near St Neots 'if there be any of the people of God that are nigher to you, you may go to them'. But Brother Mitchell who moved to Steeple Morden, twelve miles away in south Cambridgeshire, was still required to come to Caxton Pastures (*ibid*. pp. 59, 71) although the Royston meeting was much nearer. Jasper Dockraw of Bassingbourn, near Steeple Morden, did confess his difficulties to a member of the Royston meeting but was not excused his absence from the Caxton general meeting on this account, for 'I told him they were one congregation, and we another, we did not meet together' (*ibid*. pp. 99–100, entry for 1654). By 1656, a formula of dismission was developing when a member moved from the district, but even then the original congregation of baptism retained authority over the baptised (*ibid*. pp. 184–7). The process was organised by 1677 in Bunyan's Bedford Church (*Church Book of Bunyan Meeting*, fo. 63) but it was the end of the century before a printed dismission form was evolved by the church there, which contained gaps for the relevant names to be filled in (*Church Book*, fo. 79a).
[69] *Fenstanton Records*, p. 99.

346

ing in a village like Orwell, when a quarter of the heads of households were nonconformists, and where as many as seven warrants for the arrest of the 'phanaticks' were applied for and executed by these people's own co-villagers, in a single year.[70] Nor is it possible to gauge the acrimony that must have existed when the validity of Congregationalist marriages was doubted, and the 'offenders' presented, again by the villagers themselves, to the ecclesiastical officials. When one of the main effects of separatism was to split both congregations and families between different sects in the argument that immediately seemed to follow the establishment of one form of dissent in a village,[71] the whole community and its composite households must have been divided in a way previously unknown.

In exchange for this alienation from their natural communities, the converts received the constant care of their new brethren for their spiritual, and even physical, needs. It is impossible not to be impressed, in reading the records of the seventeenth-century dissenting churches, by the amount of pastoral care and patient attention given to the members. For all that there may well have been some degree of social isolation to contend with, and certainly for isolated converts there was a lack of contacts with whom the new preconceptions and beliefs could be shared and discussed. Sister Barfurd of Haslingfield who 'wept for joy to see us' when she was visited by the Baptist evangelist in 1653[72] showed effects of this isolation, which was of course much worse for the aged and infirm, who could make no excursions to conventicle meetings.

The problems of scattered membership were common to all the dissenting groups, and not confined to any one. It was this which made it an obvious step after the restoration to enact legislation against travelling on Sundays, and made it relatively easy for the authorities to pick up people like Boniface Norris, the Quaker, who was nearly eighty and unable to travel on foot 'as he was rideing to a Meeting on a first day about two Miles from his outward being'. The Old Meeting at Bedford, which was Open Baptist in principle, drew its members mostly from Bedford and a few villages round. The main monthly meetings were always held in Bedford until persecution drove the congregation to hold them in other places from 1663 onwards. Even in the 1650s, there was difficulty over attendance and keeping contact with the members. In 1656 two brethren were chosen at each monthly meeting to visit the congregation and 'stir up' the brethren to come. 'If they come not, the Church will expect an account of the reason of their absence.'[73] After

[70] See above, p. 301.
[71] See above, pp. 294–7.
[72] *Fenstanton Records*, p. 75.
[73] *Church Book of Bunyan Meeting*, fo. 16.

1663, monthly meetings were held in Haynes, as well as Bedford. In 1670, Gamlingay in Cambridgeshire also became a meeting-place. This system continued into the eighteenth century. For all that, in 1711, the Gamlingay brethren asked for their collective dismission from the Bedford church 'by reason of their distance from us'. This was granted 'as tending to the greater glorification of God . . . they at such a distance from us not being able to keep the ordinance of Christ with us'.[74]

This problem of communications may very well explain why the small market towns of Cambridgeshire, the Lintons, Sohams and Gamlingays, tended to be centres of dissent. The reason was not primarily that dissent flourished amongst the artisans, nor even that the larger size of these towns made the gatherings of a meeting of a reasonable number easier; it was that they were in the first place centres to which the villagers for miles around were accustomed to go regularly in any case, on which local trackways and roads naturally centred. The Congregational minister of Linton was described in 1690 as 'inclinable to set up a fixed Congregation, at a convenient distance from sundry places'.[75] The market towns were the inevitable gathering-centres. The trust deeds of the early dissenting chapels show this clearly. John Webb of Balsham was suffering for his Quakerism by the late 1650s, and a conventicle was listed at his house by the bishop in 1669. John Webb was still holding regular meetings at his house in Balsham in 1670, from the Quaker records, and Richard Webb of West Wickham, and Walter Crane of Horseheath were attending them. All these men were, however, listed under the general heading of the Linton meeting, in the Quaker 'Volumes of Sufferings'. The Quaker register which begins in the 1650s only includes the Linton meeting in this area. In 1733, the first surviving trust deed of the Quaker meeting-house at Linton lists Richard Webb of West Wratting, Senior, as the only surviving trustee of an earlier deed. It seems very likely that he was the surviving representative of this traditionally Quaker family, which had always held meetings in areas well away from Linton, and yet were drawn into the Linton meeting.

The way in which market towns drew in small groups in the territory about is as clearly shown in the earliest surviving Congregational trust deeds. Only four of the ten trustees of the Congregational meeting-house in Linton in 1698 came from Linton itself. Three came from Hadstock, just over the river in Essex; one from the next village of Bartlow; one from Horseheath a couple of miles away, and one from Great Chester-

---

[74] *Ibid.* fos. 110–11.
[75] 'Review of the State of the Severall Counties in England and Wales 1690–2', ed. A. Gordon, *Freedom after Ejection* (1917), pp. 11–12.

ford in Essex about ten miles away.[76] The larger villages had the same centralising effect as the market towns. The first half dozen feoffees of Melbourn Congregational Chapel in 1723 included only a single Melbourn man. The rest came from five different villages in the vicinity over a radius of ten miles. It was against this background of physical and spiritual loneliness created by the physical problems of distance that the elect of the 'gathered' churches were assembled from the Cambridgeshire villages under the commonwealth.

The cleavages caused by dissent within the villages, and the isolation of the converts portrayed in the church books, occasionally appear tragic when they are translated into human terms. The impression of spiritual distress and painful seeking, comes across in these word-by-word reports in reported speech much more vividly than it could from any effort of historical reconstruction.

Most tragic of all is one of the spiritual biographies which can be reconstructed, which shows how some of the searchers failed to find any lasting conviction. It is that of William Marriat and his wife of Eynsbury in Huntingdonshire, who seem to have begun their seeking as General Baptists.[77] It illustrates the state of complete religious confusion which the ordinary parishioner could get into, in the climate of the 1650s, after the changes of the last hundred years. On the second pastoral visit made to William Marriat after his falling away, he betrayed that he had been taking a defiantly independent attitude and had been listening to the Quakers. He said, 'I do believe that other people which do not observe those ordinances are the people of God as well as you.' Three months later, he and his wife came to the general meeting at Bourn,[78] and said they would willingly come to the meetings, but could not break bread because 'we have no right to it, because we have no faith in God. We cannot call God Father ... when we walked with you, we expected much, but were deceived in our expectations; therefore we went higher, but God hath brought us low, and it is good for us so to be.' Whatever sect had had their allegiance in the intervening time had also failed them. Marriat added bitterly, 'I see no comfort in meetings, they are only to ripen the brain; for what I was and how I was esteemed among you formerly, some of you here present know. But now I see that it was nothing but the ripeness of my own brain, and the quickness of my wit.' Despite his humble request that he and his wife should remain in communion even if they remained 'in ignorance

[76] C.U.L., W. M. Palmer Collection, B4/1, Notes on Linton Congregational Church and Notes on the Quaker Trust Deeds at Linton.
[77] It is to be found in *Fenstanton Records*, pp. 30, 39–40, 50–52, and 54.
[78] In Cambridgeshire.

and without faith, or any knowledge of God' the Marriats were excommunicated a month later. William Marriat's sense of spiritual dereliction was expressed in his response to the sentence of excommunication when it was delivered to him. 'I cannot blame you, for if you should have had communion with us, it would have overthrown all by the roots.'

I think I have said enough to show that both Puritan and separatist thinking existed amongst the laity in the diocese of Ely before the commonwealth, in certain well-definded areas which continued to be foci of dissent much later. More important, perhaps, I hope I have shown also that religious thought, anxiety, and devotion were real factors in the life of the ordinary villager, however humble he, or she, might be. We ought, however difficult it is, to stop thinking of such people purely – or mainly – in their economic capacity. Even if the third or 'working' order of man did not fight – and in the seventeenth century, he probably did – he certainly prayed.

Conclusion

Dissent and separatism were strong and firmly rooted in three groups of Cambridgeshire parishes after the restoration. Although these were parishes where Congregationalist, Baptist and Quaker evangelists had worked during the commonwealth, their work was not responsible for the existence of the Puritan state of mind amongst the laity that could lead to separatism; they were responsible for fostering, directing and spreading it, but not for initiating it. The existence of large numbers of parishioners in 1640, anxious to be rid of episcopal government and set up 'government according to the scriptures', concentrated in exactly the same areas as in 1676, demonstrates this very clearly. The fact that only a fifth of these petitioners were wealthy enough to appear in taxation lists brings home with even more force the fact that Puritan religious convictions were, in this county, a grass-roots phenomenon amongst the very humble, which pre-dated the commonwealth. A certain amount more flesh is put on these bare bones by the numbers of husbandmen and labourers with 'tender consciences', who were found to present articles against the Laudian or royalist clergy.

A considerable number of Cambridgeshire villages were anti-Laudian or even anti-episcopal in the 1630s. But we cannot take the history of their convictions back, and prove that, as the post-restoration Congregationalists had it, there was a body of 'old Brownists' in the diocese. The lack of interest in heresy shown in the episcopal visitations, the absence of records of special commissions to deal with heresy, and the destruction of the court of High Commission records in the south, effectively prevent this. The evidence that does exist is pitifully slight; we know that a Marian conventicle probably met at Willingham, and that a husbandman of Willingham was sufficiently moved by conviction to go into Essex, to make contact with the Colchester church there. We know that the Family of Love flourished, in the 1570s, in areas where Quakerism was found in the 1650s. We know that William Weston, as he looked through his Wisbech prison bars in the 1580s, was sufficiently impressed by the numbers he saw attending 'prophesyings' there to estimate them at thousands. It would be surprising, in view of the

351

depth of Puritan feeling at the village level in the diocese in the 1630s, if there was no continuity to be found, and if the late sixteenth-century peasant, like his seventeenth-century descendants, was not disturbed by, and involved in, argument about the Elizabethan settlement. But we cannot prove it. We cannot even prove, from the wills of the peasantry, what their convictions were, since we know that almost all the surviving wills from the 1570s onwards, written by these scribes, who were often villagers themselves, have neutral dedicatory clauses, or ones which express a general reformed faith in salvation through Christ. The occasional wills which stand out, as expressing the personal faith of the dying man or woman, all express a deeply personal dependence on God as Father, and Christ as Redeemer and Mediator.

We know, then, that the ordinary villager had religious convictions of his own, although we cannot trace the antecedents of these convictions back further than the 1630s. Nor can we account for them. No single social background is common to all the communities which were deeply affected by dissent. Manorial fragmentation did have some effect, but there were too many exceptions to the rule. The influence of the clergy dispossessed for Laudianism did not always, or often, prevent the growth of dissent; nor did the existence of a non-subscribing minister necessarily foster it. Schools with a continuous life tended to exist in the larger and more prosperous settlements, where there were, naturally, more dissenters. But this correlation, like the correlation between manorial subdivision and dissent, seems merely to have been a by-product of sizeable villages. No determinism, economic, social, educational or geographical, will fully account for the existence of religious conviction; which is as it should be.

The evidence for individual religious belief among the peasantry is, and always will be, thoroughly unsatisfactory. Yet there is enough to show that the importance of the parish church and its rival, the meeting-house, which between them dominated the village, was very great to the laymen, even if it cannot be statistically calculated. The local historian is not dealing with communities whose interests, in the sixteenth and seventeenth centuries, were confined to the bare economic necessities of life, even though the materials he has at his disposal on the economic life of any community are often so much richer than any others.

Appendix 1 The Butlers of Orwell

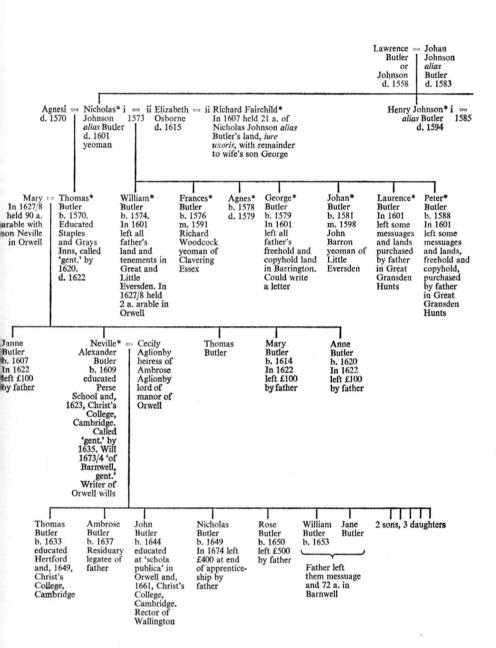

Appendix 1 The Butlers of Orwell

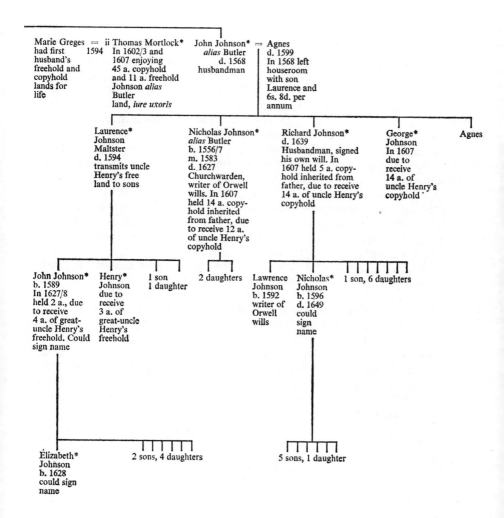

Marie Greges = ii Thomas Mortlock* | John Johnson* = Agnes
had first | 1594 | In 1602/3 and | *alias* Butler | d. 1599
husband's | | 1607 enjoying | d. 1568 | In 1568 left
freehold and | | 45 a. copyhold | husbandman | houseroom
copyhold | | and 11 a. freehold | | with son
lands for | | Johnson *alias* | | Laurence and
life | | Butler | | 6s. 8d. per
| | land, *iure uxoris* | | annum

Laurence* Johnson Maltster d. 1594 transmits uncle Henry's free land to sons

Nicholas Johnson* *alias* Butler b. 1556/7 m. 1583 d. 1627 Churchwarden, writer of Orwell wills. In 1607 held 14 a. copyhold inherited from father, due to receive 12 a. of uncle Henry's copyhold

Richard Johnson* d. 1639 Husbandman, signed his own will. In 1607 held 5 a. copyhold inherited from father, due to receive 14 a. of uncle Henry's copyhold

George* Johnson In 1607 due to receive 14 a. of uncle Henry's copyhold

Agnes

John Johnson* b. 1589 In 1627/8 held 2 a., due to receive 4 a. of great-uncle Henry's freehold. Could sign name

Henry* Johnson due to receive 3 a. of great-uncle Henry's freehold

1 son 1 daughter

2 daughters

Lawrence Johnson b. 1592 writer of Orwell wills

Nicholas* Johnson b. 1596 d. 1649 could sign name

1 son, 6 daughters

Elizabeth* Johnson b. 1628 could sign name

2 sons, 4 daughters

5 sons, 1 daughter

355

Appendix 2 Notes on Graphs 3 and 5

The harvest years and data on grain used in Graph 3, p. 79, are those used by Dr Bowden, in the *Agrarian History of England and Wales*, IV, 818–20. The barley price series used is the Cambridge one, and so should be a reliable guide to Chippenham conditions. The rye series, where it exists, is that from Loder's account book. Dr Bowden's 'harvest' year is in fact the accounting year, and runs from 29 September one calendar year, until 28 September the next. This year, however, reflects the quality and abundance of the harvest already in the barns on 29 September, not that of the one sown and actually harvested during it. The courts at Chippenham were usually held yearly, in late September or early October. This presumably meant that the day of the court was rent-day, and the time was carefully chosen to fall after harvest, when the tenants were in a position to pay their rent after selling some of their crops. At this annual court, all the deaths and sales since the previous one were, supposedly, reported.

This court always just falls within the beginning of the harvest (that is, accounting) year. It must, however, reflect the (court) dealings which took place over the whole of the previous year. In order to compare the numbers of transactions in a court year with those in a harvest year, I have therefore taken it as if a court held at the very beginning of a harvest year fell at the very end of the last one. For example, a court held in October 1598 I have taken to reflect the doings of the harvest year running from 29 September 1597 to 28 September 1598, and therefore the actual quality of the harvest brought in in the summer of the calendar year 1597. I have assumed, in doing this, that no tenant would sell in October 1598 because the harvest just brought in is very poor. He is not going to sell in advance; like Mr Micawber he will hope that something turns up. Although he may be reduced to eating his seed corn later in the harvest year 1598, it is only after that he will have to raise a mortgage, or sell a part of his holding, in order to eat. If this happens, his doings, I take it, will in turn be reflected at the next court, in October 1599.

Transactions at the handful of courts held in March and April, on the other hand, I have taken to reflect the effects of the harvest of the summer immediately before, and therefore the harvest years in which they actually fall.

Most of the courts held in Willingham (Graph 5, p. 155) between 1575 and 1603, unlike the Chippenham courts, were held in the late spring or early summer, in late April, May or June (twenty-two out of thirty-seven). The others were spread throughout the year. Most of the court transactions, if the transactions in a pastoral village were influenced by the harvest year at all, must have been influenced by the harvest brought in the preceding summer. I have therefore used Dr Bowden's accounting year, without adjusting the dates of the courts. On the single occasion when a court was held in October, I have taken it that the transactions referred to the harvest year which had just ended, as I did at Chippenham. Courts held in November, December and January, I have taken to reflect the harvest that has been gathered in the immediately preceding July and August.

It seemed worth adding the prices of wheat to the Willingham graph, because it formed a much more substantial proportion of the crop than at Chippenham.[1] It also seemed necessary to add cattle prices to the graph, in view of the proven dependence of Willingham men on their cattle. The inventories and wills give the impression that Willingham people were principally interested in dairying, and here the prices of dairy animals rather than those of all cattle should have been graphed, but there is a hint in one of Sir Miles Sandys' complaints to Chancery that beasts were fattened at Willingham too,[2] so I have used the general prices for cattle. The price series are again taken from the *Agrarian History of England and Wales*, IV, 819–20 and 826–7.

[1] See above, pp. 62–3 and 128–9.

[2] See above, p. 130. Fattening did certainly go on in the Cambridgeshire fens, and the uplanders profited. There is an interesting example in the will of Richard Kettle of Orwell, that parish lacking in pasture, which in March 1586 left his son two steers 'that be nowe in the Fenn'.

Index of contemporary names

Villagers, clerics, authors and pamphleteers

Abbreviations: C – Chippenham, O – Orwell, W – Willingham; other place-names are given in full; Q – Quaker. Figures in *italics* indicate illustrations.

Adam, of O: Grace (*neé* Caldecot, wife of Robert A.), 117; John, *senior* (son of Thomas A.), 117, 118, 327; John, *junior* (son of John A., *senior*), 118 *bis*; Margaret (wife of Thomas A.), 117; Robert, 117 *bis*, 326 n; Thomas, 117, 117–18

Adams, of O: Alice (wife of John A.), 113, Christopher, 96, 99; Elizabeth (Muggletonian) 325 & n, 326 *bis*; John, 113, 301, 302; monuments, 26 n(68); Robert, 336, 343, 344 n; 'Widow' (Muggletonian) 230

Affield, John, of Harston, 38

Alban, Thomas, of Shepreth, 40

Allan, John, of Balsham, 182

Allen: Edward, of W, 196, 330; John, of W, 332; Nicholas, vicar of C, 338 *bis* & n

Allingtons, the, 30

Ambler, Thomas, of W, 330

Amey, Thomas, of Harston, 41, 44

Andrewes, Lancelot (Arminian Bishop of Ely, later of Winchester), 105, 265

Angwood, Henry, of W, 164

Argent, George, 237

Ashmen, William, of W, 194–5

Aspland, Henry, of W, 131 n(48), 156, 157

Atkin, Timothy, of Melbourn, 268

Audley, of O: family, 126 n(20); Mrs Jean, 97, 98 *bis*

Aungier, William, parish clerk of Toft, 268

Aves, John, of C, 65, 210, 213 n, 339 *bis*

Aynsloe, John (Q, teacher and writer), of Over, 214–17 *passim* & n(39), 284, 292, 295 *bis*; *quoted*, 290–1, 292

Bancroft, Richard 260–1 *passim*

Barefoot, Luke, of Eltisley, 254

Barfurd, Sister, of Haslingfield, 347

Barliman, John, of W, 143

Barnard, of O: Edmund, 104, 327; Hugh (son of Edmund B.), 104, 107–8; John (son of Edmund B.), 104; Richard, 302; Robert (son of Edmund B.), 104; Robert (labourer, *probably* son of Hugh B.), 107–8; William, MA, rector of O, 203, 324, 325, 333

Barnard, Ursula, of Milton, 342; her will *quoted*, 342 *bis*

Baron: Thomas, of Hardwick, 37; William, of Comberton, 31

Barton, of O: Edmund, 116; Grace (*née* Caldecot), 116; John, *198*; Mary, 325, 326 *bis*

Baxter, Richard (Presbyterian divine), 274–5 *passim*; his 'voluntary association' (1653), 275

Bedall, Henry, of W, 194

Bedford, Francis, 4th Earl of, 121 & n(3), 127

Bendich, Mr (a landlord), 307

Benning, Ambrose, of O, 324

Bentley, John, of C, 63 *bis*, 85 *bis*

Benton, of W: Mark, 151; Matthew, 151

Biddall, of W: Cecily (wife of William B.), 128, 132–3, 140 *bis*, 164; family, 132, 140–1; Henry (son of William B.), 140–1 *passim*; John (son of William B.), 140, 141, 159; Richard (son of William B.), 140–1, 162; Roger, 143; Thomas (two of), 132 *bis*; William, *senior*, 128, 140, 141, 159, 162, 164; William, *junior* (son of William B. *senior*), 141; William ('the weaver'), 141

Bird, Robert, of O, 326

Bissell, of W; Henry, 196, 330; Simon, 194

Biswell, John, of W, 150

Blackaby, Mr ('a godly minister'), 237 *bis*

Blacklin, Anne (Q), 281, 282

Bland, Edward, rector of Toft, 252

Blowes, John, of Bourne, 214

Blythe, Margaret, of C (*formerly* wife of Anthony Hills), 83 & n

Boston, of Longstanton: family, 36 *bis*; Thomas 36

Bourghchier (Bourchier), Thomas (Archbishop of Canterbury, 1454–86), 175

Bourne, William, of Cherry Hinton, 212

Bowghton, John, of W, 142, 143

Bowles, of W: Thomas (fisherman), 143, 209, 330 *bis*, 336; William (son of Thomas B.), 209, 330, 332, 336

Bradshaw: Nathaniel, rector of W, 20, 227, 275, 293 *bis* & n, 302, 317; William, of Bassingbourn, 249

Braine: Edward, incumbent of Grantchester, 261; Thomas, incumbent of Comberton, 261

Branch, of C: Henry, 75; Jane (wife of Henry B.), 75

Brasier, of W: John, 157, 162; William, 150, 164

Brayshaw, John (notary public), 333 n

General Index

Notes

1. Figures in **bold type** indicate whole chapters or sections; those in *italics* indicate graphs, illustrations, maps or statistical tables; 'p' means 'passim' (here and there) – scattered references.
2. The numbers of notes are given, in brackets, only where it is necessary to assist identification.
3. 'Cambridge colleges' are indexed alphabetically under that heading.
4. Places named are in Cambridgeshire unless otherwise stated.

300–6; *influences on*: of lordship, **306–15**; of the clergy, **315–18**; of schooling, **318**; spiritual and physical care given by, 347; scattered membership among, 347; economic status of (1674), *305*; villages with large numbers of (1676, *Table 19*), *308–9*; villages without (1676, *Table 20*), *310–11*; Notes to Tables 19 and 20, *312*
dowries (*see also* women, provision for), 112 *bis*, 118, 142 & n (66), 143, 159
Dry Drayton, 51–2, 230; wills and their writers (1558–1630), **327–8**; Rev. Richard Greenham, and his predecessor and successor at. 327–8
Dullingham, 190, 279; 'parson' of, 207, 273 n (his alleged nepotism, 207); Baptist church, 279
Duxford: 'woman of', 255; parishes of St John and St Peter, 272 n

East Hatley, 253, 258, 273 nn, 317
Eastern Association, xxi *bis*; C. A. Holmes's thesis on, 3 & n
economic conditions, **1–167**; general, **3–57**; Chippenham, **58–92**; Orwell, **93–119** Willingham, **120–64**; general conclusions, **165–167**; differentiation in families, 299
education (schooling), **169–218**: schools and schoolmasters: general view, **171–83**; in Cambridgeshire, **183–91**; writing: in Orwell, 197, **200–5**; in Willingham, **192–200**; reading, in the village community, **206–18**; private tuition in villages, 186 & n(48), 190; types of, in village schools, 187–8; influence of, on religious beliefs, **318**
Education Act (1870), 173
'educational revolution' of late 16th and early 17th centuries, 173
'egresse and regresse', rights of, 113 *bis* & n
Elizabethan: genesis of dissent, 223; settlement (religious), 237, 250, 268, 352
Elsworth, 264 n(111)
Eltisley, 207 n, 227, 228 *bis*, 234 n(33), 254, 264 n(111), 269, 276–7, 286 & n, 292 *bis*, 345 *bis*; parish church, 292
Ely, 189; bishops of, *see* Index of Names
Ely, Consistory Court, 72, 210 n, 249, 253, 299 n; 'office copies' of wills in, 323 & n, 334
Ely, diocese of, xxii, 16 n(43), 59, 61, 212, 256, 266, 269, 350; the laity in, 238, **239–71**; livings (clerical) in, 175, 251; all parishes in, to have a Bible, 242; clerical absenteeism, 251
Ely, Isle of, xxii, **3–5** p, 6, 12, 28 n, 176–8 & n(21), 180, 214, 217–18, 256 p, 262, 264 n, 279
emigration: from villages, 90, 103, 118, 201; to America, 264 nn(110 & 111), 265
engrossers and engrossing, 36, 45, 72, 76, 80–2p & n(55), 85–7 p, 90, 101, 103, 108, 140, 158, 160 *bis*, 165, 176, 301, 338
Episcopalians, 274, 275 & n, 290
Ermine Street (Roman road), 94

Essex, 29 p, 181, 236 *bis*, 260, 264 n(111), 277, 282 & n(43); archdeaconry courts of, 258 & n(83)
estate surveys, 56 *bis*
Eton College, 190 & n, 195
Eucharist, the (*see also* Communion, Holy), 239, 241, 242
Eversden, Great and Little, 109 *bis*, 270 & n
Eynsbury (near St Neots, Hunts), 246 n, 349

Families of three generations, comparative rarity of, 114–16 & nn, 117
'Family of Love' (Familists, a sect), 208 *bis* & n(9), 246 n, 247 *bis*, 255–7, 259 *bis* & n(89), 262, 264, 296, 351
farmers, land-owning: capitalist (14th century), 47; yeomen (16th century), 48; small (16th & 17th centuries), 49–52, 53, 55–7, **58–92** p, 75–6, 91, 101; large (16th & 17th centuries), 52–3, 54, 55
farmhouses in 1580s, luxuries in, 48
fen: drainage schemes, 53, 120 & n(3), 127 *bis*, 329; settlements, expansion of, 165
Fenditton (Fen Ditton), 38
fens (of Cambridgeshire): the small landholder in the (Willingham), **120–64**, *166*, *167* (*see also* Willingham); tendency of conditions in, to shorten human life, 162–3; fattening of stock in, 357 n
Fenstanton (Fen Stanton, Hunts): church (Baptist), 227 & n, 291–2, 345 *bis*, 346; Church Book, 228, 277, 291, 346; Baptists, 214, 215, 228, 276, 277, 291–2, 345; Quakers, 284–5; Congregation Registers, 291–2; General Baptist church, 276, 345, 346
Fenstanton Records, 277, 278, 280, 287, 343, 345 n
field books, village, 56, 57
fields: Chippenham, 58–65 p; Orwell, 93–9 p; Willingham, 120–34 p
Five Mile Act (1665), 293
fodder crops, new (1650s), 54
Fordham (in Cambridgeshire, diocese of Norwich), 59 n, 86–8 p, 184 & n(46), 190 n, 213 n, 272 n
forest regions, 6
Forncett, 9 n(28)
Fowlmere, 248, 273 nn
Foxton, 234, 248
Foxe's *Book of Martyrs* (*see also* 'book of martyrs'), 248
fragmentation: of holdings, 36, 46, **148–59** p, 161, 165, 180–1 (*see also* inheritance customs *and* younger sons); and growth of (religious) sects, **272–97**
Freckenham, 86
Fulbourn, 33, 184, 229; churches (two), 33; St Vigor's (parish), 253, 272 n; All Saints (parish), 272 n

Gamlingay, 40, 291, 348 *bis*; Baptists, 291 n; dissenters, 313

General index

gathered churches, 234 n(33), 236, 237, 286; membership of, **344–50**
General Baptists, see under Baptists
Gloucester, diocese of, 199 n(25)
grain prices, fluctuation of, in Chippenham, 77–8
Gransdens, the (Hunts), see Great and Little Gransden
Granta, valley of the, 16, 297
Grantchester, 7 n(20), 251, 261
Graveley, 254
Gray's Inn (London), 109, 179, 204
Great Chesterford (Essex), 348–9
Great Childerley, 272 n
Great Eversden, 109, 270 & n
Great Gransden (Hunts), 109 bis, 188; Church Book, 215 n, 225 & n(9), 230
Great Level (of the fens), draining of, 121 & n(3)
'Great Mere', 121 n(1)
Great Shelford, 7, 10, 126, 184, 346; see also Shelford
Great Wilbraham, 315; see also Wilbraham
Greek Orthodox communities, agrarian, 240
'Grindletonians' (sect), 258
Guilden Morden, 30

Haddenham (Isle of Ely), 214
Hadstock (Essex), 348
'halls' (of houses), 39, 40 p, 41
Hardwick, 37, 273 nn
harlotry and harlots, 254
Harston, 37, 38, 41, 277 bis, 279, 307, 345, 346 ter
harvests of 16th and 17th centuries, 51 n(26)
Haslingfield, 190, 347
Hauxton, 184–6, 307
Hauxton-cum-Newton, 272 n
hearth tax: as economic and social guide, 37–45, 200; payers, median wealth of (1661–70), 301 n
hearths: location of, 39–40; percentages of houses with one, two, three or four-and-more, in Cambridgeshire (1664), 42, 43, 44
Hempsall Fen (Willingham), 125
Hertford (Herts), 180, 203
Hertfordshire, xxi bis, 14 bis, 16, 293
Heynes (Haynes, Bedforshire), 348
'High Fields', 96 bis
Hildersham, 314
Hinxton, 41
Histon, 234, 315; St Andrew (parish), 272 n; St Etheldreda (parish), 272 n
Hitchin (Herts), xxi
Hogginton, 27
Holy Communion, see Communion, Eucharist and Lord's Supper
Homilies, the (16th century), 207, 253
Horningsey, 257 n, 263
Horseheath, 242, 294, 319 bis, 348 bis
horses, 65, 95, 130–1, 156
Hospitallers, Knights (of Rhodes), 58

householding: plural holdings and sub-tenancies, 20 n
houses: sizes of, and hearths in, 39–43
Huntingdon (Hunts), 195
Huntingdonshire, 195, 279, 345; Baptists, 292, 345
husbandmen: economic status of, 37–9 p, 41, 44, 75; median wealth of, 72, 210 n, 299 n; retiring, 80

'Ice Age, the Little' (1550–1850), 51 n(25)
Ickleton, 40
Icknield Way, 3, 62, 63 bis, 296
image worship, forbidden (1541), 242
immigration (into villages), 160, 162, 165
Impington, 253
'Independents' (see also dissent), 234, 249, 274 & n, 275, 277 n(26), 280
Indulgence, Declaration of (1687), 289, 294
inheritance customs: Chippenham, **85–7**; Orwell, **104–11**, 118; Willingham, **159–61**
Inns of Court (London), 179; Gray's Inn, 109, 179, 204
irreverence in church, 265, 270 & n(130)
Isle of Ely, see Ely

Justification by faith (see also salvation), 326 & n, 328, 337, 342

Kennet, river, 58
Kent (county), 29 ter, 225, 227 & n, 229
King's Lynn (Norfolk), 5
Kingston, 23, 34–5, 35 n, 214, 277
Kingston Wood, manor of, 34
kitchens, 39–40 p, 41
'kulak' peasants, 92 n bis
Kuriyan (Indian geographer), quoted, 298 & n

Labourers, agricultural, landless, wage-earning: economic status of, 31–3, 36, 37–9 p, 41 bis, 44 bis, 48–9; influx of, into an open-field village, 49 n; increase of (1544 & 1560), 66 bis, 87; median wealth of, 210 n, 299 n
laity in the diocese of Ely, 238; general view of, **239–71**
Lamb's church, Bell Alley, London, 227
Lancashire, 274, 340
land distribution: changes in (1550s, 1560s & 1590s), 55–7; Chippenham, **65–85**; Orwell, 99–104; Willingham, **134–51**
Landbeach, 5 n(10)
landholding: on the chalk (Chippenham) and in the fen (Willingham), 166, 167
landowners, small (see also farmers, small): disappearance of, **46–57**; reduced in numbers before 1760 (reasons), 49–52
Landwade, 81
Langham village (Essex/Suffolk border), 206
Languedoc (France), peasantry of (see also Beauvaisis and Picardy), xxii
Laudian(s) and Laudianism, 258, 272, 315–16,